VoIP Deployment

FOR

DUMMIES®

VoIP Deployment

FOR

DUMMIES®

by Stephen P. Olejniczak

WILEY

Wiley Publishing, Inc.

VoIP Deployment For Dummies®

Published by
Wiley Publishing, Inc.
111 River Street
Hoboken, NJ 07030-5774

www.wiley.com

For general information on our other products and services, please contact our Customer Care Department within the U.S. at 800-762-2974, outside the U.S. at 317-572-3993, or fax 317-572-4002.

For technical support, please visit www.wiley.com/techsupport.

Wiley also publishes its books in a variety of electronic formats. Some content that appears in print may not be available in electronic books.

Library of Congress Control Number: 2008939205

ISBN: 978-0-470-38543-2

Manufactured in the United States of America

10 9 8 7 6 5 4 3 2 1

WILEY

About the Author

Stephen P. Olejniczak (pronounced *O lĕn ēē'chek*) is the Director of Operations for ATI, and has worked over 16 years in telecommunications. His experience is concentrated on installation, service, billing and support of voice service. The past five years having focused his time on learning all facets of VoIP as the marketplace, technology, and supporting infrastructure has evolved.

Stephen didn't start out in life as a techie, only falling prey to the glamour and easy money after failing to find a career enabling him to use his bachelor's degree in Cultural Anthropology. He currently lives in a picturesque beach town in California with his beautiful wife Kayley and a collection of fountain pens.

Dedication

I dedicate this book to everyone in the VoIP industry, past, present, and future. Without the technological pioneers that decided to hack their own SIP code, and make calls from Los Angeles, California to Bucharest, Romania, we wouldn't be where we are today. It's their sacrifices, dealing with packet loss, latency, jitter, and the resultant call completion and poor audio quality, that have paved the way for the established technology we call VoIP. They toiled away in anonymity, devoting time to the mass collaboration projects of open source software and delivering to us the ability to change local carriers and get more for our money.

I must acknowledge the current laborers chipping away every day on the VoIP rockpile. The first industry group that requires kudos are the LNP offices of every local carrier in America. They are a small but mighty group responsible for porting phone numbers into and out of their governance. They are generally ignored, sometimes slandered, and frequently maligned by individuals venting their frustration as to why it takes so long to get numbers released. The second industry group that deserves credit are the individual businesses that have moved from traditional telephony to VoIP. Their faith in this new technology has given the market form, and legitimacy, hurtling us forward.

Finally, I dedicated this book to the predecessors to the modern *homo sapiens*. Their curiosity, use of opposable digits, penchant for tools and a drive to find a new way to solve old problems still continues propel us forward as a race. It was inevitable then that we would reach here, where VoIP is simply another technological advancement like fire, the wheel, or sliced bread, allowing everyone a better life.

Author's Acknowledgments

I must first thank my beautiful wife Kayley for giving me the time necessary to write this book. Her support and encouragement kept me on track during the project and I look forward to a return to normal life for a while.

There are many industry people that have helped to shape the content of this book, the individual with the largest contribution of information and experience is Praveen Kumar of Packet Island software. He has been very gracious with his time, affording me several interviews and demonstrations which taught me the basics of LAN design and the philosophy of VoIP Lifecycle Management. The information provided and wisdom gleaned from those conversations helped make this book as rich as it is regarding those areas of VoIP over which I had no experience.

I would also like to acknowledge Brady Kirby, my co-author of *Asterisk For Dummies* and Carl Doss (my technical editor) for pitching in and helping me out when I was stuck trying to get my Linux server to load Wireshark.

Appreciation must also be given to my editor Pat O'Brien, and Greg Croy of Wiley Publishing with whom I had many conversations, developing the idea of this book. Thanks to Laura Miller for her skillful edits.

Finally, I must acknowledge every difficult customer, convoluted VoIP problem, and challenging technician I've encountered. Every one of you forced me to learn more about this technology, the infrastructure, and diplomacy required to be a success in this industry. Thank you all.

Publisher's Acknowledgments

We're proud of this book; please send us your comments through our online registration form located at www.dummies.com/register/.

Some of the people who helped bring this book to market include the following:

Acquisitions, Editorial, and Media Development

Project Editor: Pat O'Brien

Acquisitions Editor: Greg Croy

Copy Editor: Laura K. Miller

Technical Reviewer: Carl Doss

Editorial Manager: Kevin Kirschner

Editorial Assistant: Amanda Foxworth

Sr. Editorial Assistant: Cherie Case

Cartoons: Rich Tennant
(www.the5thwave.com)

Composition Services

Project Coordinator: Katherine Key

Layout and Graphics: Stacie Brooks, Nikki Gately, Sarah E. Philippart

Proofreaders: Caitie Kelly, Toni Settle

Indexer: Potomac Indexing, LLC

Publishing and Editorial for Technology Dummies

    Richard Swadley, Vice President and Executive Group Publisher

    Andy Cummings, Vice President and Publisher

    Mary Bednarek, Executive Acquisitions Director

    Mary C. Corder, Editorial Director

Publishing for Consumer Dummies

    Diane Graves Steele, Vice President and Publisher

    Joyce Pepple, Acquisitions Director

Composition Services

    Gerry Fahey, Vice President of Production Services

    Debbie Stailey, Director of Composition Services

Contents at a Glance

Table of Contents

Introduction

*I*t was February 2003 when my boss told me that I was going to be turning up a new VoIP softswitch. This was the first time I had ever heard of a softswitch, and about the second time I had heard of the term VoIP. There was a loose association of companies, hardware vendors, software guys, programmers, salesmen, and support staff that had to be wrangled together to make it happen. At the same time, I was also scheduled to take a vacation to The Netherlands and had planned a ten-day trek of museums, flea markets, and antiques shops. I never made it to Europe, but I did bring up an array of Asterisk servers.

That was my own personal trial by fire with VoIP. I researched the technology as much as I could, but there wasn't anything available to provide a basic understanding of the technology. I dug in to it, but as much as I tried, I couldn't find anything to tell me how VoIP was structured, or the basis of how it worked. The technicians I queried for information were all very tight-lipped and wanted to charge me $125 an hour to reveal the inner-workings of this new, cutting-edge technology.

Eventually I learned the nuts and bolts of VoIP. I spent a few years migrating phone numbers and troubleshooting inbound VoIP service, before we rolled out the outbound service years later. I watched as customer perceptions of VoIP changed from fear or apprehension to acceptance and aspiration.

This book is everything I wished that someone would have told me back when I was tasked with pushing through that first Inter Operability test. It is the basis for my confidence in VoIP's ability to transform the telecom industry, and the reasons why it works.

About This Book

VoIP Deployment For Dummies is unlike any other book on the market covering any aspect of VoIP. I designed the contents of it to continually answer the question "Why does this matter to me?" If the subject didn't matter, it was removed. More importantly, I looked to find the things in VoIP that had a direct impact on me. I looked at all of the times I was frustrated with VoIP and pulled apart, both *why* I was frustrated and *what information I needed to know* to resolve the problem. If I didn't know that Wireshark existed, or how to filter a capture or read the SIP with Wireshark, I'm sure there were a lot more people out there with the same problem.

I read every book on SIP, VoIP, and Wireshark I could, and even within the thousands of pages available on the subject, there were still huge gulfs of information that were missing. The day-to-day things like DTMF tones and faxes seemed to be absent, as well as information about the VoIP market and its structure.

This book covers everything you need to know about VoIP. It's relayed in a logical, and down-to-Earth style where you won't feel like you've gotten yourself in over your head. Once you know everything in this book, feel free to continue your education with other sources, but what's in here is a solid base from which you can understand the totality of VoIP.

What You Don't Have to Read

As a standard rule, don't read what you already know. This book is designed to be read by chapter as it interests you. It is not required that you read it straight through, and if additional clarification is required on a subject, I'll direct you to the chapter where it's covered in depth.

Foolish Assumptions

I wrote this book assuming that you're interested in VoIP and had some experience with telephony or programming. I didn't assume that you had any extensive training in VoIP or any VoIP-supported field (such as telecom, LAN design, or software development). It is reasonable that some readers will have extensive backgrounds in one or another aspect of these supporting disciplines, but there will always be one part where you're weaker.

For years, telecom has been divided into two camps, with the data people in one realm, and the voice people in the other. Very few people learned both disciplines, and as such, the people migrating to VoIP are coming from on or the other side of the fence. They bring with them their specific strengths, but also their weaknesses from not knowing the other realm of telecom.

I do assume that if you are using Asterisk or any other open source software running on Linux that you have some basic knowledge of the operating software. If you need to learn more about Linux, I recommend other *For Dummies* books such as *Red Hat Fedora Linux 2 For Dummies,* by Jon Hall and Paul G. Sery.

If you're a programmer or are jumping in to VoIP with experience in LAN design or networking, I recommend my first book, *Telecom For Dummies* as a basic primer for the telecom industry. It covers all aspects of telecom ordering and provisioning and is a wealth of information on troubleshooting all varieties of standard telephony problems that are not covered in this book.

How This Book Is Organized

The book is structured as a progression from general to specific VoIP information. It is layed out in the same logical manner you'd go about researching VoIP during a deployment on your network. The initial chapters cover the rudimentary structure of VoIP and provide an overview of the supporting structures of VoIP. More detailed information is then provided as the key elements of network assessment are covered, allowing you to qualify your LAN before and during deployment. The progression follows through to a section on management of the VoIP LAN you've deployed, covering troubleshooting and maintenance before handing you the pearls of wisdom in the Part of Tens.

Part I: VoIP Essentials

The basic structure of VoIP is revealed in this section of the book. It provides an overview of VoIP in general terms and addresses some of the facts and fallacies associated with the technology. All of the basics of VoIP are explored, from the hardware required to the protocol options available. A detailed view of SIP is provided as well as SDP, RTP, and the dial plan that makes up all of the call routing and handling within your VoIP phone system.

Part II: Assessing Your Network's VoIP Readiness

This is the working information necessary to determine if your LAN is prepared for VoIP deployment. Latency, jitter, and packet loss are covered in depth, as is LAN design and configuration. The standard business aspects of VoIP telephony that are frequently ignored are also covered, devoting time to the handling and options for fax transmissions and DTMF tones. Finally I cover all of the configuration settings and information your carrier may need to know when you order VoIP to ensure a smooth deployment.

Part III: Maintaining Your Network and Service

This section covers all aspects of troubleshooting, providing step-by-step information on how to troubleshoot specific issues. Various call types are dissected, with the individual variables and responsible companies identified. Troubleshooting logic is presented to help identify issues by narrowing down the scope of the problem, and the diplomacy of troubleshooting is also presented.

Part IV: The Part of Tens

I have placed all of the pearls of wisdom I have in this section. I address the general misperceptions of VoIP, where they came from and why they aren't (or are) true. All of the things that make VoIP great come next, followed by ten things to avoid. Many of them can cost you money, or land you in jail, so it's a good section to read. Finally the book is wrapped up with ten places to go for help when you feel you have nowhere else to turn.

Icons Used in This Book

The icons in this book are meant to grab your attention. Here's what they mean:

This icon indicates that you need to be extra cautious, lest you become subject to a common pitfall or problem.

Tips provide insight into configuring, developing, or understanding something better regarding PPS.

This icon denotes a key point of understanding, or serves as a reminder for how to handle something particularly tricky.

Feel free to skip anything listed as Technical Stuff unless you either really like tech stuff, or you're having a specific issue where you need to learn as much as possible about an aspect of VoIP. I don't drill down into the individual code making up the constituent software of VoIP, but I do allude to it here and there in these sections in case you want a direction for more inquiry.

Where to Go From Here

The Table of Contents is the best place to begin. Scan it and look for anything you aren't confident you know. If you've had any exposure to VoIP at all, some of the book may just be a refresher course for you, and some may not apply. If you're just starting out and haven't formally been taught anything about VoIP, dive in to Chapter 1 and then peruse the Table of Contents. Every chapter is independent and doesn't require that you've read the previous chapter to understand it, so it's okay to jump around from chapter to chapter. As one chapter piques your curiosity, you can always jump back to the Table of Contents to find other areas where it's covered as well. Many aspects of VoIP, like faxing and DTMF digits, are covered from a different angle in more than one chapter. All of the basic VoIP information you need is in here, so read it, skim it, skip what you don't need to know, and most of all, enjoy!

Part I
VoIP Essentials

The 5th Wave   By Rich Tennant

"This program's really helped me learn a new language. It's so buggy I'm constantly talking with overseas service reps."

In this part . . .

1 provide the information necessary to grasp VoIP, its structure, its myth, and the supporting elements that make it great. VoIP transmissions are not built like a normal phone call, and the unique nature of their design lend themselves to possibilities, both good and bad, that aren't available with traditional telephony.

The process for Local Number Portability (LNP) in which phone numbers are migrated from traditional local carriers to VoIP carriers is covered in detail. The process, as well as the structure of the VoIP market is addressed to illuminate the challenges with this, seemingly simple task.

The specifics of the SIP and SDP elements of a VoIP transmission are dissected, revealing their functions and the expected banter between both ends of a VoIP call. Almost every aspect of a VoIP call is negotiated between the end points, and sometimes intermediary proxy servers, so great care was given to define the aspects of the communication so any issues can be identified.

This section finishes with an overview of a dial plan, the software of a VoIP phone system governing the routing of calls and deployment of applications. Aspects of it are covered for cost savings, useful features, and to identify the wealth of options available with a standard VoIP phone system.

Chapter 1

Reviewing VoIP Basics

In This Chapter

▶ Seeing what makes up a call

▶ Separating the fact from fiction

▶ Gathering the hardware you need

▶ Sending non-voice transmissions

▶ Migrating phone numbers or getting new ones

*V*oice over Internet Protocol (or VoIP, as it's more commonly known) is truly a disruptive technology, bringing in new possibilities while departing from traditional telephony in structure. It packetizes normal voice phone calls and transmits them over the Internet, using the same sort of path on which you send and receive e-mail and Instant Messages, or surf the Web. VoIP has changed how network technicians, engineers, and programmers view telecommunications, how it's transmitted, where it can be delivered, and the lack of flexibility in traditional telephony. It empowers small business to build its own phone systems by using open source software, giving it the power to add features, use multiple carriers to save money, and turn to troubleshooting tools previously reserved only for carriers.

While the technology has evolved, the market has responded. Years after VoIP was rolled out within the networks of long-distance carriers in America, it has gained a foothold in the telecommunications market, but it remains an enigma to many. Many people still hold on to their pre-conceived notions of what VoIP is and how it works.

This chapter explains the basics of VoIP, and it also covers what hardware you need to use it, the challenges of the technology, and some of the added hurdles that it creates.

Parts of a VoIP Call

VoIP isn't one single protocol or software package that converts your analog or digital phone call into something that can run over the Internet. *VoIP* is a group of specialized software elements, each performing a specific task.

Every phone call (whether VoIP or non-VoIP) has two basic components, each using an allotted amount of bandwidth to do its specific job. These call components are

- ✔ **The voice portion:** Also called the *media* of the call or the *payload.* The digital, analog, or VoIP representation of your voice is transmitted through the voice portion. Without this part of the call, you can't hear the words, laughs, sighs, or . . . anything from one end of the call to the other.

- ✔ **The overhead:** Where everything that isn't the voice portion of the call is transmitted. It handles the housekeeping and maintenance of a call. In this section of bandwidth, the messages to establish the connection of a call are transferred (called *call setup*), as well as the mundane task of clearing a call through a network after both parties hang up (called *teardown*). This overhead section can also handle a variety of other tasks, such as transmitting codes that translate as ringing, busy signals, or recordings about failed calls (for example, if you dialed a disconnected number). This portion of the call also transmits your Caller ID, as well as the connect and disconnect signals used to begin and end billing on your call.

Figure 1-1 compares the voice and overhead portions of a standard analog and a VoIP phone call.

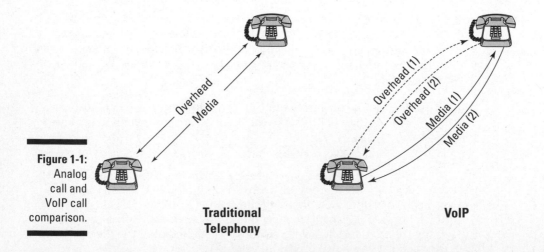

Figure 1-1:
Analog
call and
VoIP call
comparison.

**Traditional
Telephony**

VoIP

Figure 1-1 shows how the overhead and media portion of a traditional call are located in a contiguous section of bandwidth from start to finish. When the individual calls enter the network of your long-distance carrier, your call is then routed into a larger circuit, along with hundreds and thousands of other calls. All the calls have a similar structure, in which the bandwidth is portioned out for each element of the call from point to point along the way. The overhead of the call handles all the call setup and tear-down information from both ends of the call, and the media portion of the bandwidth similarly handles transmission of the speech from both ends. While your call is routed from your local phone carrier to your long-distance carrier, and on to the local carrier that services the number you dialed, both elements of the call continue to be bonded together.

Technically, not every non-VoIP call has the voice and overhead portions of the call sandwiched next to each other from start to finish. Several different protocols are used to send and receive traditional telephony calls:

- ✔ In standard loopstart, groundstart, or E&M wink circuits, Figure 1-1 is an accurate depiction of how a call is transmitted. All of these protocols transmit calls while maintaining the conjoined bandwidth of 64 Kbps for the combined overhead and the voice portion. The unique nature of these three protocols are in the Glossary.

- ✔ If the call is sent by using ISDN, then the overhead is aggregated on one channel of the circuit, not as a portion of the single channel. The overhead is stripped from the individual calls and given 64 Kbps of bandwidth instead of the minimal room given on a standard telephony call. This allows it to perform all its required duties for many calls, and has additional features that aren't available with loopstart or groundstart calls.

- ✔ If the call in Figure 1-1 is sent with SS7 signaling, then it has some of the flexibility of VoIP and a somewhat similar structure, but the overhead is still a continuous stream of data between you and your carrier, not the transmission of overhead packets on an as-needed basis that you see with VoIP.

   If you're interested in finding out more about all these other signaling types, I recommend *Telecom For Dummies* (Wiley Publishing, Inc.), by yours truly.

VoIP is structurally different from a traditional telephony call in three ways:

- ✔ The overhead of the call isn't bonded to the media of the call, so the overhead and media can be transmitted via completely different routes.

   Not only can the overhead of the call find its own way from end to end, it can also be transmitted between different endpoints than the media of a call. The detached nature of the overhead allows for much greater flexibility in call transmission as the voice portion of the call can be easily redirected to a new location while still maintaining the overhead between the same two points.

✔ The overhead of the call (depicted as dashed lines in Figure 1-1) isn't a constant flow of information in a VoIP call — it's sent only when needed.

Traditional telephone lines are constantly checking in to both ends of the call to ensure that there aren't any problems on the line. VoIP is a much more self-confident protocol — it sends the call and transmits additional information to manage the call only when necessary (such as when the call needs to be re-directed or someone hangs up the phone, ending the call).

✔ All media and overhead streams can take their own paths between start and end points. Traditional telephony assigns a section of bandwidth for the overhead and the media transmission of the call. Traditional telephony uses 64 Kbps of bandwidth for every phone call. Once the route path is established, both ends of the call use the same 64 Kbps for the bi-directional transmission of overhead and media. VoIP uses a different design that allows each stream of media or overhead to choose its own path to the destination IP. Because of this stream freedom, Figure 1-1 identifies media and overhead paths with individual directional arrows, rather than the two arrows shown on the traditional telephony call.

These three structural differences allow VoIP calls to be managed and routed in ways a traditional telephony call never could be. VoIP allows you to resend a call from its initial start or end point to a new start or end point. Figure 1-2 shows how a VoIP call can be redirected to another destination. In the example, a call between a remote phone and a business's main office is then transferred to a remote office.

This traditional mindset about call forwarding has two main problems:

✔ **You're using a lot of unnecessary bandwidth.** By accepting the call into your VoIP server at the main office and generating a new call to the remote site, you're using about 168 Kbps of bandwidth for the two sets of media streams and another 62 Kbps for the two sets of overhead streams. So, this one transmission uses a total bandwidth of approximately 230 Kbps. If you forward calls often, they can start to strain your available bandwidth.

✔ **You're using hardware that can fail or add to the latency of VoIP packet transmissions.** Every server interacting on a VoIP call adds a small amount of *latency* (delay), giving you another variable that you have to consider when troubleshooting calls. Avoid any latency that you can on VoIP calls, such as interaction with unnecessary servers, especially if either network is already over-taxed or you're transmitting faxes or key pad touch tones (which are highly sensitive to latency).

Problems with intermediary VoIP servers can also kill VoIP calls. VoIP troubleshooting, like all systematic problem-solving in telecom, can quickly degenerate into finger-pointing. Temporarily redirecting the media of a call to completely avoid a network removes that network as a possible source for whatever issue you're experiencing. If the issue is only present when your call crosses the suspect network, open a trouble ticket and have them resolve the problem. If the problem persists either way, you've at least proven that portion of the call to be clean.

Figure 1-3 shows how the standard call from Figure 1-2 should have been transferred. The overhead streams are still spanning between the main office and the customer phone, but the media streams are crossing only from the remote office to the customer, eliminating all latency on the media into and out of the main office and freeing up almost 200 Kbps of bandwidth on the main office IP connection for other calls.

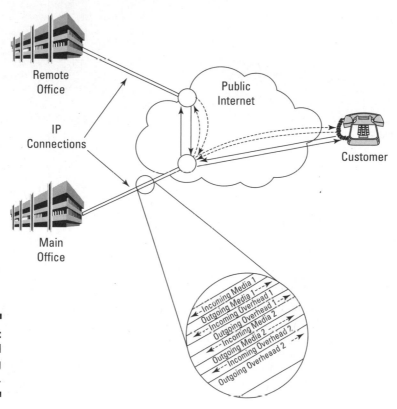

Figure 1-2:
Traditional forwarding of VoIP call.

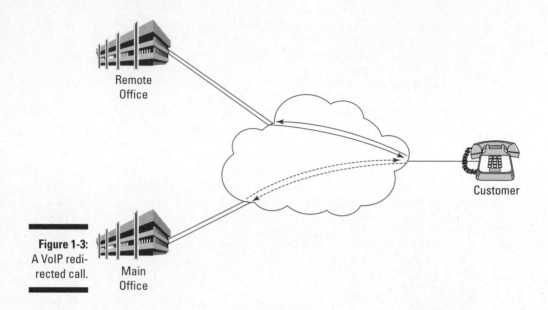

Figure 1-3:
A VoIP redi-
rected call.

As useful as this type of redirect is, many carriers don't like it because it requires their servers to work a bit harder. VoIP redirects the media portion of the call by sending a message to the server at the other end to roll the media to the new location. If you're a VoIP provider, this can amount to a lot of messages you're sending to your carrier's server to redirect the calls. Just like VoIP servers work to eliminate latency on the transmission of calls, the carriers try to reduce how hard their servers have to work.

Beware the rogue media stream. As awe inspiring as it is to see a media stream running off into the ether with no overhead in sight, a media stream can always go rogue. If the end IP destination requested in the redirect message is incorrect, some poor innocent IP is bombarded with a media stream. If the IP isn't set up to receive VoIP transmissions, the entire stream is probably rejected, with minimal impact to server receiving the unwanted data. If the receiving server is set up to receive VoIP, it might spin out of control and flood it, preventing it from servicing legitimate VoIP calls in an unintentional *Denial Of Service* (DOS) attack. Even though it wasn't your goal to overload their server, the RTP still prevented their intended customers from reaching them, so they'll call it a DOS attack, until we coin another acronym for involuntary SPAM.

Dispelling VoIP Misperceptions

Some of the confusion surrounding VoIP isn't unique. Fifteen years ago, people had the same fears, concerns, and misperceptions about the hottest technology of the time — ISDN. Today, the marketing machine for VoIP has promised that it will do everything but julienne potatoes, all for free or a low monthly package fee.

VoIP isn't as great or as horrible as anyone portrays it.

Using more bandwidth

Just because VoIP is slick and new doesn't mean that it's entirely more efficient than traditional telephony. VoIP has both uncompressed and compressed call options. Each has its pros and cons (covered in Chapter 2), but they're all contained within the same VoIP structure.

A standard non-VoIP call consumes slightly more than 64 Kbps of bandwidth, and you can place 24 consecutive calls over a normal dedicated 1.5 Mbps circuit. VoIP calls require more bandwidth to handle the additional overhead associated with packetizing it for transmission. If the media portion of the call isn't compressed, the total bandwidth consumption of a VoIP call can exceed 120 Kbps. A full 1.544 Mbps circuit of uncompressed VoIP allows you only about 13 calls, barely more than half the total calls possible if the circuit were traditional telephony.

The good news is that the most common type of VoIP compression allows you to transmit over twice the number of consecutive calls over a 1.544 Mbps circuit. You can save a lot of bandwidth by using VoIP, but how much you can save depends on whether you're compressing the media on the call. (Chapter 3 explains compression.)

Realizing that VoIP isn't free

One of the biggest marketing campaigns surrounding VoIP was the idea that all VoIP calls were free. At one point in time, that may have been true. Before 2007, the U.S. government didn't know how to tax VoIP calls, and so those calls were tax free. Before 2005, most VoIP calls were from one VoIP phone or computer on the Internet to another VoIP phone or computer on the Internet. By avoiding the infrastructure used by traditional telephony calls, it also avoided all the fees. As far as anyone else knew, the transmission wasn't anything other than someone surfing the Web or sending an e-mail.

The business of VoIP has changed since then, and many people simply use VoIP to access a local or long-distance phone carrier. Companies such as Vonage or your local cable TV company (if it also sells local phone service) are typical VoIP providers. These companies set up a VoIP connection between your home and their switch, but if you're calling your aunt in Florida or your grandma in Philadelphia, the call is still passed over the same legacy telephone network that it would if you dialed from a non-VoIP phone. Because the call uses the same switches and systems as a traditional telephony call means that the call is assessed per-minute rates in the same manner.

Any call that you make to a standard telephone number is charged a per-minute rate somewhere along the way. Even if you pay a flat monthly fee for unlimited long distance, your carrier is banking on the fact that it's charging you enough to cover all the minutes it's being billed for your calls.

Accepting that VoIP may not be cheaper than traditional phone service

VoIP's launch marketing hype said that, although it may not be free, at least it's cheaper than using the traditional analog phone lines and digital circuits. But it actually isn't always cheaper. All the long-distance carriers are rolling out VoIP service, but not every small and medium-sized business can save money by using it.

Business customers traditionally purchased dedicated circuits from their long-distance carriers, which allowed them to aggregate traffic and get a lower per-minute rate on their calls. Most carriers have kept the same pricing for the per-minute cost of their calls because the calls' networks and routing still go through the same systems. The main differences in the cost of VoIP, when compared with traditional telephony, are access fees and hardware costs.

Factoring in access fees

The phone carrier providing traditional dedicated circuit charges a monthly fee for the lease of the *local loop,* the cabling that connects your business to your carrier. A VoIP connection requires that you have not only a connection to a carrier, but also a port to the Internet, which usually costs an additional fee. You can generally use an Internet connection from another carrier to reach your long-distance provider, but then you have to worry about latency. Every server you encounter between your own server and your carrier represents a delay that can degrade the quality of your VoIP calls or simply cause your calls to fail. Before jumping into VoIP, be sure to compare how much IP bandwidth you need to match the total quantity of calls and consider all the loop fees and port costs.

The bandwidth used to place VoIP calls and traditional telephony calls can vary. A standard dedicated circuit that has 1.544 Mbps of bandwidth (called a T1 or DS-1 in America) is designed with 24 channels, each capable of processing a call. If your peak calling time has 24 calls going at one time and you don't want to compress your VoIP calls, you need to order two T1 circuits. With two circuits, your cost doubles because you have to pay two local loop fees and two Internet port fees. If you compress your VoIP calls, you can use one T1 circuit for 48 consecutive calls.

Table 1-1 and Table 1-2 show how your choice in compressed or uncompressed VoIP has a direct impact on your bottom line. Contact your Internet provider for the exact local loop and Internet port costs.

Table 1-1	Monthly Charge Comparison for Uncompressed VoIP and Traditional Telephony				
Telephony Type	**Maximum Calls**	**QTY of T1s required**	**Local Loop Monthly Charge**	**Internet Port Monthly Charge**	**Total Monthly Charge**
Uncompressed VoIP	24	2	$300 ea	$200 ea	$1,000
Traditional Telephony	24	1	$300 ea	N/A	$300

Table 1-2	Monthly Charge Comparison for Compressed VoIP and Traditional Telephony				
Telephony Type	**Maximum Calls**	**QTY of T1s required**	**Local Loop Monthly Charge**	**Internet Port Monthly Charge**	**Total Monthly Charge**
Compressed VoIP	48	1	$300 ea	$200 ea	$500
Traditional Telephony	48	2	$300 ea	N/A	$600

Figuring out the hardware costs

Unless you're creating a brand new company and phone system from scratch, you have to spend some money to either replace existing hardware or augment your network to handle VoIP. You don't have to spend this money if you stay with your existing configuration, so you need to weigh this cost against the financial and business benefits of deploying VoIP. I cover the types of hardware in the section "Identifying the Hardware You Need," later in this chapter.

Worrying about compatibility

Whenever any new technology is released, everyone always worries about compatibility. You may be wondering, "Will I be able to communicate with other VoIP devices?" I have a Fuji digital camera that uses a memory card that works with only Fuji and Olympus cameras — and it doesn't work in the photo printers at the local drugstore, either.

Looking at the compatibility headaches that came with other technologies, international organizations such as IETF (Internet Engineering Task Force) and the ITU (International Telecommunications Union) established guidelines called RFCs (Request For Comments) about how to transmit VoIP calls. This international cooperation allowed everyone to work together to develop systems and logic for VoIP transmissions, instead of everyone making up their own versions and letting the market decide which technology would survive.

Even though these organizations set down the guidelines for the transmission of VoIP calls, programmers still wrote software based on their own interpretations, and the industry quickly realized that those small nuances made all the difference.

VoIP carriers identified this challenge and developed InterOperability (InterOp) testing to ensure that the custom software built for a small business would work with the custom software built for a long-distance carrier. For a period of time, every carrier had an InterOp program with a testing window of a few days to a few weeks. In this testing window, VoIP customers and carriers validated that both ends of a VoIP call could accommodate how that call was being packaged, processed, and managed.

That was then, and this is now. In spite of the fact that you can sit down and create your own version of the VoIP protocol, you don't need to because you can find free software on the Internet that does it for you. You can download Asterisk or AsteriskNOW from `http://asterisknow.com/` and instantly have every bit of software you need to send and receive VoIP calls. The VoIP industry now has a greater level of uniformity in software, and you rarely encounter incompatibility between VoIP devices anymore. Carriers no longer have to worry about InterOp testing (though some still offer it because they've built infrastructure to support it and they have an extensive pre-established set of test cases that need to be accomplished that normally can't be concluded in a normal activation). They instead schedule a normal installation, just like they would if you were activating a traditional telephony circuit.

Many small businesses didn't appreciate the elimination of InterOp testing because they used the InterOp test environment to test and confirm their own internal dial plans or configurations. InterOp was designed to ensure that a business's VoIP server could effectively communicate with the VoIP server of its carrier, but slick technicians extended the testing to confirm that their new find-me-follow-me service was functioning properly or work through some bugs in their internal dial plans.

VoIP installation (covered in Chapter 8) is a very straightforward process. Incompatibility between VoIP hardware is now as likely as incompatibility between traditional telephony hardware.

Rejoicing in good quality calls

The quality of your VoIP call depends almost entirely on the network over which it's transmitted, from end to end. Long-distance carriers have been using VoIP within their own controlled networks for years. Almost every long-distance call you make is VoIP at some point during its transmission. VoIP is even more prevalent on international calls because the carriers that specialize in this niche market use standard VoIP compression techniques so that they can maximize the profit they get out of their current connections.

One of the first VoIP calls I received was from a programmer in Romania. I used a softphone that was installed on my work PC. The call had a lot of static and sounded like a radio transmission from Mars.

Now, almost every traditional telephony call you make is an example of the call quality you can expect on VoIP. It's no longer a free service with skittish quality; it has established itself as a legitimate form of telephony that's used, and offered by, all major carriers.

Understanding the VoIP Landscape

VoIP is a hybrid of data structure and voice application, so all the flexibility of data programming can now be applied to telephony applications.

Previously, phone systems were filled with proprietary hardware and software. If you wanted to add five more phone lines, you had to hope that your system had the room for an additional card — and the standard upgrade cards probably had more or less ports than you needed. After you finished installing the phone lines, your hardware vendor still had to sit on site to program the lines and give them the standard voicemail box.

The creation and release of VoIP has inspired a generation of programmers who didn't stop at devising a way to send voice calls over the Internet. They took on the office phone systems, as well, and decided to write open source software, such as Asterisk, on which other programmers could build. Now, you can have a fully featured voice telecom application running off a standard server with interface modules that are as easy to install as a new video card.

The largest structural downside to VoIP is the legacy data network over which the calls are transmitted. The Local Area Networks (LANs) and Wide Area Networks (WANs) were built years ago for the smooth transmission of data, and not for a real-time application such as voice transmission.

Here are the challenges that VoIP faces because it has to use existing LAN hardware:

- **Packets Per Second:** Servers, routers and network hardware are rated based on an idea of Packets Per Second (PPS). Data traffic doesn't really concern itself with PPS because, instead of sending a large volume of small packets on the LAN, it solves the problem by sending fewer packets, with each individual packet containing more data. But the real-time demands of VoIP discourage sending large amounts of data in individual packets. Losing a single large packet of data on a voice call might keep the call from connecting or affect the quality of the call. VoIP requires ten times as many packets to send the same volume of information as a data transmission.

- **Retransmission potential:** The primary protocol used to transmit data across the Internet is the Transmission Control Protocol (TCP). It confirms all packets are received by sending a count of how many packets were sent before the transmission is completed. If the receiving end received less than the total number of packets reported to have been sent, the missing packet can be resent without corrupting the transmission. Voice calls aren't that forgiving. They're transmitted with a leaner protocol called User Datagram Protocol (UDP), which doesn't allow packets to be retransmitted. If a packet doesn't arrive, it can't be retransmitted; if it arrives out of sequence, it's discarded.

  The inability to retransmit lost or corrupted data removes the possibility of a simple redundancy tool in VoIP transmissions, and is why every network engineer deploying VoIP is concerned about any delays in the delivery of VoIP packets.

- **Traffic pattern:** Data transfers tend to be long transmissions with a consistent flow of packets from end to end. Uploading or downloading a large file may take 30 or 45 minutes, during which time the packets are diligently being sent and received. Voice traffic has a patchier transmission style — your office may receive a barrage of calls between 9 a.m. and 10 a.m., and then the volume may drop off considerably before another spike hits in the afternoon.

All the issues in the preceding list are a challenge for VoIP to function within an environment that didn't anticipate its arrival. The market is continually responding to new technological needs, and I'm sure that newer, faster equipment will evolve to cater to this growing market.

Identifying the Hardware You Need

You can deploy VoIP as superficially or as deeply into your network as you want. You don't have to replace all your existing phones, your phone system, and the copper wire that connects them together with new VoIP equipment. If you're keeping all your analog phones and infrastructure, at a very minimum, you need a server to act as a gateway.

The term gateway has several different definitions, generally broken down into two categories:

- ✔ **Network gateway:** A device owned by a large long-distance or local phone service provider. It has a high call capacity and interacts through ISDN and SS7 signaling with the intermeshed connections of long-distance and local carrier networks referred to as the PSTN (Public Switched Telephone Network) that provide the paths to complete every call that either originates or terminates in the United States.

  ISDN and SS7 signaling are defined in the Glossary.

- ✔ **Enterprise gateway:** A device located at a non-carrier (most often, one transmitting at least two million minutes of calls per month) that interacts with the PSTN by using less complex protocols than a network gateway.

In the realm of VoIP, a *gateway* is a device that converts the language of the data received to a different protocol (or even a variant of the same protocol) so that it's compatible with the destination. The most basic example of a VoIP gateway is the Analog Telephone Adapter (ATA), which is a small hardware device that's delivered when you sign up to switch your home phone to VoIP.

Figure 1-4 shows how the ATA connects to your phone and sits between it and your VoIP carrier. It communicates to your carrier by using VoIP, but it converts the signal to analog so that you can use the same telephone you've always had. This type of service is generally sold as an add-on to your cable Internet or Dedicated Subscriber Line (DSL) service, but the standard bandwidth you use surfing the Web generally doesn't degrade the quality of a single phone line.

As long as you keep your voice and data networks separated, you can hold in check the variables that can affect call quality and completion. Figure 1-5 shows the most modest deployment of VoIP in a small business or office.

The small office in Figure 1-5 has existing analog phones and copper cabling that are being reused after adding a server that runs AsteriskNOW and using an Internet connection dedicated to VoIP.

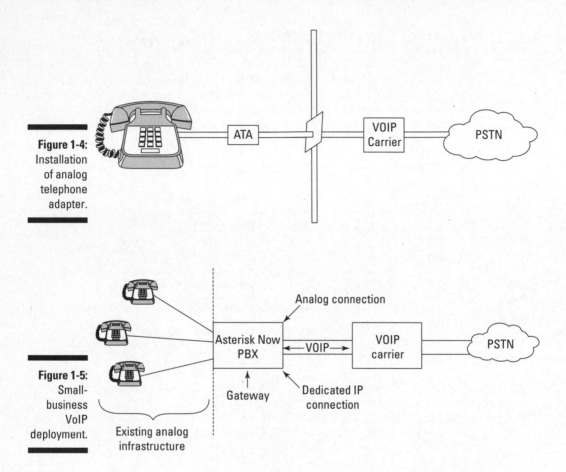

Figure 1-4:
Installation
of analog
telephone
adapter.

Figure 1-5:
Small-
business
VoIP
deployment.

If you are deploying VoIP by replacing your phone system, as shown in Figure 1-5, the main financial expense to absorb is for a strong server and analog cards that have enough ports to support your office requirements. The good news is that you don't have to replace any phones or cabling to make it all work. You can still pick up your old analog phone and dial out because the server converts the call to VoIP and sends it over the Ethernet port. The call runs through the IP connection to your VoIP carrier, which forwards it on through the Public Switched Telephone Network (PSTN) to connect to the phone number you dialed.

AsteriskNOW is my VoIP phone system of choice because the software is feature-rich and easily accessible, and anyone technically skilled enough to install a new motherboard on a computer can install it (including any analog port cards you may have) easily. This solution allows you to use both the traditional analog phone lines you receive from your carrier and an Ethernet port to send and receive VoIP calls.

You can load Asterisk on any server that's running Linux. The interface cards are made by a company called Digium (located at www.digium.com) and aren't cheap, but they work like a charm. The analog cards are optioned with either

✔ Foreign Exchange Station (FXS) ports that connect to your analog telephone

✔ Foreign Exchange Office (FXO) ports that connect your server to the your local carrier through the phone jack on the wall.

When you install the analog cards for Asterisk, don't forget to plug the power into them. FXO ports on the cards receive power from your local phone carrier through the cabling that ends in the jack on the wall. If you want to send calls to phones on the desks of your employees, you need to make the connection from the card to the internal power feed within in the server. If you don't see the green light illuminated to the telephone jack on the back of the card, that port doesn't have power.

Figure 1-6 shows a simplified, but fully integrated VoIP and data network. In this scenario, all the copper phone lines that usually connect telephones to the phone system have been replaced with Ethernet cables, and all analog phones have been replaced with VoIP phones. The same Ethernet that the VoIP phones use to connect to the VoIP proxy server also allows the office PCs to surf the Web, send and receive e-mail and Instant Messages, and access the printers and servers on the LAN.

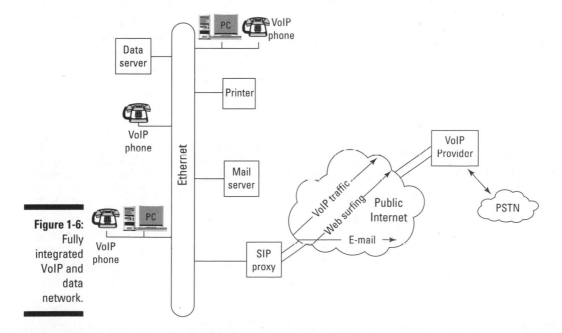

Figure 1-6: Fully integrated VoIP and data network.

This type of deployment requires much more analysis and planning before you take the plunge. All the devices on the LAN can crowd your network with packets, generating delays that can result in failed calls, and poor call quality. Part II of this book covers getting ready for deployment in detail.

The three preceding scenarios show how you can deploy VoIP with as much integration as you desire or require. As long as you have a gateway device to convert VoIP to analog, you can retain legacy hardware and still enjoy the benefits of VoIP. These scenarios are all very basic — you can find many more VoIP hardware devices available than I list in Figures 1-4, 1-5, and 1-6.

VoIP isn't a protocol to transmit voice telephone calls over the Internet, it's more the concept of doing so. Several signaling standards can be used to accomplish VoIP, but at the moment, the market is favoring only two choices — either H.323 or Session Initiation Protocol (SIP). I cover these protocol choices in greater detail in Chapter 2, if you want to know more.

The most popular protocol being used right now is SIP, so I use it as the basis for my hardware and software discussions in this book.

Understanding nodes

A *SIP node* is a generic term used to describe any hardware device that interacts with a SIP call. A SIP node can be the originating SIP hardphone, an intermediary server, or a receiving softphone. Regardless of its place in the call path, each node contains two key software elements:

- ✓ **User Agent Client (UAC):** The UAC initiates communication to the next node downstream in the call path and requests information or acknowledgements from it.
- ✓ **User Agent Server (UAS):** The UAS receives the communication from the UAC of the node upstream on the call, processes the request, and responds back to it.

Because every SIP node employs these two elements (either in part or in full) during a call, they're also sometimes referred to as SIP User Agents (UA).

Dealing with SIP end points

SIP end points are the first SIP node originating the call and the last SIP node receiving the call. They can include servers that may generate or receive phone calls, but the term *SIP end points* generally refers to the two types of SIP phones:

✔ **SIP softphone:** *Softphones* are software-based applications that display a small dial pad on your computer screen (similar to the calculator you can find in the Microsoft Windows Accessories folder). You can usually configure a softphone easily, and it allows you to make calls to other IP phones by using the same Internet connection to your PC that you use to surf the Web and send e-mail. The mouthpiece and earpiece of a traditional phone are replaced with the microphone and speakers on your computer.

I always found the reality of having someone's voice coming through the speakers of my computer a bit disconcerting. Well, only half as odd as screaming into my computer when I couldn't hear them.

✔ **SIP hardphone:** Any object that you can use to send and receive voice phone calls (that isn't a computer displaying a softphone) is a *hardphone.*

The traditional candlestick phone is a hardphone. The white and brass princess phone is a hardphone, and the black two-line phone with wireless handset on your desk is a hardphone.

Using the many servers

The downside of SIP is the more phones you have, the less likely you'll be able to deliver or manage everything that SIP can provide within the confines of that SIP hardphone. You can easily fix this problem by deploying servers in your network that have specific functions. You can have one server that provides the functionality of all the following servers, you can pair the functions, or you can distribute them as you see fit in a cluster of servers.

Securing the LAN with a SIP Registrar

When a SIP hardphone is booted up, it normally signs in with a designated database server called a SIP registrar. The server collects information about the SIP phone, identifying the phone's location so that the server can effortlessly send calls to that phone when the server receives an incoming attempt for that extension.

Benefiting from a Feature Server

SIP facilitates the transmission of VoIP, but all the great add-on options are available from associated open source software, such as Asterisk.

Don't try to cram all these fun attributes on the individual PCs that contain soft phones — instead, house them in a centrally located feature server. The services available from a standard server that runs Asterisk include not only normal elements you expect from a traditional phone system, but also some other specialties that you may have had access to from your local phone carrier or a third-party telecom provider. Some of the services that you may have on your feature server are

- ✔ Voicemail, with the recorded messages sent to preset e-mail addresses as .WAV files
- ✔ Call queues
- ✔ Call forwarding
- ✔ Conference calling, with call recording
- ✔ Call hold
- ✔ Call parking (placing the call on hold and transferring it to an extension)
- ✔ Least Cost Routing (LCR; see Chapter 4)
- ✔ Music on hold
- ✔ International call blocking
- ✔ Auto-attendant or Interactive Voice Response (IVR) systems
- ✔ Blacklisting (call routing based on the call's Caller ID)

Aggregating with a SIP Proxy

A *proxy server* acts as a link between the SIP devices on your LAN and the outside world. It serves as a single focal point to receive calls to distribute throughout your company, thus making your carrier's life easier. It also monitors the outbound calls and can be designed to restrict access for some extensions that may be unsecured (such as a lobby phone). It manages calls between the outside world and the LAN only — SIP phones on the network can contact each other without interaction with the SIP proxy (unless the proxy is also the SIP registrar).

Figure 1-7 shows SIP Phone A and SIP Phone B on a LAN. Because they're both registered with the same SIP register server (which is also the SIP Proxy, in this example), they can call each other without any assistance. If someone calls on a SIP phone that isn't listed with the SIP Registrar or from a traditional phone number that must be routed through the PSTN, the call goes to the SIP Proxy Server. This server helps to secure the telephony network. Without the SIP Proxy acting to receive and manage all communications into and out of the office, each SIP hardphone would have to speak directly through the Internet connection to the VoIP provider. Although this approach isn't a huge technical issue, it's a security issue because now you have multiple IP addresses that can make outbound calls and are vulnerable to being compromised to commit fraud instead of just one.

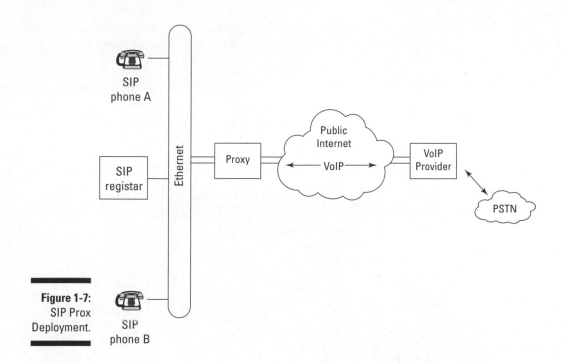

Figure 1-7:
SIP Prox
Deployment.

The processor speed of each proxy dictates the rate at which you can send new calls to your carrier. Most companies that have a normal work force of 10 to 20 employees don't need to send calls at a rate faster than two or three calls per second (CPS). If your business is telemarketing- or telecom-related, you may need to send up to 70 or 80 calls per second. You can find the calculations to determine your maximum CPS in Chapter 5. If you need more than ten CPS, your carrier will most likely provide multiple Proxy Servers or Session Boarder Controllers (SBCs) on its side to allow you to get the number of calls per second that you need. You may get four SBCs to send your calls to, with 9 CPS per SBC — allowing you to send a maximum of 36 CPS during your peak time without killing your carrier's system.

Overrunning the prescribed CPS from your carrier makes your carrier upset with you. Every carrier SBC services hundreds of customers. If one customer overloads the switch and slams it with 100 CPS when it wasn't supposed to send more than 10 CPS, the system will most likely start to progressively increase the delay in responding to incoming calls, and calls will fail. Not only will calls fail from the one customer who's slamming the switch, but every other law-abiding customer's CPS will also fail. The network security department of your VoIP carrier watch for this variety of Denial Of Service (DOS) attack and quickly resolve the problem. If you're the CPS violator, you may receive a quick call from your carrier's network security department requesting that you cease and desist, or the carrier may just turn off your access to its system. Always watch your output and maintain friendly relations with your carrier.

Transmitting the Non-Voice

VoIP was designed for the transmission of voice conversations over an IP network. It evolved to sample and reproduce the human voice, matching the quality of existing telephony. It has succeeded in that endeavor, but two other essential aspects of telecommunications frequently use non-voice transmissions — touch tones and faxes.

Pushing touch tones

Technically, the sounds you hear when you press the digits on the keypad of your phone are called DTMF (Dual Tone Multi Frequency) tones. They were designed as two tones sent at the same time (hence the "dual tone" part of their name), a feat that can't happen in normal human speech. Because of the complex nature of the sound, VoIP has a difficult time reproducing it when the voice portion (media) of the call is compressed.

Unfortunately, touch tones are commonly used during business calls. Every voicemail system says something like, "Press 1 to page this person." Or you may encounter a complex auto-attendant system that asks you to input your phone number, account number, or extension of the person that you want to speak to. VoIP has found ways to make DTMF tones work, but the solutions vary, depending on whether you're using compressed or uncompressed transmissions.

I cover the options for DTMF in detail in Chapter 6.

Faxing over VoIP

The squeals, squalls, and hissing that you hear during a fax transmission definitely don't fall in the realm of sounds made by a normal human voice. They're specifically designed to transmit data representing a visual image and, like DTMF tones, provide a challenge for voice-centric VoIP. The VoIP community of engineers and programmers have expended a great deal of effort to establish a viable way for faxes to be sent within a VoIP infrastructure.

You can get a breakdown of your best options in Chapter 6.

Porting Phone Numbers

VoIP has been helped along in popularity and growth by the widespread availability of high-speed Internet connections and the fact that people can migrate their phone numbers from their current local phone providers. *Local Number Portability* (LNP) is the process by which a phone number is moved from one local phone carrier to another. It's a relatively new process that has a few challenges to be overcome.

Keep these key points in mind when you move your phone number to a new carrier:

✔ **You lose all your features.** Every feature that you have on your phone line at this time that *isn't* provided by your phone system is provided by your local phone carrier. Your new local phone carrier needs to provide call forwarding, voicemail, three-way calling, distinctive ringing, Caller ID blocking, and any other features you require. Always ask to ensure your new carrier can provide the features before you sign a 12-month contract and move your phone number.

✔ **You can't move a virtual phone number.** Some phone numbers don't exist on a physical phone jack on your wall or a piece of copper wire coming into your office. These phone numbers are virtual numbers that exist only to provide a feature.

A classic example is the distinctive-ringing number you order for your children so that you know when someone's calling to talk to them. The phone number that your local phone carrier provides doesn't physically exist anywhere other than a database in the carrier's network. When a call arrives in the local carrier's central office, it sees the number dialed and sends the distinctive ring to your house.

✔ **You need to provide a Letter of Authorization.** This letter is a security measure for both you and your carrier. You fill out the Letter of Authorization (LOA), sign and date it (less than 30 days before your request), then submit your phone number for migration. This documentation keeps the carriers honest and provides a paper trail in case someone from a company with 100 phone numbers transposes some digits and mistakenly migrates your home line.

✔ **The time frame to migrate a number varies by carrier.** Every local phone provider of any size has its own department devoted to processing the incoming and outgoing migration of phone numbers. Although every local phone provider has a porting relationship with every other local phone provider, the nature and structure of that relationship varies. Larger local phone providers may be *e-bonded* (electronically linked) with automated systems that can validate and release a phone number to a new carrier in five days. Smaller carriers may process the requests manually with a short staff and, depending on who's sick in the department and whether it's a holiday, the time to migration may be one month or more.

✔ **You may not be able to get a directory listing.** You may not get your phone number listed in the white pages of your local phone directory when you migrate that number. Depending on the carrier you select, it (or the carrier it uses to actually receive your phone number) may not want to support the staff required to process, maintain, and manage the service. Ask whether your new carrier provides directory listing.

✔ **Your carrier can't legally prevent your number from migrating.** The phone number that rings into your office is yours — and with perseverance and diplomacy, it can migrate.

Reviewing the LNP process

The LNP process can be an extremely frustrating experience for everyone involved, especially when the business whose numbers are migrating doesn't know the steps involved. Unfortunately, unlike cell phones, the land-line realm of telecom can't migrate your phone number over in a matter of minutes. It takes days, and the process has three distinct steps.

Say that you're moving your phone number from Pacific Bell to Level 3. After you submit your order to Level 3 (along with your current LOA), Level 3 follows this process:

1. Level 3 requests a Customer Service Record (CSR) from your existing carrier. This process can take as little as a few hours if the releasing carrier (in this example, Pacific Bell) is e-bonded with the carrier making the request (Level 3), or it can take as long as weeks. Pacific Bell returns your CSR, and Level 3 uses the information to match up the LNP request, making sure that someone didn't transpose a phone number or list completely bogus or invalid information.

2. Level 3 issues an Add Service Request (ASR) to Pacific Bell to move the phone number to Level 3. Requesting the CSR from Pacific Bell doesn't tell the company that you intend to move the phone number, and the system to pull the CSR information may not be directly linked to the internal LNP process within Pacific Bell. The issuance of the ASR to Pacific Bell is its first official notification that you are porting your phone number from the company.

3. Pacific Bell issues a Firm Order Commitment (FOC) to Level 3 and identifies the date on which the number will be released.

After the carriers complete all the steps, the number is pre-built within Level 3's network on the night before it's to be released, so the following morning at 9 a.m., it cuts over without a disruption of service. The transition happens seamlessly, and you can't even tell that your number's been moved.

Understanding rejections

Not every porting request flows perfectly smoothly. An order can be rejected by your current local carrier (Pacific Bell in the preceding example) at any point during the migration process for a number of reasons. The rejections are rarely malicious — they're used to protect you and your phone numbers. If the process had no checks and balances, anyone could accidentally migrate your phone number away without your consent. Here are some of the more common rejects you may encounter:

✓ **Name or address mismatch:** This rejection is generally issued when someone transposes digits on a phone number. When your new local phone carrier matches up your order to migrate your phone number with the company or residence named on the CSR, if the phone number and company name aren't the same, the order is rejected. You can resolve this rejection by

  • Checking to ensure that you wrote the correct phone number down.

  • Providing a copy of your local phone bill, listing your company name and the phone number in question. This documentation should allow you to push through the issue (unless you have a resold account, as explained in the following section).

✓ **Pending order:** If your phone number has any pending orders on it at the time of migration, the existing local phone carrier rejects the migration request. Ordering new voicemail service on your business line a day before you request to migrate the number sends mixed signals to your carrier.

As a rule, a carrier rejects any migration request while the phone number in question has any pending orders. You can clear this rejection either by

  • Calling into your existing local carrier and cancelling the pending order

  • Waiting long enough for the pending order to complete and then resubmitting the LNP request.

✓ **Billing Telephone Number (BTN) doesn't match or is inconsistent with the phone number:** The BTN is the main phone number used in the billing system of the local carrier to identify all phone numbers for your company. Large companies with multiple locations may have unique BTNs for each site to make it easier for their carrier to invoice and manage the account. The BTN mismatch rejection is more complex than a simple name and number mismatch. The phone number and company name may match up, but the address isn't in the same city or state as the phone number. If you're trying to migrate a phone number in Milwaukee, Wisconsin and you list a BTN for your remote office in Marfa, Texas, the LNP request will probably be rejected. Just like on a name/address mismatch, you can resolve this problem by supplying a copy of your bill and following up on the order daily as it progresses through the LNP process.

✔ **PIC Freeze:** A Primary Interexchange Carrier (PIC) freeze is a logistical security device that many people have on their phone lines to prevent changing their long-distance carrier without their consent. This process also applies to the migration of local phone numbers. Your local carrier rejects any attempt to migrate your phone number as long as you have the PIC freeze on that number. You can clear this hurdle by calling your existing local carrier and having the PIC freeze removed. Then, you have to resubmit the number for migration.

Grappling with resold accounts

Every VoIP provider that you can receive phone service from doesn't have several millions of dollars in phone switches, cabling, and a batallion of employees to service their networks. A VoIP carrier has to spend massive amounts of time and money to become an established local phone carrier. Such a huge barrier exists to entering the market that many companies bypass becoming a carrier themselves. Instead, they take a short-cut and simply contract with a company that has already gone through the process. The companies that don't own their own networks are technically resellers of VoIP service. There can be several VoIP resellers between the company using the service, and the carrier that's ultimately providing it.

One of the greatest frustrations with the LNP process is the blanket of mystery that covers phone numbers provided through VoIP resellers. This situation leads to a chain of customers and providers that looks similar to Figure 1-8.

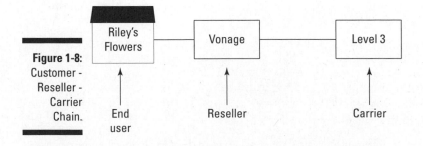

Figure 1-8: Customer - Reseller - Carrier Chain.

An _end user of record_ generally identifies the person who receives service on a phone number and is financially responsible for that number. The challenge facing the industry in the situation of resold accounts is that the end user of record changes, depending on who you ask.

The carrier in Figure 1-8 knows only that the phone number in question is on an account for Vonage. When the CSR is received by a carrier attempting to initiate a migration for it, the billing entity on it is generally listed as the reseller. Because Vonage isn't a true local phone provider, it doesn't receive the migration request — so the name, phone number, and address of the end user can't be validated in the same way that a non-resold number can. You can generally clear this reject by submitting a recent copy of your phone bill that shows your company name, address, and the phone number that you're trying to migrate.

But the situation can get even more complex and muddled. Some resellers package VoIP with additional services and private-label it for sub-resellers. Another link appears in this chain of companies, further obscuring the true identity of the legitimate end user who picks up and answers the line when someone calls the number. If a secondary-reseller is in the mix, submitting a bill copy may still not resolve the problem because the address and company name listed won't match anything the VoIP carrier or the first reseller can use to validate the request (because the true end user is only known by the secondary reseller). When all else fails, bring together everyone from the LNP departments of every company in the chain and talk it out. It's amazing how everything begins to work when you bring everyone together.

Only _local_ phone carriers own and supply phone numbers, which is why I continually refer only to local phone carriers when discussing the porting process. The line between who's a long-distance and who's a local carrier can often get blurred because of mergers, but a carrier must be licensed in your state to provide local service and have a network of large phone switches built to provide local phone service (categorized as Class Five switches) in order to have numbers to port.

Dealing with the costs

Migrating phone numbers from one local phone carrier to another used to be free in the innocent frontier days of VoIP. Local phone carriers sat one or two people in an office and let them handle the dirty business of LNP. When VoIP grew, and more and more people began migrating their home phone numbers and small business lines to VoIP-enabled local carriers, the job began to occupy more people and more resources.

Then, one day, local phone carriers' accounting departments decided to run a cost-benefit analysis of the process and — not to anyone's surprise — they found that they were losing money. Magically, overnight, the service that used to be free now had all kinds of ancillary fees, such as

- **Installation/migration fee:** A per-number charge that's assessed for the processing, migration, and activation of a phone number from one local phone carrier to a new local phone carrier. The fee can vary, but a $25-per-number charge isn't unheard of.

- **Monthly recurring fee:** This fee is generally under $1 per number per month and helps to offset cost required to maintain the routing information for the phone number in the national routing database.

- **Change/modification fee:** You have to pay this charge if you need to modify information to a number during the migration process. These fees can vary.

- **Snapback:** The Snapback process is the LNP version of dealing with buyer's remorse. If you request to have your phone number migrated, and 24 hours either before the number is to port or after the number has ported to the new carrier, you demand that it be returned to your old carrier, the carriers can do it quickly through a process called Snapback that instantly returns the ownership of a phone line to the prior local carrier. Snapback can only be done up to a few days after the initial release of the number, while the routing and infrastrucuture is still in place at the prior carrier. The downside of this procedure is that it frequently costs $200 or $300 for each phone number returned.

If you're migrating more than 20 phone numbers from a single carrier, ask your new carrier whether it can process the order as a bulk order for a reduced activation fee. You may be even more successful at reducing the installation fee if you're moving from one reseller to another who both use the same network. Figure 1-8 gives a good example — if you, the end user, move to another Level 3 reseller from Vonage, the numbers don't have to migrate to anywhere. They still remain with Level 3, who merely has to change the reseller account on which they reside. Internal migrations are generally less painful and costly for the carriers, and so those carriers are more inclined to provide financial clemency if you ask.

Many companies don't need to migrate every phone number in their office. The financial cost per number encourages many companies to simply migrate the phone numbers known to the outside world, such as the main office line used for incoming calls and the fax line. In these migrations, your existing carrier may ask whether you want to cancel or migrate the remaining phone numbers. Be very careful to identify any and all numbers that you need to migrate before telling them to cancel the rest. Any number that you cancel can be immediately released to the available pool for anyone to reserve. If you don't correct the situation before the number is fully cancelled, it can easily be gone and lost forever — with no way to recover it. Check your phone numbers twice (or three times) before you cancel any of them.

Identifying who's responsible for what

If you work in a small business that's migrating its phone numbers, you're responsible only for correctly filling out an LOA and any additional paper-work, and possibly supplying a copy of an invoice that shows your company name, address, and the phone number(s) you're porting. If you work in an enhanced VoIP company that has a book of customers on one side of your network and a carrier from which you receive your VoIP service on the other side, more responsibility is resting on your shoulders.

A VoIP reseller must not only provide an LOA and a copy of a bill, but also gather status on all LNP orders in process, identify all LNP rejections, and proactively resolve the rejects by supplying additional documentation or negotiating the release on conference calls. Unless your carrier specifically states in your contract that it is accepting the responsibility to manage the LNP orders and proactively solicit documentation from your end users, and negotiate the release of rejected numbers, it offloads that responsibility to you. Because you have the direct relationship with your end users, and because it would violate the terms of the contract you have with your car-rier as a value-added reseller, this complex and unforgiving job rests in your capable hands.

Your carrier is responsible for processing the orders you supply in a timely and accurate manner, and providing you with the means to identify rejec-tions on individual phone numbers. You might get a weekly spreadsheet with this information, or your carrier might provide an interactive Web site. You just need to remember that the reseller is responsible for deciphering the rejections and taking the appropriate action.

If you're a VoIP reseller, you also need to manage all migrated and new phone numbers assigned to you. Because your VoIP Carrier is charging you an activation and monthly fee on these numbers, you need to keep an accurate accounting of those fees to reconcile your invoice every month.

Your carrier should also provide you with a Port Out Notification whenever a phone number is migrated off your account. You have to account for all the ins and outs of your phone number inventory if you want to ensure that the ancillary monthly fees are accurate — especially if your carrier charges for numbers migrated away from you.

Request that your carrier provide your phone number information in a consistent format. Create a process around that format whereby you can simply cut and paste the phone numbers into a database or spreadsheet. Avoid entering phone numbers manually because the potential for human error is far too great — you can end up assigning a phone number that hasn't been reserved for you to an anxious customer who doesn't understand why his or her phone number doesn't actually exist.

Ordering New Phone Numbers

You can often order new phone numbers more easily and at a lower cost than you can migrate existing phone numbers. Your carrier doesn't have to negotiate the release of the phone numbers with another carrier, and it may even have numbers in stock to dole out to you. Remember these two things about new phone numbers:

- **Your new carrier can't guarantee you a specific area code or prefix.** If you live in a city that has an *area code overlay* — where two different area codes service the same geographic area — your carrier can give you either area code, regardless of the one you request. The same goes for the next three digits of your phone number, known as the *prefix*. You may want an 805 area code and 966 prefix for your numbers, but if 805-756 numbers are the only ones available, those are the number that you get.

- **Your new carrier can't guarantee all your phone numbers at the same time.** If you're requesting more than 100 phone numbers from a specific geographic area or market, you may have to wait over a month to receive all of them. New phone numbers are doled out once a month, in lottery fashion, to all local phone carriers. If your carrier can't gather all the phone numbers you want from its inventory or after the first round of new number allocation, you have to wait until at least the following month.

Chapter 2

Signaling with SIP

*V*oIP isn't a protocol, it's more of a concept. A community of programmers wanted to send voice calls over the Internet, and they made it happen. With VoIP, one piece of software doesn't do all the work. A team of individual software elements, doing specific jobs, works together to make it all happen. They're all vital participants, and losing any one element of the team stops VoIP from working.

This chapter familiarizes you with the signaling software element of VoIP, which functions like a project manager. The protocol described in this chapter doesn't do any of the heavy lifting in VoIP transmissions; it identifies the VoIP hardware responsible for the call and the basic rules of engagement between them. It doesn't break the voice portion of the call into packets or handle the transmission of the packets. It just makes sure that both ends of the call are in communication. Several VoIP protocols exist, and each choice affects the hardware you need, the networks to which you can connect, and possibly how you need to design the voice portion of your LAN.

Reviewing Signaling Choices

Computers are frequently identified by their operating systems. An Apple Macintosh or a Dell PC tells you the overall structure of the software that's used on the computer. VoIP has a similar equivalent in the VoIP software that's dedicated to call signaling that identifies the VoIP hardware engaged in both call signaling for the voice and media transmission. This software manages the overall structure of the VoIP calls. It's responsible for

✔ The languaging (the coding or wording) used in all communication

✔ Transmission of the message header, including

- Origination phone number and IP

- Number dialed or IP

- Prescribing the maximum number of times the call can be forwarded

- Listing the accepted commands

- Specialized software for managing the call's voice path (media)

- Specialized software for managing the packetization of the media

These responsibilities allow the protocols to signal, record, and deliver enhanced call features, as well as perform the standard functions of establishing the call and tearing it down once one person hangs up.

You have several signaling choices, but VoIP carriers usually offer one of only two:

✔ **Secession Initiation Protocol (SIP):** This set of guidelines, set down by the Internet Engineering Task Force (IETF), covers the transmission of voice, video, and Instant Messaging. It's the most popular protocol in the VoIP arena today, and it's structurally faster than the other choice (H.323), requiring only one message to invite a call, rather than the eight messages used in H.323. SIP also benefits from using a conversational approach to VoIP transmission that uses plain text (not code). This plain-text format enables you to read, decipher, and troubleshoot a VoIP call much more easily than with H.323. SIP is the leading protocol used in new VoIP deployments, and I use SIP in my discussions throughout this book.

✔ **H.323:** This set of guidelines was designed by the International Telecommunications Union (ITU) working group and supports the transmission of both video and voice.

It's the older of the two leading protocols and has two main drawbacks:

- **The protocol isn't in plain text.** H.323 code is, well, code. Unless you're a H.323 programmer, you probably can't make heads or tails of it — which makes troubleshooting calls for yourself much more challenging than reading the plain text and conversational banter of SIP.

- **End points have a strict registration process.** Individual H.323 VoIP phones register with a server that ensures only the IP address on that phone can send or receive calls with that phone number or extension. This restriction allows for a registered VoIP phone to be moved anywhere on a LAN and used (because the IP address is already known to the registrar server, called an *H.323 Gatekeeper*). Here's the downside — if you need to reassign the phone to a new extension or phone number, you have to take the time to reprogram that phone.

VoIP hardware, and sometimes service, is frequently dedicated to either SIP or H.323. An H.323 hardphone doesn't work in a SIP environment. It's the VoIP equivalent of trying to convey information with one person speaking Japanese and another speaking German. Each person is spewing out words, but neither end of the conversation can understand the other. Some VoIP carriers may also restrict you to either SIP or H.323 because their servers can be compatible with only one of the two protocols. (VoIP can automatically negotiate some options of a call such as compression or IP addresses, but the primary VoIP protocol of SIP or H.323 must already be agreed upon before any successful messages can be sent.)

SIP functions in a conversational manner. One end of a call requests either information or that the other end of the call take an action. The other end of the call responds to the request in a prescribed manner, and the dialog continues.

The SIP requests sent to gather information or take action on a call are defined by their function and are called SIP *methods.* The SIP methods are replied to by *SIP response codes,* indicating varying levels of success, failure, or providing additional information in the event that the desired destination has moved or is temporarily unavailable.

The SIP methods and responses are inherently linked. Every SIP response is a reply to a SIP method, and sometimes the last SIP response transmitted dictates what SIP methods can be used going forward. You can understand the general relationship of a SIP call by looking at a standard call setup.

Figure 2-1 depicts the flow of SIP methods and responses for a normal completed call. The events unfold from top to bottom (the SIP methods are identified with a gray background) and each line representing an individual packet transmitted in the direction of the arrow beneath it. The call is initiated with a SIP method called an INVITE message, coming from VoIP Phone A. VoIP Phone B responds to the INVITE with a pair of SIP responses, first sending a 100 trying response and then following it with an 180 ringing, before it picks up the call, at which point, it sends a 200 response. VoIP Phone A then establishes its audio stream, allowing both parties to speak and be heard before VoIP Phone B terminates the call by sending the SIP method of BYE. VoIP Phone A responds with a 200 OK, and the call ends.

Either phone can send a SIP method during the call. The preceding example shows that VoIP Phone A initiated the call with an INVITE, and VoIP Phone B terminated the call with a BYE.

A single SIP method can receive more than one SIP response. The preceding INVITE received both a 100 Trying and a 180 ringing SIP response. No rules require a 1-to-1 ratio of methods to their corresponding responses.

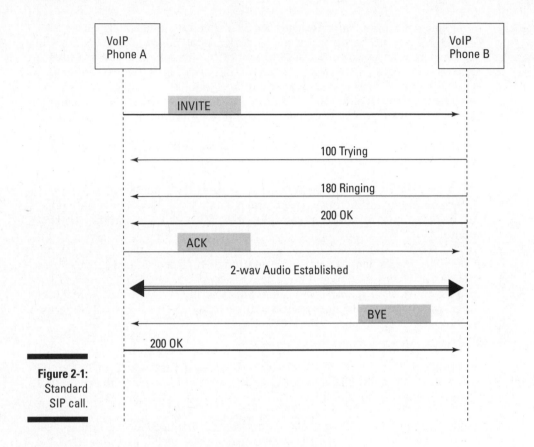

Figure 2-1:
Standard
SIP call.

Introducing SIP Methods

VoIP uses only a few SIP methods today, but more methods are being released while the technology and market evolve.

SIP is also a key element in transmitting other forms of non-verbal communication, such as Instant Messaging. This chapter covers only the SIP methods for VoIP transmissions, not the other SIP offerings.

Sending an INVITE

The SIP method to initiate a phone call is the INVITE, and it's defined in the international guidelines for SIP put forth by the Internet Engineering Task Force (IETF) in its memo RFC 2543. The INVITE method identifies the host, the intended recipient, and the other accepted SIP methods that are accepted for use by the originating SIP device during the call.

A snapshot of a standard SIP INVITE looks like this:

```
Request-Line: INVITE sip:+14145551212@100.100.100.100
        SIP/2.0
Method: INVITE
Message Header
  Via: SIP/2.0/UDP 200.200.200.200:5060;
        branch=z9hG4bk3c919aa7; rport
  From: ì128155512121î ,sip:12815551212@200.200.200.200.;t
        agas5fd2fc12
  To: <sip:14145551212@100.100.100.100>
  Contact: <sip:12815551212@200.200.200.200>
  Call-ID: 2c2b3c1e3e71246a486007ff66fa728c@
        200.200.200.200
  CSeq: 102 INVITE
  User-Agent: Asterisk PBX
  Max Forwards: 70
  Date: Tue, 09 Oct 2007 16:37:58 GMT
  Allow: INVITE, ACK, CANCEL, OPTIONS, BYE, REFER,
        SUBSCRIBE, NOTIFY
  Content-Type: application/sdp
  Content-Length: 267
```

Investigating the Request-Line

The code in the preceding section shows a very straightforward INVITE method. The `Request-Line` of the header starts with the word `INVITE`, and if you missed it, the second line reiterates the method by telling you `Method: INVITE`. SIP always tells it like it is.

A traditional VoIP call from one SIP softphone or device to another SIP endpoint has a different-looking `Request-Line` than the one in the preceding section. Rather than a phone number and an IP address, the INVITE is directed toward a destination that's named more like an e-mail address, such as

```
Request-Line: INVITE: sip:stephen@wiley.com SIP/2.0
```

A SIP address of `stephen@wiley.com` is referred to as a SIP URI or *Uniform Resource Identifier*. It identifies both the user (`stephen`) and the server (`wiley.com`). That server knows the location of user `stephen` and is responsible for connecting SIP calls to him. (The proxy server knows the users by using another SIP method called REGISTER, which I cover in the section "Logging in with REGISTER," later in this chapter.)

In this respect, the SIP URI functions like the final routing point for a local phone provider. If the Public Switched Telephone Network (PSTN) had to find a direct path all the way to the home or office of everyone called, it would take more than a minute to make the connection. Instead, the PSTN terminates your call to the central office of your local carrier, which provides connectivity to not only you, but to all the other homes and businesses in your area. This reduces the amount of routing options available to the PSTN to find your phone and ring it, so the entire process can be done in milliseconds instead of minutes.

If you're not functioning in a public network and instead are working within a secure network, the SIP URI would change to `sips:`, like this:

```
sips:stephen@wiley.com
```

A SIP URI functions a bit like a standard Web site's Universal Resource Locator (URL), such as `www.ebay.com` or `www.google.com`. These URLs don't identify the specific servers or hardware that support the eBay and Google Web sites — but it references to the IP address does that. But you can remember a URL much more easily than an IP address.

The Domain Name System (DNS) references URLs to their public IP addresses. In the server, the *DNS client* (sometimes called the *DNS resolver*) is the application that matches the URL with the IP address. In the same way that URLs are linked to the servers' IP addresses, the URIs must also be resolved to their constituent IP addresses.

You may not need to worry about this added DNS resolving step if you're sending only one call every few minutes. The challenge comes when you're sending a high volume of calls that require DNS resolution to the Edge Proxy Server (EPS) or Session Boarder Controller (SBC) of a long-distance carrier. They function as your gateway between you and the non-VoIP world of the PSTN that's used to provide connectivity between every analog phone line and digital circuit in the world. The quantity of calls that these EPSs and SBCs receive prevents them from taking the time to resolve every URI to an IP address, so most carriers now require you to use Fully Qualified Domain Names (FQDNs) that are mapped to a specific IP address. In the preceding example, the `Request-Line` includes both a phone number and an IP address:

```
Request-Line: INVITE sip:+14145551212@100.100.100.100
              SIP/2.0
```

The constituent parts of that address are still the same as in the preceding `Request-Line` example — but in this instance, the user is +14145551212, and the server providing connectivity to that user is identified by the IP address of `100.100.100.100`. If this INVITE (say, for a call to your grandmother in Milwaukee, Wisconsin) was sent to your long-distance carrier to complete, the IP address listed probably isn't actually a server on which Grammy's SIP hardphone is registered. The address represents the phone number you want to contact, and the SIP EPS or SBC of your carrier acts as a gateway between your VoIP connection and the PSTN. This type of addressing allows you to convey a call and reach any phone number in the world through your long-distance carrier's IP address.

SIP ignores dashes in a phone number, so the address could also be written as

```
sip:+1-414-555-1212@100.100.100.100
```

The structure of a phone number with a preceding +1 is an industry standard called E.164. It lays out the parameters for domestic and international phone numbers, as described by the international organization of telecom professionals called the ITU-T (International Telecommunications Union Telecommunications Standardization Sector). E.164 numbers establish the quantity of digits available for both the international country code and domestic phone number. Currently, the international country code and the domestic phone number (including the area code, sometimes called the city code in international dialing, and local number) can't exceed 15 digits. The Internet Engineering Task Force (IETF) took the E.164 standard and enhanced it to work with VoIP endpoints. The IETF developed a procedure called ENUM, that brings together VoIP-originated calls from URIs and allows them to connect to traditional phone numbers anywhere in the world.

Getting into the Message Header

The SIP Message Header contains the basic contact information and rules of engagement for the call:

```
Via: SIP/2.0/UDP 200.200.200.200:5060;
        branch=z9hG4bk3c919aa7; rport
  From: ì128155512121î ,sip:12815551212@200.200.200.200.;t
        agas5fd2fc12
To: <sip:14145551212@100.100.100.100>
Contact: <sip:12815551212@200.200.200.200>
Call-ID: 2c2b3c1e3e71246a486007ff66fa728c@
        200.200.200.200
CSeq: 102 INVITE
User-Agent: Asterisk PBX
Max Forwards: 70
Date: Tue, 09 Oct 2007 16:37:58 GMT
Allow:  INVITE, ACK, CANCEL, OPTIONS, BYE, REFER,
        SUBSCRIBE, NOTIFY
Content-Type: application/sdp
Content-Length: 267
```

The key elements of the Message Header portion of the INVITE establish the origination and termination points for the SIP signaling. The Via line of the INVITE identifies the destination server the IP address and port (in this case, IP 200.200.200.200 and port 5060) to which it should send all SIP messaging. This IP address is frequently the same as the one listed in the From line. It also identifies the version of SIP used (in this case, version 2.0) and that the preceding INVITE example is using UDP to transmit the SIP messaging.

TCP/IP (Transmission Control Protocol/Internet Protocol) is the most common protocol to transmit data across the Internet. It transmits typical computer data reliably because it resends lost packets or transmissions if they fail to arrive at the final destination. (You need to receive a complete computer file, even if the pieces arrive out of sequence and you have to reassemble them in the correct order.) VoIP uses the User Datagram Protocol (UDP), which is much better suited to the real-time application. UDP is a leaner protocol that *doesn't* resend lost packets. If a packet is lost or arrives out of sequence, it's less disruptive to discard the packet than to attempt to input it into the media stream out of sequence and play a delayed audio packet in a normal sounding conversation.

Branding the transmission with a Call ID

Every SIP call is branded with a call ID located in the `Call-ID` line of the code. In the example in the preceding section, the call ID looks like this:

```
Call-ID: 2c2b3c1e3e71246a486007ff66fa728c@200.200.200.200
```

The ID isn't the entire string of data, only the letters and numbers before the @ symbol and the IP address. The call ID is unique for each call. The call ID performs its task by is reiterating the call ID in every message of the SIP banter between the end points that allow the SIP methods and responses to be linked to the specific call over which they manage.

Limiting the forwarding

Limiting the number of times a call can be forwarded may seem counterintuitive. But all VoIP transmissions are very sensitive to delay. Each time a call is forwarded, that call experiences a few milliseconds of delay. The initial INVITE message in our example places a limit of 70 on the number of times this call can be forwarded.

This isn't an industry standard. Your SIP software can be modified for any number you want in the `Max Forwards` field.

Each time the call is forwarded, the number sent in this section of the SIP header is reduced by one to ensure the call does not exceed the `Max Forwards` number presented in the initial INVITE message for the call.

Chapter 5 covers latency in detail.

Allowing methods

Not every server accepts every SIP method. SIP is also used for Instant Message and video transmissions. Many of the SIP methods used in those mediums don't work in voice transmissions, so the initial INVITE message outlines the methods that the originating server accepts. In the example in the section "Getting into the Message Header," earlier in this chapter, the server responds to all the standard SIP methods for VoIP:

```
Allow:  INVITE, ACK, CANCEL, OPTIONS, BYE, REFER,
        SUBSCRIBE, NOTIFY
```

These methods are described in the following sections.

Sending another INVITE

Just because the INVITE message is the first SIP method sent, that doesn't mean it isn't ever used again in the call. VoIP calls frequently include an additional INVITE message from either the originating or terminating server as a means to negotiate new features (such as special compression software for faxing) or redirect a call to a new server for a conference call, voicemail, or auto-attendant feature.

The use, look, and feel of the Re-INVITE (as it's commonly known) is covered in detail in Chapter 10.

Moving a call with REFER

SIP calls are extremely dynamic, and can be rescinded and redirected quite easily. The SIP method REFER (defined in IETF memo number RFC 3261) provides an alternative URI or address in case a third party needs to receive the call in lieu of the current recipient. On the surface, this method looks like a simple Re-INVITE, but it differs in the fact that *all* the SIP messaging is transferred to the new SIP endpoint in a REFER method, instead of simply redirecting the audio portion of the call. Figure 2-2 compares the REFER and Re-INVITE methods.

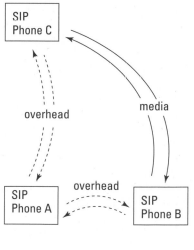
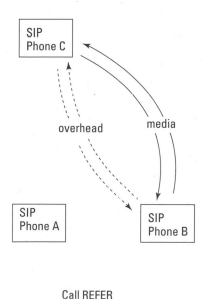

Call Re-INVITE

Call REFER

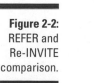

Figure 2-2: REFER and Re-INVITE comparison.

In this example, the REFER-ed call no longer passes any messaging between the initial SIP Phone A and SIP Phone B. This type of redirect sends not only the media portion of the call carrying the voice portion away from SIP Phone A, but also the overhead. A simple Re-INVITE keeps the SIP overhead processing through SIP Phone A, which acts as an intermediary on the new call. The voice path is the only portion of the call that's completely separated from SIP Phone A.

The REFER method both looks similar to and requires the same SIP response as a SIP BYE method and can be used at any time during a call. It includes a `Refer-To` header field that contains the URI of the SIP device to which the call is being referred. Here's a simple `Refer-To` header:

```
Refer-To: sip:patrick@olejniczak.edu
```

Some long-distance carriers don't like you REFER-ing calls to your friends. The challenge with the REFER method is more logistical than structural. If every end point you're dealing with is accessed through the Internet, then a REFER works without causing any legal or financial concerns to your VoIP carrier. If SIP Phone B is actually a business line in Boston that uses a VoIP carrier to reach the PSTN, then using the REFER method becomes more complex. This extreme example shows the pitfalls of REFER when handling end points that must be reached through a long-distance carrier. If you call from your office in Boston to a remote employee in London, your long-distance carrier charges you a standard per-minute rate for that call from Boston to London. If you then REFER that call so that your London affiliate can speak to your external sales director on a SIP phone in Nairobi, you just eliminated Boston as any kind of reference point that your long-distance carrier can use for billing. You're left with a call from London to Nairobi and a long-distance carrier trying to figure out how to accurately rate this new call between England and Kenya. Since the first established point of the call was England, that is seen as the point of origin. That requires that your long-distance carrier be an authorized outbound carrier with the proper British accreditation on file to do business in England. If your carrier isn't registered as a long-distance carrier in England, it now has a legal/jurisdictional problem, as well as trying to determine the correct per minute rate for a domestic U.S. call that only exists between London and Nairobi.

Confirming a call with an ACK

The SIP method ACK that's described in the IETF memo number RFC 2543 is essentially used as an acknowledgement (ACK) to a SIP response. ACK is most commonly employed as an acknowledgement to a 200 OK SIP response received after the media portion of a call is established. It can also function to acknowledge other, Non-2XX SIP responses.

This very simple method is designed with detailed information on the call negotiating elements of the message body covered in Chapter 3. The use of ACK is not confined to use with the 200 OK response, but also confirms aspects of the call offered in other SIP responses. A basic ACK response is

```
Request-Line: ACK sip:13165551212@69.100.100.100.100: 5060
          SIP/2.0
   Method: ACK
Message Header
    Via: SIP/2.0.UDP 207.100.100.100: 5060; branch
          z9hG4bk0b13d547; rport
    From: ì12565551212î <sip:12565551212@207.100.100.100>;t
          ag=as5fd2fc12


    To: <sip:+13165551212@69.100.100.100>;tag=AD6D.25F1
    Contact: <sip:12565551212@207.100.100.100>
    Call-ID: 2c3b3c1e3e71246a486007ff66fa728c@
          207.100.100.100
    CSeq: 102 ACK
    User-Agent: Asterisk PBX
    Max-Forwards: 70
    Content-Length: 0
```

An ACK transmission usually doesn't contain any additional data or media because its sole purpose is to simply acknowledge a response.

Logging in with REGISTER

A traditional SIP or SIPS URI requires that the server listed in the URI know the user's location. This is a simple SIP URI:

```
sip:stephen@wiley.com
```

For the URI to function, the `wiley.com` server must know where `stephen` is to send his VoIP calls. To notify the server about the location of the `stephen` SIP phone, that phone periodically sends a REGISTER method to the server. The server that receives the method is called a *registrar,* and it maintains a database of users and their locations, so calls can be routed appropriately.

One of the great features of SIP is that it permits more than one end point to log in to the registrar for the same user. So, both a SIP hardphone at work and a SIP softphone on a PC at home can send a REGISTER method to `wiley.com`, allowing calls to be sent to both locations so you never miss that important call.

A registration doesn't last forever. The response to a REGISTER should list the time at which the registration period ends in the `Expires` header. You can request that your REGISTER be valid for a specific duration when your phone sends the REGISTER method to the registrar, but the registrar doesn't necessarily award you the entire duration that your phone requests. If the response to the REGISTER method *doesn't* include an `Expires` time, your SIP node is most likely registered for the default time of one hour.

The REGISTER method is used *only* to establish routing for incoming SIP calls. The enrollment of a user on a SIP registrar doesn't prevent that user from making outbound calls. SIP can qualify outbound calls through a standard challenge-and-password security mechanism, but these validation systems aren't SIP. They're based on HTTP authentication.

Signing off

Two SIP methods can end a SIP call. Which method your phone uses depends on whether you're terminating a call that had the bi-directional voice portion of the call established. A SIP call that processes a normal INVITE message that is responded to with a 200 OK and an ACK indicates the call has full, bi-directional audio that must be torn down, instead of simply cancelling an INVITE. The audio may have been formed before anyone even speaks a word on the call. This is common when calling from, or to a large phone system that prompts you to dial an extension or places you on hold until someone can pick up the line. Even though you can't speak to another person, you can still hear the recorded messages of the destination phone system, and they can hear the touch tones you press. You not only use a different method to end a call, depending on the situation, the SIP method also functions differently.

There are two SIP methods to end a call:

✔ **BYE:** The SIP method that ends a call after the voice portion has been established through the normal SIP banter of sending out an INVITE, and receiving a 200 OK replied to with an ACK.

It's just like any normal call — you dial a number, someone answers, you have a conversation, and one person hangs up the phone. In this case, the VoIP hardware associated with the first person hanging up the call sends a BYE, and the recipient VoIP hardware responds with a 200 OK.

✔ **CANCEL:** The SIP method that ends a call if the bi-directional audio portion of the call hasn't been established.

If you hang up a call before the person (or phone system of the person) you dialed picks up the line, you reach a number that has been disconnected, you get a busy signal, or your call attempt leads to anything other than a solid connection, you must use a CANCEL method, which the VoIP hardware receiving it responds to with a SIP response of 487 request terminated.

Determining your OPTIONS

SIP allows you to gather information about a destination server or node without sending it a traditional INVITE message. The OPTIONS method solicits information about the capabilities of the remote device without engaging it in a call. The SIP messaging for an OPTIONS method looks very similar to an INVITE:

```
Request-Line: OPTIONS sip:13165551212@69.100.100.100.100:
         5060 SIP/2.0
  Method: OPTIONS
Message Header
  Via: SIP/2.0.UDP 207.100.100.100: 5060; branch
        z9hG4bk0b13d547; rport
   From: ì12565551212î <sip:12565551212@207.100.100.100>;t
        ag=as5fd2fc12


  To: <sip:+13165551212@69.100.100.100>;tag=AD6D.25F1
 Contact: <sip:12565551212@207.100.100.100>
 Call-ID: 2c3b3c1e3e71246a486007ff66fa728c@
        207.100.100.100
 CSeq: 102 ACK
 Accept: application/sdp
 Max-Forwards: 70
 Content-Length: 0
```

The key difference between the OPTIONS method and any other SIP method request is the addition of an `Accept` line in the header. This line identifies the desired media capabilities. The preceding example of an OPTIONS method indicates that the originating SIP device accepts SDP (Secession Description Protocol) for its media. SDP and the associated signaling components are reviewed in Chapter 3.

The SIP device receiving the OPTIONS method replies to it by using a similar SIP response as to an INVITE. The standard response is a 200 OK that lists the capabilities of the node that's queried. Here's a typical response to an OPTIONS method:

```
SIP/2.0 200OK
Via: SIP/2.0.UDP 207.100.100.100: 5060; branch
        z9hG4bk0b13d547; rport
   From: ì12565551212î <sip:12565551212@207.100.100.100>;t
        ag=as5fd2fc12


  To: <sip:+13165551212@69.100.100.100>;tag=AD6D.25F1
 Contact: <sip:12565551212@207.100.100.100>
 Call-ID: 2c3b3c1e3e71246a486007ff66fa728c@
        207.100.100.100
 CSeq: 102 ACK
```

```
Allow: INVITE, ACK, CANCEL, OPTIONS, BYE
Accept: application/sdp
Accept-Encoding: gzip
Supported: foo
Content-Type: application/sdp
Content-Length: 274
```

Updating your call

After you send an INVITE, you may need to renegotiate some aspect of the call. If you haven't yet received a 100 TRYING or 200 OK from your initial INVITE, you can't send another INVITE to change the parameters of the call. You can, however, send an UPDATE to negotiate the modification before the initial INVITE is confirmed.

Either end of the VoIP call can send the UPDATE. The response to the UPDATE is delivered in the 200 OK associated with the initial INVITE message. This method updates any aspect of the SIP or media negotiation in the initial INVITE, from the IP address you're using to receive the SIP information to a modification in the type of compression you want to use for the media portion of the call. The response to the UPDATE establishes a clean slate for the SIP banter when the destination SIP node sends the 200 OK, for the initial INVITE, all of the changes offered and accepted in the UPDATE method are listed.

After the destination end SIP node answers an INVITE with a 200 OK, the VoIP hardware on either end should send a re-INVITE to update the information on any aspect of the call instead of using the UPDATE method. SIP treats the UPDATE method as an urgent transmission and responds immediately, without the need for user approval. Use UPDATE only when you really need it — in all other cases, just re-INVITE.

If the call fails and the destination end SIP node sends a standard SIP reject response to the initial INVITE, such as a 404 Not Found, SIP node receiving it ignores the UPDATE, and the call simply fails.

Making provisional information final

PRACK acts as an ACK for provisional responses (I explain provisional responses in the section "Responding to Methods," later in this chapter). If a normal INVITE receives a response of 180 Trying, it can reply to it with a PRACK.

The PRACK method maintains the integrity of a SIP call when the response from the far end is either delayed or not expected in less than three minutes. Most PRACKs are sent in $2 \frac{1}{2}$-minute increments to reinforce the provisional responses received and keep the call alive until the final responses arrive.

Spanning technologies with PINT

Gone are the days when VoIP was used almost entirely to span calls from one IP device on the Internet to another. VoIP has integrated itself into the very fabric of the traditional, non-VoIP PSTN. That negotiation of VoIP and PSTN required some help along the way. The challenge is that some cool telephony services are available only in the dusty, traditional world of telecom. PSTN/Internet Interworking (PINT) service tries to bridge the gap between the neat features on the old technology and the flexibility of VoIP. The PINT protocol uses SIP, and it enables the standard SIP servers and clients as PINT servers and clients.

Figure 2-3 shows how the PINT client, which is also a SIP client, uses the existing SIP proxy to travel the Internet and reach the PINT gateway that sits on the edge of the PSTN. The PINT gateway negotiates requests from PINT clients over the Internet using SIP with the delivery of their requested services or sessions from the PSTN.

PINT is important not only because of what it does, but also because it has three unique SIP methods associated with it:

- **SUBSCRIBE:** A PINT client uses this method to let a PINT server know that it's interested in a specific PSTN feature. Maybe you want your daily horoscope or the status of a phone call, or you need specific information on the disposition of a fax to see if it is ringing, negotiating, complete and transmitted successfully. If the information you require is the disposition of a call originated by an INVITE from the PINT client or SIP proxy, the details of the media portion of the call are listed in the SIP response to the INVITE message.

- **UNSUBSCRIBE:** A PINT client uses this method to let a PINT server know that it's no longer interested in the PSTN feature for which it initially logged in. This method is the standard way to signify that the PINT client no longer expects a requested PSTN feature to be delivered.

- **NOTIFY:** This method keeps the PINT client updated on the disposition of the PSTN feature for which the PINT client is SUBSCRIBE-d. A NOTIFY update is sent to the PINT client whenever the status of the request for PSTN service changes, including the successful delivery of the PSTN service or notification of a delay incurred in the request.

A PINT gateway can send an UNSUBSCRIBE, regardless of whether the PINT client requested it. The PINT gateway may time out the request, even if the PINT client has no desire to terminate the request.

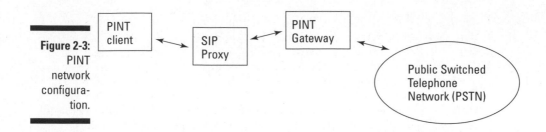

Figure 2-3:
PINT
network
configura-
tion.

SUBSCRIBE methods have an `Expires` header that specifies when the information you're requesting (if you're asking for the disposition of a transmitted fax, for instance) will be purged. If you SUBSCRIBE to pull information but don't receive that information before the deadline specified in the `Expires` header that the PINT gateway sends, the information you've requested won't be sent. The PSTN features requested are only available to you during the life of the SUBSCRIBE request. The expiration for the PSTN service requested by the PINT client is either listed in the SIP response to the initial INVITE message or as a response to a SUBSCRIBE or UNSUBSCRIBE method.

Responding to Methods

The SIP methods are often tied to, or limited by, the SIP response received. All SIP responses are presented in three-digit numeric codes and referred to in denominations of 100 that identify the permutations of success, failure, or disposition of action requested in the preceding SIP method. SIP numbered responses range from 100 to 699, as shown in the following sections.

SIP responses aren't infallible. They're generated in response to specific situations and events, and every SIP node sending a response has its own qualifications for when one response is required over another. If someone wrote his or her own SIP code, he or she could configure it to send a 604 response in a situation in which other devices might send a 503 or a 410. Most of the time, everyone plays by the same rules and you get expected and mundane SIP responses. You see more 100 Trying, 180 Ringing, and 200 OK responses than all the others combined. When you're using the SIP response codes to troubleshoot, don't get hung up on the specifics of the code. Just use the response as an general indication about what the code most likely represents, and you'll do fine.

Aside from the numerical breakdown of SIP responses into the 1XX, 2XX, 3XX, 4XX, 5XX, or 6XX group, they fit into two larger categories:

✔ Final responses provide actionable intelligence. If you get a response telling you that the call connected and the audio portion is established, you can accept that information, act on it, and finish establishing your call. The final responses are sent by reliable means to the server that sent the INVITE, and they trigger the progression of call establishment, disconnect, and are acted on by VoIP phone systems to route calls.

✔ Provisional responses aren't sent by reliable means. If all VoIP was conducted only between two VoIP servers using a well managed private Internet connection between them, the issue of provisional responses wouldn't be that important. A controlled environment like a private network almost eliminates the possibility of lost packets or failures due to connectivity. Every message is sent reliably, and so no provisional responses need to be sent while a server waits for a response from the far end. The challenge comes because most VoIP calls now enter the PSTN with every other non-VoIP call, so the gateway at your VoIP carrier needs to connect the high-speed VoIP phone at your house to the analog, rotary-dial phone at grandma's house. A VoIP call needs to know what's going on all the time. If it doesn't receive a prompt response from the far end of the call, it thinks something bad has happened. *Post-Dial-Delay* (PDD), that 5- to 35-second delay before you hear the line start to ring, is a common condition when dialing someone internationally, and even domestically. PDD on a non-VoIP call doesn't cause any problems, but a delay of as little as a second starts to make VoIP anxious.

100s: Receiving information

The SIP responses in the 1XX series are provisional responses that just keep you updated on the progress of a call. They're sent mainly to let you know that the SIP server at the other end hasn't forgotten about you, in spite of the fact that the line isn't ringing yet. The provisional responses are sent if the server thinks that you'll be waiting at least 200 milliseconds before it has a final response to send to you. The responses are SIP packets sent in the overhead of the call, and are only realized by a caller when they trigger your phone system to do something, like play ringing in your ear before the person you called answers. The three informational responses you see the most are

✔ **100 Trying:** The most typical first response you receive back from a submitted INVITE. This response simply tells you that the INVITE method was received and is being processed, but that all the connections on the back end of the call aren't done yet. The call may need to be converted from VoIP to pass through the PSTN, or it may simply need to be forwarded downstream through more servers.

✔ **180 Ringing:** This response is usually sent after a 100 Trying and is used to trigger your SIP phone or VoIP phone system to play back a ringing sound in your ear. The traditional analog phone you called is ringing, but since bi-directional audio hasn't been established on the VoIP portion of the call, the VoIP gateway sends you the 180 Ringing to alert your SIP device to play its internal ring-back recording.

✔ **183 Session Progress:** This response is sometimes sent in lieu of the 180 Ringing when your call is immediately received into a VoIP phone system. The phone remains silent (no ring-back is played) while you wait for the call to connect to the number dialed.

200s: Achieving success

SIP responses in the 2XX series are final responses. The most common 2XX series SIP response is the 200 OK. This response code contains the negotiated response to all the information proposed in the INVITE message. If the INVITE message requests a specific type of compression for the media of the call, or any type of special handling or routing, the 200 OK response confirms what the receiving server can accept. A simple 200 OK response looks like this:

```
Status-Line: SIP/2.0 200 OK
   Status-Code: 200
Message Header
   Via: SIP/2.0.UDP 207.100.100.100: 5060; branch
        z9hG4bk0b13d547; rport
   From: ì12565551212î <sip:12565551212@207.100.100.100>;t
        ag=as5fd2fc12

   To: <sip:+13165551212@69.100.100.100>;tag=AD6D.25F1
   Call-ID: 2c3b3c1e3e71246a486007ff66fa728c@
        207.100.100.100
   CSeq: 102 INVITE
   Content-Length: 202
   Content-Type: application/sdp
   Contact: <sip:12565551212@207.100.100.100>
   Allow:  INVITE
   Allow:  BYE
   Allow:  INFO
   Allow:  PRACK
   Allow:  CANCEL
   Allow:  ACK
   Allow:  OPTIONS
   Allow:  SUBSCRIBE
   Allow:  NOTIFY
   Allow:  REGISTER
   Allow:  REFER
   Allow:  UPDATE
   Session-Expires: 1800; refresher=uas
Message Body
```

The preceding response to the INVITE message identifies the SIP methods the responding SIP node uses and validates all the IP and URI information required to engage in the SIP dialog.

The 200 OK response requires its own confirmation from the receiving server. SIP isn't configured to reply to a SIP response with another SIP response, so the correct confirmation to a 200 OK SIP is the SIP ACK method.

300s: Being redirected

Not every SIP INVITE ends up receiving a neat little 200 OK with a bow on it. Sometimes, just like sending a letter to someone's house, the recipient may have moved (temporarily or permanently) or may have more than one location at which you can try to reach him or her. The 3XX SIP responses handle all these situations in which your call must be redirected. They include the following responses:

- **300 Multiple Choices:** This response lets the INVITE know that it needs to send INVITE-s to a few other endpoints and to the primary URI it initially contacted. The original SIP end point may have been too limiting. After losing too many calls while you're in meetings, at home, or on the road, you might decide to receive your calls through every means possible. SIP has the ability to send a single call to multiple end points, and so you can have your calls sent to not only the SIP softphone on the computer at your desk, but also to the SIP hardphone in the conference room, the VoIP service you have at your home, and the VoIP phone system in the office, which forwards the call to your cell phone.

  Despite all these options about where you can receive your call, you must let the server sending the INVITE know where the call is received. The initial INVITE specified a single URI and end point, so the SIP node or proxy sending the 300 response keeps the SIP nodes aware of the new end point options (which weren't listed in the initial INVITE).

- **301 Moved Permanently:** A normal response when a SIP URI has been moved, but the server receiving the initial INVITE message still knows where to find the intended extension. When you receive a 301 response, program your SIP proxy or phone system to keep the information and update your address book or database to expedite connections to the same SIP URI in the future.

- **302 Moved Temporarily:** This response is like holiday routing on your phone line. You aren't at your house in the suburbs, but by having your mail redirected to your beach house, your friends can still reach you. The 302 Moved Temporarily response does the same thing. It alerts the server sending the INVITE that you're not at the SIP URI listed in the contact header field. The server knows both where you are now and for how long you'll be there. Your new address is listed in the `Contact Header` field, and the `Expires` section of the SIP header alerts the INVITE-ing server about how long you'll be available at the alternative location.

✔ **305 Use Proxy:** A straightforward response telling the originating SIP node to refrain from sending VoIP calls directly to you, but instead to contact your SIP proxy. The originating SIP device should retain this information, just as if it had received a 301 Moved Permanently response. You can't configure the SIP hardware of everyone that might send you a VoIP call to identify and hold this information from 301 responses, but you can ensure it is set up within your own hardware.

✔ **380 Alternative Service:** This response is actually more of a failure with a silver lining. The 380 response tells you that the call attempt failed but that alternative services are available and defined within the message body of the response.

400s: Receiving a client error

4XX responses are some of the least desirable responses in the SIP world. This section of SIP responses has the largest variety of established codes, and they all indicate the many splendid ways that your call can fail.

Here's a sampling of the many 4XX response codes:

✔ **400 Bad Request:** Indicates that something in the syntax of the request was flawed.

This response generally alerts you to the source of the problem, and the `Reason-Phrase` section of the header may tell you how to fix it.

✔ **401 Unauthorized:** This rejection is usually used only by SIP registrars and indicates that you need to authenticate your registration.

✔ **403 Forbidden:** The server knows what you want but won't connect you to the required extension or SIP device.

This response is the SIP equivalent of slamming the door in your face.

✔ **404 Not Found:** The server has received your request, has checked its database of extensions and registered SIP devices, but can't find the end point you're trying to reach.

✔ **405 Method Not Allowed:** Indicates that the SIP method submitted isn't supported by the far-end server. The good news is that this response also includes a list of the SIP methods that *are* acceptable.

✔ **408 Request Timeout:** SIP is a protocol that's very aware of how much time it takes to do anything, and it likes to keep you informed. If it can't find the final SIP endpoint requested in a timely manner (maybe if that endpoint is too many hops away), you receive a 408 response. It tells you that the originating SIP proxy server really tried to find the final SIP node or execute the command — but it just took too long, so your SIP proxy server eventually gave up.

- **410 Gone:** This response tells you that the SIP URI you're looking for is gone and left no forwarding address. The server you contacted is aware that, at one point in time, the SIP URI was active.

   If the server has more information about the destination URI, such as where it moved to or when it would be back, you receive a 3XX code with that information. If you get a 410 response, move on.

- **415 Unsupported Media Type:** This rejection code is a popular one in the VoIP faxing arena. If you're using any of the advanced compression techniques for fax (which are covered in detail in Chapter 6), one of the SIP devices at the far end (or any place in the middle) may not support that technique. The incompatible device kicks out a 415 rejection, and either lists the compression algorithms it can support or identifies the wayward configuration.

   SIP is nothing if not a helpful protocol, and the 415 rejection is nice enough to list the *acceptable* media types in the `Accept`, `Accept-Encoding`, and `Accept-Language` fields in the SIP header.

- **480 Temporarily Unavailable:** If your SIP phone has logged off because you left for the day, or if you've activated the Do Not Disturb feature on your phone, your SIP proxy sends a 480 response to anyone trying to reach you. This simple rejection means, "Try again later." Some 480 responses also tell you when to try back.

- **487 Request Terminated:** A pending SIP method waiting for a response can be stopped by either the origination or destination SIP node sending a BYE or CANCEL method. When this method is sent, the first SIP method receives a 487 response, indicating that the request associated with it was rejected because it received the BUY or CANCEL method.

500s: Receiving a server failure

The 5XX series responses pertain only to rejections or dispositions of the SIP servers that support the final SIP device.

The most common 5XX series responses you encounter are

- **500 Server Internal Error:** Similar to the server error you receive when you can't reach your favorite Web site. The server error may be temporary, and if you attempt the call again later, you may be able to connect.

- **503 Service Unavailable:** If you dial a phone number that isn't built into the dial plan of the destination SIP server, that server probably replies with a 503 Service Unavailable response. This problem may be temporary, as well, if the entire destination SIP server is down due to a power outage.

The most common reason for a SIP server returning a 503 response is because the routing for the specific SIP URI you're trying to reach isn't yet fully constructed and active.

✔ **504 Server Time-Out:** Very similar to the 408 Request Time-out response, but instead of the origination SIP proxy being unable to respond to your VoIP phone in a timely manner, it's the terminating SIP proxy that can't get a response from the final SIP node and respond to your request.

✔ **505 Version Not Supported:** The SIP protocol you're using isn't supported by the destination SIP server.

600s: Going nowhere with a Global Failure

The 6XX series responses are referred to as global failures. It sounds very daunting, but the failures aren't really global. They're specific to a final SIP node or the proxy server for the SIP node.

The 6XX response comes in only four varieties, which are similar to other responses in the 3XX, 4XX, and 5XX series:

✔ **600 Busy Everywhere:** This response doesn't mean that you can't call anyone — it's not as if the entire Internet is busy and you can't send a single INVITE. It simply means that the server you've sent your INVITE to can't reach the SIP phone or device you're trying to reach.

✔ **603 Decline:** the SIP phone or device you're calling can decide whether it wants to decline all incoming calls to it. Like the 480 response, you might get a note about when to try the end device again — which you can find in the `Retry-After` header field of the SIP transmission.

✔ **604 Does Not Exist Anywhere:** The SIP URI you're trying to reach isn't known anywhere in the universe of SIP URIs associated with the SIP server receiving your request.

✔ **606 Not Acceptable:** SIP methods that request addressing syntax, bandwidth, or media types that aren't accepted by the server receive this response. It may explain suitable addressing or media, or it may list the reasons the session can't be supported in a `Warning` header.

Chapter 3

Exploring the Message Body

. . . .

. . . .

*T*he main VoIP protocol discussed in this book is the Session Initiation Protocol, more commonly known as SIP. It's the base on which VoIP calls are built, and it's covered in depth in Chapter 2. It takes care of the general logistics between the two end points of a VoIP call and sets the basic rules of engagement about how they interact.

But SIP can do only one job. After the two ends of the call start talking, something needs to coordinate how the speech coming out of the mouths of the speakers is packaged, compressed (or not), transmitted, and uncompressed. After that effort, something still has to identify where the now-packetized samplings of the callers' voices will be sent to and received from.

Two software programs actually work together to handle all the processing of the voice portion of the call:

✔ **Secession Description Protocol (SDP):** Manages the logistics of the audio portion of the call.

✔ **Real-Time Transport Protocol (RTP):** Does the real work of coding the voice portion of the call.

RTP is a workhorse of a program, allowing multiple audio stream sessions to be established from a single IP address on one server and splitting up the calls based on unique port numbers.

This chapter talks about the teamwork between these two programs that allows your VoIP calls to process seamlessly and smoothly.

Transmitting Media with the SDP

The *media* is the section of a VoIP call transmitting the audible voice portion so that both ends of a call can actually hear each other.

The main software element associated with coordinating the media for a call is the Secession Description Protocol (SDP). It negotiates the lower-level parameters such as the specific port and IP address to receive the media between two SIP nodes.

 SDP also works with the Session Announcement Protocol (SAP) for multicast secessions where the media is sent to multiple destinations, Real-Time Streaming Protocol, and most e-mail. The SDP elements of a SIP call, located in the message body of that call, negotiate the media.

The message body of a VoIP call contains the SDP. The SIP snapshots that I present in Chapter 2 end at the message body because SIP doesn't govern any information contained in the message body, it just makes room in the protocol to accommodate that message body.

A complete SIP INVITE with SDP looks like this:

```
Request-Line:  INVITE sip:+13165551212@69.100.100.100
          SIP/2.0
  Method: INVITE
Message Header
  Via: SIP/2.0/UDP/207.100.100.100:5060;
          branch=z9hG4bk2c920aa8; rport
  From:   "18055551212" <sip:18055551212@207.200.200.200>;tag
          =as5fd2fc12
  To:  <sip:+13165551212@69.200.200.200>
  Contact: <sip:18055551212@207.100.100.100>
  Call-ID: 2c4b4c1e7e71246a486007ff66fa728c@207.200.200.200
  CSeq: 102 INVITE
  User-Agent: Asterisk PBX
  Max-Forwards: 70
  Date: Tue, 09 Oct 2007 16:37:58 GMT
  Allow: INVITE, ACK, CANCEL, OPTIONS, BYE, REFER,
          SUBSCRIBE, NOTIFY
  Content-Type: application/sdp
  Content-Length: 267
Message Body
  Session Description Protocol
      Session Description Protocol version (v) : 0
      Owner/Creator, Session Id (o): root 23184 23184 IN IP4
          207.200.200.200
      Session Name (s): session
      Connection Information (c): IN IP4 207.200.200.200
      Time Description, active time (t): 0  0
```

```
Media Description, name and address (m): audio 10704
     RTP/AVP 18 0 101
Media Attribute (a):   rtpmap: 18 G729/8000
Media Attribute (a):   fmtp: 18 annexb=no
Media Attribute (a):   rtpmap: 0 PCMU/8000
Media Attribute (a):   rtpmap: 101 telephone-
     event/8000
Media Attribute (a):   fmtp: 101 0-16
Media Attribute (a):   silenceSupp: off - - - -
```

The first half of the code, from the `Request-Line` to the `Content-Length`, is all SIP information. The message body, which starts on the line following `Content-Length`, identifies that the Session Description Protocol governs everything beyond that point.

The SDP takes over, identifying itself as coming from a user named `root` at the IP address `207.200.200.200`, using RPT for media packaging on port `10704`. Using SDP, the calling endpoint can request that the destination SIP node use specific coding logic, the rate at which the audio of a call is sampled, and even a packaging protocol other than RTP (although endpoints rarely request a non-RTP packaging protocol).

Describing the SDP session

Each line of code within SDP contains a unique lowercase letter in parentheses that identifies the task for which it's responsible. These task descriptions fall into one of two groups:

- **Session-level description:** This information pertains to all sessions processed by the SDP.

  The IP address for the media server that sends and receives the audio portion of the call is a prime example of session-level description information. Regardless of who sends or receives a call from a location, the same media server for that location is used.

- **Media-level description:** This information applies to the individual call.

  The specific port on the media server used for a specific call is defined in this section of the SDP, as are the unique protocol and features requested for the call.

In the example code in the preceding section, the session-level description portion of SDP includes the first five lines of the SDP code. SDP can be used in many kinds of applications, so the lines of SDP code that VoIP uses are only about 50 percent or 60 percent of the total SDP fields.

The other possible SDP fields include lines for an e-mail address, phone number, and additional session information.

The session-level description used with SIP includes these fields:

- ✔ **(v):** SDP version. The preceding section's example code uses version 0.
- ✔ **(o):** Owner/creator and session ID.
- ✔ **(s):** Session name. The example session isn't named anything fancy, just branded with a default value of `session`.
- ✔ **(c):** Connection information. This identifies the version of Internet Protocol software used to generate the packet, along with the IP address from which the SDP was transmitted.
- ✔ **(t):** The time the session is active.

The (o) line of code contains several bits of information that break down as shown in Figure 3-1.

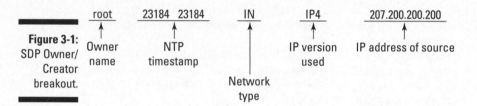

Figure 3-1: SDP Owner/ Creator breakout.

The example call owner's name in the (s) field is `root`. This name is based on the SIP node originating the message — it could be `sansay-VSX`, `Asterisk-Venus`, `Fido`, or however you identify your SIP servers. If the machine has no name, the space in the (o) line begins with a hyphen to show that no name was attributed to your server (like if you never rename your PC from "my computer").

The following information in the (s) field is the Network Time Protocol (NTP) Timestamp. NTP is an extremely accurate method for determining time and was built to accommodate the variable latency in data networks. The key feature of NTP that makes it so useful to VoIP transmissions is that it's accurate to within 10 milliseconds over the Internet. A standard packet of voice generally represents only 20 milliseconds of sound. If NTP had any more variance than it does, transmissions could easily end up out of sequence. The last half of the (o) line of code identifies the type of network (`IN` — representing the Internet) and IP version used by the originating device, and that device's IP address.

The (s) portion of the code is populated with the session name. Making this line of code even more boring, the example session name is called, generically enough, `session`.

The connection information in the (c) portion of code reiterates the IP version and IP address of the origination SIP node used to receive the SDP messaging from the destination SIP node. This information *can* be different than the IP version and address in the owner/creator line if you're using a separate media server. With VoIP, the media stream doesn't have to terminate to the same server that handles the SIP messaging. Some network designers prefer to have separate media servers to avoid using processor power to provide voicemail and conference call functionality that could be devoted to SIP messaging to set up and tear down calls.

The (t) line of code identifies the start time and stop time of a conference session. This example call isn't a conference and therefore doesn't have start and stop times. In all the traces for VoIP calls that I can remember, this field simply had 0 0. If you find something else, then congratulations, you've identified a conference.

Gathering the media-level information

The media-level description section (m) of the SDP gives information unique to an individual call. The first line of code in this section lays out the specifics needed to ensure that both ends of the VoIP call know the correct port and IP address to send the audio of the call.

The media of a VoIP call exists in two separate streams of packets that don't share similar paths from end to end. Each stream passes through the public Internet to reach the far-end device, using whatever route is available to it based on IP provider and congestion. Every IP provider has their own connection to the Internet backbone, some requiring interaction with more servers along the way (more hops), so the route they take into the Internet will be different. The independent nature of the media streams means that each end of the SIP call has to use SDP to negotiate the connections and ensure continuity on both ends.

Describing the media

The media-level description section of the example call looks like this:

```
Media Description, name and address (m): audio 10704
    RTP/AVP 18 0 101
Media Attribute (a):   rtpmap: 18 G729/8000
Media Attribute (a):   fmtp: 18 annexb=no
Media Attribute (a):   rtpmap: 0 PCMU/8000
Media Attribute (a):   rtpmap: 101 telephone-
    event/8000
Media Attribute (a):   fmtp: 101 0-16
Media Attribute (a):   silenceSupp: off - - - -
```

The (m) line of code identifies that this is an `audio` transmission that's using port `10704` to transmit and receive the media of the call. After the media is established, it's constantly sent between the two devices. Additional calls are assigned new media ports, ranging from `10000` to `20000`. When calls conclude and the ports become available, they're reused.

The rest of the (m) line indicates the SIP node originating the message requests that Real-Time Transport Protocol and Audio/Video Profile (listed as `RTP/AVP`) be used during the call. The final section of the (m) line is a series of numbers called RTP payload types (PT). These numbers correspond to Coder-Decoders (codecs) that package the voice portion of the call to be transmitted over the Internet. Codecs are covered in detail in the section "Introducing Codecs," later in this chapter.

The sequence of the RTP PT identifies the preferences of codecs, listed in descending preference. You can maximize your Internet bandwidth by listing a compressed codec first, and then an uncompressed codec. The destination SIP node will respond with the first codec listed that it supports. If it doesn't support the compressed codec, the call will be established as uncompressed, but the placement of the codecs clearly shows what you prefer as your first choice. This section's example identifies only two RTP PT:

- **18:** The first choice, which corresponds to the G.729 compressed codec
- **0:** The second choice, which corresponds to the PCMU (Pulse Code Modulation U) uncompressed codec

So, the origination SIP node is negotiating to use the G.729 compressed codec on the media streams for this call. If the far-end SIP device can't offer G.729, the originating SIP node provides a second option of taking the call as PCMU.

Provide more than one codec option when negotiating the RTP. Not all carriers and SIP end points offer all codecs, so it's better to provide options for the far end to choose from, rather than dictate which codec you require (by listing only one RTP PT) and potentially fail the call in the process.

Table 3-1 lists some of the active RTP payload types currently available.

Table 3-1	RTP Payload Types (PT)	
PT	*EncodingName*	*Clock Rate (Hz)*
0	PCMU	8000
3	GSM	8000
4	G723	8000

PT	EncodingName	Clock Rate (Hz)
5	DVI4	8000
6	DVI4	1600
7	LPC	8000
8	PCMA	8000
9	G722	8000
10	L16	44100
11	L16	44100
12	QCLEP	8000
13	CN	8000
14	MPA	90000
15	G728	8000
16	DVI4	11025
17	DVI4	22050
18	G729	8000
33	MP2T	90000

Providing unique attributes

The `Media Attribute (a)` section of the SDP allows it to both

✔ Choose which lines of code it needs for the application

✔ Provide specific requirements for the application

In this chapter's example, this section describes the nuances of voice codecs that are specific to VoIP transmissions. In this area of the SDP code, multiple lines are allowed for a section. You can't send SDP with more than one (o) or (m) line without confusing the transmission. But the (a) section of the SDP requires several entries because it defines the requirements for the payload types and adds any additional requirements requested by the originating SIP node for call completion. Here are the media attributes for this chapter's example:

```
Media Attribute (a):   rtpmap: 18 G729/8000
Media Attribute (a):   fmtp: 18 annexb=no
Media Attribute (a):   rtpmap: 0 PCMU/8000
Media Attribute (a):   rtpmap: 101 telephone-
     event/8000
Media Attribute (a):   fmtp: 101 0-16
Media Attribute (a):   silenceSupp: off - - - -
```

Every call INVITE must have at least one `Media Attribute` `(a)` line of code clarifying the parameters of the codecs requested. The first line of the preceding code clarifies that the RTP payload `18` represents the G.729 CODEC and is to be sampled at a clock rate of `8000` hertz (Hz). Different codecs have different clock rates (as identified in Table 3-1), so the exact rate appears in the `rtpmap` information, ensuring that both ends of the call are sampling at the same rate.

The other `rtpmap` offerings clarify the payload type of `0` as `PCMU`, and payload type `101` as a `telephone-event`. Both payload types have the same clocking rates, identified by the `/8000`.

The second line of code lists an `fmtp` source attribute. It represents format parameters requested in the RTP PT identified. In spite of the fact that the first `fmtp` in the preceding code identifies the RTP PT of `18`, adding additional clarification to it, this line of code isn't structurally linked to the preceding `rtpmap` line of code. The media attributes can be listed in any order. The `fmtp` listed on this line identifies that, for the G.729 codec (identified by RTP PT `18`), the originating SIP node requests that `annexb=no`.

Annex B is a special variant of the generic G.729 codec that enables silence suppression on these compressed calls. VoIP doesn't send audio packets when nobody is speaking on a conversation. If *silence suppression* is enabled, white noise is played during these times so that neither party believes the call has been disconnected. Our example requested `annexb=no`, so the silence suppression won't be activated on a call that uses the G.729 codec.

After a codec is designed, built, and released to the waiting and adoring public, it can't really change basic elements of its makeup. Modifications to codecs are released, but those modifications are listed as new extensions or annexes of the original codec. G.729 isn't the only codec with an annex available. G.726 also has an annex released for silence suppression (G.716 AnnexA), and some of the older codecs for video, such as H.263, have annexes that span from A to X.

The clarification of the payload type in the `fmtp` line can include several parameters. The second `fmtp` line of code pertains to the `101` `telephone-event` and identifies `0-16` as its additional formatting information. The 101 telephone-event identifies a way of transmitting DTMF tones that aren't sent through the audio portion of the call, but instead are sent as notations in the overhead stream and are defined in the IETF memo RFC2833. DTMF is nothing more than a fancy way to refer to the tones generated by your phone when you press the numbers on your keypad. When you push the 1 button to "continue in English" with your local utility company's answering service, the sound made by that key is a *DTMF tone*.

DTMF tones include sounds not made by the keypad of your phone. The SDP world also includes ringing tones, busy tones, and all other audible sounds passed on a phone that aren't attributed to a human voice. More than 200 DTMF `telephone-events` apply to the `101 telephone-event` line, representing non-verbal sounds that can be transmitted in the audio portion of the VoIP call. The first 15 DTMF `telephone-events` must be supported on all VoIP calls. If your VoIP service doesn't support more than the required 0 to 15, you can omit this line of code.

The DTMF events are grouped based on their application, their geography, or the signaling to which they apply. You can see them listed in Figure 3-2.

You can accept the DTMF events for more than a contiguous block of events. If you want to also receive audio on a busy tone (code 72) and dial tone (code 66), your SIP server would present the offering as

```
Media Attribute (a):   fmtp: 101 0-16,72,66
```

The numbers don't have to be listed in ascending order, except when a hyphen denotes a span of acceptable parameters. You *can't* represent an acceptance of the first 16 attributes as

```
Media Attribute (a):   fmtp: 101 16-0
```

All additional payloads that your SIP server deem acceptable are separated by a column without any spaces.

DTMF tones can be transmitted either as sound in the media stream of the call (the same way your voice is transmitted) or as message events in the overhead of the call. (If you're interested in how this works, Chapter 6 covers the specific mechanics of how DTMF events are transferred, and Chapter 11 shows how to track DTMF events during troubleshooting.)

The final line of code listed in the example `Media Attribute (a)` section is the disabling of silence suppression on any of the calls. The clarification of `annexb=no` earlier in the code covers calls that are negotiated as G.729, but it doesn't affect calls established as PCMU. This final bit of code takes care of any confusion:

```
Media Attribute (a):   silenceSupp: off - - - -
```

DTMF Event	Description
0	0
1	1
2	2
3	3
4	4
5	5
6	6
7	7
8	8
9	9
10	*
11	#
12	A
13	B
14	C
15	D
16	Flash
23 - 31	Unassigned
32	Answer tone (ANS)
33	/ANS
34	ANSam
35	/ANSam
36	Calling tone (CNG)
37	V.21 channel 1, "0" bit
38	V.21 channel 1, "1" bit
39	V.21 channel 2, "0" bit
40	V.21 channel 2, "1" bit
41	CRdi
42	CRdr
43	CRe
44	ESi
45	ESr
46	MRdi
47	MRdr
48	MRe
49	CT
52 -63	Unassigned

(DTMF DIGITS; Data and fax)

DTMF Event	Description
64	Off Hook
65	On Hook
66	Dial tone
67	PABX internal dial tone
68	Special dial tone
69	Second dial tone
70	Ringing tone
71	Special ringing tone
72	Busy tone
73	Congestion tone
74	Special information tone
75	Comfort tone
76	Hold tone
77	Record tone
78	Caller waiting tone
79	Call waiting tone
80	Pay tone
81	Positive indication tone
82	Negative indication tone
83	Warning tone
84	Intrusion tone
85	Calling card service tone
86	Payphone recognition tone
87	CPE alerting signal (CAS)
88	Off-hook warning tone
89	

(E.182 Line Events)

DTMF Event	Description
96	Acceptance tone
97	Confirmation tone
98	Dial tone, recall
99	End of three party service tone
100	Facilities tone
101	Line lockout tone
102	Number unobtainable tone
103	Offering tone
104	Permanent signal tone
105	Preemption tone
106	Queue tone
107	Refusal tone
108	Route tone
109	Valid tone
110	Waiting tone
111	Warning tone (end of period)
112	Warning Tone (PIP tone)
121 -127	Unassigned
128...137	MF0... 9
138	MF K0 or KP (start-of-pulsing)
139	MF K1
140	MF K2
141	MFS0 to ST (end-of-pulsing)
142...143	MF S1... S3
144...159	ABCD signaling (see below)
160	Wink
161	Wink off
162	Incoming seizure
163	Seizure
164	Unseize circuit
165	Continuity test
166	Default continuity tone
167	Continuity tone (single tone)
168	Continuity test send
170	Continuity verified
171	Loopback
172	Old milliwatt tone (1000 Hz)
173	New milliwatt tone (1004 Hz)
173 - 205	Unassigned

(Country-specific Line Events; MF Tones & Signals; Trunk Notification and Events)

Figure 3-2: DTMF telephone events.

Responding to SDP

The SDP in the initial INVITE message is simply an opening negotiation. It generally provides a list of codecs and features that the origination server wants. Everything requested in the INVITE isn't necessarily provided in the response. You may have requested G.729 as your primary codec and G.711 as your second choice, but the far-end device supports only G.711 and the compressed codec of G.726. In this case, the call would be negotiated with G.711 — your second choice.

The example code in the section "Transmitting Media with the SDP," earlier in this chapter, requests G.729 as the primary codec (with PCMA as second choice), silence suppression to be deactivated, and the DTMF events of 1 to 16 to be accepted in the overhead of the call. VoIP is just like standard telephony in the fact that, for a telephone call to be successful, both ends of it must be configured the same and work in the same way. You can't have one end of a call sending G.729 compressed media, and the other side transmitting uncompressed G.711. The codec is negotiated on a per-call basis, and the average VoIP call includes only one RTP port, with one codec agreed upon to code the outgoing media and decode the incoming media.

The SDP information in the 200 OK response that's sent against the example INVITE looks like this:

```
Media Description, name and address (m): audio 52150 RTP/
        AVP 18 101
Media Attribute (a): ptime: 20
Media Attribute (a): rtpmap: 101 telephone-event/8000
Media Attribute (a): fmtp: 101 0-15
Media Attribute (a): sendrecv
```

The first line of the response identifies that it has accepted the INVITE and that the RTP media streams for this VoIP Call are to be received on port 52150. The (m) line also identifies the negotiated CODEC for the call, identified by the RTP payload type of 18, indicating that G.729 is the logic used to code and decode the media portion of the call.

The SDP information in the preceding 200 OK response is much more specific than the codec choices and parameters offered by the initial INVITE. Although the initial INVITE message provides a few options for acceptable ways the call can be constructed, the response locks in the specifics on the call. Every line in the response further clarifies some aspect of how the call has been established.

Boxing out some time

The first Media Attribute (a) in the response lists the packetization time, or *ptime,* required for the call. This parameter defines the duration of audio captured from the call and coded into each audio packet sent in the RTP stream. The value to the right of ptime: is the number of milliseconds captured in each audio packet. The most common amount of time used in the packetization of voice is 20 milliseconds (ms). But some companies use values of 10, 30, or 40 ms. Ptime is an important consideration in your VoIP deployment. The amount of audio captured in each packet affects the impact on your audio quality if an individual packet is lost, and on how many packets per second your servers must handle to pass the same amount of audio.

Figure 3-3 illustrates how the ptime you choose for your transmission impacts your network. The transmission requires 20 packets at a sampling rate of 10 ms each to successfully transmit one-tenth of a second of audio (100 ms). A simple increase in sampling size to 20 ms cuts the quantity of packets required to send the same 100 ms of audio in half. The increase in volume can easily overload your routers, creating an increase in lost packets. This kind of systemic congestion can clog your network, cause poor call quality, and lead to completion errors on call attempts.

Your VoIP welfare depends on you knowing the quantity of packets used to send an audio transmission, especially if you've integrated VoIP into your LAN. You need to pay attention to packet volume because routers and LAN equipment are rated based on the quantity of packets per second they can handle.

A standard LAN environment used to transmit data isn't as concerned with the quantity of packets flowing through the network because most data packets are ten times as large as a VoIP audio packet, and data can be retransmitted if any packets are lost or stolen.

So, if small packets cause congestion problems, you can choose the largest packet size available. You can effectively cut the quantity of packets in half if you go from a 20-ms packet to a 40-ms packet. Reducing half of the packets running through your LAN or WAN should make it run smoothly because it now takes only five packets to transmit the same 100 ms of audio.

But when you use a large packet, you have to accept a trade-off. The larger 40-ms packets are carrying quite a bit of audio for your call. If a single 40-ms packet is lost, or arrives out of sequence at the receiving router at the far end of the call and has to be thrown out, the people engaged in the call notice. The technical term for when a packet is dropped is *clipping*. For example, you're speaking to your friend and say, "Do you want to go out to dinner tomorrow?" But she hears, "Do -ou wan- to -o out -o di—er to—orrow?"

10 ms Packets

20 ms Packets

30 ms Packets

Figure 3-3:
Ptime
options.

40 ms Packets

The larger the packet, the more damage packet loss does to the audio of the call, even if only a single packet is lost. If the same quantity of packets were lost, but the sampling rate was 20 ms, the impact on the call quality might be negligible. The problems tied to both ends of the spectrum of calls, the smallest and largest, make them undesirable choices. 20 ms is the most common packet sampling size, but if you're running across you own private LAN, of if you have confidence in your IP provider, you may also be able to use a 30-ms packet without problems.

Establishing the telephone-event parameters

The two lines following the ptime line in the example code (in the section "Responding to SDP," earlier in this chapter) cover the telephone events setup to which the responding server agrees. The code shows that the event is confirmed at a 8000 Hz setting, but it also indicates that the originating SIP node isn't getting all the DTMF events it requested. The code covering this section is

```
Media Attribute (a): rtpmap: 101 telephone-event/8000
Media Attribute (a): fmtp: 101 0-15
```

The `fmtp` DTMF events requested in the initial invite were 0-16. By transmitting a request for DTMF events 0-16, the responding server had to imply that no other DTMF events were supported in the overhead of the call. It couldn't reply with any new DTMF events, but it can (and did) reply with less. DTMF event 16 wasn't supported by the responding SIP device, and so it listed 0-15 in the response.

The final Media Attribute is `sendrecv`, which indicates that the RTP port of 52150 listed in the (m) line is to be used as the single point of contact where the INVITE-ing server will both transmit the outbound media stream to and receive the inbound media from. If the destination SIP node wanted to restrict the transmission so that it uses the RTP port identified in the 200 OK response only to send the media stream, not receive a media stream, the response would have been

```
Media Attribute (a): sendonly
```

Introducing Codecs

Codecs are Coder-Decoder algorithms that package the voice portion of the call so that it can be transmitted over the Internet. You have several choices in codecs; each comes with its own benefits and detriments.

When choosing the correct codec for your application, check these three elements:

- ✔ **Compression ratio:** Compression is the financial silver lining of VoIP. The greater the compression on a call, the more calls you can place on a circuit. Traditional telephony allows only 24 active calls on a single DS-1 circuit before you must buy another circuit from your carrier. Every additional circuit involves an installation fee, monthly fee, and the need to purchase more hardware to connect to the circuit. By using one VoIP DS-1 for the same quantity of active calls as two or more traditional DS-1s, you don't have to incur all the additional expense.

- ✔ **Call quality:** Some compression techniques reduce quality. These two elements are generally inversely proportional. You need to find the greatest compression that still gives you good call quality.

- ✔ **Propagation delay:** Whenever a call must be converted from VoIP to analog or vice versa, the process takes some time. In your daily life, the 50 milliseconds required by a codec to compress and packetize a voice call is inconsequential; in the VoIP world, anything that generates a measurable time delay is a concern as it increases the chances for packet loss, poor call quality, and call failure.

Your network manager or VoIP deployment software needs to monitor transmission latency. Every delay incurred from end to end on the transmission of a VoIP call increases the likelihood of lost or misdirected packets. A total delay of more than 200 ms indicates a call prone to packet loss, failure, or rapid degradation in call quality. (Latency is covered in Chapter 5.)

Table 3-2 lists a handful of codecs that have different blends of compression and call quality.

Table 3-2	Codec MOS and Propagation Delay		
CODEC	*Prop Delay*	*Bit Rate (Kbps)*	*MOS Score*
G.711	0.75 ms	64	4.1
G.723.1	30 ms	6.3	3.9
G.726	1 ms	32	3.85
G.728	3–5 ms	16	3.61
G.729	10	8	3.92

The bit rate in Table 3-2 indicates the bandwidth used in the transmission of the call's media. The amount of bandwidth used in the transmission of calls varies from codec to codec, based on the compression technique employed. G.723.1 uses only 6.3 Kbps to transmit the same sampling of voice that requires 64 Kbps with G.711.

The compression used can reduce the bandwidth requirements for only the media of the call. It doesn't reduce the bandwidth requirements for the overhead of the call, the SDP, the SIP, or any other protocols used to place the transmitted data into a packet for transmission across your LAN or the Internet.

The average *Mean Opinion Score (MOS)* for the CODEC is an industry-embraced rating system used to identify the quality of a phone call. The quality of the call can range from 1 to 5. The MOS scores break down as follows:

- **1:** Bad call quality. Static or noise on the line makes communication impossible without each party in the call yelling at each other.

- **2:** Poor call quality. The static and line noise are constant and present, but the parties can have a conversation if they concentrate.

- **3:** Fair call quality. The call has bouts of static or line noise, but it isn't overtly disruptive to the conversation.

- **4:** Good call quality. The conversation has no static, line noise, or echo of any kind. It might have trace amounts of telephony-induced background noise, but that noise is barely noticeable.

- **5:** Excellent call quality. The sound has no distortion, and both parties can hear each other as if they're sitting in the same room.

The MOS score used as the baseline for voice calls on an analog or digital (non-VoIP) network is 4.0. This standard for quality on traditional telephony lines (also called *toll quality*) is used with greater regularity in the VoIP area than in the non-VoIP world of telephony. The many variables that can impact VoIP call quality make using MOS scores a valuable management tool, and I discuss it in greater detail in Chapter 5.

The best-performing codec in Table 3-2, in regards to the lowest propagation delay and the best MOS, is G.711 — the generic, uncompressed codec. RTP can convert a sample of voice into a G.711 packet in less than 1 millisecond, and G.711 has an inherit MOS of 4.1. The G.711 codec varies only slightly across the world. The United States and Japan use a variant called G.711µLaw, also called G.711u or Pulse Code Modulation U (PCMU). The name PCMU comes from the logic used to sample the audio that it packetizes. The rest of the world uses G.711ALaw, also called G.711a or Pulse Code Modulation A (PCMA).

The G.729 codec is the most aggressive codec that still retains a consistent call quality. It boasts an 8-to-1 compression and can be used without incurring excessive delays in the process.

G.729 is a wonderful CODEC, but it frequently includes a financial premium. Open source software, such as Asterisk, provides all the necessary software to use the G.711 uncompressed CODEC. But if you want to use G.729, you must purchase a group of licenses to enable it. Each license costs about ten dollars and enables the codec to code and decode for a single call.

If you plan on having more than one G.729 call active at any given time, you need to buy more licenses. The licenses aren't that expensive and don't expire, so get the maximum quantity that you may possibly need to prevent complications and potential failed calls when you run out. Unless you create special software to monitor your G.729 license consumption, you don't know when they're all fully employed. In spite of the fact that you may have more than enough bandwidth available to send or receive the next call, your server will deny it. If any additional calls require G.729, they fail to a normal busy signal until one of your active calls that's using G.729 ends and the license becomes available again.

Using Your Codecs Wisely

Your SIP phone or proxy server may be happily negotiating calls from a variety of codecs and running along just fine, but depending on how you've configured your network, they could be working harder than they need to.

This section includes a few scenarios that highlight benefits and pitfalls you may encounter when deploying VoIP.

Deploying a proxy server that re-INVITEs calls to the end SIP device or node has tremendous benefits. Figure 3-4 shows the standard configuration used by carriers and customers alike.

If your SIP proxy is an Asterisk server, you can see how it requires two G.729 licenses to complete the call on the left in Figure 3-4. Each leg of the call functions as a unique and separate VoIP call, using its own G.729 codec, despite the fact that they're technically two halves of the same call.

Allowing your proxy to re-INVITE the call directly to the remote VoIP phone frees up the G.729 licenses. The media of the call runs though your SIP proxy for a few milliseconds until the remote VoIP phone responds to the re-INVITE, but after the remote VoIP phone sends a 200 OK, the media is effectively transferred, and the two G.729 licenses are returned to an available status in your SIP proxy.

If the far-end server doesn't allow you to re-INVITE the G.729 call, your VoIP proxy server must use two licenses for one call because each unique RTP stream requires a G.729 license. In this situation, you can run out of licenses while a call is in progress. For example, say the incoming leg of the call is effectively negotiated at G.729, using the last available G.729 license. When your VoIP proxy makes the outbound call, it attempts to negotiate it as G.729, but that leg fails because you've run out of licenses. The person on the other end of the call probably hears only dead air.

Conserving G.729 licenses isn't the only benefit of re-INVITE-ing a call. Figure 3-5 demonstrates the bandwidth you can save.

The left side of the figure identifies an uncompressed G.711 call being processed by a SIP proxy and forwarded to an off-site VoIP phone. The proxy is using approximately 230 Kbps of IP bandwidth for a single call between a remote SIP phone and a VoIP carrier. G.711 calls consume huge amounts of bandwidth when compared to traditional non-VoIP telephony calls, and by forwarding the call in this manner, you double the IP consumption.

The call example on the right in Figure 3-5 shows the same call, but with the media re-INVITEd to the remote VoIP phone. With this configuration, the SIP proxy uses a maximum IP bandwidth of 31 Kbps. The overhead of the call in the SIP and SDP messaging isn't sent continually, so you don't usually consume much bandwidth on your proxy.

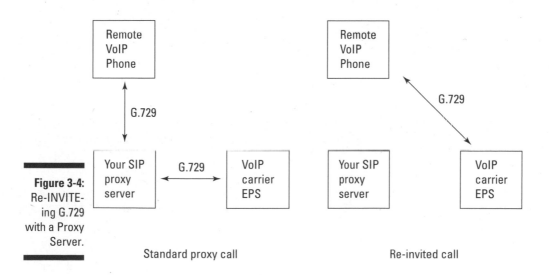

Figure 3-4: Re-INVITE-ing G.729 with a Proxy Server.

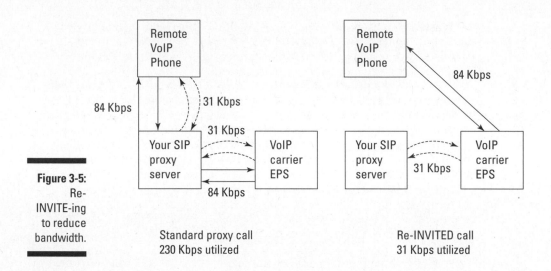

Figure 3-5:
Re-
INVITE-ing
to reduce
bandwidth.

Re-INVITE-ing a call eliminates the SIP proxy as a potential suspect in call quality issues. If the Remote VoIP phone is within a short geographic distance, possibly on your LAN and within your office, this may not be a large concern. If the Remote VoIP phone is in a satellite office across the country, you could be incurring unnecessary latency and server hops. If the proxy server of our VoIP carrier is in Miami, your SIP proxy is in Los Angeles, and your remote VoIP employee is in New York City, you're crossing the country twice with every voice packet. Sending the second INVITE message (the re-INVITE) from your SIP server in Los Angeles requesting your carrier send the media to the port and IP address for your New York employee directly avoids all the server hops, hardware, and potential traffic congestion while your VoIP call crosses the country. With call quality issues, every server the call hits is a potential source of latency, packet loss, and call failure. Eliminating all unnecessary hops allows you a much more consistent call quality.

There are some instances where a call can't be re-INVITEd. The most common reason for this is shown in Figure 3-6.

The Remote VoIP phone in Figure 3-6 may not accept the protocol negotiated between your proxy and the carrier. So, your SIP proxy must sit between both ends of the call, transcoding from G.729 to G.711. You don't want your SIP proxy used to transcode VoIP calls for two reasons:

- **Transmission delay:** The transmission is delayed while your proxy decodes the G.729 from your VoIP carrier and recodes it at G.711. Always try to avoid adding latency to any part of a VoIP call because the cumulative latency from end to end results in packet loss and call quality issues.

✓ **Wasted bandwidth:** You're using precious bandwidth to your SIP proxy when you can't re-INVITE a call that you're forwarding. The Internet bandwidth into your LAN is a fixed commodity that must be used wisely. If you've integrated your VoIP infrastructure and your LAN, the bandwidth is being used to surf the Web, send and receive e-mail, transfer large documents, and Instant Message as well as send and receive your VoIP calls. This all creates a lot of pressure on a limited resource. If you can't avoid generating latency in a call, at least try to avoid wasting bandwidth. Latency adds to the likelihood of packet delay or loss. If you run out of bandwidth, your calls fail. If you have only ten phone lines in your office, the 11th call probably receives a busy signal. The same thing holds true for your VoIP proxy. After it runs out of bandwidth, it can't accept more calls. You can always solve the problem by just buying more bandwidth, but that costs money. By simply re-INVITE-ing the calls, you free up the bandwidth to your VoIP proxy and enable it to process many more calls.

The only thing worse than using your VoIP proxy to transcode from one codec to another is to employ your VoIP proxy to forward calls, running the overhead and media through your proxy without changing anything. The VoIP proxy isn't wasting time transcoding the calls, but it is utilizing a lot of bandwidth in the process. If enough calls come in to occupy your remaining G.729 licenses, your calls will fail to a busy signal.

Use your bandwidth wisely. Even a small congestion issue can result in packet loss, and poor call quality.

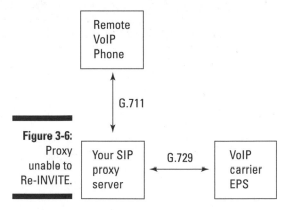

Figure 3-6:
Proxy
unable to
Re-INVITE.

Chapter 4

Understanding the Call Plan

In This Chapter

▶ Finding out what makes up a phone system

▶ Understanding the basic VoIP phone system features

▶ Looking in to some more advanced features

*V*oIP has had a big impact on the telecommunications industry by developing and releasing open source software that can replace a traditional phone system. These free and downloadable programs allow any computer or server to transform into a technologically advanced phone system. The systems use easy-to-install cards that have phone jacks on them so that you can connect the system to the phones in your office to the lines from your local carrier. You can have more phone lines available to you by using both your Internet line and your traditional phone lines for communications.

Telecommunications technology is now in your hands. Companies no longer have to rely on the expensive proprietary phone systems, which require special hardware and limited features — companies can simply build their own phone systems. You can find many open source phone systems (I'd have to write another book just to cover them all). This chapter focuses on the features available in one of the most popular open source platforms going today — Asterisk. I cover the features available to you on a basic VoIP phone system and how you can use those features.

Your old phone system may look downright *boring* after you finish this chapter.

Reviewing Your Phone System

Regardless of the phone system you have, whether it's a spiffy new VoIP system that has all the available features or a simple legacy setup that you use to deliver calls to the five people in your office, they all have the same component parts. The three elements common to every phone system are

✓ **The hardware:** This element includes anything you can touch, such as

- Your telephone

- The cable that connects your phone to the phone system

- The box that houses the software for your phone system. It may be a proprietary Avaya Communications Manager system or a Shuttle PC you bought on eBay that's running AsteriskNOW.

- The interface card that accepts the cable from your phone. This card may also have additional ports that allow you to connect to phone lines provided by your local phone provider, long-distance carrier, or Internet provider.

- The cable that runs from your phone system to the Internet, your local phone provider, or your long-distance provider.

✓ **The telephony signaling:** This aspect of your phone system handles the actual transmission and receipt of phone calls into and out of your office. Chapters 2 and 3 cover the specifics of the telephony aspect of VoIP transmissions.

✓ **The features:** This part of your phone system is facilitated by a logical and orderly piece of software called your *Call Plan.* This software establishes your voicemail, contains the recorded messages used to prompt callers to "press 1 for customer service," and defines the parameters of every feature provided by your phone system.

VoIP still keeps all the elements of a standard phone system, it just uses all of the elements a bit differently. If your entire office uses only VoIP (no analog lines), you don't need the traditional copper phone lines that come into your office from your local phone carrier. You can replace them with a single, dedicated Internet connection that has enough bandwidth for your voice and data needs.

SIP, SDP, and RTP (check out Chapters 2 and 3 if these terms seem foreign to you) take care of the telephony signaling in a VoIP phone system. The mechanics of the telephony are already set up for you in the VoIP software on your router or the open source software (such as Asterisk). You don't have to build, create, or modify the software that you use for the telephony aspects of VoIP. If the development team of your open source software finds a bug, it will update the newest release of your software; you don't have to dig into the SIP and insert lines of code to resolve an issue.

In the *Call Plan* (also called the Dial Plan), you take the basic features offered in any system and tailor them to your needs. Figure 4-1 shows how the Dial Plan functions like a huge flow chart of if-then statements, in which every call is presented with options. If the caller presses 1, then the call is routed to the queue of extensions that take calls for customer service. If the caller presses a direct extension — for example, 271 — the call is routed to that extension.

After the call is delivered to the extension, the Dial Plan is still active. If the call isn't answered in 30 seconds, the call is then redirected to the voicemail box for the extension. Figure 4-1, an overly simplified example, shows only the interaction on a single inbound call. It doesn't break down the complexities of how a call is handled if the specific call queue receiving it is full, in which case, the call is sent to a general voicemail box for the queue. At the same time, a person can use many of the Call Plan features when he or she has a call in a pending status by pressing 0 (zero) to talk to the operator or # to access a dial-by-name directory.

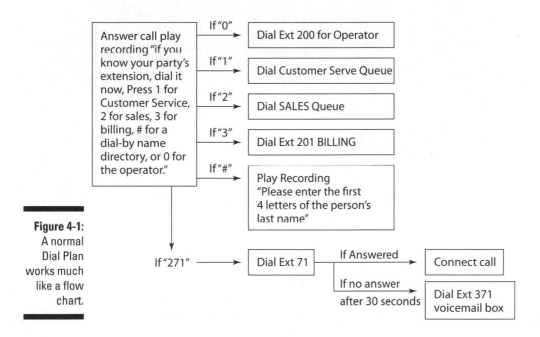

Figure 4-1:
A normal
Dial Plan
works much
like a flow
chart.

The Dial Plan combines the capabilities of the phone system with the specific requirements of your business. Even though the phone system or Cisco router can handle advanced VoIP fax compression codecs, your Dial Plan may still need to identify the specific calls that require the codec. Failing to make the link between the phone number belonging to your fax machine and the need to request the special fax compression codec can result in failed calls or calls negotiated with a less-than-optimal compression.

A professional should develop or deploy any of the open source software that you use. If you're not familiar with the Linux operating system, haven't had a class or two in programming, and don't also have the patience of a saint, then let someone else deploy the Dial Plan portion of your VoIP phone system.

Basic VoIP Phone Features

Your business probably needs a few common telephony functions, such as voicemail or access to conference calling. Almost every phone system released in the past ten years has some voicemail capabilities, but conference calling has only been provided by specialized companies. These are only two of the features that are frequently used. The following sections give you the scoop on the most frequently used functions.

Starting with voicemail

Voicemail is as common in today's phone systems as a dial tone. You may know the basic voicemail setup, in which someone leaves you a message, then your phone notifies you in one way or another. You might see a small red light start blinking on your phone, or you may hear the dial tone stutter the next time you pick up your phone to dial out. These methods of notification can let you know that someone left you a message — but only if you're in the office.

VoIP phone systems don't have this limitation. The very flexible VoIP system allows you to set up as many voicemail boxes as you need. I've personally never pushed the limits of how many voicemail boxes I could put on a VoIP phone system, but as long as your server has memory, you can continue to build those voicemail boxes. VoIP systems are also more flexible in the specific mechanics of the voicemail than traditional voicemail systems, allowing you to specify parameters, such as

✔ Megabyte size allocated for messages to be received. This identifies how much memory you're devoting to the voicemail box to hold the recorded messages.

✔ The amount of time that elapses before a call is transferred to voicemail.

✔ The length of an outgoing message.

✔ Primary Voicemail extension. This is the extension you dial to retrieve your voicemail messages and manage your voicemail box. Despite the fact that someone has to dial extension 145 to reach you, you dial the primary voicemail extension of 200 to retrieve your messages or change your greeting.

✔ The pass code to retrieve messages.

These parameters are all variations on the same features that you may already have. VoIP phone systems provide voicemail with more options than traditional phone systems because VoIP is a telephony application with a data mindset. So, when your customer leaves you a voicemail about cancelling that meeting or rerouting that order he or she placed from New York to Miami, that voicemail is recorded in a simple, .WAV audio file. You can play .WAV files on almost any computer in the world, and because your phone system is running VoIP, it's already connected to the Internet. Your voicemail can send a copy of the recorded .WAV file that your customer left to your e-mail address as a message attachment.

Set all voicemails so that a copy of the recorded message is sent to the recipient's e-mail address. Sales staff or other individuals who travel on behalf of the company can stay in touch by using this feature. You may begin to check your e-mail before you even think about calling the office and digging in to your voicemail. You can also very easily forward the message to another person or department so that he or she can respond while you're at that trade show or on a sales call.

Building a conference (call) room

Whenever you need to speak to more than two other people, your boss invariably tells you, "Set up a conference call." The conference call is, technically, just a series of calls received on the same phone number or extension where every caller can speak to each other. Every company should have the ability to host its own conference call. It shows a level of corporate sophistication and legitimacy when you can tell your customers, "We'll use our conference room, here's the dial-in number."

You can use many conference-call hosting services, but most of the VoIP phone systems have provisions that allow you to create an extension for the purpose of conference calls. You need three logistical pieces to set up a room ready to host your conference calls:

- **The extension number used for the conference room:** You can set up a normal extension that the callers dial after they reach your main auto-attendant greeting of, "Thank you for calling our office. If you know your party's extension, dial it now. . . . " For example, the extension 271 doesn't ring to the office of Mortimer Fowler in sales, like it normally does — it's identified in the Dial Plan so that it rings to your conference extension.

  You can also assign a unique phone number in your office to the conference room. In this case, your Dial Plan identifies the phone number dialed as belonging to the extension for the conference room, and it routes the call accordingly.

- **The pass code to gain entrance to the call:** The numeric code, usually four digits, that allows only the select participants to enter the call. Even though you can be routed to the extension for the conference bridge as long as you know the number, if you don't know the pass code, you can't enter the call.

- **The moderator code:** Only the moderator of the conference knows this numeric code, usually four digits, which he or she uses to open the bridge. Before the moderator enters this code, all the attendees of the conference call are on mute — they can't talk amongst themselves, or even know that anyone else is waiting to join the conference call, until the moderator arrives and enters the code. After he or she enters the code, everyone is taken off mute, and the call can begin.

Any VoIP phone system worth its salt offers additional features for your conference calling, such as

- Announcements when new participants join the call
- Playing music until the moderator arrives and enters the moderator code
- Recording the conference call
- Announcing when participants leave

Establishing a call queue

A call queue puts incoming calls in a neat line, making the callers wait until an employee in the designated queue can take their calls. A call queue is a simple but effective way for a small number of employees to service an influx of calls.

The first time I heard the term "queue," I had just arrived in London, England, for a study abroad program. We were directed to the queue for the buses, where a perfect line of people stood, one behind the other, waiting for their turn to enter the available bus.

You can have your call queues designed as simply or with as much complexity as you require. Figure 4-2 shows three different call queues, each containing specific extensions that act as agents to receive the calls. These are three simple sets of queues, all with overflow to another queue. The trigger to open the second queue as overflow can be anything, from the number of calls to the average hold time — you can decide on that parameter and instruct your programmer building the Dial Plan to create the hierarchy.

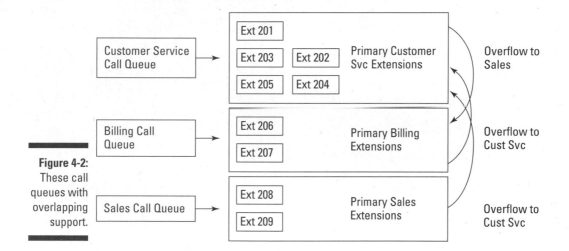

Figure 4-2:
These call queues with overlapping support.

After you set up the extensions and the overflow of your call queue, you only have to decide how the calls are delivered into the queue. You have a series of extensions that can receive any call, and most VoIP phone systems allow you to choose from some standard methods of delivery:

- **Fewest Calls:** This option tracks the number of calls the agents have accepted and sends new calls to the agent who has the least amount of completed calls. This scenario may seem like a good idea, but if an unruly customer takes up an hour of time for a single, customer service rep, this option will slam the rep with calls for the next few hours while he or she tries to catch up to the call count of his or her peers.

- **Least Recent:** This option allows calls to be sent to the agent who has been idle (without a call) for the longest duration of time.

- **Random:** The phone system randomly assigns calls to any of the agents available on the system.

- ✔ **Ringall:** This option rings all the agents who are logged in to the system; it doesn't assign the call specifically to any one agent. The first extension to answer the call gets it.

- ✔ **Roundrobin:** Each agent receives a call in a set pattern when you use this option, just like dealing the opening hand of cards to players in a poker game. Everyone gets one card (or call) in the same order each round.

The individual extensions must be logged in to the queue in order to be seen as available. So, you can rotate staff into and out of the queue for lunch, breaks, and when the evening crew replaces the morning operators, without calls going to the extensions of people who have gone home for the day.

Building out an extension

Individual extensions identify the employee phones, office fax machines, and internal features (such as voicemail or conference bridges) supported by the phone system. Each extension must be built in the Dial Plan so that the Dial Plan knows that extension's location, as well as the extension's permissions or restrictions to send and receive calls. The configuration established in the Dial Plan allows the extensions to

- ✔ Receive inbound calls
- ✔ Dial local calls
- ✔ Dial long-distance calls
- ✔ Dial international calls
- ✔ Establish itself as an agent in a specific call queue
- ✔ Register the name of the person at the extension for the dial-by-name directory

Advanced VoIP Phone Features

If you're implementing a VoIP solution, it probably includes a sackful of features that can help you manage and improve your business's phone system.

Saving money with Least Cost Routing

The rates that a long-distance carrier charges you reflect the rates that the local carriers who supply service to the phone numbers you're dialing charge that long-distance carrier. Depending on how much volume a long-distance carrier (such as Qwest or Sprint) has with the local carrier (such as Ameritech or Bell South), it may pay more or less than its competitors. In the end, every long-distance company has its own cost to domestic and international locations based on its current traffic and how effectively it can negotiate a deal. So, no two rate plans from competing long-distance carriers are ever the same. You can always find destination countries and locations that cost less with a particular carrier. The perfect solution is to use both carriers and always send your calls to the carrier with the lowest rate.

You can make this dream a reality with most VoIP phone systems. Picking the best rates from two or more carriers is a function called *pattern matching*. This simple technology identifies patterns in data that, in the case of phone systems, routes phone calls onto a specific carrier.

Designing and deploying a system to send calls over only the most cost effective carrier takes some effort, but if your phone bill is more than $500 per month, it may be worth it in the long run. Ideally, you create a large *Least Cost Routing (LCR)* matrix of routing decisions in your phone system, based on the first six digits of any domestic or international phone number you might dial. LCRs require you to match up the rate plans offered by your carriers to determine which is more cost effective, and then link those rates to the first six digits of the phone numbers that meet that criteria.

This can take a lot of time because two carriers seldom provide their price lists to you in the same format. One carrier may contract with you for a flat per-minute rate of ten cents per minute for all calls within your state and five cents per minute for all calls to any other U.S. state. Your second carrier may have different rates per state, or to an even more granular level of regions within each state.

The final step before deploying the LCR is matching up all the rates to the area codes located in the specific states. Your carrier may be able to translate your standard price list into one based on the area codes. The second option is to purchase a recent Local Exchange Routing Guide (LERG) database from Telcordia at www.telcordia.com.

American domestic phone numbers are generally assigned to local phone carriers based on

- ✔ The area code (also called the NPA, or Numbering Plan area code)
- ✔ The first three digits of the local phone number, called the prefix, exchange, or NXX (digits 1-9 represented by N and digits 0-9 represented by X).

If you want to find out which local carrier supplies service to your grandmother in Milwaukee, you can look up her phone number, 414-744-XXXX, and identify Ameritech Wisconsin as her carrier. So, Ameritech provides service to every phone number in the 414-744 area code and prefix, and your long-distance carrier should have the same rates for all numbers with that area code and prefix. Anyone can identify the local carrier for any domestic U.S. phone number by going to the `www.localcallingguide.com` Web site and clicking the Search Area Code/Prefix/OCN link.

You can easily make a rudimentary LCR system for international calls. You don't have to drill the international numbers down too specifically. For example, your Sprint contract may have a much better rate for Germany than your Qwest contract, so your phone system simply has to route based on the 011 international dialing prefix and the international country code consisting of the following two to four digits to cover the entire country.

Using an LCR can save you quite a bit of money, but you must have either your analog lines assigned to the different carriers or individual dedicated circuits terminating to different carriers. Your phone system can identify the physical interfaces of the analog or digital line in Port 1 as Sprint and the line in Port 2 as Qwest. After you establish the physical link from the carrier to the port, you can then route all the Sprint preferred calls to Port 1 and all the Qwest preferred calls to Port 2.

You can use an LCR even more easily by using VoIP connections. All long-distance carriers are rolling out VoIP products to replace their traditional dedicated connections. A VoIP connection allows you to connect to a quality Internet provider and connect to multiple long-distance carriers by using the public Internet. As long as you choose a dependable IP provider, you shouldn't have many issues. You simply identify your carriers by the IP address of their proxy servers, allowing you to bring on more carriers without additional cost.

If you want to employ LCR over your existing analog lines, you don't have to change the primary long-distance carrier assigned to them with your local phone carrier. By building in the ability to dial the 1010 access codes for other carriers over your analog lines, you can bypass your primary long-distance carrier and have the call passed to a different long-distance carrier to terminate the call.

For example, say you have one phone line that's set up with Qwest for your long-distance service, but Sprint has a cheaper rate to Japan. You can send your call to Japan by entering the Sprint access code (also known as a dial-around code) before you enter the 011 international dialing prefix and the number you're calling in Tokyo. The whole string of digits to be dialed, including the Sprint access code, the country code for Japan, and the city code for Tokyo, would be 1010333 011 81 423 XXXXXX.

You *must* have a contract for service with the long-distance carrier on which you're sending the 1010 call. Sending calls over a long-distance carrier that you don't have a contract with by using a 1010 code can cost you a lot of money or result in your call being blocked. Until you sign up for service, the long-distance carrier doesn't know who you are or whether you'll pay it. So, it charges the maximum rate possible on these non-contract 1010 calls. You could wind up paying $2 per minute on top of a $5-connection fee. The charges appear on your local phone bill, and you have no way to dispute them.

Many people have tried to dispute these charges, stating that the long-distance carriers somehow grabbed the calls and sent them over their network. That isn't possible as long-distance carriers receive the calls either as the default long-distance carrier that your local carrier assigns to you or by you dialing a 1010 number. They have no way to receive calls from you that neither you, nor your local carrier has sent to them.

Protecting against fraud with pattern matching

Pattern matching can protect you against fraud. Many companies conduct all their business domestically and don't need to dial international destinations. Most of the expensive telecom fraud is the result of someone gaining access to a business phone system and then placing thousands of calls to international destinations. The biggest market for telecom fraud is for calls to the most expensive countries, generally in the Middle East (including Egypt, Iran, Afghanistan, Pakistan, Saudi Arabia, and Iraq). So, you need to use the same pattern matching logic used in your LCR system to identify calls dialed to these international destinations to route these calls to a dead extension or one that plays a recording that says, "Your international call has been blocked by the company phone system."

If you conduct some international business, you can focus your pattern matching on looking for calls to specific countries in which you aren't currently doing business. The pattern matching then includes the 011 prefix and the country code that require special handling. You get protection but can still reach your legitimate international contacts.

Pattern matching looks for the entire string of data in order to route the call.

Here are a few pattern-matching configurations:

```
All "011*" calls are sent to the default carrier
All "01181*" calls are sent to a dead extension
All "01144207*" calls are sent to a dead extension
```

If these three pattern-matching rules are the only ones present in the system, all 011 dialed international calls are passed through to your default long-distance carrier for completion, but all calls to Japan (country code 81) and inner London, UK (country code 44, city code 207), are blocked. Even though inner London calls are sent to a dead extension, you can make calls to other parts of England without a problem. Only phone numbers that include the entire pattern of 01144207 are selected for unique routing. If someone dials 011 44 208 (outer London), the dial doesn't match the preset pattern and therefore is sent to your default long-distance carrier for completion.

Some international destinations don't require a 011 prefix. Several countries are technically international for U.S. callers, but if you're in America, you can reach those countries by simply dialing 1 and ten digits, just like a domestic call. These countries, which are in what's called the North American Numbering Plan (NANP), include Canada, the U.S. Virgin Islands, St. Kitts, Jamaica, Grenada, Guam, and most of the Caribbean. High-end telecom fraud usually doesn't target these countries, but several phone-sex companies are based in these areas. The phone-sex and gambling industries reacted to the ease with which companies and local phone carriers could place the 011 block on outbound calls, so most of the companies moved into the Caribbean to market with a domestic-looking phone number. If you have any concerns about this type of fraud, simply build a pattern-matching scheme for the area codes found in Table 4-1.

The North American Numbering Plan (NANP) was developed to make international calling easier. It set a 10-digit phone number structure including a three-digit area code and a seven-digit phone number for calls to Canada, the Caribbean, and the United States.

Table 4-1	North American Dialing Plan Area Codes
Country	**Area Code**
American Samoa	684
Anguilla	264
Antigua	268
Bahamas	242
Barbados	246
Bermuda	441

Country	*Area Code*
British Virgin Islands	284
Cayman Islands	345
Dominica	767
Dominican Republic	809
Dominican Republic	829
Grenada	473
Jamaica	876
Montserrat	664
St. Kitts/Nevis	869
St. Lucia	758
St. Vincent/Grenadines	784
Trinidad & Tobago	868
Turks & Caicos	649

Routing incoming callers with pattern matching

Pattern matching can enhance your ability to serve your customers. You can modify your Dial Plan to match the Caller IDs on calls going to your customer service queue with a database of your existing customers. You can identify a client who's calling in for assistance and route him or her to the correct department for the specific product or service that he or she purchased from the company.

You can also use pattern matching on incoming calls to blacklist callers. If a customer is past due on his or her balance, you can create an extension for your Accounts Receivable department to which that customer's call is routed before he or she even has the chance to press a single button.

You can develop blacklisting even further. Use it to handle harassing calls without having to file a restraining order. You can become as creative as you want — send the call to

✔ An maze of automated voicemail prompts for increasingly bizarre things

✔ A continuous loop of an annoying song

✔ The most boring book on tape you can find

Assembling an Interactive Voice Response (IVR) system

An Interactive Voice Response (IVR) is the basic routing mechanism used in many phone systems today. It asks you to "Press 1 for English or 2 for Spanish" or "Press 1 for customer service, 2 for sales, 3 for billing, or 0 to reach our operator." Everyone has these systems because they're efficient. You can decide how complex and in depth you want your IVR to be.

When you use a VoIP phone system, you can record any prompts that you want. You can solicit information from the caller by using a prompt such as "Enter your account number," or you can provide service to the customer without having to engage a live agent for the call by using a prompt such as "To hear your current account balance, press 1."

Designing an IVR takes some work, but it can integrate with a database to reference account information and relay it to your customers. This area of a Dial Plan is limited only by your imagination. If you can dream up a need to relay information, you can create an IVR that allows someone to hear that information.

Using VoIP to call forward

A VoIP phone system doesn't only use VoIP signaling to communicate with VoIP phones and VoIP carriers, it also uses VoIP internally. Your VoIP phone system may also connect to standard analog line from your local carrier, but by using VoIP internally, you get the flexibility of VoIP on every call, regardless of whether it started out VoIP. You can take an inbound call that originated on an analog line from your normal local phone carrier and transfer it to your office line. If you don't pick up the call, your VoIP phone system can send a SIP INVITE for the call to an outside line to attempt to reach you on your cell phone. If your cell phone doesn't pick up in four rings, your phone system can then rescind the call and send a new SIP INVITE to your voicemail box in the office. The recorded message that the caller leaves is saved as a .WAV file and e-mailed to you.

Many enhanced VoIP carriers provide this service, generally referred to as the find-me-follow-me service. Staff who are frequently out of the office, or unavailable for some reason or another, can better stay in touch through this service. As soon as a staffer becomes available, he or she can't help but know you called.

Turning on the lights with X10

One of the most cutting-edge software applications available is a programming language called X10. It works well in a Linux environment and allows you to manipulate electric devices.

The setup is pretty straightforward. Replace some of your electrical outlets with either X10 receiving electronic outlets or external receivers. Then, plug in lamps, appliances, coffee makers, toasters, and anything else you want to remotely control. A singe device (a *transceiver*) that's plugged in to an electrical outlet activates the receivers.

The transceiver allows phone-based remote access to the basic functionality of the electronic devices connected to the receivers. For example, you can remotely turn on the lights in your office by setting up an IVR that integrates with the X10.

You can use this functionality by integrating an X.10 system into the Dial Plan. Your Dial Plan designer needs to build a series of prompts and routing within your IVR, including a specific extension for the system and a password to protect access to it. For example, after dialing in to the system, selecting the extension for the X.10 system, and entering the password, the IVR that your programmer designed can then run through a series of prompts to activate and deactivate your electric devices. Each prompt can be designed to handle any task you need, with one of the IVR recordings stating "To turn on the lights in the reception area, press 5 and to turn off the reception area lights, press 6."

You may need to do some additional homework to integrate X.10 with all the features you need, but the VoIP systems (such as Asterisk) have a system application that allows them to pass command-line data to be executed. You have to create individual sections of the Dial Plan for the X10 connection, but if you have the time, it's a unique way to activate appliances, servers, and security devices.

Modern homes are built with two 110-volt circuits in the breaker box. These circuits break down the 220 volts that your power company supplies to your home. Some of your electrical outlets are on one circuit, and some are on the other. When using X10 technology in your home, you usually need a *phase coupler* to connect the two 110-volt circuits. The phase coupler facilitates X10 communications throughout your home.

Using the console mode of your phone system

Almost every VoIP phone system allows you to see its inner workings in real-time. You can see the Caller ID of every incoming call, the manner in which it arrived (from an analog port or through VoIP), and whether the caller pressed 1 for customer service or 3 for billing. You can even watch the call being sent to the final extension and answered. It's kind of like taking the back off your watch and watching the gears running.

Watching the lifeblood of your phone system course before your very eyes isn't just for fun, it's also helpful. Because this option allows you to see the events while they're happening, you can use it to help troubleshoot issues when calls go awry. If you have a complex LCR system built and multiple long-distance carriers possible for each call, you may want to access the console mode when you make a test call to identify the carrier that received the call. Reporting a call failure to a carrier, pushing for action on it all day, and then finding out after eight hours of follow-up that the call never hit its network can be frustrating, to say the least.

The system shows you whether the call was sent to a carrier or whether it even left your phone system. If some form of the Dial Plan syntax is wrong, viewing the call in the console mode may show you where the call actually ended up when it was supposed to go to your voicemail. The Dial Plans are generally loaded with code that flashes by in an instant while the calls are processing. If you designed the code, it'll all make sense to you, and I'm sure you'll have the problem resolved in no time. If you aren't the programmer who created the Dial Plan, most of the information is identified in simple terms, such as "Destination: Port 1 IP 205.100.100.10." This allows anyone with a little technical savvy to at least get some useful information like the destination port receiving the failed call, or any error or warning messages that appear, to relay to the designer when you speak to him or her.

Using your Call Detail Records

VoIP phone systems, such as Asterisk, record vital information about every call they process. The date, time, duration, number dialed, and outbound port that processed the call generally start the Call Detail Records (CDR) held in the system. The CDR is a file, like any other in the Dial Plan, so you can build your Dial Plan to gather data from each call and store it in the CDR. You can flag specific calls with the tag of FORWARDCELL if it was sent from the office line to the person's cell phone. If your office uses the find-me-follow-me capabilities of VoIP, this feature can help you keep track of multiple outbound calls that start from a single inbound call.

The main reason to access the system CDR is to reconcile your monthly phone invoice. The more money you spend on your phone bill every month, the more you need to use this system to verify the bill's tally of total calls and total minutes that you receive from local or long-distance carrier at the end of the month.

Don't expect the total minutes on the invoice from your carrier to exactly match the data you pull from your CDR. I've been comparing CDR data to invoices for 16 years, and I've never seen an exact match. You always encounter variances, but overall, you want the difference below 5 percent. If your carrier has in excess of 10 percent more minutes or calls than your CDR, you may want to investigate. If the variance jumps up between 5 and 10 percent, monitor it closely as it probably indicates that a new problem may have just impacted the billing, and next month the difference may be 12 percent. If the next month variance drops to 3 percent, don't waste any more time on it.

Your numbers may not match the total calls and minutes from your carrier for several reasons:

- **Carryover and lag in reporting calls.** Your carrier may need several days to receive all the CDR for every call you make, so a bill created at the end of the month may not contain calls that your business makes in the last two days of the month. But don't worry — they'll show up on next month's bill. An invoice always has some bleed-over calls from the previous month. This lag can be as minor as the calls showing up a week late or as severe as calls showing up months late.

- **The exact start times and stop times are never the same.** The exact millisecond that your carrier identifies as the beginning of billing on a call is never the exact same millisecond that your phone system recognizes. This creates the disparity between the total call duration you see according to your CDR, and the total call duration registered by your carrier.

- **The billing increments may be different.** Say you have a large volume of short-duration calls. Your phone system may measure your call to the second, but your carrier bills in six-second increments. This difference could cause a discrepancy of 30 percent or more between your CDR total duration versus your carrier's total. If this happens, you need to reconcile the total number of calls over the duration, rather than the precise lengths of calls.

- **Your carrier doesn't charge for failure.** Your carrier should have fewer calls than your CDR, on average, because carriers don't invoice you for failed calls, but your CDR faithfully records those failures.

You can use your CDR to check the overall accuracy of your carrier invoice, but don't expect a perfect match. If you stumble across something completely at odds with reality, such as your carrier charging you for calls to phone numbers that you have no record of ever calling, ask your carrier to conduct a full, immediate review.

Part II

Assessing Your Network's VoIP Readiness

The 5th Wave   By Rich Tennant

"We mapped our corporate value stream, Phillip, and your department was such a mudflat that we're going to eliminate everything but the clams and scallops."

In this part . . .

The scariest part of VoIP used to be the deployment stage. There seemed to be no tools at our disposal to pre-qualify a LAN to ensure it was running efficiently now, or how it would react once VoIP was deployed. Times have changed and there are more tools available to help us ensure a successful deployment. This section covers all aspects of preparation and deployment of VoIP.

The very structure of the LAN is analyzed first, and the topics of latency, jitter and packet loss are identified as the main concern in a VoIP deployment. Several options are provided to streamline both LAN and VoIP traffic, while introducing concepts such as Class of Service, Quality of Service, and Mean Opinion Score.

Once the structure of your LAN is covered, the specific features you require from VoIP are addressed. Touch tone (DTMF) and fax transmission methods are not ideal candidates for VoIP transmission and so they have been managed through work around options that are offered. These are only two of the many configuration elements required to be identified when ordering VoIP service from your carrier. The specific data they need to know, from packet sampling size and call per second rate, to maximum concurrent calls and your choice of codecs is reviewed as well.

The section also includes a detailed review of two software packages allowing for more visibility into VoIP than any other form of telephony. The VoIP Lifecycle Management software package from Packet Island allows you visibility into your LAN like never before, with data and metrics for every call and every reason you could experience a dip in call quality. Wireshark is the second essential software for anyone using VoIP as it allows any user to capture and analyze a VoIP call at the same level of detail available to a network technician at your carrier.

This section tells you how to make it all happen.

Chapter 5

Reviewing Your Network

*I*ndustry estimates indicate that up to 85 percent of company LANs aren't ready for VoIP deployment. Even if you don't currently have a problem with the ebb and flow of data through your LAN, you don't know the true impact of VoIP on your network until it's deployed.

Converged network LANs that include real-time applications, such as VoIP and video, are as prevalent today as the broadband Internet connections that feed these applications. LAN hardware is inexpensive, and much of the software used to deploy VoIP is open source and free for the taking. The major financial hurdles in network design and deployment have been removed.

Network design and analysis is critical for a successful VoIP deployment. Even on a new network, you need to perform due diligence to prevent problems down the road. VoIP is a mix of voice telephony elements and data transmission structure, but it's like a distant cousin of either network. The data transmission and programming worldview spawned the idea of voice transmissions controlled from open source software. Anyone with the basic programming skills can modify that software down to the smallest detail. However, the LAN elements in which most of the programmers work aren't designed for the unique transmission profile of VoIP. In that regard, the technology is a curious visitor in both realms. You have to analyze your LAN thoroughly before deployment if you want VoIP to work once it's integrated.

This chapter covers the basic needs and concerns of any network that's facing the integration of VoIP. I review the network design, topology, and techniques available to you that can increase your chances for a successful VoIP deployment.

Analyzing Your Network Design

Networks grow organically, rather than through a pre-designed structure. Every addition made to the LAN, whether it's a new router, printer, or small adjunct subnet, will have an impact on the LAN's overall effectiveness.

Before you begin to buy your new VoIP hardware, take a good look at your existing LAN. The best way to get a general overview of your network is by making a network diagram of your LAN, including all the devices; IP addresses; types of cabling such as Ethernet or Cat5; and connections to remote sites, the Internet, and any other WAN interfaces. This diagram provides a birds-eye view of what's happening to your data, which fits into one of the five basic LAN designs.

Figure 5-1 shows the basic LAN designs employed in networks today. Depending on the application running on your LAN, and how the applications and your LAN are managed, they can all transfer data without a problem. Some of the designs offer more challenges when you need to troubleshoot a problem, simply because of their structure. The LAN designs listed in Figure 5-1 are

- **Bus:** This type of LAN has a single backbone onto which all the devices are connected. Because they all share a common conduit, the surge of data from any device on the LAN can impact every other device every time someone transfers a file.

- **Point to Point/Line/Daisy Chain:** A variation of the bus type architecture, except that each piece of hardware in the chain acts to maintain continuity. If any computer or server in the chain fails, it effectively splits the chain, and the devices on one side of the Daisy Chain can no longer communicate with the devices on the other side.

- **Ring:** Like a daisy chain, only connected from end to end. In this type, if a single node malfunctions, all the devices can still communicate by transmitting through the other end of the ring.

- **Star:** A very useful and controlled LAN layout. It's also called a Hub and Spoke because it resembles a wagon wheel, in which a central routing device — called a *hub* — connects work stations, printers, or devices. This configuration allows your central server great visibility into the entire LAN because this layout allows a central point to see everything on the LAN. The downside, of course, is the potential for failure. If the hub dies, the entire LAN stops working.

✔ **Tree:** A variation on the Daisy Chain design in which individual devices act as an intermediary between a main server and additional devices. If you have this type of LAN, you can install devices at the location where the LAN branches into two segments to establish a separate network, generally called a subnet, that can pass packets within the subnet and send packets on to the rest of the LAN only if necessary. Your LAN can be segmented and controlled more easily, but you have to work harder to analyze it because subnets function like separate entities and so can be difficult to manage as a part of the entire LAN.

Your LAN may not be an exact representation of any of these types, and it may incorporate design elements from more than one type. Branches of your LAN may be attached at a given point because the network engineer can create that layout more easily than he or she could run new cabling back to the main router.

One of the key selling points of VoIP during its early years was its ability to reduce the amount of cabling you needed to establish an office. The mindset was that by running Ethernet to every computer, you could connect into the same feed for your VoIP phone. But if you take that approach, you inject all the traffic from your PC onto the cabling that runs your VoIP. So, every e-mail that you send or receive, every file that you download, and every PowerPoint presentation that you move across the LAN consumes vital bandwidth that you also need to transmit a quality VoIP call.

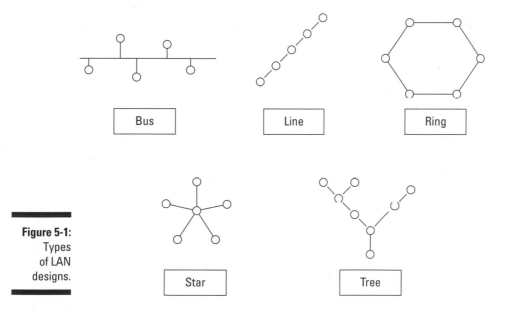

Figure 5-1:
Types
of LAN
designs.

This doesn't mean that you have to run an entirely new set of cables to every desk in your office. Integrating VoIP on an existing data LAN can be accomplished while running over the same cabling, but the solutions of today require some advanced configurations that are covered later in this chapter as well as Chapter 6.

Introducing VoIP Lifecycle Management

The need to plan and manage the impact of VoIP deployment on an existing LAN has become a process called *VoIP Lifecycle Management (VLM)*. No one created this process in a single ah-ha moment; customers, carriers, and VoIP engineers developed it over time while companies began deploying VoIP. They realized that as soon as VoIP was active on the LAN, it had a large, negative impact in ways they never expected. Challenges still appeared from time to time, even after the companies addressed the immediate problems. Six months or a year later, after everyone thought they had the VoIP part of their LAN under control, their businesses grew or evolved. They deployed more VoIP phones and sent more data through the LAN. The hardware grew old and overworked, and it began to fail.

The constant evolution of data and voice consumption on any LAN means you can never stop maintaining and managing it. After years of reacting to the new situations created by VoIP, customers, carriers, and VoIP engineers realized they need to manage the application before it breaks. Those who ignored this need to plan, analyze, and test are still dealing with major problems on their VoIP networks today.

There are three stages of VoIP Lifecycle Management:

- **Stage 1 — Analysis:** The first step in any solid VoIP deployment. It involves analyzing your existing network to confirm it can handle the increased workload of a VoIP deployment. The section "Analyzing Your Bandwidth," later in this chapter, covers this stage of VoIP Lifecycle Management.

- **Stage 2 — Installation/verification:** This stage covers the process of activating VoIP on your network, validating all the hardware, and testing all aspects and features employed on VoIP. Chapters 8 and 9 talk about this stage of VoIP Lifecycle Management.

- **Stage 3 — Ongoing monitoring:** This phase of Lifecycle Management never ends. Every month, quarter, half-year, or year, you need to re-evaluate your network to identify trends and prevent problems before they impact service. Companies don't stay the same; they're always either expanding or contracting. Regardless of which way your business is moving, it'll have different data and voice requirements six months from now, compared to today.

Industry estimates identify a 50-percent chance of failing to successfully transition to VoIP if you ignore the stages of VoIP Lifecycle Management.

It's rare if any company has definitive data on bandwidth consumption, peak usage, collisions, errors, and hardware degradation on data LANs, pre-planning for VoIP deployment is all the more essential. You can much more easily do the research now while everyone in your office is calm, instead of trying to fix a problem a few months from now when everyone's nerves are frayed and they just want their calls to complete cleanly.

Managing Latency

Latency is a delay in the transmission of a data packet. It's also the most common concern during any VoIP deployment. Even after you clean, design, and work out all the signaling details between your LAN and your carrier on your network, you always have to worry about the specter of latency as it leads to poor call quality and even call failure.

You can't entirely avoid latency because every piece of hardware that interacts with a VoIP packet adds a few milliseconds of latency to that packet. You probably don't notice the overall impact as long as the total latency from end to end is below 200 milliseconds (ms). After you cross the 200-ms threshold, your calls experience a noticeable degradation of quality.

The exact point at which call quality begins to drop is subjective. The 200-ms mark is about the middle of the road for the upper limit of tolerable latency. Some manufacturers, such as Cisco, have a stated policy cautioning their customers against any transmissions with more than 150 ms of latency, but other providers are more forgiving and caution their customers only after 300 ms of latency.

PING your prospective carrier's router to determine a benchmark for the latency you can expect on your VoIP calls. PING is a simple command that you can execute from a command prompt on your PC. Try to PING from the server that you plan to use to send the VoIP calls.

From a PC running Windows XP, follow these steps:

1. **Click the Start button on the lower-left of the toolbar.**

2. **Choose All Programs⇨Accessories⇨Command Prompt.**

   The Command Prompt window appears.

3. **In the Command Prompt window, type the command PING and the destination IP address to which you want to connect.**

   This example PINGs the IP for www.google.com:

   ```
   C:\ PING 74.125.19.99
   ```

4. **Click the Enter key on your keyboard to being the ping test.**

You receive a quick check of the path used by your IP provider from you to the destination IP. The response I received wasn't encouraging:

```
Pinging 74.125.19.99 with 32 bytes of data:
Reply from 74.125.19.99: bytes=32 time=75ms TTL=247
Reply from 74.125.19.99: bytes=32 time=76ms TTL=247
Reply from 74.125.19.99: bytes=32 time=74ms TTL=247
Reply from 74.125.19.99: bytes=32 time=79ms TTL=247

Ping statistics for 74.125.19.99:
       Packets: Sent = 4, Received  = 4, Lost =  0 (0%
          loss),
Approximate round trip times in milli-seconds:
       Minimum = 74ms, Maximum = 79ms, Average = 76 ms
```

If this was a VoIP call, I'd still have 120 ms before I had to worry about call quality degradation — so overall, it's okay, but not great.

Not every carrier has an IP address for its VoIP proxy server that you can test it. Many carriers deactivate a part of the Internet Protocol (IP) software called the Internet Control Message Protocol (ICMP) Protocol Stack, preventing you from either PING-ing their IP. If your carrier has a PING-able IP, PING it. If not, ask whether the carrier has an IP on its network that can act as a suitable alternative.

If your PING returns with lost packets, be very concerned. Lost packets quickly deteriorate your call quality. Under optimal conditions (with no packet loss), an uncompressed call using the G.711 codec has an expected MOS score of 4.4, and the compressed codec of G.729 has roughly a 3.6 MOS score. (I talk about MOS scores in the section "Coming to Grips with MOS," later in this chapter.) The quality of the calls deteriorates substantially when packets are lost. The compression used with G.729 amplifies the issue as the process of converting the audio into compressed packets takes more time than forming uncompressed packets. The additional latency adds to the existing transmission latency, increasing the risk of packet loss. A packet loss of only 7 percent degrades the call quality of a G.729 call to approximately 1.5. The same 7-percent packet loss over G.711 still remains over 2.0.

Dealing with jitter

Simple latency is a fact of life. Everything takes time on a VoIP call, from encoding the voice into packets, to sending it through the LAN and WAN, to decoding it on the other end. If you could somehow anticipate the latency on each call and adjust accordingly on both ends, latency would no longer affect either call quality or completion.

But latency isn't constant. If the IP for your VoIP calls is also supplying the Internet connection for e-mail, IM, and Web surfing for your office, the strain on the bandwidth fluctuates while people conduct their daily lives. If someone downloads the complete *IEEE Computer Society Digital Library,* the usage spikes, and the latency that was consistently 30 ms because of other VoIP traffic now increases to 120 ms for the next 20 minutes, until the download completes, at which time, the latency returns to 30 ms. These swings in latency are called *jitter.*

Jitter is one of the most troubling aspects of latency because it results in packets arriving at the far end in an unexpected cadence, where the amount of time between arriving packets fluctuates to the point where they arrive out of sequence, making it that much more difficult to reassemble them in a consistent flow. Some devices can reduce the jitter, but those devices can be more of an overall hindrance than a help if improperly configured.

Devices such as *jitter buffers* and *Packet Loss Concealment (PLC) devices* may look like a solution. They collect the individual VoIP packets, arrange them in sequence, and then send them out in a uniform cadence.

You want your packets to transmit in a consist rhythm, but by holding on to the packets before sending them, the jitter buffers actually create more latency than they avoid. While the buffer adds latency, the packets for transmission may begin to collect in the buffer faster than the buffer can transmit them. This backup becomes a problem when outgoing VoIP packets fill the storage capacity on the jitter buffer. After the buffer is full, the next VoIP packet delivered overwrites an existing packet in the buffer. The arrival of subsequent packets in the buffer wipes out more of the existing packets, and your call quality quickly begins to drop. Jitter buffers can effectively be used as long as they are one element used to deal with the latency instead of the only management device on an overloaded or poorly built network.

Identifying flap

Networks are dynamic, living, and breathing entities. They both route traffic from one point to another and also redirect that traffic around congestion and areas of the network where packets are flowing slower than expected. The term *flap* refers to a sudden or temporary change in routing between end points. Figure 5-2 shows what a flap looks like.

Figure 5-2 demonstrates a transmission that has a single route flap. The primary route for the VoIP call from Seattle to Washington, D.C., goes first into Minneapolis, then on through Chicago, Pittsburgh, and finally to Washington, D.C. The transmission encounters congestion in Pittsburgh, so the very next packet sent from Seattle is now routed south through Salt Lake City, Dallas, and Atlanta before hitting Washington, D.C. As long as all the packets arrive at their destinations in a timely manner, you don't experience any problems with the transmission. Route flaps do have a problem: They usually result in some packets arriving out of sequence. Because a VoIP call is a real-time application, the system can't ask for packets to be resent or wait for missing packets to arrive before forwarding them. A receiving VoIP node can't use the out-of-sequence packets and so discards them. The packet loss may not have occurred due to a failing piece of hardware, but the same call quality degradation occurs, regardless of whether the packets are lost in a network, overwritten in a jitter buffer, or discarded because they arrived out of sequence.

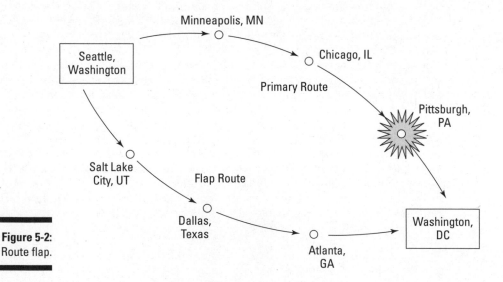

Figure 5-2:
Route flap.

The example in Figure 5-2 illustrates a call with a single route flap employed on the transmission. The problem of out-of-sequence packets becomes much larger when the Internet provider employs multiple route flaps. Each additional route flap increases your chances of a packet arriving out of sequence. The more route flaps encountered on a VoIP call, the more packets are discarded when they arrive out of sequence at the destination, and the call quality begins to drop.

Out-of-sequence packets from a route flap don't cause much trouble during the middle of a call, but if you're transmitting anything that isn't voice during a route flap, such as DTMF (Dual Tone Multi Frequency) xtones (meaning touch tones) or faxes, it can result in the receiving VoIP node failing a transmission or misinterpreting the data sent.. If final DTMF packets arrive out of sequence and aren't discarded as they should be while the END notifications are sent, your hardware may perceive those packets as new DTMF digits. If you see a double representation of DTMF tones being sent or received, take a packet capture of your calls. Chapter 11 shows how you can take DTMF captures by using Wireshark to help you isolate the issue. If your hardware doesn't discard out-of-sequence packets, contact the manufacturer to update the software, firmware, or hardware to correct the problem.

Analyzing Your Bandwidth

Traditional LANs that ran data were more brawn than brains. They were designed based on expected data transmission and use, and then over-engineered for the given application. The switches, routers, and hubs were designed to be stronger than the network needed at the time, and bandwidth was also piled on to take care of peak times. In reality, you can't tell with any certainty the specific hardware, software, and bandwidth that an application requires.

Most LANs in the United States don't have any management software or tools to identify network congestion. They simply make a reactionary, best-guess effort with diagnostic tools that generally rely on the perception of latency or congestion by employees. If pulling a file across the LAN seems to take a lot longer today when compared with yesterday, you don't have many available options to identify why that file is taking so long to transfer.

At this time, you can't find any tools used by LAN technicians to identify if you're pushing the maximum Packets Per Second (PPS) on your switch, router, bridge, or firewall. You can't easily tell whether one of these components has a software bug that's injecting latency in transmissions or a component is shorting out and dying a slow, painful death. You can get a bit of insight by using one of two basic options — SNMP and Wireshark (formerly called Ethereal), which I talk about in the following sections.

Pulling general information with SNMP

The tools available for LAN analysis are blunt instruments at best, but they have always worked fine for the analysis of data on a LAN. The need for performance information on a data LAN isn't as crucial as the information required on a VoIP LAN as traditional data transmissions can be resent if they arrive at the destination corrupted. VoIP transmissions are real-time applications and don't have the option to be resent if a packet is lost.

The most common LAN management tool available is the *Simple Network Management Protocol (SNMP)*. SNMP is a team of software elements residing in nodes on a LAN that collect management data on the health of the LAN. The system functions based on a main management device called a *Network Management System (NMS)* that controls and monitors the other SNMP-enabled devices. These devices, called *managed devices,* are different than ordinary hubs, routers, printers, bridges, and switches because they have a software element installed in them (called an *agent*) that allows them to gather management data and relay it up to the NMS.

The statistical information available on SNMP-managed networks include counters for these values:

- Alignment Errors
- Single Collision Frames
- Multiple Collision Frames
- Deferred Transmissions
- Late Collisions
- Excessive Collisions
- MAC Transmit Errors
- Carrier Sense Errors
- Internal Max Receive Errors
- Symbol Errors

The SNMP error counters collect information on the events and make them available to the NMS so that your network manager can read and interpret them. Unfortunately, the information represents only a total number of errors or collisions over a given period of time. The information doesn't tell you when the errors occurred. If the SNMP notes 100 Single Collision Frames, you can't tell whether they all occurred at the same time during a unique LAN event or they happened every 15 minutes on a single managed device.

If you were dealing with data, you'd need only this collected information to measure the health of a LAN. As long as the overall numbers looked good, you declared the LAN healthy, and everyone went about their business.

Gathering the details with Wireshark

Not everyone has a managed network that runs SNMP-enabled nodes (as discussed in the preceding section). Even if you do, the reports available don't identify the exact source of a problem or how the errors or collisions occurred (whether they happened periodically or all at the same time). The other tool at your disposal is a packet-capture software called Wireshark (formerly Ethereal).

Plugging a laptop that has Wireshark installed into your main router, server or firewall allows you to capture all the packets flowing through that point of the network. Depending on how long you leave the capture open, you may need to sift through a huge accumulation of data to find an answer. As great as Wireshark is, it doesn't provide any graphs or a matrix for congestion, allowing you to quickly identify and locate the source of congestion issues. So, you have to scroll down through hundreds and thousands of lines of code on each type of traffic and review the timestamps for each stream of data while it flows through the network.

The main limitation to this type of analysis is that a congestion issue or problem must be going on while you're capturing packets if you want to actually identify the problem. If the problem you're chasing down is intermittent and occurs only 5 or 10 percent of the time, it could persist for months before you can finally identify and resolve it.

Wireshark is a new version of Ethereal. It color codes the transmission types, allowing you to quickly identify the protocols used in the packets as TCP traffic, versus SIP with SDP. It's the most helpful software available for analyzing problems on VoIP calls as it links together packets associated with individual VoIP calls, making it simple to scroll through every SIP method and response transmitted, and I give you all the details in Chapter 11.

Despite the fact that you can't find many legacy LAN tools available to help you, a growing number of software programs can fill the gap between what you used to need for data transmissions and what you need now to monitor VoIP traffic. The leader in this field is the VoIP Lifecycle Management software and hardware available from Packet Island, which I talk about in Chapter 9.

Managing Your Bandwidth

Despite the lack of available tools to see how your bandwidth is doing (as I talk about in the preceding sections), you can use a handful of techniques that allow you to control the flow of traffic in your LAN. The following sections give you the details about these techniques.

Handling latency with prioritization

Hundreds, thousands, and hundreds of thousands of data packets may be coursing through a LAN at any given time. A router receives each packet and processes it accordingly, each in its turn, on a first come, first served basis.

This process can cause a problem because packets for real-time applications such as VoIP and video are waiting on packets used to send e-mails and surf the Web. All packets aren't created equal. Some are in a rush, and some can take their time getting to a destination. Table 5-1 shows some common types of transmissions in a LAN, their bandwidth requirements, and their general levels of urgency.

Table 5-1	LAN Transmission Types	
Application	*Bandwidth*	*Urgency*
E-mail	128 Kbps–1.5 Mbps	Low
Surfing the Internet	128 Kbps–1.5 Mbps	Low
Instant Messaging	28 Kbps	Moderate
VoIP	64 Kbps	High

Just like doctors can't deal with patients in an emergency room on a first come, first served basis, you need to triage your data transmissions. All of the transmission types shown in Table 5-1 are transmitted with IP, which has the means to prioritize packets, giving some preferential treatment over others. Table 5-1 shows that e-mails and Internet surfing are low-urgency transmissions. If they lose connectivity, or if a packet arrives out of sequence or corrupted, it can always be resent without any harm done.

The real-time applications, such as Instant Messaging and VoIP, are much more sensitive and need to be processed with greater urgency. Each transmission type can be categorized in a different priority level to help refine data transmission on the LAN.

Internet Protocol (IP) identifies eight levels of priority, from 0 to 7, with 7 being the highest priority. Generally, network engineers use 7 only for mission-critical transmissions of network management or routing, and 5 and 6 typically identify real-time applications such as VoIP.

Don't use prioritization as your only means of dealing with bandwidth management on a network running both data and VoIP because

✔ **It adds latency.** The server utilizing the prioritization hierarchy must identify the priority level of the packets received in the router and usher all those packets into their appropriate queues for transmission. So, every packet — data and voice alike — experience more latency.

✔ **After a while, all the packets become 6s.** While the volume of VoIP calls increases, your router spends more time sending VoIP transmissions into the priority 6 queue. The VoIP packets may represent 50 percent or 70 percent of the traffic on your LAN. Eventually, spending the time to identify packets as VoIP transmissions and dropping them in a queue wastes more time than if every router, switch, and server sent the packets along without being prioritized.

Resolving latency with packet shaping

Prioritization alone isn't an effective tool for peacefully using bandwidth between VoIP and data packets. You can more effectively use prioritization as an auxiliary tool in conjunction with other constructs, such as *packet shaping* (also known as *rate shaping*), a standard feature on many routers. Packet-shaping devices don't handle all your LAN traffic as individual packets, they actually manage the data flowing through them by criteria such as

✔ **Traffic protocol:** They can categorize traffic by the protocol used, whether TCP, IP, SIP, SDP, or RTP.

✔ **Transmission port:** SIP traditionally uses port 5060, which the router with packet shaping can use to identify your VoIP traffic and differentiate it from someone surfing the Web.

✔ **Host connection:** Your VoIP LAN sends your VoIP traffic to the same VoIP provider, and the outbound port or IP address on your LAN can also use this data to identify your VoIP traffic.

Rate shaping allocates a specific quantity of bandwidth to each type of traffic, based on the criteria you set. For example, if you have a 45-Megabit Internet connection, you can identify 35 Meg for VoIP traffic and the remaining 10 Meg for all other data transmission.

The traffic limits set on the packet shaper are either definite or burstable. Don't make the limits set for the data portion of your network burstable. This setting allows the data traffic to invade the bandwidth allocated for VoIP calls. During peak business times, when both your voice and data networks have their greatest usage, you don't want to sacrifice your VoIP call completion and quality for a data packet that can be resent.

Separating VoIP from data with a subnet

Packet shaping (discussed in the preceding section) is a great concept. You can go one further and, instead of simply splitting the existing bandwidth, move the VoIP traffic onto its own section of the LAN. Partitioning off a section of your LAN to prevent the VoIP traffic from interacting with the router traffic further isolates the system. If every router in your LAN doesn't have to identify and manage every VoIP and data packet, that translates into less work for the routers, less latency, and a cleaner transmission.

Creating a subnet that contains only VoIP traffic is another great solution. You can partition off sections of your network into subnets, but those subnets can also add difficulty to a VoIP deployment if any VoIP node is installed outside of its subnet. Figure 5-3 shows a subnetted network in a VoIP application.

The design in Figure 5-3 looks acceptable at first glance. The network is separated into a VoIP subnet, containing VoIP phones managed by a router that has a direct Internet connection with a single connection into the main LAN. The one VoIP phone attached to the PC workstation faces a challenge. Its packets are directly immersed in every data transmission from the PC to the rest of the LAN, and those packets also have to flow through the server and the serving router before they even reach the final router connected to the Internet.

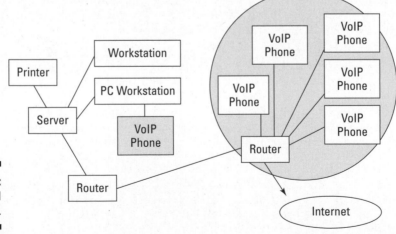

Figure 5-3:
VoIP LAN
with subnet.

In Figure 5-3, you might face some problems when you try to move the PC workstation's VoIP phone or wire it into the VoIP subnet. For example, the location of the single VoIP phone not on the subnet may be on the other side of the office building from the VoIP subnet, or it might be in a remote office if you have a campus environment. Creating the physical connection may be a logistical nightmare, but you have a solution in a VLAN (discussed in the following section).

Employing a VLAN

A VLAN is a Virtual LAN that acts like a physically separate network, despite the fact that it uses the exact same switches as your primary LAN. Figure 5-4 shows what a VLAN looks like.

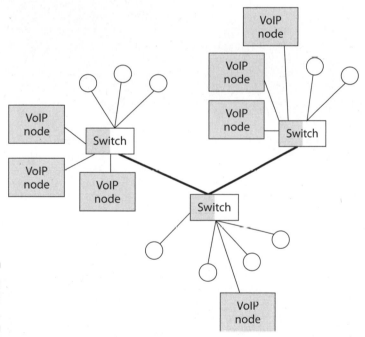

Figure 5-4:
The Virtual
LAN.

The gray boxes in Figure 5-4 are VoIP nodes and devices connected on the LAN through switches. The circles attached to the switches are data devices such as PCs, servers, and other peripherals. In the world of the network, the switches on the LAN see two separate LANs functioning side by side. The VoIP portion of the LAN contains and sees only the VoIP nodes and the sections of the switches allocated for the VoIP LAN traffic. The data LAN runs through the data side of the switches and is blissfully unaware of the fact that VoIP traffic runs beside it on the network. It's not only a peaceful coexistence, it also is the basis for a very efficiently deployed VoIP network.

Depending on the size and complexity of your LAN, you may not need to establish a VLAN. You may be able to manage your VoIP traffic effectively through a combination of prioritization and packet shaping as discussed previously in this chapter. If you are sending more than 24 calls at the same time, deployment of a VLAN is something you should discuss with your network engineer.

Keep all your options in mind and reassess your LAN every four to six months. Your business changes while it grows (or shrinks), so you need to adjust to the new mix of traffic flowing through your LAN.

Jumping In to the OSI Model

You need a basic understanding of how networks function if you want to grasp all the potential sources of latency. Fortunately, network engineers created a theoretical structure that encompasses all the individual variables on a network, which your network engineer can use when designing, configuring, implementing, and troubleshooting a network.

If you already know the Network OSI model, glance over this section for anything interesting. If you're diving in to VoIP and your resume currently covers all the intricacies of standard telephony voice calls and nothing on LAN design or management, then today is your lucky day — you get to find out all about the OSI model.

VoIP has more components to it than standard telephony. A traditional telephony environment has a limited number of variables that potentially affect call quality or completion. Traditional telephony generally has to concern itself with

- The physical lines carrying the call
- The hardware that the call encounters

The hardware and physical lines can both experience layers of problems, but in a traditional telephony environment, the specifics of those problems fall on the shoulders of the companies, carriers, and vendors that own those phone lines and that hardware. Traditional telephony requires an end user to be responsible only for his or her phone system and any inside wiring. After you clear these elements as potential sources of a problem, everything else that can go wrong on a phone call is someone else's problem.

VoIP brings the finer details and responsibilities, previously shouldered only by carriers, right into your company. Not only can you have static on a call generated from a wire that has an electrical short, you now have to take responsibility for many other layers of interaction between yourself and your VoIP provider where trouble can arise.

You need to ask yourself about any potential trouble issue, "What are the variables?" With VoIP, every interaction between your hardware and your VoIP provider is a variable. You still have to consider the potential for problems caused by the physical line, but now you also have to concern yourself with how the packets are sent and received, bandwidth use, allocation, the banter back and forth of SIP methods and responses, SDP, and RTP transmissions.

Network engineers and developers use the Open Systems Interconnection basic reference model (OSI model) as a standardized way of talking about the components required to support all network transmissions:

- ✔ **Good news:** The OSI model is broken down in a logical hierarchy that you can easily grasp.

- ✔ **Bad news:** Latency on a VoIP call can be introduced at any level of the OSI model.

Figure 5-5 shows how the model is divided into seven layers and how those layers identify the protocols used to transmit VoIP. Each layer of the model is identified by the job it performs in a transmission and relies on the layer below it for support while supporting the layer above it. The model is also used to develop applications that can exist and be modified at higher layers of the OSI model that don't require corresponding changes on lower levels.

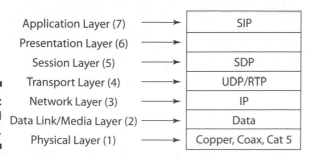

Figure 5-5:
OSI model
with VoIP.

Application Layer (7)	SIP
Presentation Layer (6)	
Session Layer (5)	SDP
Transport Layer (4)	UDP/RTP
Network Layer (3)	IP
Data Link/Media Layer (2)	Data
Physical Layer (1)	Copper, Coax, Cat 5

On your computer at work, you might be running Windows XP as your operating system, which supports the higher OSI level Microsoft Internet Explorer application to surf the Web. If you choose to use another Web browser, such as FireFox, that exists on the same application layer of the OSI model, you can easily download and use it from the same computer without having to change the operating system. The ease in which you can change higher OSI level applications without needing to manipulate the supporting software in the lower layers shows the support structure and flexibility of the OSI model.

Entering the first layer

The first layer of the OSI model is the *Physical Layer* — the part of the network you can actually touch. It's the wires, cables, connectors, and fiber used to string together all the elements of the network. This layer handles the electrical signal, mechanical connections of the connectors and jacks, and voltage specifics.

Electrical shorts in the cabling or hardware can appear in the first layer causing static, latency, and line noise on all calls, VoIP or non-VoIP. The slow failing of a hardware element in the call path usually causes issues on the first layer. The switch, router, or telephony hardware might have an electrical short that's generating errors. Even if you had a traditional phone system, you'd still have to watch out for layer 1 problems.

Even if the first layer doesn't have any noticeable defects or shorts, it still creates a small degree of latency. Transmitting any signal or message over hundreds or thousands of miles takes some time. If your calls are running half-way around the world, expect some distance-related latency.

Moving to the second layer

The second layer of the OSI model is also referred to as either the *Data Link* or *Media Layer*. This layer provides the most basic foundation for the transmission of packets through the LAN and is the portion of the OSI model where the header information in the packets being transmitted. It handles error control, synchronization, and flow control. In this layer, network switches function to direct packets. Because it's a lower level of the OSI model, it generates less latency when handling packets because the packets aren't opened and inspected or checked for prioritization before they're sent along the LAN, processes that take time.

Network switches work at the second layer of the OSI model and are concerned with frame units, physical addressing (MAC) and signal attenuation. Any challenges with the responsibilities of the second layer can cause latency, jitter, and packet loss.

Sending IP on the third layer

The complexity of the interaction between the packets of data and the hardware supporting them increases when you progress to higher layers of the OSI model.

The second layer has minimal interaction with the data, which allows network switches working at that level to process packets of data very quickly. This cursory interaction has a downside: the network switches can't perform advanced or complex routing at a per-packet level based on any specialized criteria such as prioritization.

The third layer of the OSI model is also called the *Network Layer,* which increases the level of hardware interaction with the data packets. This layer of the OSI model uses network routers as its primary hardware devices for processing packets. These routers are responsible for setting up the connections from end to end, keeping them active for the duration of the call, and tearing them down after the transmission is complete. Just like the second layer (which I talk about in the preceding section), the third layer can cause packet loss, jitter, and latency, but the third layer has the added variable of being susceptible to amplification and distortion issues in the media that can result in echo being heard on the call or variations in volume.

Transmitting UDP on the fourth layer

The fourth layer of the OSI model is called the *Transport Layer.* This layer is responsible for end-to-end connections, including flow control and error recovery. In a normal Internet circuit that runs TCP/IP, you'd find TCP (Transmission Control Protocol) in this layer. VoIP doesn't use TCP, but instead employs UDP (User Datagram Protocol) as a leaner alternative.

The packets sent by UDP are called *datagrams* and contain both a header and payload information. The datagrams are sent as efficiently as possible, but you get no guarantee that they'll arrive in sequence — or at all. As long as you and your carrier are managing your networks effectively, UDP transmits VoIP calls without any problems because it's faster than TCP.

In this level of the OSI model, the RTP (Real-Time Transport Protocol) also does its work to transmit and receive the media of the VoIP calls. It uses support from the UDP at this same level (it also gets support from the IP in layer 3 to make it all work).

This level of the OSI model is susceptible to packet loss and jitter. It also bears the additional challenge associated with transcoding distortion while packets are converted into and out of UDP that can cause the voices being sent to sound robotic.

Topping it off with the Session, Presentation, and Application Layers

The top three layers of the OSI model involve a much higher level of interaction at the individual packet level. Chapters 2 and 3 cover the detailed aspects of interaction between transmissions at these levels.

When the SDP interacts at the fifth layer of the OSI model, also called the *Session Layer,* communications between servers or PCs take place at this level, such as when you dial in through your company network to access your work PC remotely from your home. This layer provides the management structure for communication between applications and sets up the sessions used for VoIP, including most of the tasks performed by SDP.

The sixth layer of the OSI model is also called the *Presentation Layer.* It houses data representation and encryption. In this layer, data is compressed, decompressed, and encrypted, if needed. The audio of a call is also encoded into or decoded from VoIP.

This layer has inherit latency because it takes time for your codec to convert the data. In this layer, VoIP calls are transcoded from one codec, such as G.729, into another codec, such as G.711.

The highest layer of the OSI model (layer 7) is the *Application Layer,* where servers provide services for network management and SIP functions. This layer also contains the mechanics for converting sound into packets, and it may introduce additional noise on the line. This noise can be either

- ✔ **Additive noise:** For example, additive noise occurs when your VoIP hardware attempts to convert a louder-than-expected sound or sounds in the sampling algorithm. If the volume of sound from background noise is too great, you have additive noise.

- ✔ **Subtractive noise:** The opposite of additive noise. Not generally caused by a lack of sound to be converted to packets, but rather the result of packet loss in the transmission.

In addition to additive or subtractive noise on a VoIP call, the seventh layer of the OSI model also has the potential for *over-modulation,* which flattens out the inflection in the speaker's voice, making him or her sound robotic.

The world of VoIP actually has two categories of noise — the undesired and the desired:

- ✔ **Undesired noise:** The side effect of poor transmission, packets that are lost or arrive out of sequence, modulation, and electrical issues on the line. These aspects of VoIP transmission reduce call quality.

- ✔ **Desired noise:** Called *comfort noise* — the soft static or white noise you hear during a call during those moments when nobody is speaking. The VoIP phone or phone system at your building generates this noise. VoIP conserves bandwidth by transmitting audio only when someone is speaking. So, only one RTP stream needs to send any audio during that time. But hearing dead silence on a call makes most people think they've been disconnected. Your phone or phone system keeps you happy by injecting comfort noise so that you know the line is still active.

Introducing VoIP calls for testing

VoIP is a completely different creature than what normally lives on your LAN. The fat data packets sprinting though your routers are about ten times the size of your average VoIP packet. To put it in perspective, your network switches and routers have to process, on average, ten VoIP packets for every one data packet to push the same volume of information.

This comparison may seem like a bit of fun with numbers, but it has a very real impact on your LAN. The quantity of packets flowing through your LAN is very important, more so than the size of those packets. Routers, switches, firewalls, and all other LAN devices are rated by the Packets Per Second (PPS) that they can transmit. If you're already pushing your routers' PPS limits, adding VoIP to the LAN can quickly push it beyond its capabilities.

One of the most daunting tasks of a VoIP deployment involves trying to understand the impact that VoIP traffic will have on your network before you even buy your first VoIP phone or device. You must assess your network and reinforce your LAN before you deploy VoIP. Trying to patch all the holes in your LAN after you flood it with VoIP takes a lot more effort (and creates a lot more anxiety).

So, you must calculate the impact of VoIP on a network before you have any VoIP devices installed. How do you do that? Any algorithm or hypothetical calculations that you create would be little more than guessing. The exact traffic footprint of your LAN will be unique to your company. The specific quantity of data and voice packets flowing through your LAN will vary by day, week, hour, minute, and second because of variables such as

✔ Daily downloads of data for remote tape backups

✔ Peak phone usage times for incoming service calls

✔ Peak outbound phone usage for pro-active sales calls

✔ Peak data processing times because of

- Receiving orders

- Processing orders

- Processing invoices

- Job cycles for graphics or database work

- Employees downloading videos

Any of these events have a temporary impact on the overall congestion level of your LAN. The only way to effectively identify the impact of VoIP on your LAN is to inject live VoIP calls into it. Fortunately, you can find VoIP Lifecycle Management (VLM) software packages that run test VoIP calls through your LAN.

My favorite VoIP Lifecycle Management software is Packet Island, and I cover it in Chapter 9. If you want to do a quick test from your LAN, go to www.test yourvoip.com, log in, and get a quick check of the quality of a VoIP call from your LAN to one of a variety of destinations.

However you plan to execute these simulated VoIP calls from your LAN, run your test in a manner that most closely simulates your actual calling pattern. Keep in mind

✔ The quantity of calls you expect to send at any one time

✔ The average duration of calls

✔ Your peak calling time during the day

Placing one call at 5 p.m. on Friday to check the impact of VoIP on your LAN isn't a realistic test. If you have 20 phone lines and half of them are filled at your peak hours of 10 a.m. and 3 p.m., then set up a simulation for those times that will send ten calls at the same time.

Ideally, you'd set up a constant test of ten VoIP calls from the moment your business opens to the moment it closes. The only thing better than a full day's worth of test results is test results over the course of a week — or a few weeks.

Your data network is working harder on some days than on others. If you run billing every Monday, be sure to test on a Monday. A VoIP simulation on a Wednesday might show that your LAN is ready for deployment. In spite of the fact that's good news to your CFO, it doesn't reflect reality. Always test your LAN on peak data days to discover the congestion on your network. Don't test when you know your LAN doesn't have much activity just to avoid having to deal with the congestion.

Coming to Grips with MOS

Most programs that allow you to test VoIP on your LAN don't tell you the exact quantity of packets lost, or the amount of latency and jitter incurred during the life of the call. The programs usually give you the results of testing based on the MOS score (which I define in Chapter 3).

The MOS score established on the subjective quality rating of calls by a panel of listeners. I'm not saying that a battery of people independently rate your VoIP test-call quality and then average their individual scores. The VLM software programs employ testing algorithms that use specific criteria (such as latency, jitter, perceived increases or decreases in the volume of the audio, and packet loss) to arrive at a realistic MOS score for your test calls.

VLM software can determine the MOS scores in two ways:

- ✔ **Summary metrics:** This method plays a recorded message from a location on your LAN to an end destination and samples the quality at both ends. The server running the VLM software then compares the data from both sites to see how the call changed or degraded during transmission.

  Use this option, if you can. The VLM software can rate the recorded message at both its point of origin and its termination. The VLM software then compares these two readings to provide an accurate representation of any degradation in voice quality experienced while passing through your LAN. If the call quality is the same at the receiving end as it was at the point of origin, then your network is solid — the path through it doesn't affect the call in any negative way.

- ✔ **Real-time MOS score:** This method listens to live VoIP calls and identifies a MOS score by using mathematical algorithms.

Identifying a MOS score on a VoIP call is like taking your temperature when you feel sick. It gives you a number on a scale, and although that number doesn't identify exactly what's wrong with you, it indicates your general health. If you have a fever of 103 degrees, or a MOS score of 1.5, you know that you're not doing well. Either score alerts you so that you can focus your attention on resolving whatever's causing the condition. In the case of VoIP, your condition probably involves latency, jitter, and packet loss.

MOS isn't only a rough approximation of the health of your LAN, it's also a rough approximation of the quality of the call. Each call gets only one MOS score. Unfortunately, the quality of a call doesn't always remain consistent throughout the duration of the call. If a call has low audio at the beginning and excessive audio at the end, that call gets a favorable MOS score because the two issues cancel each other out when averaged. Take MOS as a general indicator, telling you when you need to do some additional research.

Chapter 6

Preparing Your Network for VoIP

. . . .

. . . .

*T*his chapter presents a testing regime that you can use to prequalify your LAN for VoIP traffic, as well as solid background on the telecom features for which VoIP isn't natively designed.

Chapter 5 covers the design and management techniques of most networks and defines some of the helpful tools and system limitations that can affect a LAN. You can use the information in that chapter as a solid base to define your LAN's overall environment. This chapter builds on that information by applying it directly to your LAN.

Industry estimates identify a 50-percent chance of a failed VoIP deployment if you don't go through the prequalification phase. Out of all the successfully deployed VoIP networks that ignored pretesting, 60 percent report monthly service disruptions, and nearly two-thirds of those disruptions impact the businesses financially. The information in this chapter gives you the edge to prevent becoming a part of those statistics.

Determining Your Peak Call Volume

Because of the dynamic nature of VoIP, you have to analyze your traffic much more than if you were ordering traditional telephony lines. The non-VoIP world is very logical: Your local phone carrier drops off ten phone lines to your office, and you can then place ten calls at the same time — one per line. This setup makes life easy for the phone company because it knows up front how many calls you can possibly make, and the one-to-one ratio keeps everything neat and tidy.

VoIP changes the dynamic. You can send multiple calls at the same time over a single Internet connection. So, your VoIP provider must ensure it has sufficient bandwidth and facilities to handle all your calls. It has no idea how many calls you could potentially send it at a given time, so before you order your VoIP service, you must determine your *maximum concurrent calls,* meaning the maximum quantity of calls you expect to have active at the same time. This is the VoIP equivalent of ordering a certain number of lines from a traditional phone company.

You can most easily identify your maximum concurrent calls by checking your current phone bill. It should have several pages of summaries to include "peak calling hours" or "calls per hour per day." The calling footprint for every company is different, but you probably have at least two spikes in your call volume per day. Business calling volume generally peaks when everyone is arriving in the morning between 8 a.m. and 9 a.m. (or whenever you start business). After employees deal with the morning's follow-up calls and urgent issues, call volume tapers off until another peak occurs in the afternoon when everyone returns from lunch, and then you may have one more spike during the last hour before the office closes.

If you don't have a helpful summary section on your invoice, isolate your sample during one of these common peak times. Because you can't get a report that tells you exactly what you need, you have to delve in to the itemized list of your calls on your invoice. The call detail section of your invoice identifies the specifics about the individual calls in lines of data called Call Detail Records, or CDR. They usually list:

✔ Origination date

✔ Origination time

✔ Phone number from which you placed the call

✔ Destination phone number

✔ Call duration

✔ Cost

If you choose the time frame from 8 a.m. to 9 a.m. for your sample, scan through your entire invoice and write down all the calls that started after 8 a.m., listing the phone number that initiated the call, as well as the start time and duration. Throw this data into a spreadsheet in case you want to manipulate the data.

After you list all the calls, take a quick look from top to bottom. Most likely, only half of your lines have a call on them at any given time. Write down a rough count of the number of calls that were active at the same time and add 30 percent more for a bit of headroom to give yourself a good starting estimate of maximum concurrent call volume.

If you really want to know the exact number of concurrent calls you have during peak times, you can take the data you collected and create a matrix for calls. Mark off a spreadsheet in one-minute increments for the entire hour, with rows representing the calls for each phone line. Draw a line on each row to identify when calls began and ended. After you plot every call on the graph for the hour, run a ruler across the page vertically and count the number of lines representing calls you cross every minute. Tally the calls at the bottom of the page and you can then see, minute by minute, the maximum number of concurrent calls placed for your office.

If you currently have a dedicated circuit or multiple phone lines, you may have your individual Call Detail Records (CDR) delivered in an electronic format on a CD-ROM. This format makes your life much easier because you can import the CDR into a database program like Microsoft Access or Microsoft Excel, then sort it by date and time to group all your calls, making this process much less time consuming than having to manually key in all of the CDR information into a database or spreadsheet.

If you run a telemarketing company, an enhanced VoIP carrier, or simply have hundreds or thousands of lines, your hardware probably can tell you your total concurrent calls.

Calculating Calls Per Second

When you have data that identifies your maximum concurrent calls, you need to figure out how fast you'll send those calls to your carrier — another concern that's rather unique to VoIP. Long-distance carriers use simple metrics to determine the statistical probability of when a call would arrive in non-VoIP, traditional telephony. The carriers use one device to provide a dial tone to every phone line, and they know (by mathematical probability) how often they need to provide call setup for an incoming call.

VoIP has changed this dynamic — with one IP circuit, you can send hundreds or thousands of calls to your carrier in a single second. But even if you *can* send 200 calls per second to your carrier, you shouldn't. If you're a small or medium-sized business, you may need to send a maximum of only one or two calls per second to your carrier. It'll love you for it, and you shouldn't have to worry about ever overloading its VoIP proxy server with incoming calls.

Your carrier won't appreciate being inundated with 100 — or 1,000 — calls in the same second. The first 100 calls overload your carrier's VoIP proxy server. This condition, whereby your VoIP carrier's proxy is incapacitated, both prevents the remainder of your calls from completing and also prevents any other customer that the long-distance carrier has assigned to that specific VoIP proxy server from completing any calls. This type of situation usually earns you a quick call from the network security folks at your carrier, telling you to stop sending so many calls. If you have a habit of flooding their network with calls, they may simply block your IP and stop providing service to you.

If you're a larger telecom customer and have dedicated circuits running the equivalent of hundreds or thousands of phone lines, you need to do some quick analysis. Three factors impact the maximum number of Calls Per Second you require:

✓ Your average call duration

✓ Your average duration of time your outbound calls ring at the destination (ring-back time) before the call connects

✓ The maximum number of concurrent calls you need

Traditional dedicated telecom services have two main benchmarks for maximum concurrent calls. Many companies that are replacing existing service with VoIP or deploying a new office and phone system frequently use these traditional telephony units of measure to place their required call volume into a known grouping:

✓ **DS-1:** Represents 24 phone lines

✓ **DS-3:** Represents 672 phone lines

If your carrier can manage even one call per second, you can make a DS-1's full 24 calls in less than half a minute.

Table 6-1 shows two calling profiles' maximum concurrent calls at an increasing number of allowed calls per second.

Table 6-1	Maximum Concurrent Calls at Different Calls Per Second	
Calls Per Second	*55-Second Total Duration*	*85-Second Total Duration*
1	55	85
2	110	170
3	165	255

Calls Per Second	55-Second Total Duration	85-Second Total Duration
4	220	340
5	275	425
6	330	510
7	385	595
8	440	**680**
9	495	765
10	550	850
11	605	935
12	660	1,020
13	**715**	1,105
14	770	1,190
15	825	1,275

The left column in Table 6-1 represents the calls per second available. The center and right columns represent the maximum number of consecutive calls possible at two call-per-second rates:

✔ **55-second total duration:** Represents the values for calls whose average duration is 55 seconds from the moment the last digit of the phone number is sent to the time the call is disconnected.

This duration breaks down, on average, to 25 seconds of ring-back time before the call is answered and a call connect duration of 30 seconds.

Your maximum concurrent call level must be attained within the time of your average total call duration. After you cross that threshold, you're gaining calls only as quickly as your active calls are disconnecting.

✔ **The right column (85-second total duration):** Shows that you can get a larger number of total consecutive calls when you have a longer total call duration (ring-back time and the total time the call is connected from end to end). An 85-second call identifies a call with a total off-hook time of 85 seconds (25 seconds of ring-back and a 60-second connect duration). The longer call duration provides 30 more seconds to send new calls before you begin disconnecting your previous calls. This enables you to reach a higher total consecutive call number.

You can use Table 6-1 to try to calculate the total calls per second that you need for the volume of calls you have on existing non-VoIP circuits. Either call-duration profile can easily fill seven to ten DS-1s with only three calls per second. The values that each call-duration profile needs to match the volume of a DS-3 (672 phone lines) appear in bold.

If your business is telemarketing, you must factor in an initial failure rate on your calls of up to 20 percent because of bad phone numbers in your dialing list. A call that receives a busy signal or recorded out-of-service message ends quickly, freeing up a line. If you're pushing to fill the equivalent of a DS-3 in calls, you have to negotiate a higher call per second rate.

Your carrier bases your number-of-consecutive-calls and calls per second restrictions on the capacity of its Session Boarder Controller (SBC) assigned to receive all your calls. You may need more calls per second or sessions than your carrier will provide. If you find yourself in this situation, ask your carrier to split up your traffic over two or more SBCs. It shouldn't have a problem meeting your 20 call per second requirement as long as two SBCs, which each have you allocated for 10 calls per second, handle your calls.

Dealing with Touch Tones

The tone you hear when you press a number key on your telephone isn't just one tone, it's actually two different tones at the same time. The touch tones (*Dual Tone Multi Frequency tones,* or DTMF tones) were designed so that your carrier could easily tell that you were dialing a phone number — your carrier couldn't mistake those tones for the sounds of a human voice.

But VoIP was designed to sample and replicate the human voice, not the DTMF tones created by your phone. This VoIP limitation doesn't affect how you make a call because VoIP doesn't need DTMF tones for dialing phone numbers. The destination number is actually transmitted in the overhead of the SIP messaging.

You may need DTMF tones after the call is established, though. For example, you may have to "press 0 for the operator" or navigate through the auto-attendant maze of your insurance company or utility provider.

You have three ways to transmit DTMF over VoIP:

✔ **In-band:** In-band transmission of DTMF places the audio of the touch-tone sounds into the media of the call. So, VoIP actually samples the DTMF tone, packages it up, and sends it through the RTP stream with your voice.

You can use in-band DTMF only if you're sending your audio uncompressed (using the G.711 codec). The compression algorithms used in the other codecs can't pick up the nuances of the DTMF, so the digits aren't transmitted effectively. If you're using any other codec utilizing compression (such as G.729), you must use RFC2833.

✔ **Out-of band RFC2833:** RFC2833 is the industry standard for sending DTMF on compressed calls. The digits are actually transmitted in the RTP of the call as a unique transmission called an RFC 2833 RTP Event. The digit pressed is listed as a number in the message, as are the volume of the tone and the length of time the key is held down. If you press the 5 key and hold it, the RTP event packets continue to send with each new RTP event packet identifying a longer duration.

I go over the look and feel of DTMF-packet transmission in Chapter 11.

✔ **SIP info:** The SIP info method of DTMF transmission has fallen out of favor with the VoIP community, and the (Internet Engineering Task Force) IETF officially *deprecates* (discourages) using it. Use RFC2833 instead. It's much cleaner and easier, and it shows up nicely on captures if you need to troubleshoot (check out Chapter 11 for details).

Determining Fax Requirements

VoIP has to overcome not just the transmissions that don't sound like a human voice in touch tones (as discussed in the preceding section), but also fax transmissions. Most VoIP books, and companies deploying VoIP, wholly ignore the need for faxing, despite the fact that it's a vital transmission medium that people still use every day. By simply scanning documents and e-mailing them, many people transmit documents just as well as they could by faxing, but faxing still has a huge market and demand that any company intent on using a VoIP infrastructure for faxing needs to address.

Faxing over an IP network, or FoIP, has more potential issues that can fail a transmission than DTMF. The analog fax machines that typically receive faxes must synch up with the SIP transmission. FoIP hardware can find synching the simplest, uncompressed call a challenge because the maximum processing speed (or baud rate) of the receiving fax can range from 600 baud to 64 Kbps, where FoIP calls generally begin at 64 Kbps.

Sending uncompressed FoIP with G.711

Unless you're set up to use specialized fax protocols, your only chance of sending a successful fax with FoIP is by transmitting it with the G.711 codec. But even using that codec can be a challenge because the codec is specifically designed for the transmission of voice, not faxes. The sampling algorithms can't successfully compress and then reconstitute the squeals and squawks of a fax transmission based solely on the audio representation of those noises.

Even when you use G.711 to transmit your faxes, the calls can still fail because of synch issues with the receiving fax machine. If the receiving fax machine is capable of performing at very high speeds, known as Super G3 level (basically anything over 14.4 Mbps), the transmission will very likely fail. The conversion of the fax to and from G.711, along with the need to synch up to the receiving machine, requires too much time and coordination for a high-speed fax. The whole process rarely works well with these higher-end fax machines, so the transmission is likely to be corrupted and fail.

Latency, jitter, and packet loss can kill a fax call. You must have a high-quality network and connection if you plan on sending fax transmissions over an uncompressed G.711 transmission.

Using T.37

The community of programmers forging ahead into the world of VoIP recognized the challenge of transmitting faxes over an IP network. They realized that the idea of sampling the audio transmission associated with a fax wasn't going to work, and they needed a new type of transmission mechanism. They decided to collect the fax data, reconstitute it as a completed image, and then save the image in a standard Tagged Image File Format (TIFF). They created a new technology for sending faxes over an IP network called T.37.

T.37 works in a simple manner, as shown in Figure 6-1.

Most fax machines can't directly receive or send T.37. The analog fax machine you bought a few years back is designed to plug in to the single-line jack on your wall and operate over a normal phone line. Most likely, it isn't built to receive T.37 and convert the signal into something it can print on a page.

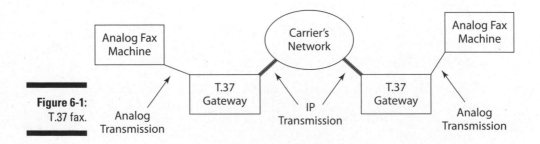

Figure 6-1: T.37 fax.

The main drawback of T.37 from the perspective of a VoIP carrier is that it demands both processor power and buffer memory. When your local carrier's VoIP network receives the fax, the call is converted to T.37, meaning that every page of the fax is fully received and converted to a .TIFF.

The proxy performing this work has to devote a lot of effort to converting the fax data. While the fax is converted to .TIFF files, the finished documents are stored on the switch, which takes up valuable memory until the final page is completed and the fax can be transmitted. The quantity of faxes transmitted around the world prevents T.37 from being an acceptable business product. Don't worry, though — the VoIP carriers created a viable alternative with T.38, which you can read about in the following section.

Getting the fax with T.38

T.38 is a more network-friendly version of T.37 (which I talk about in the preceding section). It resolves the buffer and processor issue by treating the transmission more like a voice call, rather than a fax. T.38 doesn't store the pages while it spools the entire fax document into a TIFF. It simply converts the fax and sends small packets of it, which represent portions of a fax page.

The main benefit of T.38 is compression. It provides the same eight-to-one compression in fax transmissions that G.729 uses for voice calls. You need a lot of bandwidth when you use VoIP because any bottleneck in your Internet connection is instantly realized as poor call or transmission quality in real-time applications as a result of latency, jitter, and packet loss. If your business sends a large volume of faxes, talk to your VoIP provider about T.38.

T.38 has another complication — it uses a unique format to send the T.38 packets. The transmission is sent with a modified version of UDP called the User Datagram Protocol Transport Layer (UDPTL). It doesn't use RTP like a normal VoIP call does or TCP like a normal data transmission does.

Figure 6-2 identifies one of the challenges with T.38. T.38 isn't native to analog fax machines so a network server or gateway is needed to transcode the incoming signal to the fax machine from T.38 to analog.

A T.38 deployment takes time, planning, and a highly competent technician. Your VoIP carrier must design every switch within its network that might encounter the transmission so that it can handle and transmit UDPTL packets. Some carriers have only limited deployment of UDPTL, or it may not yet have fully integrated it. If the VoIP carrier hasn't proven and tested all these switches with UDPTL, its existing network hardware can make the connection from end to end, but the transmission fails when it tries to send UDPTL packets.

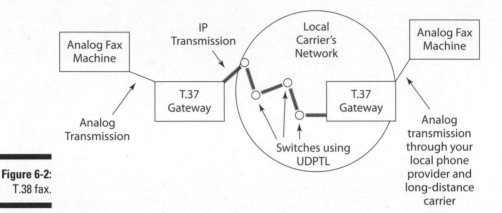

Figure 6-2:
T.38 fax.

INVITE-ing to T.38

T.38 isn't an option provided on every VoIP call. The INVITE message sent on a call that concludes as T.38 is straightforward and appears to be nothing more than a normal voice INVITE. After the VoIP server recognizes the call as a fax, it must then re-INVITE the call to T.38. You can re-INVITE a call to T.38 in two ways:

- ✔ **Program your phone system's Dial Plan for inbound calls.** You must add the phone number or toll-free number on which you plan to receive inbound T.38 faxes to the Dial Plan of your phone system to re-INVITE the call to T.38 as soon as it realizes the number/extension dialed belongs to your fax machine. Your programmer or the individual who designed your Dial Plan shouldn't find programming this very straightforward re-INVITE into your Dial Plan difficult.

- ✔ **Your carrier does all the work on outbound faxes.** Your carrier may be able to monitor your outbound calls and identify in the first few milliseconds whether the call is connecting to a fax. In this case, you don't have to program the re-INVITE into your Dial Plan.

Your carrier can more easily make this distinction in a situation where a remote employee uses the same phone line for both his or her normal phone calls and faxes. An employee or customer with one traditional analog phone line would ignore the incoming call or activate his or her fax machine when he or she needed to receive a fax and disable the fax when he or she wanted to make a call. When the carrier identifies a fax call, the employee can still switch back and forth between types of phone-line usage, and the carrier re-INVITEs only when the employee connects to the fax. If you were to build in an automatic re-INVITE to all outbound calls from your fax line, you'd simply blast a fax tone in the ear of the person every time you called. He or she would eventually figure it out and activate his or her fax machine, but allowing your VoIP carrier to sense the device at the destination is a more diplomatic solution.

If you plan on using T.38 for your fax transmissions, speak to your carrier to figure out whether it handles the re-INVITE to T.38.

Setting up T.38 specifics

T.38 is a more intensive protocol than a normal voice call, and it has additional parameters that the SIP nodes must negotiate. The initial INVITE of a call that's eventually negotiated as T.38 begins as a VoIP call with only voice options listed.

The magic happens after either your Dial Plan identifies the incoming call as a fax or your carrier auto-senses the remote fax on an outbound call. After that happens, the SIP device aware that the destination is a fax, sends the re-INVITE to the originating VoIP server of the transmission and offers T.38, along with the finer details required to make it all work. The Media Description in the SDP looks like this:

```
Media Description, name and address (m): image 43214 udptl
         t38
Media Attribute (a): T38FaxVersion: 0
Media Attribute (a): T38 MaxBitRate: 9600
Media Attribute (a): T38FaxFillBitRemoval: 0
Media Attribute (a): T38FaxTranscodingMMR: 0
Media Attribute (a): T38FaxTranscodingJBIG: 0
Media Attribute (a): T38FaxRateManagement:TransferredTCF
Media Attribute (a): T38FaxMaxBuffer: 316
Media Attribute (a): T38FaxMaxDatagram: 316
Media Attribute (a): T38FaxUdpEC: t38UDPRedundancy
```

You can find out what normal SDP negotiations look like in Chapter 3 (that chapter also gives you the details about the SDP header that I don't include in the preceding code).

The preceding code's first line shows that the transmission is an `image` using port `43214` sent via `udptl` and using `t38` — in other words, a fax. The SDP INVITE needs to present only the rate management, but most fax transmissions also include the other lines in the preceding code, as well. If the parameters do appear in an INVITE, they can appear in any order. These parameters represent

- **Software version:** If the INVITE doesn't identify a version, it populates this position with `0`. If it does note a version, that version identifies the specific release of T.38 used.

- **Max bit rate:** This line identifies the bit rate needed for the fax transmission. The preceding example indicates that it requires `9600`.

- **Fill bit removal:** This line identifies whether the transmission requires additional data to identify blank sections of the fax (called fill bits) or if they can be removed to reduce the bandwidth.

✓ **Transcoding MMR:** This line identifies whether the Modified Media Read (MMR) compression format for faxes can be used to reduce the bandwidth of the transmission. This example indicates with the 0 that the SIP device initiating the INVITE can't use the MMR transcoding.

✓ **Transcoding JBIG:** This line identifies whether the compression technique for fax developed by the Joint Bi-Level Image experts Group (JBIG) can be used to compress the data used on the fax transmission. This example indicates with the 0 that the SIP device initiating the INVITE can't use the JBIG transcoding.

✓ **Rate management:** This line indicates the T.38 fax rate management model that the transmission uses to ensure that both fax machines are functioning at the same speed. The two options are

• **LocalTCF:** A Training Check Frame (TCF) message from the receiving machine or gateway identifies the Bit Error Rate (BER) of the transmission.

• **TransferredTCF:** A TCF message transmitted between endpoints identifies the BER; the receiving machine or gateway has to use the TCF sent by the originating device.

✓ **Max buffer:** This number identifies the maximum number of bytes of data that the INVITE-ing server can store before it has to overwrite that data. After the responding SIP node negotiates this parameter, it helps the transmitting end of the call regulate the transmission to prevent the receiving buffer from being overrun. The max buffer in the preceding code allows for 316 bytes before they're overwritten. The max buffer value you see in a packet capture probably won't be 316, as this field varies, and on the low end, I've seen max buffer values of 72.

✓ **Max datagram:** This value identifies the maximum size of the payload inside an RTP packet. 316 is a common value for this parameter; it's unwise to overload an individual RTP packet.

✓ **UdpEC:** UDP Error Control modes that allow options to provide some sort of redundancy. That's difficult on a transmission where you can't resend lost packets. One option is Forward Error Correction (FEC), which sends additional information in the initial packets sent identifying the number of packets to be sent. This section's example identifies UDPRedundancy, indicating that the SIP device originating the INVITE requests UDP Redundancy Error Correction on the transmission. If the INVITE message preferred FEC over UDPRedundancy, the FEC option would be listed as:

```
Media Attribute (a): T38FaxUdpEC: UDPFEC
```

T.38 is a real-time application with no time for retransmitting. But you can increase your chances of a successful transmission. Forward Error Correction (FEC) sends additional redundant data in the transmission that provide guidelines to replace lost data during the transmission. Network engineers have used FEC for transmitting data for some time; it's not specific to T.38.

The values presented for transcoding MMR and JBIG are referred to as *Boolean values,* named after the 19th-century British mathematician George Boole. Calling them Boolean values is just a fancy way of saying that the values are either 1 or 0, with 1 representing a TRUE response, and 0 representing a FALSE response.

Testing Your LAN

Before buying your first VoIP hardphone or deploying that slick Asterisk server, you have to test your LAN to make sure that it can handle the additional packets, bandwidth, and hardware necessary to support VoIP. Chapter 5 talks about testing your LAN by using the Web site www.testyourvoip. com to make test calls. This Web site gives you a general MOS score for the specific moment in time the calls are executed. But this testing lacks sufficient depth and breadth to fully qualify your network.

MOS scores (which you can read about in Chapter 3) are only a generalized rating for a call. An MOS score doesn't identify whether the first few seconds of the call had low volume, the last half of the call had excess volume, and packets were lost during a few seconds in the middle of the call. It averages all these factors and provides a score. MOS is the starting point for LAN investigation, which you use to track down the latency, jitter, and packet loss that impacts your calls.

You need to test your network with live VoIP calls in a scaled and methodical manner over the course of a full business day. Create a cyclical testing pattern in which you place one call after another every few seconds. You want to increase the number of concurrent calls on your network until you reach the number of calls you've identified as your maximum concurrent calls. Most small to medium-sized businesses don't have many calls active at the same time — usually, up to ten concurrent calls.

Test on several days of the week and make sure that testing covers any peak time of the month (such as when monthly billing is run or during any large data tasks that your business does regularly).

You must have some type of software deployed on your network to help in the VoIP Lifecycle Management (VLM) required for a successful VoIP deployment (and covered in detail in Chapter 5). By bringing on additional calls in a slow and methodical manner, you allow your VLM software to track the impact of each additional call on your network. The VLM software that you use has a direct impact on how easily you can determine the source of latency, jitter, and packet loss. I recommend using the Packet Island software (`www.packetisland.com`) that's covered in Chapter 9.

Focusing on latency

Chapter 5 covers latency from a general standpoint, but this section identifies it in regards to VoIP network design. The testing that you conduct on your network should indicate the latency incurred while the VoIP test calls traverse individual switches, routers, and firewalls. In this regard, you want to look for the consistent sources of delay on your network so that you can get a sense of what latency to expect under normal conditions.

A little latency, all by itself, doesn't cause a large problem. You need to worry about it only when your average network latency is more than 150 milliseconds (or 100 milliseconds if your network is prone to jitter). Either scenario sets the stage for any additional latency to cause packets to arrive out of sequence or be lost.

Investigating jitter

Jitter isn't a systemic and common issue in the way that generic latency is. It isn't the minor fluctuation of 1 or 2 milliseconds (ms) in delay caused by the normal ebb and flow of packets coursing through a switch or router. The jitter you encounter during the testing process on your VoIP network design prior to VoIP deployment of more than 50 ms or more caused by hardware, software, routing, switching, or cabling must be identified and reduced below this level.

The normal day-to-day functioning of your LAN handles the transmission of e-mails, instant messages, and some casual Web surfing. This expected ebb and flow of data is disrupted when a coworker starts downloading the CD-Burn file for Linux Fedora. For the next 110 minutes (depending on the size of your Internet connection), the bandwidth on the LAN is constricted because this download consumes the majority of it.

When the download completes, the available bandwidth returns to normal levels, and the packets continue to flow like they did before the download began. Bandwidth constraints aren't the only sources of jitter — hardware with software bugs, failing hardware, and cabling issues can also produce intermittent spikes of latency.

The source of jitter can be an extreme challenge to identify when designing and proving out your network for VoIP deployment. Like any intermittent problem, you have a chance to find it only if you're capturing data from the LAN at the time the problem occurs. Jitter doesn't always present itself in the form of bandwidth consumption for a network back-up or file download. Many instances of jitter related to hardware and cabling come in the form of small spikes of latency lasting only a few seconds, at most.

Jitter is frequently the extra boost that pushes the normal latency level in your LAN to the point that it begins dropping packets. The good news is that identifying jitter allows you to prepare for these spikes, so they don't cause packet loss. Now, you just have to get good VoIP Lifecycle Management software to find it.

Sniffing out packet loss

Packet loss represents more than simply a packet being misdirected between hops. Although packets can end up wayward and never make it to their final destinations, packets are more often discarded. This can happen because

- The jitter buffer overloads, and incoming packets overwrite packets already in the buffer.
- You run out of LAN or WAN bandwidth.
- Excessive latency or jitter within your LAN causing packets to arrive out of sequence and be discarded.
- The switches or routers are pushed beyond their Packets Per Second capacity.
- Routers or switches have a routing bug that causes internal congestion, which leads to packets being discarded.
- Packets being sent via different routes from origination to termination (referred to as route flaps and covered in depth in Chapter 5) cause packets to arrive out of sequence.
- Switches or routers are failing.
- Firewalls are pushed beyond their Packets Per Second capacity.
- The cabling over which the packets are traveling experiences issues or shorts.

Packet loss is the one VoIP deployment challenge that's directly responsible for poor call quality and call failure. Latency and jitter affect the transmission of packets, but if they somehow arrive at the end destination in sequence and in time, you get acceptable call quality. Packet loss literally is a loss of data, and without the packet, any information it contained is absent. If you lose enough RTP packets that contain the audio of your conversation, the call quality drops because sections of your conversation don't reach the other end of the call. If the packet sent was an INVITE, a re-INVITE, or an acknowledgement, your call could potentially never get set up or fail in midstream.

Beginning VoIP Design

Before running a series of tests on your LAN, design and structure it as efficiently as possible so that you can eliminate many issues caused by packet collision and design, allowing you to focus on the bandwidth, hardware, and cabling as your only remaining variables after testing begins. Chapter 5 covers the individual elements used to design an efficient VoIP network; in this section, I present those elements in a plan for deployment. Following these steps provides you a well-built network in which you use your bandwidth and hardware as efficiently as possible:

1. **Remove unnecessary hops.**

   Eliminate any unnecessary routers, switches, and hardware between where the VoIP call originates and where it finally hits the PSTN.

   You can't control how your Internet provider routes the call, but you can eliminate unnecessary hardware within your LAN.

2. **If you're deploying VoIP on an existing LAN by using the same cabling, switches, and routers, build the network infrastructure for your VoIP traffic as a Virtual LAN.**

   Isolate the VoIP traffic from your existing data network as much as possible. If the data packets don't even know the VoIP packets exist, the data packets can't as easily get in your way.

3. **When you have your VoIP traffic on its own LAN, give the voice packets their own section of bandwidth from any other packets that may be riding with them as an additional refinement in your LAN design.**

   The implementation of rate shaping is most important at choke points in your network, such as firewalls, where the data and VoIP traffic both hit the same piece of hardware.

4. **Add prioritization to your routers and firewalls to ensure the voice traffic receives the best treatment.**

   Add this prioritization to network choke points so that the VoIP traffic isn't incurring latency waiting on lower-importance data traffic.

You need to hire a LAN professional to deploy these requirements, but it's money well spent. A clean and efficient network requires less bandwidth and hardware to support it.

Diving In to VoIP Network Analysis

The series of test calls that your VLM software generates from your LAN over the course of a day, days, or weeks generates a lot of data. You want to make quick work of reviewing the information, drilling down to find the base level of latency, reasons for jitter, and sources of packet loss. Analyzing the data collected by your VLM software from your test calls follows the same philosophy as troubleshooting.

The first rule of troubleshooting is to always trust your data. It's the empirical information from your network, void of any emotional wants and desires. If the data indicates that your routers, switches, and firewalls are all dropping packets because they can't handle the increased flood of VoIP packets, don't decide to just buy a bigger Internet pipe because that's cheaper than a new router. The only way to fully resolve a problem is to act on the information provided in testing.

Handling systemic issues

The first report you probably see from your VoIP analysis is the MOS score for your calls. These MOS scores give you a place to start on analysis because they're a good general indicator of the overall health of your network. If you performed your test calls in a cycle, you first see the impact of an ascending quantity of concurrent calls on your network infrastructure, including hardware, cabling, design, and your connection to the Internet.

The pattern of degradation in Figure 6-3 indicates that a systemic issue is causing poor call quality — that some aspect of your LAN is being pushed beyond its limits. The two most likely culprits for this type of failure are bandwidth and hardware.

If you identify that you have a systemic issue, check your bandwidth. Your testing results should include a breakdown of bandwidth usage by data type — VoIP or TCP. If you allocate only a small portion of your dedicated Internet connection (for example, 128Kbps) to e-mail and Web surfing, then you can use all the rest (in this example, a little more than 1.4 Mbps) to send your VoIP calls.

To check your bandwidth, you have to do some math. The bandwidth used by your VoIP calls varies, depending on the codec you're using.

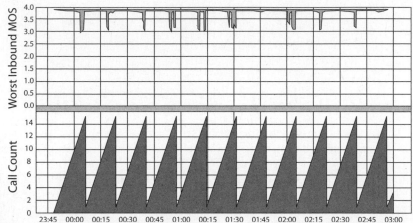

Figure 6-3:
Test call
results with
MOS.

Table 6-2 makes quick work of the numbers. If every call sent in the test example in Figure 6-3 was transmitted with the uncompressed G.711 codec, you can expect packet loss and MOS degradation when the final call is sent because you've run out of available bandwidth. The total bandwidth required for 15 uncompressed calls is about 13 Mbps more than this example network has available. If you're in this kind of situation, just call your IP provider and order more bandwidth.

Table 6-2		Bandwidth Consumption		
Codec	*Overhead*	*Payload*	*Total Mbps Per Call*	*Total Mbps for 15 Calls*
G.711	31	64	95	1425
G.729	31	8	39	585

If all the calls were sent with the compressed G.729 codec, then bandwidth isn't the issue in this example. You could actually send an additional 15 calls with G.729 and still have bandwidth to spare. The data tells you the MOS score dropped at some point in the testing process, so you now have to investigate the hardware on your LAN to identify which switch, router, or firewall is failing because you're pushing it beyond its ability.

Working over intermittent problems

You may have difficulty finding intermittent issues. The perfect testing environment would sample your network every 20 milliseconds to track every packet generated. But you can't really use a sampling rate that aggressive because the process of sampling the packets would induce latency, and the sheer volume of packets and data generated would overrun any hard drive. Ask your VLM software provider about that software's sampling frequency.

Many intermittent issues affecting VoIP last for only a few seconds. If the software you're using samples less than once a minute, you can easily miss vital data that you need to locate the source of the problem.

If your sample includes random calls that have a low MOS score, then you need to do a little more investigation. Identify a specific call and use your VLM software to isolate every possible variable on the LAN that could have affected it. Every VLM software package doesn't provide detailed data on every switch, router, hub, and server on your LAN, but pull the most detailed information from it that you can. You need to be able to use the test data to isolate the information down to a specific hour, half hour, minute, or second. The more specific your data, the more easily you can find the offending variable. Your search should cover

- ✔ Bandwidth use by network traffic and other calls
- ✔ Latency induced by a switch, router, or firewall
- ✔ Packet loss induced by a switch, router, or firewall

When you find the cause of the issue, check for more calls that have the same MOS score and perform the same analysis on them. This additional analysis either reinforces that you found the correct source of the problem on your first call or indicates additional hardware or bandwidth concerns that you also need to address.

Retesting it all again

Your initial testing indicates areas of your network that need upgrading. You may need to replace routers, order additional IP bandwidth, and configure VLANs, employ rate shaping and prioritization, eliminate unnecessary hops, and maximize traffic flow. Around this time, everyone in your office starts asking you, "Is it done yet?"

Stay strong and tell everyone to give you some more time. After you implement solutions for all the known issues, run the exact same cycle of tests again. You should get acceptable MOS scores across the board. But don't take the good test scores at face value. Look at the test results for a handful of calls to check the bandwidth used and the performance of all the new hardware. You also may find and need to resolve another issue before you can officially deploy VoIP with a clear conscience.

Introducing non-network issues

Your VoIP calls must also contend with the normal array of problems that can befall any phone call. These issues fall into two general categories:

- ✔ **Call-quality issues:** These issues include static, echo, and clipping.
- ✔ **Call-completion issues:** These problems result in call failure.

I go over all these issues as they pertain to VoIP transmissions in Part III of this book, where I also talk about standard troubleshooting logic and methods. Some VoIP-specific problems in call quality can also arise, such as improper encoding and decoding of the audio packets, which can cause the sound to be distorted and make the voices on the call sound robotic.

If you run across a call-quality or completion issue that sounds just like something you heard on a non-VoIP call, the issue is probably linked to the traditional telephone network.

Realizing the Pros and Cons of Caller ID

VoIP has its own unique billing concerns that the market is just now catching on to. The one issue that has the largest impact on how calls are rated relates to VoIP's ability to uniquely identify the origination phone number that creates a call. The phone number identified in the Caller ID window of the receiving telephone completely depends on the phone number supplied in the FROM field of the SIP header. But any programmer who has finished an entry-level class in C++ can probably figure out how to change this field.

Many telemarketing companies have a legitimate need to modify the phone number you see in your Caller ID window when they call you. Telemarketing companies, which by law have to present a valid Caller ID when they solicit new customers, use the phone numbers belonging to the companies they are dialing on behalf of as their Caller ID to legally solicit customers. Many people receiving telemarketing calls use the phone numbers logged in to their phone's Caller ID records to initiate return calls to people and companies. This is an efficient way to reach the business trying to sell you something, and by giving you its phone number, you don't waste time talking to the company it uses to place the phone calls. The Caller ID number is frequently a direct phone number that may be local to the people being called, or it may be a toll-free number to encourage a return call.

Telemarketing companies work for other businesses to place calls to existing or prospective customers. An example of this is if a telemarketing company named TeleX is dialing 100,000 existing and prospective customers for Circuit City to leave a 30-second message on their answering machines about an upcoming sale at the Circuit City in their neighborhood. Circuit City wants the people called to contact them at their local retail store if they have questions about the sale, so TeleX uses the phone number for the local retail store as the Caller ID when it calls the 100,000 homes in the area. This is a legitimate manipulation of Caller ID as it fulfills the federal requirement for displaying a valid call-back number.

In either case, the telemarketing company may be following federal laws, but if it's using VoIP, the telemarketer could be in for a billing surprise. The FROM field on the call is the only piece of information that most long-distance carriers use to derive the number that populates the Caller ID window of the receiving party *and* acts as a billing point of reference. This is exactly how traditional telephony calls from your analog phone are rated, but the complication with VoIP is that the Caller ID can be easily manipulated, and the phone number shown from an analog phone can't.

A telemarketing company located in Dallas that calls a potential customer base in Florida for a Florida client may send a Florida phone number as the Caller ID. The local carrier in Florida identifies that the call originates in Florida and requires that the long-distance carrier provide the intrastate rate for the call. As a general rule, the intrastate rates for a phone call are generally much more expensive than the rates for calls coming from outside the state. Because the long-distance carriers are charged the higher intrastate rates, they pass those charges on to the telemarketing company sending the in-state Caller ID triggering the charges.

The same type of charges would generally apply if a telemarketing company assigned a toll-free number as the origination Caller ID. The process would take a few more steps, but in the end, the same type of rating would be applied. Toll-free numbers aren't geographically tied to any area, unlike a phone number that can be attributed to a physical phone line at a home or business. So, the VoIP carrier tags calls that employ a toll-free number as the origination Caller ID as Indeterminate Jurisdiction (IJ). The local phone carriers want to charge the higher rate for any calls they can, so they charge the long-distance carriers sending these IJ calls as intrastate. The long-distance carrier can much more easily pay the intrastate rate and pass the charge on to its customer, instead of engaging in a protracted debate with the local carriers to prove the call was interstate.

Cell phones are usually billed based on the phone number attributed to the cell phone. If you have a California cell phone and place a call back home while you're on vacation in Texas, the call is seen as intrastate California. Since you are paying for air-time minutes and not based on jurisdiction, it doesn't matter to you. It does matter if you call a toll-free number from your cell phone as a California toll-free number will be billed as an intrastate call. There is a solution in the works using an additional field of data in the call stream called a Jurisdictional Information Parameter (JIP) field that identifies the physical location of a caller (serving cell tower for instance) as a billing reference point instead of the phone number attributed to the cell phone. This is still a work in progress and isn't fully deployed on all long-distance networks.

Changing the origination phone number used for outbound calling with the intent to manipulate the jurisdiction of the call is illegal. If you're dialing from Colorado to customers in Denver, you may be tempted to throw a Texas number as your origination phone number for the calls. You receive the lower interstate rate on the calls, but your long-distance provider realizes that you're engaging in devious business practices. Your carrier may not catch on right away, but when it does, you face having calls rerated or your service terminated. If you're an enhanced VoIP provider or a certified long-distance carrier in the eyes of the FCC, you face a whole litany of fees, fines, and possibly even a tangled web of legal troubles.

Telemarketing companies that illegally manipulate Caller ID, as well as value-added VoIP resellers, may also realize another side-effect of billing based on Caller ID — curious local taxes. Carriers that employ calling-card platforms may have to deal with this situation often because most calling-card calls are dialed to the same state from which they originate, even though the calling-card platform may be located in another state. The calling-card companies forward on the phone number of the payphone being used to reach the calling-card platform and the intrastate rating of calls trigger the assessment of local-, county-, and state-level taxes for these calls. In the example of the telemarketing company in Dallas, it could potentially see local Florida taxes on its invoice for the calls it dialed to Florida on behalf of its client.

Dialing Out to Toll-Free Numbers

All the VoIP billing issues that can crop up also have a potential silver lining.

The FCC requirements dictate that all outbound VoIP must have the ability to transmit valid 911 information. The local phone carrier used to be responsible for providing your address when you call 911 for an emergency.

Despite the merging of long-distance and local phone companies, the networks servicing each market are structurally different. Local phone carriers, like the traditional "baby Bells" (Pacific Bell, Bell Atlantic, and Southwestern Bell) provided a dial tone to phone numbers, as well as access to toll-free numbers and long-distance carriers, by using a piece of hardware called a class 5 switch.

In contrast, long-distance carriers use a class 4 switch. A class 4 switch is completely geared toward finding out which local carrier owns the number you dialed and routing your call to that carrier. This kind of switch is structurally different from a class 5 switch because class 4 switches lack a class 5 switch's intelligence and infrastructure, which allow you to have all those great local features, such as

- Dialing 911 for emergency services
- Dialing 411 for directory assistance
- Dialing over different long-distance networks, specifying the carrier by dialing its 1010+ access codes
- Dialing toll-free numbers

Residential and small business customers generally reach their long-distance carrier through their local carrier. Their analog phone line is ultimately wired into their local carrier's class 5 switch. Because the local carrier first processes their calls, all the features of the class 5 switch are at their disposal, even if their VoIP carrier is a traditional long-distance carrier.

Larger business users generally opt for a dedicated digital connection that bypasses their local carrier's class 5 switch and is ultimately wired directly into the class 4 switch of their long-distance carrier. They give up the features that the local carrier offers and get long-distance per-minute rates that may be half the price of rates available from the analog lines.

In the access to these local carrier services, you can see the VoIP silver lining. At this moment in time, some carriers (such as QWEST) are processing all their outbound VoIP calls through a class 5 switch to meet the federal requirements allowing VoIP to connect to 911 for emergency services. This interaction with the class 5 switch, although fleeting, is all an outbound VoIP customer needs to dial a toll-free number. The customer still enjoys the lower dedicated digital rate he or she used to have with his or her DS-1 or DS-3 circuit, but now he or she can dial toll-free numbers and special numbers, such as 911 and 411. If you are a small business with only five or six phone lines, this doesn't mean anything to you. Once you grow and need your first dedicated circuit, suddenly you'll have access to much lower rates, without all of the restrictions imposed on a traditional telephony connection.

Chapter 7

Providing Configuration Information

*1*f you have a small or medium-sized business, you may establish VoIP service with a carrier very similarly to how you establish a connection through a DS-1 or DS-3 dedicated digital circuit. The order flow — including matching protocols, configurations, and options — follows the same process, regardless of whether it's a DS-3 or VoIP connection. Matching up the configurations on both ends of the connection is just as important with VoIP as it is with traditional telephony. You won't be able to pass a valid call if your VoIP is set up to send SIP and the carrier runs H.323, just like any protocol mismatch on a DS-1 configuration.

This chapter covers most of the questions you may encounter on the VoIP questionnaire that you get from your carrier to define both your SIP configuration, as well as specifics of your calling pattern. Every company has its own strengths, weaknesses, flexibilities, and absolutes, so every VoIP questionnaire is different. But in this chapter, I not only mention and define the standard issues raised by a carrier, I also explain why the choices are important.

Carriers understand that nuances exist between the configuration of their Edge Proxy Server (EPS) or Session Boarder Controller (SBC), and their customers' individual routers and servers. The unique business applications and features that customers require all translate into the specific SIP configuration that the carrier must match to ensure the successful completion of a customer's calls.

VoIP as Local Loop Replacement

Businesses across the world finally see VoIP as a legitimate technology. Its previous reputation as inexpensive but unstable has changed because many companies are embracing VoIP's flexibility and features. This growing demand for VoIP isn't going unnoticed by the long-distance carriers who are rolling out VoIP products geared toward this market.

The long-distance carriers don't use VoIP as an end-to-end transport medium, but simply a technology that allows the carrier's customers to reach the carrier's network. Figure 7-1 compares a traditional digital circuit connection into a long-distance carrier with a new VoIP connection.

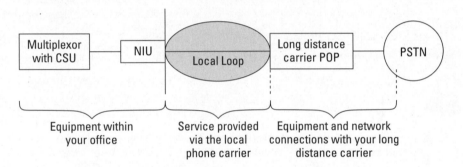

Traditional Dedicated DS-1 connection to a long-distance carrier

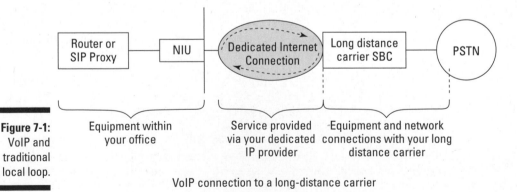

Figure 7-1: VoIP and traditional local loop.

VoIP connection to a long-distance carrier

The diagram on the top of Figure 7-1 shows a traditional dedicated connection between a business and its long-distance carrier. The *local loop* is the cabling that spans from the Network Interface Unit (NIU) to the long-distance carrier's Point of Presence (POP). The local loop's section of cabling usually runs to your building by the local phone carrier in the area, for which you're charged an installation fee and a monthly recurring fee.

The schematic on the bottom of Figure 7-1 shows the same connectivity to your long-distance carrier, but instead of having a dedicated cable connecting your office to the POP, you access the POP via the Internet through your dedicated Internet connection. You may prefer the VoIP connection to a traditional local loop for several reasons:

- **A potentially less-expensive connection:** Your long-distance provider generally accepts VoIP traffic from you, as long as you're contracted with a reputable Internet provider with a direction connection to the Internet backbone. Your long-distance provider calculates the cost for the local loop by the distance from your premise to the POP.

  If you're in a remote location, the monthly fee could be thousands of dollars just to reach your long-distance carrier. A local IP provider may be able to deliver the necessary bandwidth for a fraction of the cost.

- **Maximum bandwidth for voice and data:** A traditional office pays for two dedicated connections — one for the Internet and one for a long-distance DS-1 or dedicated circuit. Combining them allows you to pay only one monthly fee, rather than two.

- **More long-distance carriers available:** Because you're not hard-wiring your network into your long-distance carrier, you can use multiple long-distance carriers. VoIP requires only your VoIP server to be programmed with an IP address for the carriers you want to receive the SIP and RTP packets. You can very easily have two or more long-distance carriers, using the same dedicated Internet connection for VoIP calls. So, you can route your calls based on who has the lower rate to the given destination, maximizing your savings.

- **Effective long-distance carrier redundancy:** After you have two or more long-distance carriers established, you can easily make changes to your Dial Plan to send all of your calls to your second carrier in case that your first carrier has a catastrophic failure. You can address even small regional outages that affect one carrier by sending the calls over an alternative carrier.

These reasons are pushing many companies to migrate to VoIP. I anticipate that the trend will continue when new offices choose VoIP hardware from the outset, instead or wrestling with the decision to replace existing hardware.

Ordering VoIP

If you're ordering VoIP service for your home or an office that has only a few phone lines, your VoIP provider may send out a small Analog Telephone Adapter (ATA). This device acts as an interface between your traditional analog phones and your carrier's VoIP server, converting the calls to VoIP and sending them out over your Internet connection. The ATAs are preprogrammed, so all the configurations, settings, and variables are taken care of in a nice neat package.

If you're ordering VoIP for a large office in which you need at least ten lines, the process with many carriers follows the same procedure and timeline that ordering a dedicated circuit does because the provisioning process for both orders within the carrier, encompassing the order entry, allocation of bandwidth, facilities, design of how the calls are routed through the network, and assignment of some kind of billing reference number is almost the same. Establishing the VoIP connection between your SIP proxy and the SBC of your VoIP carrier is only the first segment in this entire provisioning process. Figure 7-1 shows that at the point where either a traditional telephony circuit or a VoIP connection enters the carrier, the carrier then routes calls from either interface through similar equipment and network connections.

Figure 7-2 shows how, aside from the method used to get the calls to the long-distance carrier, everything within the carrier's network is the same on a traditional circuit and a VoIP connection. After the individual calls hit the network, SBC (for VoIP), or the dedicated interface card (for DS-1s) package the calls that into aggregated groups of contiguous bandwidth called *trunk groups* that act to direct the calls and link a billing reference number to the calls. That reference number can be the trunk group name itself, a specialized number called an Auth Code, or the DL value that assigns the calls running through the trunk group to your account. Finally, the calls travel out of the long-distance carrier's network through outbound circuits that pass your calls to the Public Switched Telephone Network (PSTN).

Anyone with a VoIP connection can populate the FROM section of his or her SIP header with any phone number, regardless of if it belongs to him or her, or if it isn't even a legitimate phone number. VoIP doesn't have a way to restrict anyone to only use phone numbers he or she owns as the origination phone number in his or her INVITE message. So, you have to consider the origination phone number listed on a VoIP call an unreliable means of billing with your VoIP carrier, or at least a suspect one. You must somehow tie the calls to your origination IP address, ensuring that only the calls that you actually place are billed to you. If your carrier used only your legitimate origination phone number to attribute your calls, it would throw any call that has a bogus or unknown origination phone number into an errors file with no way of being able to bill for it. Every call is billed by linking your outbound calls to either your origination IP or a trunk group that has its own billing reference.

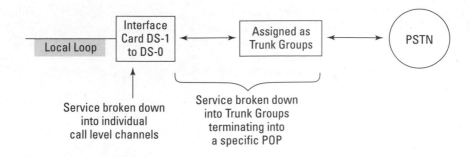

Traditional Dedicated DS-1 configuration within a long-distance carrier

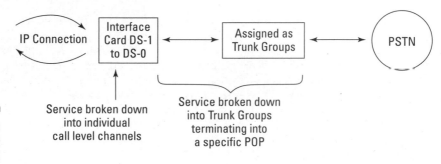

Figure 7-2:
VoIP and
traditional
provisioning.

VoIP configuration to a long-distance carrier

All the billing and routing elements that your VoIP carrier needs to provide VoIP service translates into a common provisioning timeline of 30 to 45 days. Larger VoIP orders, those that require the equivalent of 500 or more phone lines, may have to run trough a vigorous screening process before they even reach Day 1 of the 30- to 45-day provisioning process.

Looking at Your Standard Usage

The protocols, options, and parameters required to connect to your VoIP provider cover only the interaction between your SIP server and the SBC of your carrier. The billing elements of your connection constitute the other half of the provisioning timeline and have their own concerns.

Your *calling footprint* (or *calling profile*), which represents the states, cities, and local carriers terminating your calls, becomes more important when you require more than 500 consecutive calls. If you're replacing a traditional voice DS-3 (containing 672 phone lines), your carrier may ask for a one-month sample of your traffic so that it can analyze it.

Validating port quantity

Your long-distance carrier generally wants an average month's worth of your Call Detail Records (CDR). It analyzes this data to validate that you truly need all the ports you're ordering. Every carrier has their own benchmark for justification of VoIP ports. The average requirement is for about 1,000 minutes per port. If you're ordering 500 ports, your carrier expects half a million minutes of usage on the CDR you provide.

If you don't use the total minutes required for the ports you're ordering, your carrier may reclaim the unused ports. All long-distance carriers constantly work to manage their capacity. They generally reclaim any facilities that aren't being used and give those facilities to another customer who needs them. After your carrier alerts you that it's targeted your circuits for reclamation, you generally have 30 days to ramp up the usage or lose them.

It may provide you with a 30- to 90-day ramp-up period to reach the billing level to which you committed, but after that, contract usage minimums may kick in. If your carrier estimates that the 1 million minutes should equal $10,000 per month and you bill out only $500, you could be looking at a $9,500 short-fall fee.

The good news about having your ports reclaimed is that any monthly recurring fees associated with the ports are generally eliminated. The fact that your carrier is seizing services for which it's contractually obligated to provide gives you some degree of leverage. Your carrier wants to give the ports to someone who'll use them to generate revenue. At the same time, you have a legal footing in your contract stating that you ordered them and are paying the monthly fee, so you should have access to them. The best deal for both parties involves you releasing the ports back to your carrier and your carrier discontinuing your monthly recurring fees for the ports. You no longer have the capacity, but you've fostered a good relationship with your carrier. Most carriers understand that your growth projections aren't always realized. They are trying to work with you to grow your business, and since they qualified you for the additional bandwidth when you placed the order, they are generally understanding when you have to temporarily scale back. This goodwill comes in very handy when, later, you want them to give you additional ports when your usage warrants it.

Analyzing your calling profile

Besides figuring out how many ports you can have (which I talk about in the preceding section), a carrier needs to look at your CDR to determine where you're calling. Not only does it need to know the city and state that you're calling, it also needs to determine the local phone carriers responsible for the phone numbers you normally dial.

The geographic locations that you call, and the quantity of calls sent to those locations, are very important to your carrier. Most long-distance carriers don't have the capacity to send an additional 100 consecutive calls to rural Montana or a small town in Virginia. If your calling profile frequently sends a high volume of calls to a specific area, your carrier may need to add additional facilities to the area. Your carrier always wants to be aware of your calling patterns before installing your service, instead of having to deal with call completion issues that it could have avoided.

It may request that you put the information it needs in a Minutes of Usage (MOU) report, sorted by destination. Generally, you can create this kind of report only if you have specialized telecom software programs to analyze your traffic and break it down by geographic areas and by terminating local carriers. If you can't provide the MOU report, just send your carrier the month's worth of traffic and have it analyze it; it should be happy with either.

A long-distance carrier doesn't often run out of capacity when completing your calls. It generally has several additional routes and underlying carriers available to complete calls if its primary facilities are full. But the secondary or tertiary route choices are frequently more expensive for the carrier, which is another reason carriers want to know ahead of time where you're calling. The 30-day interval between when it receives the CDR and when you're finally installed gives your long-distance carrier the time to negotiate more capacity from its underlying carriers before it costs the carrier.

Don't overload the local carrier's central office switch. Local phone providers that serve small towns don't have excessive facilities coming into them or going out from them. If you send 100 calls to a town with only 200 residents, you can easily overrun the local carrier's network, causing all but a handful of your calls to fail. Just like sending too many calls per second to your carrier's SBC, this behavior quickly results in a call from the Network Security office at your long-distance carrier telling you to stop. Pace calls to small towns. You'll have a much higher completion rate and avoid calls from network security.

Your carrier also thoroughly analyzes the financial aspect of your call profile. The local carriers that own the phone numbers you dial charge your long-distance carrier to complete the call. If the phone number you dial belongs to

Verizon, for example, then Verizon charges your long-distance carrier a set rate to complete the call. Generally speaking, calls to the traditional Regional Bell Operating Companies (RBOCs), such as Pacific Bell, Southwestern Bell, and Bell Atlantic, are some of the least expensive calls. Your long-distance carrier probably pays these companies millions of dollars per month and has negotiated some very favorable rates.

The quantity of calls you have terminating to local phone carriers that are not the direct descendants of those early RBOCs, such as cell phones or VoIP carriers (a group of companies referred to as Completing Local Exchange Carriers or CLECs because they are in competition with the RBOCS), can have a large financial impact on your long-distance carrier. The CLECs charge much more to terminate calls to the phone numbers they own than the RBOCs do. Long-distance carriers frequently employ an 80/20 clause in their contracts for service, which requires that at least 80 percent of your traffic must terminate to RBOCs. Consult your contract to see whether it has such a clause. Failing to meet the call-profile percentages can result in some pretty heavy financial fees or charges.

Listing Your Servers

The VoIP worksheet that your carrier sends to you is set up to handle all configuration information required from the most complicated end-user network it can imagine. So, the form probably asks you for information that doesn't apply to your network.

You probably find the most questions that don't actually apply to your network in the section about your servers. The VoIP worksheets assume that you're using separate servers for the SIP messaging and the media (RTP). You may have an array of SIP servers, backup servers, and media gateways; a DTMF collector; and a collection of feature servers. Some VoIP deployments include all these devices, but not many. Your VoIP provider needs specific information about the servers you have, including

- Manufacturer make and model number
- Software revision
- IP address

Even if the carrier gives you the IP address of its SIP hardware, its firewall still blocks you until it has your IP address established on its network.

Using multiple servers in your VoIP network to process calls provides redundancy in the event that one server fails. This type of configuration also combines the processor strength of all the servers, increasing the quantity of calls per second you can send. Keep in mind that with a cluster of servers, you must have an efficient system to update routing changes and configuration information through all your SIP servers.

Ask your carrier how its SBC will respond if one SIP server in your cluster fails. Ideally, it should be able to send messages to your servers to qualify they are active and bypass any router that fails to respond. Qualifying your servers before your VoIP carrier sends calls allows your carrier to skip any unresponsive server. So, you receive every call on a viable proxy, instead of having intermittent call failures when the one server fails to respond to the INVITEs of incoming calls.

Your carrier needs to know the physical location of your SIP servers for billing and tax purposes, despite the fact that the connections between your carrier and you are all virtual. Most long-distance rates fall into either an intrastate or interstate category. Depending on the logic used by your VoIP provider, it may use the physical location listed for your servers as the sole means of determining the jurisdiction of your calls.

Don't assume that because your servers are located in Milwaukee, every single call you make will use that location as the billing reference point. An alternative choice of billing logic your carrier may use is the phone number in the FROM section of the SIP header or other proprietary fields available from your carrier. Speak to your VoIP carrier about how it determines the inter- and intrastate jurisdictions of your calls, instead of assuming that it bases those jurisdictions on your physical location.

Covering Signaling Basics

Your protocol, the size and type of your Internet connection, and the details about how your calls will be packetized (which software mechanism you use and your preference or codecs) are all required by your VoIP carrier to configure its SBC to accommodate your configuration, allowing your VoIP calls work. Each option you choose has ramifications for your carrier and your company. The signaling and configuration portion of a SIP questionnaire is vital, so double-check the info before you send the order form to your carrier.

Choosing a protocol

The first question on most VoIP questionnaires asks you what VoIP protocol you use. Are you using SIP or H.323? This question is on the top of the list in many VoIP order forms because it has an effect on how and where your service is provisioned. Your provider needs this simple (but very important) answer because it can't change from SIP to H.323 as easily as other options during activation.

Carriers have separate servers for H.323 and SIP, which have different IP addresses assigned to them. For example, if your SIP hardware is damaged in the 30 to 45 days between when you ordered the service and when it's scheduled for installation, don't expect your backup H.323 system to work. The entire front-end of your VoIP service, the server assigned to you by your carrier, the IP address of its server, and your access to that address all have to be repositioned. Your carrier can implement most other changes without much difficulty, but you have a two-week delay if you need to change your protocol from SIP to H.323 (or vice versa).

Getting down to specifics

Identifying whether your protocol is H.323 or SIP is only the first step in configuring the VoIP carrier's SBC. Your carrier also needs you to confirm that your SIP proxy will send the traffic with the UDP transport method, not TCP. Even though you have only one logical choice, it may request that you confirm that choice.

Your carrier also asks for the signaling port that your SIP proxy uses to send and receive your SIP messages. The standard port for signaling is 5060 for most carriers. You can select a different SIP port for signaling, but any deviation from the 5060 port raises a red flag at your VoIP carrier, and your VoIP carrier may fixate on that as the source of any issue, if you have call-completion issues.

Stick with what's expected, if you can. Non-standard configurations generally delay troubleshooting because everyone triple-checks your configurations to ensure that they're not the source of the failure.

The final pieces of essential signaling information between you and your carrier are your codec selection and packet sampling size. List all the codecs that you plan to use, noting which codec you prefer to use all the time, and which codecs are your second or third choices, should your primary codec be unavailable. During the INVITE and 200 OK sequences, your SIP proxy negotiates the codec used on a call, but your carrier must know which codecs you intend to use. Many carriers support only G.711 and G.729, so a request for G.723 and G.726 may require your service to be provisioned to another part of their SBC or may result in a notification from their order-entry staff that the codecs aren't supported.

The packet size used between most carriers and companies is 20 milliseconds (ms). Some carriers may actually negotiate the packet sampling size in the initial INVITE and 200 OK exchange. If you require anything other than 20 ms, speak with your carrier to ensure that it can accommodate you.

Agreeing on how to dial the call

VoIP standards cover every aspect of VoIP transmissions, and the way in which phone numbers are presented in the SIP header isn't immune. The International Telecommunications Union (ITU) recommendation for phone numbers, referred to as *E.164,* is the basis for how all phone numbers appear in a SIP header. The recommendation requires a preceding "+1" before the normal area code and seven-digit telephone number. Many servers still require the VoIP carrier's SBC to manipulate the standard format, and their SBC may need to strip either the + or the entire +1 prefix on incoming calls or add it to outgoing calls. Generally, most carriers can accommodate these minor deviations from the E.164 standard.

During the early days of VoIP, small boutique carriers specializing in VoIP provided service. They weren't large long-distance companies offering a VoIP product, but were instead small start-up companies that owned and operated their own VoIP switches and converted VoIP traffic before passing it off to long-distance carriers that used traditional telephony. These small and specialized carriers frequently offered their customers more flexibility on how those customers wanted their incoming phone numbers presented to their SIP proxy. If you wanted every call to begin with 5, 9, or 57, they could and would do it. The technician who compiled the software probably worked on staff, so he or she could easily build something unique for you. The VoIP products provided by large long-distance carriers today aren't that flexible. The most you can hope to receive from them is to have the + or +1 removed. They most likely deny anything else that doesn't match up to their interpretation of the industry standard.

Your SIP proxy addresses your VoIP carrier's server by using its IP address, not a traditional SIP URI. So, a traditional SIP URI like this won't be accepted by its SBC:

```
sip: stephen@wiley.com
```

The URI used by a VoIP provider to connect your outbound calls to traditional telephones generally constructs its URIs in a similar manner, but the last half if it consists of information that doesn't require the extra step of resolving the SIP URI to the IP address supporting it. Most SIP URIs for VoIP connections are composed of the E.164 number you want to dial, followed by an @ symbol and your long-distance carrier's IP address:

```
sip:+19495551212@24.100.100.100
```

Going with an IP provider

Your carrier knows that the Internet provider you use to send calls can impact your VoIP call quality and completion. It needs to ensure that you have a quality Internet provider and sufficient bandwidth to carry everything you're planning to send to it.

The information that it wants regarding your IP connection includes

- ✔ The name(s) of your Internet provider(s)
- ✔ The quantity of IP circuits that you have
- ✔ The bandwidth of your current IP circuits
- ✔ Whether the IP bandwidth carries other traffic

Your VoIP provider doesn't check up on the IP provider you list. It simply wants to ensure that you have sufficient bandwidth for the quantity of calls you require and that you're using a quality provider. Your VoIP carrier is just asking to be inundated by trouble reporting calls from you on lost packets and poor call quality if it allows you to use an IP provider that's 15 hops away from either the Internet backbone or the SBC assigned to you.

Try to have more than one IP provider if you can because it adds another layer of redundancy to your connection.

The final IP-bandwidth-related question asked relates to whether any other traffic uses the same IP circuit. These other applications impact how much bandwidth is available for VoIP and could factor into call quality or completion issues you report to your VoIP carrier after deployment.

Your VoIP provider may provide a contractual agreement for Quality of Service (QoS) only if you purchase its IP bandwidth to reach it. This policy makes sense because it can't really guarantee the quality of transmission over someone else's bandwidth. But using the IP service provided by your carrier is frequently inconvenient and expensive, and any solid tier 1 IP provider should be able to connect your VoIP calls with the same statistical probability of completion and latency as your carrier's bandwidth can.

Detailing the Call Volume

Your long-distance carrier generally uses the Call Detail Records (CDR) or Minutes of Usage (MOU) report for a call profile only to validate billing and routing issues. Despite the fact that your carrier possesses the data, it doesn't dissect it to determine the specifics of your call volume and call rate.

Your long-distance carrier needs this information to manage your expected call flow because it needs to know how many SBCs you require on its end. The specific information it requires includes

✔ The total number of concurrent calls you need

✔ Peak calling times

✔ The average call hold time (including ring-back)

✔ Peak calls per second

Chapter 6 covers these points in detail and tells you how to determine the values for each.

Your carrier may ask about international calling. If you plan to place any international calls, what percentage of your total call volume do you expect to be international? This question establishes some security on your service, instead of helping with configuration. Just like non-VoIP circuits, fraudulent calls are typically dialed to international destinations. Your carrier should note the percentage of traffic listed and alert you if your traffic pattern suddenly jumps above that threshold.

Telecom fraud is your problem to control. The only time the responsibility of fraud rests in the hands of your long-distance carrier is if it specifically lists a provision in your contract for service stating that it agrees to take on that responsibility. A long-distance carrier very rarely extends that kind of coverage, so you're financially responsible for every penny of usage over your lines (either with or without your consent). Your carrier is charged for even the fraudulent calls from the underlying carriers, and the local carriers who completed the calls for them. If your long-distance carrier does give you any credit, it does so as a courtesy and not as a contractual obligation.

Addressing the Non-Voice Features

A section of the VoIP questionnaire covers your need for DTMF touch tones and fax. The carrier probably offers the two standard touch-tone options of either in-band or RFC2833, with each option probably tied to the voice codec that you use. Chapter 6 covers touch tones in depth, but here are the DTMF option match-ups:

✔ In-band DTMF for uncompressed G.711

✔ RFC2833 DTMF events for compressed G.729

You can use RFC2833 with G.711 without a problem, but you can't use in-band with G.729. The compression is based on sampling and reconstructing the human voice, not complex DTMF tones.

Selecting a fax choice

Just like DTMF, you have two options for fax transmission, categorized by whether you want to compress the transmission (I go over these options in Chapter 6):

- Uncompressed faxing over G.711
- Compressed faxing with T.38

By default, VoIP calls are INVITEd with only voice codecs. To handle the unique need for T.38, the destination SIP device re-INVITEs to T.38 after the call is established as a normal voice call. The re-INVITE message contains only T.38 in the SDP offering to ensure the call is established as T.38, if possible. If the T.38 transmission fails, you or your carrier can re-INVITE it as G.711 in an attempt to complete the fax.

Your VoIP carrier doesn't necessarily support every fax choice or option associated with T.38. You may love compression that uses some special tweak to remove excess packets, but your carrier may not offer it. If you plan to use T.38 for fax transmission and rely on a unique feature that provides error correction or added compression, double-check with your carrier to make sure that it supports it.

Opening up SIP-T

SIP-T is a protocol used to interface VoIP calls with the non-VoIP Public Switched Telephone Network (PSTN). The integration of SIP-T with the PSTN doesn't need a huge and complex change in coding because the predominant signaling protocol in the PSTN, called *Signaling System 7 (SS7),* shares many similarities with SIP structure.

In theory, your VoIP carrier's network uses SIP-T to gain information from the PSTN that it doesn't normally deliver in the standard SIP protocol. SS7 signaling contains more data in the overhead than SIP does. Several bits of information available in the SS7 call stream may persuade you to use SIP-T, including several different fields where unique phone numbers can be input to act as a geographical billing reference point for the call to determine inter- or intrastate rating, and a two-digit number called an ANI InfoDigit that helps process toll-free calls.

SS7 signaling provides several positions in the overhead of the call stream to identify the origination phone number. The origination phone number position has so many options because at the long-distance-carrier level, every call is rated based on the origination and termination numbers. All the technological advancements in customer hardware, allowing the origination caller ID to be manipulated make this rating process more complex than it used to be, so now every carrier must design a hierarchy from which to select the data to rate the calls. If one origination phone number isn't available, it chooses the second, third, or fourth option. These data fields in the call stream include

- **Called Party Number (CPN):** This number appears in the Caller ID window of the phone dialed.

- **Billing Telephone Number (BTN):** Linked to a dedicated circuit, this number acts as a billing reference point. Calls from dedicated digital circuits (T1s or DS-3s) don't have a phone number attributed to them, so the long-distance carrier may apply a BTN.

- **Jurisdictional Indicator Parameter (JIP):** A cell tower or switch that identifies the physical location of where the call originated assigns this number to cell-phone calls, instead of simply using the origination cell-phone number to rate the call and determine jurisdiction. If you take a your cell phone from the Philippines to Los Angeles and dial an L.A. toll-free number, the carrier providing the toll-free service thinks the call originated in the Philippines unless its network uses JIP.

- **ANI II (also called ANI InfoDigits):** VoIP customers who use SIP-T do so most often because of ANI II. The *InfoDigits* are two digits that carriers and customers who have thousands of toll-free numbers uses to categorize the type of phone originating a call.

A business may need ANI InfoDigits to identify which calls placed to your toll-free number were originated from a payphone. Every call made from a payphone entitles the Payphone Service Provider (PSP) to a fee called a payphone surcharge. The PSPs are very diligent in their pursuit of getting paid. If you're running a calling-card company or service that needs to factor in these payphone surcharges when they happen, you need to use SIP-T to receive the ANI InfoDigits and ensure you are paying the surcharge on all applicable calls. You can find more information on payphone surcharges and toll-free numbers in my book *Telecom For Dummies* (Wiley).

ANI (pronounced either *aye-enn-eye* or *An-EE)* stands for Automatic Number Identifier, and it's just a techie way to refer to a telephone number. You may also hear TN (for telephone number). An ANI isn't anything fancy, complicated, or special; it's just the ten-digit phone number at the other end of your call.

SIP-T is frequently an all-or-nothing feature. If you're a VoIP service provider or have a large VoIP deployment that covers many offices and locations, all your hardware must be able to handle the SIP-T information. You can't generally employ this feature on a per-call basis or establish it by using a re-INVITE, like you can with T.38. This switch-level setting affects all calls from your carrier.

Confirming Your Privacy

You may find yourself in a telecom situation in which you must provide Caller ID. A federal mandate says that all telemarketers must present a valid Caller ID when they call a home or business. This identification allows a person who receives a telemarketing call to easily call the company back if he or she is interested in its product or service, or simply wants to be placed on its Do Not Call (DNC) list.

Aside from this scenario, you can block your phone number on outbound VoIP calls. Use a *privacy header* that stipulates in the INVITE message to your VoIP carrier that it shouldn't forward the information in the FROM line of the SIP header as the Caller ID. Despite the fact that most carriers offer this feature, you still have to specify in the VoIP questionnaire when you order the service whether you want to use privacy in your calls.

Privacy not only tells your carrier to avoid broadcasting the information in the FROM line of the SIP header, it also allows you to avoid placing any viable information in the FROM line to begin with. This absence of information creates a challenge for both your long-distance carrier and the local carrier that owns the phone number to which you're dialing. VoIP calls are virtual and can originate from anywhere in the world. Without a valid phone number somewhere in the SIP header, neither carrier can legitimately identify the jurisdiction of the call. If the call terminates in the same state from which it originates, the local carrier, and subsequently the long-distance carrier would rate the call at the intrastate rate, rather than the less-expensive interstate rate.

Because local phone carriers need a billing reference point translated from information in the SIP header, you can't use privacy alone. You must accompany it with one of these two fields:

- **Remote Party ID (RPID):** The old feature
- **P-Asserted-ID (PAID):** The new feature

Either method works, but you may need to specify with your carrier which option you want to use if you require privacy.

A privacy-enabled call header in an INVITE message looks like this:

```
FROM: "Anonymous" <sip:anonymous@anonymous.missing>;
        tag=1805744722
Remote-Party-ID: <sip:4145551212@wiley.com>; party=
        calling;
id-type=subscriber; privacy=full; screen=yes
```

You can see that the FROM line of the header in the preceding code doesn't present any valid information about the geographic origin of the call. So, your VoIP carrier uses the phone number in the `Remote-Party-ID` line of code as the billing reference point, but that number doesn't appear in the Caller ID window of the person receiving the call. The final line of the header establishes the fact that the VoIP carrier shouldn't use the information in the FROM line of the header to display as the Caller ID:

```
privacy=full
```

Your VoIP Carrier only sends the information in the FROM field of the header as the Caller ID if you set the privacy as

```
privacy=off
```

The P-Asserted-ID works with privacy, alerting your carrier to withhold the information in the FROM field of the SIP header by listing the type of information being withheld. A SIP header that has the Caller ID withheld looks like this:

```
FROM: "Anonymous" <sip:anonymous@anonymous.missing>;
        tag=1805744722
P-Asserted-Identity: <sip:4145551212@wiley.com>
Privacy:id
```

To convert this header so that the information in the FROM field of the SIP header appears as the origination caller ID, you simply need to remove the `Privacy` line. A SIP header that contains the information in the following code displays the phone number 414-555-1212 (which appears in the FROM header) in the Caller ID window of the phone dialed:

```
FROM: "Stephen" <sip:4145551212@wiley.com>; tag=1805744722
P-Asserted-Identity: <sip:4145551212@wiley.com>
```

Be sure to check with your VoIP provider to see whether it supports both options and whether it has a preference. You can activate VoIP's privacy options on a per-call basis, rather than as a default for all outbound calls. Identifying which calls you want to send with privacy requires some advanced programming, but if you need this feature, it's available.

Remote Party ID and P-Asserted-ID headers identify the geographic point of origin of a phone call. They function as a billing reference point if the privacy indicator tells your VoIP carrier's SBC to ignore the phone number listed in the FROM field. Every carrier is different, so yours may or may not use the Remote Party ID field or P-Asserted-ID field. If it accepts these fields, ask your carrier about the logic used to determine which field is used first as the billing reference point, and when it is ignored for the second or third available field.

Most carriers use a cascading logic in their billing. If they have to discard the first choice for a billing reference point for some reason, they look at the second option and then the third option, if necessary. If your FROM field contains a valid phone number and a P-Asserted-ID, your carrier can choose the phone number in the FROM field as the main billing reference point in all circumstances or as a second choice only if the P-Asserted-ID field is blank.

Before you send your first call over your VoIP carrier, ask your carrier the specifics about its VoIP billing logic:

- What billing fields does it recognize (PAID, RPID, or FROM)?
- Which field does it select first?
- Which field does it select second?
- How does the billing logic react to a bogus phone number or a toll-free number as the first billing reference? Does the VoIP carrier's billing system use the data and instantly declare the call to be of indeterminate jurisdiction and rate it as intrastate? Or does the carrier's billing system reference another field to identify a valid phone number it can use to determine the jurisdiction?
- Does it use a default reference point if all the phone number information in the FROM field, Remote Party ID and P-Asserted ID is invalid?
- If it has a default reference point, does it charge all indeterminate calls over a certain percentage of your usage for the month as intrastate calls?

Chapter 8

Activating VoIP

- -

- -

The process for VoIP activation has evolved quite a bit in only a few years. The early days of VoIP saw customers and carriers engaging in extensive testing between their hardware and software. Industry engineers and customers felt great anxiety if the hardware and software on both ends could actually work with each other, consistently and in all circumstances. The concern was warranted at the time as many deployments used custom VoIP software created as one programmer's interpretation of the guidelines. The nuances in the SIP methods sent and expected SIP responses returned may not function with every other SIP device that may have employed an alternative take on the guidelines.

To prove that end-user and carrier hardware would work together, VoIP carriers developed InterOperability (InterOp) testing. You generally did this kind of testing outside the normal scope of provisioning, and it could last weeks or months. You always had to worry that the different hardware might not work together. You could have a mission-critical feature on one side that the hardware on the other side simply couldn't support. Even if all the hardware supported the basics necessary to establish and tear down a call, you still had to figure out how the SIP banter between the VoIP endpoints would proceed in order to facilitate the unique applications in your Dial Plan.

Those days are mostly behind VoIP users now. You're just as likely to run across a piece of non-VoIP hardware that doesn't work with a standard long-distance carrier as you are to have an Asterisk, server-based VoIP configuration fail to function with your VoIP carrier's SIP proxy.

Scheduling Your Install

VoIP activation shouldn't take more than a day if you're properly prepared.

The good news is that VoIP has a much easier installation process than traditional dedicated circuits. The non-VoIP world generally requires a rigid scheduled installation, where the carrier technician and your technician slowly and methodically activate the individual circuits. They must activate the circuits at the circuits during a scheduled conference call with all technicians on line because if your carrier sends a live signal to you before you have your hardware installed, the absence of deployed equipment on your end activates alarms in the long-distance carrier's network. To avoid any alarms, your carrier makes you confirm that your hardware is active and connected before it opens up service from its end.

VoIP doesn't share these limitations. Your VoIP carrier can easily give you its IP address and open its SBCs to accept calls from your IP, before you even program anything into your SIP server. I highly recommend having a carrier technician available during your installation, but if you can't find one who's available, you can probably conduct all the required testing yourself. With the help of tcpdump or Wireshark captures (covered in Chapter 11), you can easily forward any curious or unexpected messaging that you receive to your carrier.

Drawing Up a Test Plan

A VoIP deployment has too many pieces of hardware, programming, and variables to leave anything to chance. During the rush to test everything, you may forget a piece of hardware, phone, or feature. You may not have to worry about the oversight if you have your own in-house VoIP technician conducting the activation. But most small to medium-sized businesses don't have a technician. Even large businesses that aren't telecom-related usually contract to an outside vendor to test their VoIP.

Your outside vendor probably doesn't draw up his or her own test plan for your office. He or she may know the locations of your VoIP phones but not how your business operates or the applications built in to your LAN that you use on a daily basis. So, you ultimately have to list all of the tests that need to be conducted for them.

Figure 8-1 shows the three general areas that you test during VoIP activation:

- ✔ The LAN
- ✔ Interaction with the VoIP carrier
- ✔ Legacy analog devices (if any)

The areas in the preceding list aren't the only ones that can potentially cause problems on a phone call. You always have the possibility of static or mis-routed calls somewhere between your VoIP carrier and the PSTN, or within the PSTN itself. Your VoIP carrier works out those sorts of issues. Your VoIP deployment focuses on testing and resolving issues over which you have visibility and control.

Construct your test plan to include a series of tests that check the overall InterOperability of your SIP server with your VoIP provider's server. You execute these tests to ensure that the SIP methods presented from one end receive an acceptable SIP response from the other end. You can conduct all these tests from any VoIP phone on your LAN because the information you're validating as working properly concerns only the flow between your SIP server and your carrier.

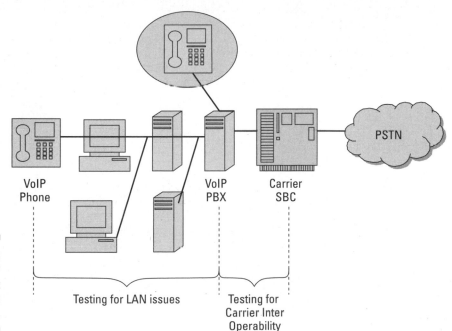

Figure 8-1:
VoIP
deployment
testing
areas.

Proving out call setup and tear-down

Begin testing with the most general interaction and then move to the specifics. If the most basic phone call to a local phone number doesn't complete, you don't really need to check the latency on a five-minute call. Testing needs to prove out the basic call setup and tear-down before you work on testing different call types and features.

If you can call out from a SIP phone on your LAN to a regular analog phone out in the world, you know that your SIP proxy is relaying the SIP header information in a manner that your carrier can effectively use. When you can complete calls, you can be relatively confident that all the information in the FROM and TO fields of the SIP header are populated correctly. A standard battery of tests includes

- **An inbound call to a VoIP phone from the PSTN, connect with PSTN hang-up:** This test ensures that the SIP header information coming in form your carrier is interacting correctly with your SIP server to establish the call. After the call is connected, have the PSTN end the call by hanging up to ensure that your carrier is sending a valid BYE signal and that your hardware is accurately responding to it.

- **An outbound call to PSTN, connect with VoIP hang-up:** This test confirms that the SIP header information you're generating is acceptable to your carrier, and it can route your call. After the call is connected, disconnect it from your VoIP phone to ensure that the BYE signal is being effectively sent from your VoIP phone through to your carrier.

- **An outbound call to a PSTN number, hang-up before connection:** VoIP usually ends an *active call,* one in which the bi-directional audio has been established, by sending the SIP method of BYE. To hang up a call before the audio is established, VoIP uses the SIP method CANCEL. Using CANCEL has a specific procedure, and the SIP node receiving the CANCEL method must send the appropriate response code of 487 Request Termination.

- **An international outbound call:** The outbound dialing configuration of your VoIP proxy sometimes loses the finer points of E.164 numbering on international calls sent with SIP. An international call can fail because your SIP Proxy doesn't follow the E.164 numbering format.

The tests conducted to validate the SIP banter between your SIP proxy and the hardware at your VoIP carrier for normal call completion also check for packet loss. Losing an INVITE or BYE packet can kill your call or prevent it from being established. Execute a packet capture by using tcpdump or Wireshark (see Chapter 11 for specifics) on every test call that you execute. The captures don't take up much memory and execute rather quickly. You can find them an invaluable resource if you encounter a call completion problem because the technician proving out your network on the VoIP deployment can send them to your carrier to confirm or validate how your VoIP carrier handles your VoIP calls. Save the packet capture files and refer back to them when you're researching call quality or completion issues that you may experience during testing.

Ensure that your VoIP Lifecycle Management (VLM) software is running when you conduct the tests. Every call throughout the day of testing provides more information about the interaction of the new VoIP traffic with your LAN.

Confirming treatments for failed or busy calls

The transmission of SIP methods and responses between your SIP proxy and your VoIP carrier for completed calls or calls that you know were dialed to a good termination number only prove out the general nuts and bolts of the SIP banter between your network and your carrier. You probably know that most of the calls you dial are good numbers, so you don't end up receiving notification that the number you dial is no longer in service.

You probably don't intend on calling a disconnected phone number, or one where your call is intercepted by an operator recording of "all circuits are busy," but they do happen. These operator-intercept calls are one of the challenges with VoIP. Your SIP server must send or receive a response that the other side of the call has to be able to interpret in an intelligent manner. The test calls to check that the operator-intercept messages and other responses on unsuccessful calls include:

✔ **An outbound call to a known bad number:** Your carrier can respond to your attempt to call a phone number that has been disconnected or is no longer in service in a few ways. Here are the standard operator-intercept options:

- A standard 4XX SIP response. This is the standard SIP response to a failed call attempt. If your carrier is set up to only provide the SIP messaging, your hardware will have to accept the specific 400 series SIP response and interpret it to let you know the call failed because the audio of the recording that "the number has been disconnected" is not played to you by your VoIP carrier.

- An audio recording sent via one-way RTP. Your carrier may not send you the SIP reject response at all, but instead send you an RTP stream of audio playing the appropriate message. This audio is received before a 200 OK message because it is a failed call, so your SIP server must acknowledge the audio and send a CANCEL to end the call.

> • Both a 4XX SIP response and the audio recording. This is the pre-ferred method as it provides both options and makes it easier for your SIP proxy to identify the reject SIP response and issue the CANCEL.
>
> ✔ **An inbound call to a SIP phone that's busy and has no voicemail:** This test confirms the response provided to the incoming call is properly translated by your VoIP provider as a standard busy signal.

Whichever option your carrier uses to send you the operator-intercept information, ensure that your SIP server knows what to do with it after it's delivered. A little confusion by your SIP server over how to interpret the response won't generally cause a catastrophic problem. It's more likely that your SIP server will just ignore an unexpected response or audio in a one-way RTP stream. In this situation, your SIP server may hold the call in an active state until either your SIP proxy or your Dial Plan realizes that the call hasn't received any packets for a duration of time and cancels it.

Checking your fax transmission

VoIP may be all about the voice, but you still need it to send your faxes. The success of your fax transmissions is influenced by several factors that I talk about in Chapter 6.

Place one test call for each compressed and uncompressed transmissions for fax if you have T.38 capability because you may end up using both kinds of transmissions. The test calls include

✔ An inbound fax over G.711

✔ An outbound fax over G.711

✔ An inbound fax over T.38 (if applicable)

✔ An outbound fax over T.38 (if applicable)

If either your fax or VoIP hardware can't use T.38, you may have limited faxing capabilities because G.711 has problems connecting faxes to remote fax machines that function at speeds over 14.4 Mbps. If you don't have T.38, you may want to keep an analog phone line for faxing until you can upgrade to T.38.

Execute a packet capture on your fax transmissions by using tcpdump or Wireshark to truly see what's happening with the negotiation of the call. Even if your transmissions complete fine, you can use this information to see the elements of the transmission so that you can understand what's required to make the transmissions happen. Figure 8-2 shows the standard run-through for a normal T.38 transmission. The transmission contains three elements:

✔ The T.38-enabled fax machine

✔ The SIP proxy on your LAN

✔ The SBC of your VoIP provider

Figure 8-2 shows a standard VoIP tree, identifying the SIP methods and responses generated by the individual devices, as well as the recipients of the messages.

T.38 fax transmissions are generally established as a standard voice call and then re-INVITEd to T.38. The example in Figure 8-2 sets up the call as a standard G.711 voice call until your T.38-enabled fax re-INVITEs the call to T.38. This re-INVITE cascades the request to your VoIP carrier's SBC that acknowledges it, establishing the bi-directional stream necessary to transmit the T.38 fax.

When the fax transmission is complete, the T.38 fax machine sends a BYE to disconnect the call, and your SIP proxy reINVITEs the RTP stream back to it as G.711 before ending the call itself by sending a BYE to your carrier.

This banter can fail in many places. Any SIP device or node interacting within the call could respond to a T.38 INVITE with a 415 Unsupported Media Type response. This response indicates that the device you re-INVITEd to T.38 doesn't support T.38 — your best hope in this situation is to try again by re-INVITE-ing at G.711. Your VoIP proxy may have to follow some rather involved steps to set up and tear down a T.38 fax transmission. If you have any problems sending or receiving T.38 fax transmissions, capture your test call by using tcpdump or Wireshark so that you can review the banter between the SIP nodes and your carrier.

Touching tones with VoIP

Chapter 7 covers your options for sending and receiving DTMF (touch tones), but you still have to confirm that you're processing the inbound and outbound DTMF digits. You need to test all the DTMF types that your LAN uses. Place outbound calls from a VoIP phone on your LAN to a remote phone in the PSTN, as well as vice versa. You need to conduct these test calls:

✔ An inbound call with DTMF in-band, using G.711

✔ An outbound call with DTMF in-band, using G.711

✔ An inbound call, using RFC2833

✔ An outbound call, using RFC2833

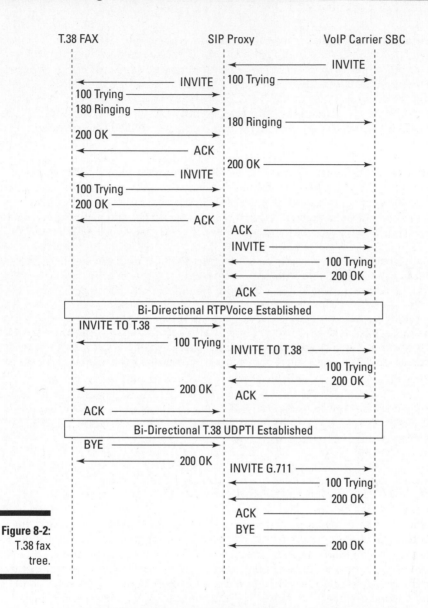

Figure 8-2:
T.38 fax
tree.

The test calls don't have to be specific phone systems that prompt you to
"Press 1 for accounting; press 2 for sales . . . " You can make the calls to your
home phone or an analog phone in another office. As long as someone can
answer the line and you can press three or four digits on the keypad of your
phone, you have a valid test call.

You can use in-band DTMF only with the uncompressed G.711 codec. The method of sampling the human voice that G.729 uses can't reproduce uncorrupted DTMF digits, so in-band DTMF can't recreate a viable DTMF tone once the far end attempts to reproduce if in the media stream of the call from the compressed data. You can use RFC2833 with either G.711 or G.729 because RFC2833 sends the DTMF tones as RTP event packages that aren't included in the media stream so they aren't affected when the media is compressed.

You can't see anything special on the packet captures of the in-band DTMF examples. The process of sampling the tones and sending them in the RTP along with your voice completely hides them from a standard capture. But you can easily see the tones sent with RFC2833 in a packet capture. (Chapter 11 shows you how to filter for RFC2833 DTMF tones sent as RTP event packages.)

Testing every VoIP phone

After you complete all the tests that I outline in the preceding sections, you can feel confident that the interaction between your SIP server and your carrier is solid. Your INVITE, BYE, CANCEL, and SIP responses all fall into the normal banter between two SIP nodes. The interaction between your SIP server and your carrier is vital to productively using VoIP, but so is the interaction between your VoIP phones and your VoIP proxy on your LAN.

After you test the server-carrier communication, you need to perform the LAN portion of your VoIP activation. The test is simple but time consuming. You need to make only one test call per VoIP phone, but you have to leave the call open for at least five minutes. Your technician needs to work his or her way through your office, testing every shiny new VoIP phone. Most technicians marginalize this simple test.

Most technicians glaze over this test because they've probably spent some time in the world of non-VoIP telephony, which doesn't require these five-minute test calls. The analog phone lines don't interact with anything besides your phone system and the local phone carrier before they hit the PSTN. Most test calls made on traditional analog or digital telephony installations last about four seconds. As long as the traditional-telephony call has a dial tone, the call connects, and both ends of the call can hear the other end without static or bad volume, the call is good, and the service is accepted.

VoIP calls must interact with your LAN, so they have to function properly in the VLANs you create for them, using the rate shaping and prioritization you design. A four-second call made on a VoIP phone confirms only that your SIP server can send a good INVITE message to your VoIP carrier. It doesn't tell whether the VoIP phone is configured for half duplex transmission rather than full duplex, or whether the call is besieged by jitter for one reason or another.

You really need to have your VLM software running when placing these test calls from your VoIP phones within your LAN. The five-minute calls provide enough time for the VLM software to attribute a solid MOS score and for any small or large issues of latency, jitter, or packet loss to rear their ugly heads.

The traffic flow or management of your LAN may not be causing a call's poor quality. You might have an issue with the configuration of the VoIP phone you're using. VoIP phones have two main settings:

- **Speed:** Generally 100 BaseT
- **Duplex:** Half or Full

Having only two parameters to set seems easy enough, right? To make matters better (and worse), most VoIP phones auto-negotiate these settings to what they believe the SIP registrar requires. The downside to this auto negotiation is

- What your VoIP phone thinks is the correct configuration for your SIP server may be incorrect.
- You can't validate what setting a VoIP hard phone has negotiated.

Avoid the insanity of working through VoIP phones that attempt to auto-negotiate these settings and manually set the speed and duplex on your VoIP hardphones so that you know, beyond the shadow of a doubt, how they're configured. If a VoIP phone has a minor setting variance, you may still be able to establish a call, but that call experiences persistent quality issues. Even if you check your high-speed VLM software's reports for MOS, jitter, and packet loss, it doesn't indicate any reason for the lost packets. In that case, reset the VoIP hardphone and manually specify the settings again.

If you still experience call quality issues from the VoIP phone, identify if the problem is confined to one specific phone, or if it seems to be affecting every VoIP phone. If it affects every VoIP phone, the problem is with your LAN, and not the phone. Use your VLM software to analyze what's happening in your LAN and isolate the problem. If the issue is confined to a single phone and manually configuring it doesn't solve the problem, have your technician check the cabling to your VoIP phone for electrical shorts. If the line is fine, return the phone for one that works.

Testing residual analog phones

You may decide not to replace every analog phone or device on your network. Many open source software packages, such as Asterisk, offer analog cards that you can use to integrate your VoIP-based phone system with your legacy analog phones. Even if your VoIP phone system is simply bridging the one analog phone line in your office to the fax machine, you still need to test the legacy hardware.

You probably connect the fax or legacy analog phone to the VoIP server with the same cabling that used to connect it to the previous phone system. Therefore, almost everything you're using has been working for years, so you can assume that it works fine. You don't have to worry about the configuration of the phone because it doesn't send VoIP protocol and doesn't have to choose half or full duplex.

You do need to test the configuration of the extension in the VoIP phone system's Dial Plan. Test to ensure that it rings when its direct phone number or extension is dialed. If the port in the phone system hasn't been properly mapped, you may be able to dial only to pick up your voicemail, with no inbound or outbound capabilities. Keep your VLM software running when you make test calls from your analog phones too, because they are converted to VoIP before they are sent to your VoIP carrier, and you need to check all calls sent with VoIP for latency, jitter, and packet loss, even if they start as analog.

Validating your Dial Plan features

The first series of tests prove out the interaction between your SIP server and VoIP carrier. The second set tests for latency, jitter, and packet loss on VoIP phones (or analog phones) over your LAN. You need these key elements to work properly for end-to-end connectivity, but you also need to test one final piece of the puzzle while your VoIP tech is on site — your phone-system features.

Unless you have in-house staff that built and designed your phone system (in which case, they probably tested these features during development), have your VoIP technician validate all the internal structures and features of your phone system during the day of your VoIP deployment. List every essential Dial Plan feature that you have, which you depend on every day, and test those features. At a minimum, you need to test these features:

✔ Checking voicemail

- Leaving a message
- Retrieving a message
- Deleting a message
- Forwarding a message
- Recording primary and alternate greetings

✔ Using the dial-by-name directory

✔ Employing Least Cost Routing (LCR)

✔ Blocking access to specific extensions or general International blocking

✔ Channeling calls by using a call queue

✔ Using conference calling

✔ Navigating all options on an Interactive Voice Response (IVR)

✔ Dialing 0 for the operator

✔ CANCELing calls that fail to disconnect properly

After your technician proves out your Dial Plan, he or she packs up and hits the road. You have to make another appointment and pay a two-hour minimum fee to have him or her come back. But just because the testing is done doesn't mean the deployment is complete.

Requesting a Report on the Deployment

Before you contract with a VoIP technician to conduct the activation, ensure that he or she can provide a report on the performance of your VoIP network after he or she completes the activation. The information you receive about your network in this report is the benchmark for all future reports run on your VoIP service by either you or your VoIP technician and should cover

✔ The average MOS score per VoIP phone or extension

✔ The average latency experienced by your calls due to interaction with your LAN

✔ The average range of jitter experienced by your calls due to interaction with your LAN

✔ The average packet loss experienced by your calls due to interaction with your LAN

When you add employees, phones, computers, and services to your business, the traffic that flows through your LAN and WAN changes. After successfully deploying VoIP, the next phase of VoIP Lifecycle Management covers the ongoing maintenance and monitoring of your VoIP network. Compare all reports that you run on your network to the previous test results so that you can identify any trends in overall call quality and network health.

You can see a sample of an activation report generated by Packet Island in Chapter 9. Packet Island isn't the only company providing VoIP Lifecycle Management software services, but it's the best.

Confirming Billing Structure

After you complete testing and activation of VoIP service (which I discuss in the preceding sections), you should have the confidence to use your new VoIP network — but you still have to confirm billing. Your VoIP carrier may charge you per port used, per consecutive call, or simply with traditional per-minute rates for connected calls. When you receive your first invoice, compare it against your contract for service and make sure all of the contracted rates and charges are billed accurately, to include:

✔ Monthly recurring charges

✔ Installation fees

✔ Expedite fees (if you expedited your order)

✔ Per-minute fees

Discuss with your carrier which pieces of information in the SIP overhead it uses to determine the jurisdiction (inter- or intrastate) before you even sign the contract for service. Your carrier can derive your point of origin from these three basic positions in the SIP overhead:

✔ The origination phone number listed in the FROM field

✔ The supplemental phone number listed in the Remote Party ID

✔ The supplemental phone number listed in the P-Asserted ID

The IETF acknowledges the Remote Party ID and P-Asserted ID as standard features that can appear in a SIP header. Despite this fact, SIP transmissions generally don't have them unless you specifically design your SIP server to implement these features. For most applications, you send the standard phone number assigned to the office or extension from which you're calling. If you're an enhanced VoIP provider, telemarketer, or calling-card company, discuss the ramifications and responsibilities of these fields with your VoIP provider. You need to know which field your VoIP carrier uses to populate the Caller ID window of the called phone and which field your VoIP carrier uses to establish the state from which the call originated. Populating the fields without understanding how your carrier uses them could have a tremendous impact on your bottom line.

Not every carrier acknowledges the Remote Party ID and P-Asserted ID for billing. Even if they do, they may use the information in an order different than a previous VoIP carrier you have used. Some carriers (such as QWEST long distance) actually give primary billing jurisdiction to a proprietary P-Charge-info number that your SIP hardware must be input into your SIP header, similar to the Remote Party ID or P-Asserted ID.

The supplemental SIP fields of Remote Party ID, P-Asserted ID, and P-Charge-info help determine the jurisdiction of the phone call. So, you must populate the specific field used by your VoIP carrier with a valid phone number that can be tied to a specific geographic location. Carriers generally invoice calls that have either toll-free numbers or bogus information, such as a phone number 1234567890, in any field used as a potential billing reference at the more expensive intrastate rate. For example, say that your office is in Nebraska and you're calling Colorado, but you populate all the origination fields with 111111111. Your carrier will probably rate your calls at the intrastate Colorado rate, just as if you called from Denver. Every carrier has unique rules and regulations about call rating and jurisdiction, so find out what its rules are before you manipulate this information.

Chapter 9

Using Packet Island Software

*Y*ou can find VoIP a very frustrating technology if you don't have access to accurate diagnostic information. The old tools at your disposal for managing a data LAN with Simple Network Management Protocol (SNMP) and the various packet capture software aren't precise enough for a VoIP network. The packet capture software only allows you to gain visibility into your LAN for the brief moments that the capture collects packets, and doesn't show ongoing management specifications. Aggregated data that lists packet collisions or network events available through SNMP don't provide enough information to isolate the source. You need something that can collect enough empirical data to efficiently direct you to the root source of a problem.

Packet Island software is the most effective tool I know for this job. This chapter covers basic information about Packet Island, as well as the functioning of the Packet Island GUI.

Even if you're not using Packet Island, this chapter identifies the key elements you should look for in any VoIP Lifecycle Management (VLM) software.

Getting the Basics on Packet Island

Packet Island (www.packetisland.com) is based out of Cupertino, California, and was founded in 2004 by a couple of engineers who have deep experience in VoIP and network management technologies. They'd been in the industry for many years and were watching the VoIP market grow and evolve from the vantage point of their VoIP chip company, so they had a front-row seat for the beginning of the VoIP industry boom. When they saw that hardware prices were dropping, VoIP software was becoming increasingly open source, and broadband Internet was rolling out across America, they knew the stage was set for great things to happen.

The first stage of the VoIP boom did occur. Networks evolved to leverage the newfound hardware, technology, and access to broadband Internet. The landscape of the LAN shifted from single, large monolithic entities to an array of smaller, more dynamic and intelligent nodes, connected through public Internet connections.

Every element seemed to be in place for VoIP to take off like wildfire. Many new start-up VoIP carriers leveraged the fact that almost every home in America has access to a broadband Internet connection to begin selling VoIP to residences and small businesses from coast to coast. Nobody else could effectively compete against the traditional local phone carriers because it cost too much money to reproduce all the wiring and cabling to serve every home. Now, the Internet providers were supplying the cabling for the VoIP carriers, and the projections on growth for the market seemed open-ended.

Then, a curious thing happened. The VoIP carriers started losing customers almost as fast as they were signing up new ones. The Achilles heel of those first VoIP carrier deployments appeared: It was easy to deploy VoIP, but difficult to service it. Granted, you can run the nationwide operations for your VoIP company out of a small office in Cudahy, Wisconsin, but if your customer in rural Kentucky is having problems with the hardware you sent out, how do you help him or her? The cost for hiring an outside tech and dispatching him or her to the person's house would take all the projected profit from the account for the next year or more. And that hypothetical situation assumes that the person actually calls in to report that he or she is having problems. Generally, the person just got fed up and left without telling the carrier why.

The VoIP technology was sound, but the networks on which VoIP was being deployed were completely different. Each end user's broadband Internet connection was essentially a node on the VoIP carrier's Wide Area Network (WAN). The VoIP hardware on site enabled these remote nodes to be relatively intelligent and dynamic, but the carrier had no easy way to manage them. The traditional method of using SNMP to manage the system wasn't an option because the public Internet connections tied all the sites together.

VoIP transmissions crossed too many wide open spaces in the public Internet to manage them with normal SNMP polling, and many sites didn't even have SNMP available and activated.

The Internet has connected the whole world, and for standard data transmissions, it works great. People accept relatively slow response times for data transmission. You don't worry about a one- to four-second response time when you're surfing the Internet, and e-mail (the other large consumer of IP bandwidth) essentially occurs behind the scenes. You don't experience it while it happens, only after it's done its job.

Packet Island realized that the new LAN topology would first impact voice and video applications. It developed a set of processes, methodologies, and tools for VoIP customers and service providers. The technology built on existing management systems and works with existing SNMP technology, ensuring that it's compatible and enhances the data collected. SNMP offered aggregated statistics for the LAN, but the Packet Island software provided the specifics, allowing companies to isolate the true source of a LAN issue.

The end result is software that allows companies to perform network assessment, network verification, and ongoing monitoring and diagnostics. Its software focuses on the ebb and flow of data within your LAN, which is the environment where the individual company both faces the most challenges and has complete power to affect the situation.

The Packet Island software does what any VLM software should — it provides statistical data:

- Verifies network design.
- Detects transient LAN issues by analyzing individual data flows to identify
  - Bandwidth use
  - Hardware performance
  - Network efficiency
- Ensures IP availability, which allows you to validate the contracted Service Level Agreement (SLA) you have established with your VoIP provider for responses to trouble reports.

The impact of problems that affect a VoIP LAN are much more visible than when they affected data-only LANs. The management of the VoIP LANs becomes more complicated when you become responsible for more and more remote LANs. You might be able to make due with SNMP or Wireshark captures on a single LAN, but the amount of work required to manage 10, 50, or 100 sites across the country makes either of those choices unfeasible. With VoIP, most issues are transient, so you'd have to execute hours of packet captures to sift through hundreds or thousands of calls per day at each site to finally locate an affected call.

Deploying the Software

The VLM software must exist on a device strategically placed within your network where it can observe any and all packets that run through your LAN. The best installation site for this device is between your firewall and your switch (or router, if you don't have a switch). That vantage point allows the device to watch every packet coming into and out of your network.

Now that you know the best place to install the device, the next question is, "What are my options on how the VLM software is delivered?" You can choose from two main methods of deployment:

- Software downloaded on a PC at your site
- Installation of a purpose-built micro-device

Downloading software onto a PC and installing it in the LAN between the firewall and the switch seems like an easy solution to start with, but it does have some inherent challenges. The PC onto which the software is loaded must be completely clean, meaning that you must disable or remove all background programs, including any spam that infected the PC and any anti-spam software.

A PC-based VLM software solution offers a challenge because of the physical portability of it. You may need to move the point from which you collect the data. The tests at the standard location between the firewall and switch may need some more granular testing, which requires you to move the collection point further into the LAN on the other side of the switch. Physically lugging a PC around your LAN isn't very easy, especially if the initial test results warrant another series of tests for which you need to incrementally reposition the VLM software through the LAN, all the way to the back end of a specific VoIP phone that's having a problem.

Packet Island realize the challenges facing a PC-based collection point, and it deploys its product on a small purpose-built micro-device, roughly the size of a deck of cards. It contains an IN port and OUT port for Ethernet and a power adapter. If you can plug in a telephone, you can use the micro-device. After you install the micro-device, it goes to work, making copies of every packet sent in the network and relaying all the information to a secure Web site without adding any additional latency to your LAN.

Introducing the Packet Island GUI

The micro-device is only one portion of the entire Packet Island solution. It performs real-time measurements and uploads the data to a set of servers. You access the database through a Web GUI that allows you to see and analyze the data. The GUI has been designed with varying layers of visibility and access, allowing you to authorize subsidiary companies to view reports for their office, while preventing them from viewing data related to other locations.

VoIP carriers that use the software to manage their end users find these access controls a great benefit because the carrier can give direct access to larger customers so that those customers can pull reports for their offices. Your company may not be structured to support the frequency of testing that some end offices want, but the online GUI allows them to create the reports themselves. The tiered access to the system also allows them to access only their office without fear of cross-visibility with your other customers who may be their competitors.

The GUI, like all secure GUIs, requires you to log in with your user name and password before it allows you access to the main portal shown in Figure 9-1. This is the main screen of the Packet Island web GUI from which you can navigate and manage all offices enrolled in the service.

The companies and LANs that you've set up for testing are located in a column on the upper-left side of the GUI main page. Each VoIP LAN that has a micro-device deployed is represented by a small icon that you can click to display the devices at that site. Before pulling any data on a LAN or executing a battery of testing, select a specific device from which to gather the data. After you highlight the device and a green check mark appears next to it, you're ready to investigate that LAN.

The data in the GUI is grouped by date, so the first option that you select is the date listed in the top toolbar. It defaults to the current date, but it allows you to scroll up or down to find a specific date on which you require data. If an employee approaches you on Monday about a problem that he had with his VoIP phone the previous Friday, simply scroll to the date or press the calendar button to choose the date. After you select a date, the GUI opens to the VoIP Calls tab. Press the Show Calls button to list all the calls placed on that date.

A list of every call made on that date then appears in the section below the Show Calls button. The GUI also allows you to search for calls based on the origination phone number, terminating phone number, or IP address.

Double-clicking any call populates the bottom portion of the GUI with the specific data, as shown in Figure 9-2.

The GUI presents a standard SIP call tree for the call highlighted in the upper section of the GUI. This call tree can really help you with initial troubleshooting because you can see the SIP methods and responses used for the call. The specific call in Figure 9-2 appears to have been rejected on the first attempt with a 401 Unauthorized response before it sent a second INVITE message and received a positive 100 Trying and 183 Session in Progress.

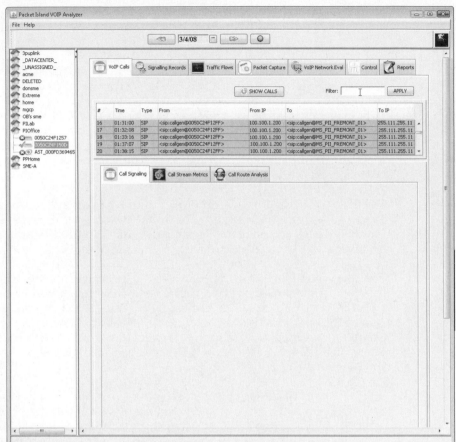

Figure 9-1:
The Packet
Island GUI
main page.

Knowing the specific SIP responses that you receive from your carrier makes troubleshooting much less frustrating. The more information you can provide to your carrier during the troubleshooting process, and the more detailed that information is, the less frustration you have to suffer and the shorter the duration of time required to resolve the issue. I talk about troubleshooting in Part III of this book.

The SIP dump section in the bottom portion of the GUI screen provides the specific SIP information for whichever message you select. Figure 9-2 has the initial INVITE message selected in the second section, allowing you to see the specific header information presented in the SIP packet, including the full SIP URI that originated the call and to which the call was terminating.

The basic information presented on the Call Signaling tab gives you a good initial point of departure in any investigation of VoIP quality or completion. You can easily scroll through several calls and identify the specific one that requires investigation.

The employee may have made two or three calls to the same terminating number that day, possibly having to redial because of poor line quality, such as static and clipping, or completion issues caused by lost SIP packets. This type of specific information makes the troubleshooting process that much more efficient. If you see two calls with short durations and one call that lasts five or ten minutes, you can focus your attention on the shorter duration calls that had the reported problems.

If the Call Signaling tab confirms that the general call setup and SIP signaling didn't have any issues, you know that the issue isn't with the SIP banter between your LAN and your VoIP carrier. The next step in troubleshooting the issue is to select the Call Stream Metrics tab to get detailed information on the call.

This tab actually has six different graphs available to you for analyzing the specific call. They all show data for the specific call highlighted and shed more light on the network conditions that occurred during the time of the call.

Figure 9-2:
Double-click a call to see that call's signaling.

Reading packets per second

The first chart option in the Call Stream Metrics identifies the packets per second transmitted on the call. Fifty packets per second is expected with the transmission of 20-millisecond (ms) packets. The quantity of packets sent during a call can vary because some VoIP carriers that use silence suppression don't send calls when no audio is being transmitted. Many carriers don't use silence suppression because that feature can lead to audio clipping issues. For most VoIP deployments, you see a steady 50-packets-per-second rate for each of the two media streams.

You can expand any area of the graph by simply selecting a portion of it with your cursor. The GUI allows you to draw a box around a section of the chart, just like making a box with the drawing toolbar in MS Word. After you select the area, click the Refresh Charts button to populate the new information. Being able to expand a portion of the graph allows you to isolate a specific 60- or 70-second portion of a 15-minute call, with every second accounted for and visible. Figure 9-3 shows an enhancement view of a selected section of a call.

All the graphs on the Packet Island GUI identify both the inbound and outbound streams separately. Broadband Internet connections, such as DSL, guarantee different quantities of bandwidth for uploading and downloading. Because most Web surfing entails very little uploading and mostly a lot of downloading, your transmission bandwidth may be minimal, so you need visibility into the different call streams.

Figure 9-3:
Packets per
second call
analysis
detail.

The call example in Figure 9-3 shows a substantial drop in packets per second at 10:08 and 50 seconds. This rate variance, identified by a dip in packets per second that doesn't immediately recover indicates that the call suffered packet loss at this time. Because this is just the initial report, even if the call did experience packet loss, you still need to identify why the packets were lost so that you can make the necessary corrections in the LAN or WAN.

You absolutely need VLM software that can provide information about the health and activity of your LAN at a second-by-second level. The majority of LAN issues that affect your VoIP call quality last only a matter of milliseconds, and any sampling rate slower than once per second can easily miss the transient issues that affect your calls. You might as well not even have VLM software if it can't find a problem.

Seeing the jitter

A degree of *jitter* (meaning delay variation) is normal. Less than 40 ms of jitter exists on most LANs without degrading call quality or completion. Many networks employ jitter buffers to eliminate this delay variation. These devices build a delay into the endpoints and wait for the packets to arrive, playing them out in a real-time sequence. But you may end up with a problem comes if the packets arrive too late or after the buffer is full. In either case, you end up with discarded packets, and your call quality suffers.

The next three charts available from the GUI all concern jitter:

- **Jitter — Mean (ms):** This graph identifies the average jitter (delay variation) experienced on the call. You can use it as a baseline if you're just checking the overall health of your LAN. Jitter is determined by the time between packet arrivals.

- **Jitter Min (ms):** This graph identifies the bottom register of jitter for the specific call.

- **Jitter — Max (ms):** You use this graph when you're troubleshooting poor call quality. Jitter can lead to packet discards, which then deteriorate your call quality.

The Jitter — Max chart in Figure 9-4 identifies that three large spikes of jitter occurred during the call, each lasting only a few seconds. The chart represents only part of the total picture. You know that the call experienced a delay variation in transmitting packets (jitter), but that fact doesn't tell you what caused the jitter. (Packet loss and jitter aren't always related.)

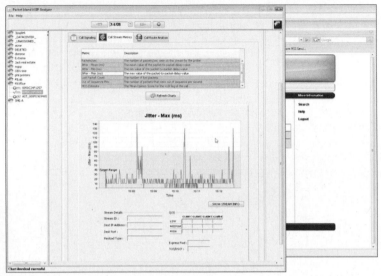

Figure 9-4:
A Jitter —
Max chart.

When analyzing the Jitter — Max chart, you need to look at the entire chart. The majority of the jitter in Figure 9-4 sits within the acceptable range, less than 40 ms. The spikes weren't systemic, so spot congestion on the LAN or WAN likely caused the jitter.

As a general rule, any jitter spikes that last longer than 80 ms indicate that packets will most likely be discarded. VoIP phones and media gateways can't absorb that much delay variation without throwing some packets away. On the other hand, 40 ms of jitter is considered normal fluctuations of latency that you can expect in a LAN.

Losing packets on the LAN

Packet loss is an easy concept to grasp but a difficult issue to confirm. *Packet loss* is, in the simplest terms, a packet that's sent from your VoIP phone but never arrives at the far-end SIP node. You could easily validate this problem if SIP and RTP sent a continuous stream of packets.

But many SIP servers use silence suppression, meaning that they don't send RTP packets when the person at their end of the call isn't speaking. Instead, they transmit a single packet (generally called a keep-alive message) whose sole purpose is to let the far end know that the call is still active, despite no audio being sent. VoIP hardphones can employ several different standards for silence suppression, so you don't have any one methodology that you can use to categorize them all. The good folks at Packet Island have researched not only the various flavors of silence suppression, but also the varying interpretations of SIP, so that it can deliver an accurate representation of lost packets.

Figure 9-5 shows that the example call did experience packet loss, and not because of systemic jitter. The spikes on the Lost Packet Count graph match the spikes on the Jitter — Max chart, confirming that packet loss caused the momentary jitter.

So, this call experienced packet loss, but not because of network congestion. This type of issue has two potential sources:

✔ **You used up all the bandwidth of your outbound IP connection.** Any deployment that uses DSL (which usually allocates more bandwidth for downloading than uploading) has a very real potential to run out of bandwidth on the uplink to the Internet. If you have a full dedicated T1 to the Internet, and not DSL, it that allows you the same bandwidth for uploading and downloading data, you don't have to worry about working with a much smaller bandwidth for uploading.

✔ **You have a hardware issue.** An improperly optioned or failing piece of hardware can generate random packet loss. Investigate this issue further by checking your router for errors or framing issues. You can easily replace a failing router after you know that it's affecting your traffic.

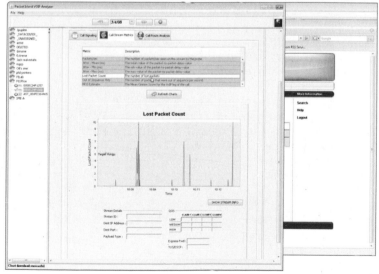

Figure 9-5:
The Lost
Packet
Count
graph.

The Out of Sequence Packets graph usually echoes the Lost Packet Count graph. The out-of-sequence packets coincide with the same time frame as the packet loss, in most cases. If the packet loss is consistent over 20 or 30 seconds, it either indicates a LAN congestion issue or a hardware issue. If the congestion is related to packet loss, then use the traffic flow graph to see whether you're maxing out your bandwidth.

Looking at call quality with MOS

The final chart available on the Call Stream Metrics tab is for the Mean Opinion Score estimate. The chart is much better than a standard MOS score for a VoIP call because it identifies the MOS score in a linear fashion for the entire duration of the call. If a portion of the call was affected by packet loss, you can clearly see when it occurred on this chart. You don't lose the information in the overall aggregation of data that creates a single MOS score for the entire call. MOS scoring, along with the methods for determining MOS scores and the pitfalls of relying on it are covered in Chapter 3.

Packet Island determines the MOS score of real-time calls by using a mathematical algorithm based on network impairments of delay, packet loss, and jitter. The MOS report gives you a good overall sense of the VoIP call's quality, but don't forget that you need to identify and resolve the jitter, delay, and packet loss.

The MOS graph provides a mathematically derived benchmark for the expected call quality. If the individual on the call reported poor quality and this graph reflects that, you're probably looking at the correct call. If this chart shows a clean 4.0 MOS for the entire duration, request more information from the person reporting the issue and check out some other calls. You may be looking at the wrong session.

In addition to LAN issues that affect your VoIP call quality, you may also have issues caused by the non-VoIP portion of your call. You may experience static, echo, and other types of additive line noise because of phone hardware or any cabling problems located at any point along the analog path of the call, from where it's converted from VoIP to traditional telephony all the way to the point of termination. If you're calling to a non-VoIP destination, your call is converted from VoIP and enters the PSTN, where it encounters a whole new set of hardware and handshaking that can influence call quality. Issues within your long-distance carrier or beyond it are the responsibility of your long-distance carrier. You can read about these issues in Part III of this book.

Showing stream info

Below each chart on the Call Stream Metrics tab is a small section dedicated to call stream information. The left side of the area covers simple address and codec information, identifying the destination IP address, port, and codec used for the transmission.

The right side of the area is dedicated to the Quality of Service (QoS) and identifies how your LAN handled the call. If your LAN or VoIP phone employ the Differentiated Services Code Point (DSCP) values in QoS, the first section, which lists four classes of service with three priority levels in each, is populated.

The bottom right section of the screen identifies the Type Of Service (TOS) identified for the call. This section is only populated if the VoIP phone you're using is working off the older Type of Service (ToS) byte instead of the new QOS option. ToS uses the expedited forwarding (Exp Fwd) that's the same as the traditional LAN prioritization of precedence level of five. The Internet Telecommunications Union (ITU) recommends this priority level for VoIP transmissions, and it's represented by 101 in the first three bits of the ToS/DSCP field.

ToS functions at the Network layer (3) of the OSI model, along with IP. So, you can use ToS only with routers and other hardware that function at layer three. Hubs and switches function below layer three, so you can't use them with this technology. If you want to know more about the OSI model, please jump over to Chapter 5.

Analyzing Your Call Route

The third tab available to you for individual call analysis, the Call Route Analysis tab, covers the route taken by the specific call highlighted. The information in this tab functions like an active trace route for your call and identifies the IP address that the call was forwarded to, as well as the minimum and maximum experienced round-trip time (RTT) to that IP address. Figure 9-6 shows the Minimum RTT and Maximum RTT for a call.

The final column in the Call Route Analysis tab indicates whether the call experienced a route flap, where some packets in the RTP stream are sent to the end destination via a different route through the Internet than the rest of the packets for the audio at any time. Route flap can be as detrimental to a call as excessive LAN jitter. A single route flap doesn't cause any damage, but multiple route flaps indicate that the RTP stream has taken multiple routes to deliver packets on the same call. Avoid route flaps, if possible, because packets arrive out of sequence and the VoIP node at the receiving end of the RTP stream eventually discards them if the delays overwhelm the jitter buffer. Fortunately for the example call in Figure 9-6, the call didn't experience any route flaps during its journey from the VoIP phone to the edge proxy server of the VoIP carrier.

The Packet Island software measures the RTT on two directions. Because the inline micro-device is sitting between your firewall and your switch, it's pulling data from its location to both ends of the VoIP call. The micro-device checks the leg of the call that runs from the micro-device itself, through your LAN, to the VoIP phone that originates the call. The micro-device takes its second set of calculations from itself, out your router, and through the Internet to your VoIP carrier's media gateway or edge proxy server.

The calculations that cover the path to your VoIP carrier's server aren't as accurate as those gathered from within your LAN. The uncharted territory of the public Internet makes the calculations less accurate. Despite that, the software provides you with trends that are accurate, over all. If you see that a specific router or ISP has consistently high levels of delay or packet loss, you should avoid or replace it.

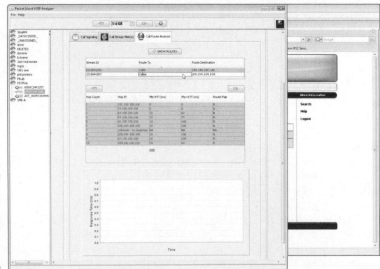

Figure 9-6:
The Call
Route
Analysis
tab.

Internet providers often offer the RTT as a part of their Service Level Agreement (SLA). Recommended limits for RTT vary, but 100 ms is a good benchmark to set for the maximum allowable. Some ISPs that have well-designed and -deployed networks offer an RTT in their contract of under 10 ms, so you can find a great variety of performance available in the Internet marketplace. Be sure to ask your ISP about its RTT guarantee when you sign your contract for service and don't forget to read the SLA to see what RTT it promises.

Monitoring Traffic Flows

The second main tab on the GUI covers signaling records and provides information that isn't necessarily call-related but pertains more to the validation of adds, moves, and changes within your LAN. You can check the new VoIP phones you haven't yet set up in the Signaling Records tab, but for detailed information on the health of your LAN, you need to check the Traffic Flows tab on the GUI.

Traffic flows are just another way to speak about the transmission of data from the point of origin to the point of termination. A single VoIP session is an example of a single type of data that makes up the entire traffic flow. Packet Island aggregates the multitude of traffic flows on your network, allowing you to see the overall impact on your hardware and your bandwidth. The information that you can find in this section of the GUI provides additional insight into why a specific call experienced latency, jitter, or packet loss.

You can resize the charts provided so that they cover only the area of time that interests you, just like all the charts in the GUI. Being able to resize the charts is extremely important because the issue that's affecting the call may have been very fleeting, lasting only a few seconds. Figure 9-7 shows the traffic running on your LAN, broken down into five categories:

- **UDP-RTP:** Comprises the VoIP traffic for the audio of the call
- **UDP — Others:** Any UDP that isn't identified as VoIP, possibly video traffic or audio streaming
- **TCP:** Contains Internet surfing and uploads/downloads
- **ICMP:** Contains the packets sent on your LAN by using the Internet Control Message Protocol
- **Misc:** Any other traffic that doesn't fit into one of the four preceding categories

The traffic flow charts identify the entire flow for the day. Expand the section of the chart to identify the specific time frame during which a reported call experienced jitter, packet loss, or latency.

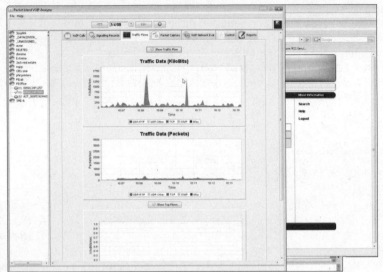

Figure 9-7:
The Traffic
Flows tab.

Whatever VLM software you use, ensure that it can identify the individual packet flows down to the level where each type of data traffic on your LAN is visible. Without the specific data, you can't make an intelligent and informed decision about how to resolve a congestion issue or even confirm that it *is* a congestion issue.

The topmost and center charts in the screen show the same time frame of data, but each chart expresses that data in a different way. The top chart in Figure 9-7 shows the bandwidth usage for each data type in your LAN. This chart clearly shows the TCP traffic, which represents Web downloads. This traffic generated two noticeable spikes during the time in question. If these spikes coincide with the same time frame in which the call experienced packet loss, you can conclude that the TCP traffic generated LAN congestion, resulting in the packet loss.

When faced with this type of problem, you have two possible solutions:

✔ Order more bandwidth from your Internet provider.

✔ Institute constraints in the rate shaping that your network employs so that you can prevent the TCP traffic from usurping the section of the band-width allocated for VoIP traffic. If you don't have rate shaping employed in your LAN, this kind of call issue indicates that maybe you should. Rate shaping, and all of the tools available to you to manage, sequester, and protect your VoIP traffic are covered in detail in Chapter 5.

The best rate-shaping devices are protocol aware. Edgewater Networks has a great product that allows you to route traffic based on the destination ports. Allocating port numbers 10,000 to 15,000 solely for VoIP usage allows you to guarantee a specific bandwidth or priority for your VoIP traffic. You can even maximize your LAN a bit more by setting a definite bandwidth for the VoIP traffic, but still allowing the data traffic to have access to it when the bandwidth is available.

You can use rate shaping only if routers and other LAN hardware are interacting at the third layer of the OSI model. You can't use rate shaping in areas of your network handled by hubs and switches because they don't look deep enough into the packets they process to differentiate them.

Remotely Capturing Packets

Many variables can potentially affect VoIP, and many of those variables are invisible, depending on your observation point. Your carrier can't see all the SIP banter on a call that happens within your LAN, and you have limited visibility into the minutiae and routing after the call leaves your LAN.

In the end, the most effective VoIP troubleshooting requires a combined effort by yourself and your carrier to unravel the mystery of why a call is failing or has poor call quality. Any issue into which you have limited visibility can quickly turn into a frustrating endeavor as the troubleshooting progresses and greater detail is required to resolve the problem. The resolution process could end up with a "best efforts" resolution that's only designed to avoid the situation and not resolve the problem.

The best tool you have at your disposal for intensive troubleshooting where you need complete visibility into a call is packet capture software such as Wireshark or tcpdump. The captures that you can create with this software enable you to provide your carrier with empirical data that illustrates what your network is seeing and experiencing. These captures eliminate all the emotion and desire that frequently corrupt the troubleshooting process. By giving your carrier these captures, you're telling it, "This is exactly what you sent to me, and this is exactly how I responded."

I worked on many trouble issues in which the resolution of an issue stopped in its tracks because the end user couldn't provide a packet capture. You may find the software a bit tricky to download and compile, and doing so for every site of a 100-node network takes a lot of time. But you don't have to worry about any of that because Packet Island made incorporated packet captures into its GUI.

Through the GUI, you can make packet captures remotely for any office or device. The capture gathers all the information that flows through the LAN while the capture is active and open. Depending on the level of activity on your LAN, a five-minute capture could grow to 5GB, or an all-day capture could top out at 700 Mbps.

Keep the capture confined, if possible. Even if you have the room to capture everything running through your LAN for a day, you don't want to sort through all that data. Coordinate with an employee on site to execute a test call directly after you open the capture, and close the capture after the call ends. The cleaner the test, the less ancillary LAN packets you have to wade through.

You can set the remote capture to remain open based on any or all of the following three criteria:

- ✔ **Duration:** Identify the quantity of seconds that you want the capture to remain open.
- ✔ **Size Limit:** The capture closes after it collects the maximum file size.
- ✔ **Packet Count:** When the capture collects the maximum number of packets, it closes.

The Packet Island GUI currently has a 1MB device limit on the capture, but it's working on relaxing that limit.

Figure 9-8 shows a capture limited to 60 seconds in length. Unless you can anticipate the total amount of traffic flowing through your LAN, avoid the size or packet limitations on the capture. You don't want to end the capture prematurely because you didn't factor in the high volume of calls generated by VoIP.

The packet capture can also collect either the full Ethernet frames or simply the packet headers. I recommend selecting the Packet Headers only because you can resolve most issues by looking at the packet headers alone. Capturing only the headers also helps to keep the capture below the 1MB limit. If you do require more information, you can always go back and execute another capture for the full frames.

The capture request takes about 15 to 30 seconds to hit the far end and begin the capture, at which time the screen of the GUI updates with a message of Capture in Progress. After the capture is closed, the status is updated to File Is Ready, but you can view the capture as it's being conducted, similar to watching the command-line interface or Console mode of your favorite VoIP phone system.

After the file is ready, download it to your local computer drive so that you can analyze it or forward it to your carrier for comparison against its capture.

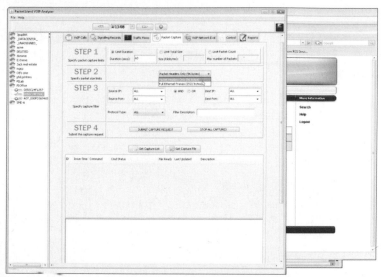

Figure 9-8:
A remote
packet
capture.

Evaluating the VoIP Network

The first few tabs of the GUI can help you identify individual call issues. They allow you to pull apart what has happened on the LAN during the course of a normal day, but they don't give you the ability to directly test the LAN. The VoIP Network Eval tab of the GUI takes care of this testing.

You may not be able to reproduce some intermittent issues during an individual packet capture, or you may simply want to reevaluate your network. The latency, jitter, and packet loss benchmarks established by your initial VoIP deployment may be ancient history after you hire five more employees and add additional servers. Regardless of the reason, the best way to check the health of your network is to execute a cycle of VoIP calls over a duration of time, pushing your LAN to its limits and checking it for environmental changes.

The VoIP Network Eval tab of the GUI, shown in Figure 9-9, places all the steps for designing and executing the tests in a numbered sequence. Just follow these steps:

1. **Select a target.**

   The section labeled "Step 1 - Select a Target" allows you to identify a specific IP address to test.

2. **Define the test.**

   The specifics of the test include

   - Codec

   - Packet interval

   - Max concurrent call (Do you want the test to ramp up to that level or simply remain constant at that level?)

   - Duration of call

   - Start time for test

   - End time for test

   - Description tag (Add text in the text box listed at the bottom right of the "Step 2" to identify the specific test you're running if you want to be identified in some way.)

3. **Schedule the call generation.**

   You can start the test at the time that you specify in Step 2, or you can stop all calls in a test that's currently active.

4. **Schedule the route analysis.**

   Start and stop trace routes on the calls.

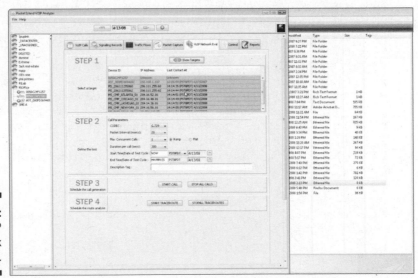

Figure 9-9:
The VoIP
Network
Eval tab.

Always ramp up to the level of the max concurrent calls you select. The process of adding one call in a methodical sequence until your reach the maximum concurrent call level provides a consistent impact on your network. If you have a maximum call level of 15, you want to identify if and when it pushes your LAN to its limit, at which point, the MOS score drops, and the packet loss begins.

The generated test calls appear alongside the normal office calls that are already flowing through your LAN, and you can view the test calls in the VoIP Calls tab on the GUI, identifying MOS, jitter, and packet loss for each call.

Reporting on Your VoIP LAN

The final tab on the Packet Island GUI is the Reports tab. It's an essential part of any VLM software, generating hardcopy reports of the overall health of your VoIP LAN. Store these reports for comparison against other reports from different times so that you can identify systemic trends in usage, network efficiency, and hardware performance.

The Packet Island GUI provides access to four reports:

- ✔ **VoIP Assess (Standard):** Contains only one page of data with summary information on call quality (MOS scores), latency, jitter, and packet loss.

- ✔ **VoIP Assess (Premium):** Contains about 30 pages of verification covering overall call quality (MOS scores) for individual VoIP phones, as well as aggregate data on percentages of total calls that had good, fair, and bad call quality, along with detailed reports on bandwidth usage.

- ✔ **VoIP Verify (Standard):** This report covers all aspects of VoIP deployment and provides the benchmark for latency, jitter, packet loss, and MOS for your entire network as well as the individual VoIP phones.

- ✔ **VoIP SLA (Standard):** Information on live calls going through the network identifying call quality summarized by time of day, and contrasted against the other traffic flowing through your LAN during the same time frame.

Generating assessment reports

The assessment reports are calculated based on the battery of test calls created on the Network Eval tab of the GUI. You can access the report as soon as the test completes — Packet Island sends the report to the e-mail address you specified when you requested the report.

The premium VoIP assessment report provides a general view of your VoIP LAN's health by first listing the MOS scores for each level of concurrent calls, from one to the maximum number requested. This information gives you a basis for the detailed reports that follow, which cover

- MOS inbound
- MOS outbound
- Jitter inbound
- Jitter outbound
- Packet loss (inbound)
- Packet loss (outbound)
- Traffic flows
- Call route information
- Router response based on increasing quantity of calls

Conduct a scaling VoIP call test prior to actual VoIP deployment at a rate higher than you expect to actually need. If your expected maximum concurrent call level is 10 calls, execute the test to scale up to 15 calls so that you can see how much headroom you have in your LAN when your company does expand. You need a high packet rate to fully test the capacity of your routers. You want to determine where your failure point is in a laboratory environment, rather than after VoIP is deployed and the small LAN issues become huge, expensive problems.

Requiring a verification report

One of the most important reports you generate (and one you should require from any VLM software you use) is a verification report that covers all aspects of the final VoIP deployment. This report should cover more than the MOS, latency, jitter, and packet loss of the newly deployed phones; it should also provide a detailed flow analysis of bandwidth usage and a report of call quality and test calls made from every VoIP phone on your LAN.

Figure 9-10 shows a page from a Packet Island verification report that identifies that five VoIP phones were tested during the deployment. All the phones are listed by SIP URI, phone make and model, and specifics of the last call executed on the phone, along with the codec used and the lowest MOS score for the phone.

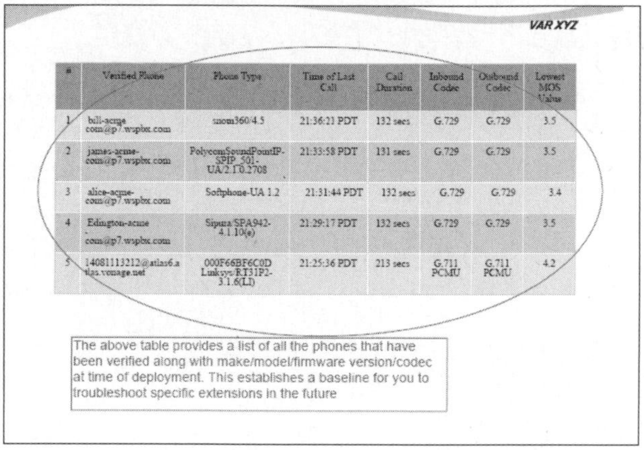

#	Verified Phone	Phone Type	Time of Last Call	Call Duration	Inbound Codec	Outbound Codec	Lowest MOS Value
1	bill-acme com@p7.wspbx.com	snom360/4.5	21:36:21 PDT	132 secs	G.729	G.729	3.5
2	james-acme- com@p7.wspbx.com	PolycomSoundPointIP-SPIP_501-UA/2.1.0.2708	21:33:58 PDT	131 secs	G.729	G.729	3.5
3	alice-acme- com@p7.wspbx.com	Softphone-UA 1.2	21:31:44 PDT	132 secs	G.729	G.729	3.4
4	Edington-acme com@p7.wspbx.com	Sipura/SPA942-4.1.10(a)	21:29:17 PDT	132 secs	G.729	G.729	3.5
5	14081113212@atlas6.a lls.vonage.net	000F66BF6C0D Linksys/RT31P2-3.1.6(LI)	21:25:36 PDT	213 secs	G.711 PCMU	G.711 PCMU	4.2

VAR XYZ

The above table provides a list of all the phones that have been verified along with make/model/firmware version/codec at time of deployment. This establishes a baseline for you to troubleshoot specific extensions in the future

Figure 9-10:
A VoIP
phone
report.

The verification report that you create during VoIP deployment provides proof that the VoIP technician installing your hardware did a complete and accurate job. Use the verification report to enforce the requirement that your installation tech conducts a five-minute call on each VoIP phone. This report tells you whether the call duration was 5 seconds or 300 seconds. You can compare and contrast the performance of each VoIP phone with how the other phones rated under similar conditions by using these tests.

If your second VoIP phone had an average MOS score of 2.5 and the first phone had an average 3.5 MOS during the same level of latency and jitter, your install tech needs to isolate the reason for the underperforming phone. He or she may need to replace the cabling to the one defective phone or force the duplex configuration on it. This report can clearly identify an issue that the installer needs to correct before he or she wraps up the job.

A VoIP phone can renegotiate its speed and duplex setting if it loses power. If a VoIP phone loses power and renegotiates its settings, the only way that you can validate the configuration of duplex mode between a VoIP phone and a switch is SNMP. SNMP must be deployed on both the VoIP phone and the switch on your LAN if you want visibility into the SNMP data. In situations where you don't have SNMP visibility into your VoIP phone, force the speed and duplex on every phone and switch in the network so that you can guarantee they're all set correctly.

Using the SLA report on live calls

The Service Level Agreement (SLA) report is drawn from data on live calls. This report provides a quick snapshot of the overall health of your network for the time frame that you specified when you requested the report. You can run the report at any time, and you should run it periodically to monitor the evolution of your LAN traffic.

The report identifies specific calls that experience a call quality of 3.2 or less. The report classifies these calls as having a poor MOS rating and displays them as an overall percentage of total calls, as well as specifically identifying the calls with the worst MOS scores.

Figure 9-11 shows information presented in an SLA report for jitter. The pie chart shows that 2.6 percent of the calls during the reporting time were of poor MOS quality. The lower portion of Figure 9-11 shows the four calls that had the lowest MOS score. This report indicates both good and bad news. The good news is that 97.4 percent of the calls had fair or good call quality, according to the MOS scores. The bad news is that you still have some lingering LAN or WAN issues that are affecting your calls, which you need to address.

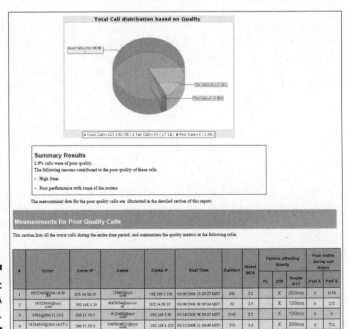

Figure 9-11:
An SLA
report.

The SLA report identifies the worst-offending calls by date, time, MOS score, and IP address, so you have sufficient information to research the individual calls. You can investigate each call through the normal process that uses the VoIP Calls tab. After identifying the date of the defective call in the main page of the GUI, scroll by time down the calls listed and find the specific call with the poor call quality. The available tabs and charts available in the Call Signaling, Call Stream Metrics, and Call Route Analysis tabs for the call show the jitter, latency, loss, and data flows that impacted the call quality and can explain the drop in quality on the specific call.

Managing It All with Packet Island

The work doesn't end the day you successfully deploy your VoIP network with IP phones. Your technician may have left the building after he or she checked all the cabling, forced the configuration of speed and duplex on every VoIP phone, and tested every device, node, and feature on your phone system. But your system always has the potential to experience service impacting issues.

One month after the successful installation of your VoIP service, rerun a sample battery of test calls. If your network has any lingering issues, they may surface at this time. Depending on how much work you need to do to correct routing, hardware, and other LAN issues after you make these test calls, you may want to continue rechecking all your data once a month for the first three or four months to ensure that you've addressed everything.

Conduct testing once a quarter, or at least once every six months, after you're satisfied with the performance of your VoIP LAN. Execute a series of tests that set up the concurrent calls to your projected maximum for 24 hours, or even multiple 24-hour periods, to get a solid report. Then, dissect the data to identify any patterns in MOS degradation related to the time of day or the day of week, and see whether your data shows a correlation between declining MOS score and an increase in the concurrent call quantity.

The Packet Island GUI and micro-devices allow you to effectively run reports for every site and analyze the data. If you're a VoIP provider, you can deploy the micro-devices at your customer sites for monthly or quarterly network assessments. Many customers become frustrated and disillusioned with VoIP before they engage anyone to troubleshoot it. The Packet Island solution allows you to pro-actively identify and research issues before your customers even know that their router is failing or that they need additional bandwidth.

Chapter 10

Investigating SIP Call Generation

SIP uses a specific sequence of methods and responses to set up a call. The manner by which a method or response is transferred through the intermediary SIP nodes from the origin to the final SIP device, as well as how the far end reacts to the SIP messaging, is all rigidly structured. If a receiving SIP device sends an unexpected response code to an INVITE message, the call can fail, and the SIP transmission can be stuck in limbo.

I talk about the standard SIP and SDP messaging in Chapters 2 and 3. This chapter focuses on the interaction between the endpoints and the flow of messages you should see in a standard VoIP call. The structure of the messaging for each call is very important. If you see any variation in your SIP banter, compared to the examples in this chapter, you should investigate.

Recognizing the International Standards

The Internet Engineering Task Force (IETF), located at www.ietf.org, is the repository for the international standards for SIP signaling. Each unique aspect of SIP banter is spelled out in the curiously named *Request For Comments (RFCs)*. These documents specify the required responses to SIP methods and the manners of interaction between SIP nodes. The IETF Web site lists all the current RFCs on file. Here are some of the RFCs that you may be interested in:

✔ **RFC 1889:** RTP (Real-Time Transport Protocol)

✔ **RFC 2543:** SIP (Session Initiation Protocol)

✔ **RFC 2658:** RTP for PureVoice audio

✔ **RFC 2733:** RTP payload format for generic error correction

✔ **RFC 2833:** RTP payload for DTMF digits

✔ **RFC 2848:** PINT Service Protocol (SIP/SDP for IP access to telephone calls)

✔ **RFC 2976:** SIP CANCEL specifics

✔ **RFC 3261:** SIP REFER specifics

The RFCs are the standards used in the telecommunications industry, keeping everyone operating from the same rulebook. They're simply guidelines, and they include a bit of room for interpretation. This flexibility ensures that some nuances of how the RFCs are employed vary from company to company or individual to individual. New RFCs may clarify these minor variances, but no international VoIP jury or enforcement department exists for RFCs. But remember that large carriers structure their SIP signaling by using the RFCs as a reference point because those carriers strive to ensure continuity.

Not everyone follows the RFCs all the time, especially some smaller, boutique carriers that own their own VoIP switches. If you want to use the SIP method of BYE in all situations — even when a CANCEL would normally be used — you can. SIP is merely a common language used between two devices; you can modify it in any way you want. If you want to modify SIP, your carrier needs to make a special modification to the SIP stack, so see whether your carrier specializes in accommodating the nuances of its customers. But don't expect a high level of flexibility from a VoIP product delivered by a major carrier. It's disinclined to make changes to its SIP stack that deviate from the RFC. If its switch went down, lost power, or was upgraded to a new software revision, everything could go back to defaults, which would erase all of the custom programming and create a nightmare as it tries to rebuild every custom response for all of its customers. Carriers can deliver consistent and stable VoIP for the long term only by abiding by the RFCs. So, if you have a quirky SIP setup, expect your carrier to require you to change your configuration so that it matches the RFC because it probably won't even consider modifying its code for your particular setup.

Reviewing a Completed Call

VoIP calls are set up and torn down through a very specific and methodical banter between the SIP nodes. The absence of any one of the key SIP transmissions can result in problems or failure of your VoIP call.

Figure 10-1 shows a SIP call tree identifying the basic banter required for a completed VoIP call. The first three messages are required to establish any call. They include

✔ An INVITE from the origination VoIP node to the destination VoIP node

✔ A 200 OK response from the destination end to the origination VoIP node

✔ An ACK from the originating device back to the destination VoIP node

The receipt of the ACK message identifies the point in the call where the individual RTP streams are established in both directions and the call begins, with both ends of the call capable of receiving the audio from the other end.

Figure 10-1 is a condensed version of a SIP call — it doesn't include any other messages that aren't absolutely essential to make the connection. More messages may flow back and forth, including additional INVITE messages and confirmation responses that may occur between the initial INVITE and the ACK that identifies when the RTP streams have been established. But if you boil down any VoIP call, you absolutely need only these three messages to establish the call.

After the call is established, it continues with both people chatting and listening until the conversation concludes and someone hangs up. In Figure 10-1, you can tell that the origination VoIP node hangs up first because that node sends the BYE message to the destination end of the call. The destination VoIP node acknowledged the BYE with a 200 OK, and the call ends.

I go over SIP methods (such as ACK, BYE, CANCEL, and INVITE), as well as SIP responses (such as 180, 200, 404, and 503), in Chapter 2. Flip back to that chapter if you want more information on the specifics of what these methods and responses are, as well as their purpose in the SIP universe.

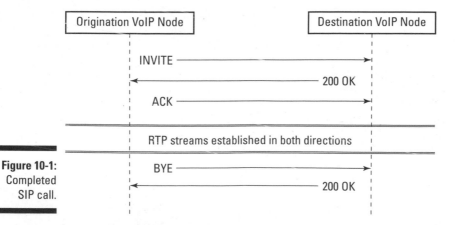

Figure 10-1:
Completed
SIP call.

Figure 10-1 shows only the distilled SIP banter required to complete a call. The destination device usually sends a 200 OK response as its second or third response. Almost every SIP call that you investigate provides at least one 1XX provisional response before the destination device sends a 200 OK.

Figure 10-2 is a snapshot of the normal banter found in a SIP call. The call includes the required elements of the INVITE, 200OK, and ACK to establish the call, but it also includes two provisional SIP responses delivered from the destination VoIP node back to the originating VoIP node of 100 Trying and 180 Ringing.

The 100 Trying response confirms that the destination device received the INVITE and indicates that the session is off to a good start. The 180 Ringing response tells the originating VoIP node to play its ring-back recording. These responses both give good indications that the call is going through fine. If the dialed number was busy at the time that the originating VoIP node tried to reach it, the call sequence may be more like Figure 10-3.

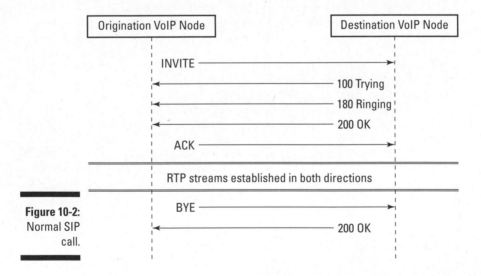

Figure 10-2:
Normal SIP
call.

Because the call in Figure 10-3 didn't have the completed INVITE/200OK/ACK sequence, the call was never truly established. Because the call was never established, the originating VoIP node can terminate the call simply by sending the ACK method to the 486 Busy Here SIP response received by the destination SIP node. Figure 10-3 would look exactly the same if the destination SIP node sent the response 503 Service Unavailable or 404 Not Found, rather than 486 Busy Here. Any of these responses allow the call to end without anything more than a single ACK from the end of the call that receives the reject response.

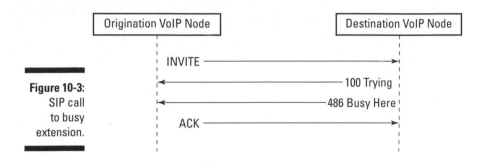

Figure 10-3:
SIP call
to busy
extension.

Viewing a Multi-Node Call

Very few SIP calls occur between two endpoints without more SIP nodes between them. Almost every call is handled by a proxy or node relaying the SIP and RTP information to the far end of the call. You need to understand the flow of the SIP messages while your calls stretch out and cover more and more nodes. Each proxy server adds a bit more latency to the transmission of SIP packets and acts as another potential point of failure on the call, so when troubleshooting any VoIP issue, you need to view them all together.

In addition to the call quality concerns, the different SIP methods and responses cascade differently when they're sent down the intermediary SIP nodes. Intermediary or proxy devices respond to some SIP methods instantly, but some SIP methods require the intermediary SIP nodes to wait for the message to make its way to the final SIP node before providing a response.

Figure 10-4 shows more detail on a standard SIP call than the preceding figures in this chapter. The preceding figures showed only the final endpoints, but Figure 10-4 includes one of the intermediary SIP nodes. A SIP call may have many individual nodes from end to end, but you may not always have visibility into them; many VoIP carriers and resellers don't provide detailed network information identifying the processing SIP servers.

The SIP proxy transmits the SIP provisional response of 180 Ringing only after the intermediary SIP node receives this SIP response from the far end. The nodes receiving the 200 OK responses and the SIP methods respond immediately to them.

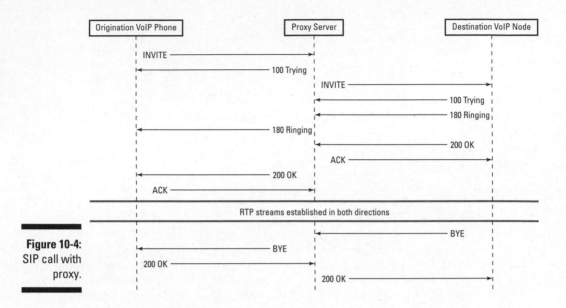

Figure 10-4:
SIP call with
proxy.

The teardown of the RTP streams of the call is done in the coordination with the process of sending the SIP method BYE. The node receiving the BYE method responds to with a 200 OK. The transmission of the SIP method BYE indicates that the associated RTP stream from the node originating the BYE method is to be dismantled. The SIP node receiving the SIP method of BYE acknowledges that the incoming RTP stream is no longer active, and disables its own outbound RTP stream while it sends the 200 OK confirmation. A normal proxied SIP call forwards the BYE to the end device and returns the 200 OK only after the proxy receives it. This ensures that the RTP stream spanning from the SIP node originating the BYE to the final SIP node receiving the BYE is discontinued before the returning RTP stream is discontinued in coordination with the transmission of the 200 OK.

Canceling a SIP Call

If the destination VoIP device sends a 1XX provisional response or a 2XX OK response, the originating SIP node must terminate the call with either a standard BYE or a CANCEL. Both SIP methods have their specific purpose. If the originating SIP node sends a CANCEL when a BYE is required, the SIP method may be rejected or ignored, and the call will not disconnect properly, just like sending a BYE when a CANCEL is required.

The CANCEL method differs from the BYE method in two ways:

✔ **The CANCEL method can be used only if the call disconnects before the ends can establish the RTP streams with a 200 OK/ACK handshake.** After the audio portion of the call is established in both directions with the 200 OK/ACK messaging, a BYE must be used.

✔ **The CANCEL method is non-negotiable and waits for nothing.** If 50 servers lie between the originating VoIP phone and the final VoIP device, every one of the 50 servers responds to the CANCEL with the appropriate 487 Request Terminated response and a 200 OK before forwarding the CANCEL downstream to the next server. This process tears down each hop in the call, instead of waiting for a 200 OK from the far end to remove the RTP as required when processing a BYE.

You can see these differences in Figure 10-5.

Figure 10-5 shows how the originating VoIP phone disconnected the call shortly after it heard the far end ringing. The proxy server passed on the INVITE, and the far end received and forwarded a 180 Ringing just before the originating VoIP phone sent a CANCEL. This call scenario happens often, for example, when the caller realizes that he or she dialed the wrong number.

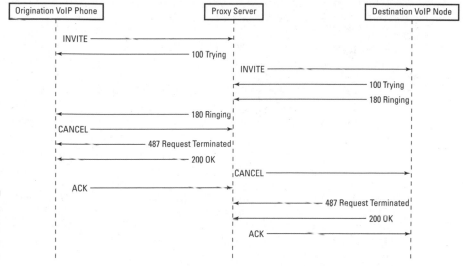

Figure 10-5:
SIP Cancel
with Proxy

When the originating SIP phone hangs up, the CANCEL message is sent from that phone to the proxy server. The SIP proxy doesn't challenge or wait for any response from the far end when it receives this SIP method, it immediately sends the appropriate 487 Request Terminated and 200 OK (RFC 2976) to the originating SIP phone. The SIP proxy relays the CANCEL to the destination VoIP node only after the RTP stream has been torn down from the originating VoIP phone. This process of canceling each segment of the VoIP call continues, one server at a time, until all RTP streams are removed.

SIP uses the CANCEL method for more situations than just when you decide to hang up a call before the far end answers it. CANCEL can also terminate a call that fails to successfully connect to the far end. The call failures vary, and can include

- ✔ A recording of "Your call cannot be completed as dialed"
- ✔ A recording of "The number you have dialed is disconnected or no longer in service"
- ✔ A recording of "All circuits are busy"
- ✔ A fast busy signal
- ✔ A regular busy signal

Some phone systems can find these types of responses troubling; every carrier and phone system may be configured to process these types of calls differently. Your phone system and the gateway of your VoIP carrier need to establish a special coordination to process calls that receive error messages or operator intercept recordings. No one has created a codified rule about which SIP response code must be used for each recording or failure response. Depending on how your VoIP carrier has configured its gateway, your VoIP carrier may respond with a 404 Not Found or a 503 Service Unavailable, or something else that it believes to be the more accurate representation of the number you've dialed. This allows for interpretation; a recording stating that your call "cannot be completed as dialed" may be seen as a 403 Not Found to one carrier, and a 503 Service Unavailable to another.

Your VoIP server must then receive and process that information. If you don't have anything within your VoIP proxy or the Call Plan of your phone system established to handle a 410 Gone or 403 Forbidden response, your server generally sits and waits for another SIP message to arrive that it does understand.

One complication in how you configure your SIP hardware or Dial Plan to respond to these operator intercept calls is that every VoIP carrier has a variety of ways it can give you the failure messages or recordings. It can

✔ **Provide an audible treatment.** A VoIP carrier using this option supplies a one-way RTP stream that transmits the audible recording from the terminating local carrier. The audio you hear of "The number you have dialed is disconnected," for instance, is actually being transmitted directly from the local carrier responsible for the phone number you dialed. So, you're listening to the exact information provided by the local carrier, rather than your phone system's interpretation of the SIP response.

✔ **Provide a SIP response code and no audible treatment.** This option places more responsibility on your phone system. You may receive just a 404 or 503 response, without the audio recording that's normally played by the terminating local carrier. Your phone system must either read the SIP response and play a recording from its own library of audio files or disconnect the call and leave you wondering what just happened.

✔ **Provide an audible treatment and a SIP response.** You can both hear the original recording from the local phone carrier and also receive a SIP response that allows your VoIP server to have two options on how to process the call. You always want more information, rather than less, and this option gives you the most information. You don't run the risk of your VoIP phone system cross-referencing the SIP response to a less-than-accurate recording, and your phone system can record the SIP response provided to assist in troubleshooting the call, if necessary.

If your VoIP deployment covers your office or standard business use, this problem of handling operator intercept calls won't have a large impact on your day-to-day life. As long as your carrier has you set up for either the audio treatment or the SIP response with audio treatment, the person dialing the call hears the accurate recording and promptly hangs up the call.

If your business uses VoIP for telemarketing and the entire dialing process is automated, you may find this concern of how your SIP server responds to operator intercept calls to be a larger issue — especially if your automation handles a call to the point at which your SIP server recognizes a live voice on the far end before sending the call to an operator. The auto-dialer configurations, or any system that makes outbound calls, must know how to handle the response code you receive. If your Dial Plan is set up to respond solely to SIP response codes and your carrier sends you only the audio treatment, the SIP session can lock up.

If you're using VoIP in a fully automated scenario, be sure to speak to your VoIP carrier to determine how it processes these calls. Most small businesses experience a low percentage of calls that fail because of misdialed or disconnected phone numbers. It may be 3 percent of your overall dialing, if that much. The percentage is much higher for telemarketing companies that can experience 20- to 25-percent failure rates on their outbound dialing because of phone numbers on their call lists that are no longer in service. That rate of failure can have a large, cumulative effect on a telemarketing company's ability to dial if its SIP server handles the call treatments inefficiently or just ignores the treatments.

Building time-out limits into your SIP server prevents sessions from needlessly remaining open. You can feel confident that if your SIP server doesn't receive either a SIP message or an RTP packet in 30 seconds, the call has probably failed. Your SIP server should tear down sessions that have timed out because it's good housekeeping and avoids allocating resources to a session that's no longer valid.

Calls that receive failure responses of 4XX or 5XX haven't completed the INVITE/200OK/ACK sequence that establishes the RTP streams in both directions. If these calls remain open, the originating SIP device must tear down the VoIP session by using the SIP method CANCEL.

Looking In to a Re-INVITE

The ability to re-INVITE a call is one of the great benefits of VoIP. VoIP servers and nodes do it so frequently that most people almost ignore the logistics of it. Your VoIP provider may be using this technique to deliver your RTP, cutting down on potential latency, jitter, and packet loss.

I cover the benefits of re-INVITEs in Chapter 3.

Either end of a SIP call can send a supplemental INVITE message through to the other end. Any SIP node can send a re-INVITE for several reasons, including

- Moving the RTP stream to reduce latency, jitter, packet loss, and bandwidth use

- Moving the RTP to a feature server for voicemail, a dial-by-name directory, a call queue, or other applications not available at the primary VoIP server

- Requesting a new codec or feature not offered in the initial INVITE, such as

    - RFC2833 DTMF

    - T.38 for fax

The call flow on a re-INVITE call is slightly different than a normal proxy call because only the SIP information continues to flow through the intermediary node, not the bandwidth-hungry RTP. The RTP stream may never pass through the intermediary node until the end of the call when the SIP proxy may re-INVITE it back, similar to how a CANCEL works.

Re-INVITE isn't a REFER. A Re-INVITE sends the RTP stream to a new destination IP address while maintaining the SIP overhead messages flowing through it. The SIP method REFER sends both the SIP messaging and the RTP to the new destination IP. You may find this rerouting useful in some scenarios, but generally speaking, you don't want to cast off calls that you've received to remote sites. The call was sent to you in the first place for a reason, and you probably need to maintain some visibility into it. If the call experiences audio or completion problems, you can much more easily analyze what happened to it if you hold on to the SIP overhead.

Figure 10-6 identifies a T.38 call that starts out with a standard voice INVITE and progresses to re-INVITE to T.38. SIP devices capable of using T.38 commonly use this practice because any originating SIP server can more easily send every call out as a standard voice call, rather than maintain some type of database that identifies which phone numbers or IP addresses xxx use for faxing and therefore require T.38. You can more easily modify the Dial Plan for the individual phone line within your VoIP phone system that uses T.38, instead of changing up your SIP stack to provide T.38 as an option, which would affect every call.

The re-INVITE call progresses through the initial INVITE/200OK/ACK stage, just like any normal voice call, establishing both the RTP streams. After the streams are established, the receiving T.38 fax machine sends the re-INVITE message, requesting T.38. The proxy receives and processes the INVITE, immediately sending a 100 Trying response before forwarding the INVITE to the VoIP carrier.

The ACK responses establish the UDPTL streams that send the T.38 packets. The fax information is transmitted through the UDPTL streams, just like a voice conversation is transmitted over RTP streams.

After the fax is complete, the receiving T.38 fax machine sends a BYE and the proxy responds with a 200 OK, effectively removing the outbound UDPTL stream from the T.38 fax machine. The specific server in Figure 10-6 didn't simply forward the BYE to the SBC of the VoIP carrier, but instead sent another re-INVITE to establish a more controlled release of the call. The INVITE sent by the proxy after the fax was successfully transmitted performs two functions:

- It converts the call back to an uncompressed G.711 voice call.
- It establishes the media stream (RTP) between the VoIP carrier SBC and the SIP proxy if the media stream for the T.38 fax previously had been directly connected to the T.38 fax.

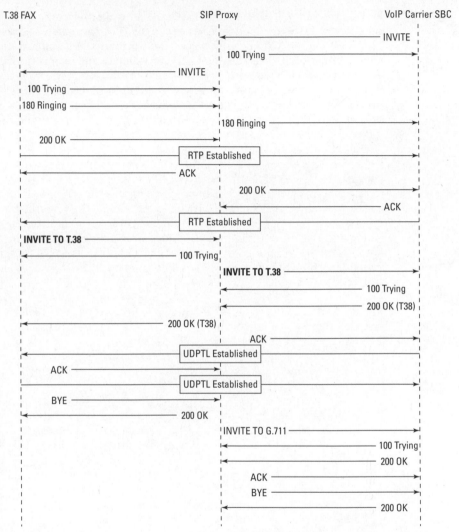

Figure 10-6:
SIP
Re-Invite
with T.38.

Completed calls in which the media (RTP or UDPTL) streams have been re-INVITEd are torn down in a similar manner to CANCELed calls. The SIP messaging still flows through the intermediary SIP proxy, so that proxy may respond with a 200 OK to the BYE method received from the SIP node initiating the call tear-down before either sending the BYE down to the final destination SIP node of the call or waiting to receive a 200 OK from that destination SIP node.

The RTP media streams can appear in a VoIP call prior to the 200 OK/ACK handshake. Just like a VoIP carrier can provide out-of-area and operator-intercept recordings to you as in-band audio, the carrier can also do the same thing with the ring tone that you hear. The delivery of an RTP stream back to the originating SIP node prior to the 200 OK/ACK messaging isn't uncommon, and every carrier may send either the 180 Ringing response, the audio treatment of the ringing sound, or both. If you buffer the audio of the call for any reason, or if your system is very sensitive to when the RTP starts and stops, speak to your carrier to identify its policy on advance RTP.

Using SIP Call Trees

The SIP call tree shown in all the figures in this chapter is a standard analysis tool in VoIP that provides a quick overview of a call, listing the sequence of SIP methods and responses used. A call tree generally lists the IP addresses of the SIP nodes engaged in the call and includes a running timestamp down the left side to identify the chronology of the messages. Call trees can also identify other aspects of a call, such as DTMF events, T.38 packets, and ports used for the SIP signaling and the RTP.

You frequently look at a SIP call tree as the first step in investigating a call issue. The call tree can indicate whether an INVITE was rejected or your carrier was unable to complete your call for some reason. You may need only these overviews to confirm that you need to report the problem to your VoIP carrier or call to your hardware vendor to address an issue with the Dial Plan of your VoIP phone system.

Wireshark is my analysis tool of choice for investigating SIP issues at the individual call level. It's such an important VoIP tool that Chapter 11 covers it in detail, along with tcpdump, another packet capture software that is used more for capturing data than analyzing it. You and your carrier should see the same call trees. If you ever see an INVITE or a response in your call tree that your carrier didn't receive on its call tree, investigate your Internet provider because as long as the packet left your SIP proxy, your Internet provider must have lost or discarded that packet.

Chapter 11

Analyzing Calls with Wireshark

*Y*ou can use the structure of VoIP to help you troubleshoot any problem. All the messaging that flows from your SIP server to the SBC or proxy of your carrier is physically flowing through a server on the edge of your LAN. The information moving between your SIP server and your carrier includes all the SIP methods and responses exchanged in the banter of setting up and tearing down calls. Gaining access to this conversation allows you to analyze the inner workings of the call, shortcutting the troubleshooting process and reducing the impact of the issue on your company. Fortunately, you can find free software only a download away that allows you to see everything going on between your SIP server and your VoIP carrier. It's called Wireshark.

Wireshark is the world's best network protocol analyzer. The only problem with this amazing tool is the curious absence of documentation about how to use it for VoIP analysis. Most people associate software built to capture packets on a computer or a LAN with malicious hackers using it to snoop on people's computers to find passwords. Despite the history of this type of software, you can use it as a powerful tool for VoIP analysis. This chapter covers all the bits and pieces that you need to know about Wireshark.

Introducing Wireshark

Wireshark is easy-to-use software that allows you to capture and analyze packets running through your LAN.

Many people who work with LANs and were around during the initial phase of VoIP know Wireshark by its old name, Ethereal. Since those days, the Wireshark team splintered away from Ethereal and continued to develop and refine the software. The newest version is color-coded and chock full of new features and options.

If you're running a SIP server, you need Wireshark. The software has two functions, one simple and one complex:

- ✔ Capture all packets flowing through the hardware on which Wireshark is deployed.
- ✔ Analyze the captured packets in an intuitive and logical manner.

Capturing the packets is an easy task. The software makes copies of every packet flowing through that piece of hardware on the LAN for as long as you keep the capture open. After you close the capture, the file is complete. You can copy, and transfer it anywhere for analysis.

Wireshark isn't the only software that performs packet capturing, and many people actually use other programs, such as tcpdump, for this step in VoIP call analysis. Wireshark and tcpdump each have complementary strengths, so I give you the code needed to install each in this chapter. You may be able to more easily capture data by using tcpdump, but you can more easily view the data in a dynamic display by using Wireshark. The two types of software don't conflict, and you can have both systems available on the same server without a problem. You can decide which software you install and use for a particular task — capturing or viewing. I recommend using Wireshark to view any capture file. The only real question is if you prefer to use the command line of tcpdump or if you have the ability to use the interface for Wireshark.

You can find varieties of Wireshark for many operating systems, from Linux to Mac to Windows. Whatever operating system your SIP server is running, you should be able to find a compatible Wireshark version.

After Wireshark or tcpdump completes the packet capture, you can move the resulting file of data to a PC that's running Wireshark for analysis or e-mail the file to a technician. You can much more easily dissect the capture from the comfort of your desk than to engage in analysis of a packet on your server that executed the capture. Wireshark truly shines when it comes to network protocol analysis. It provides definitive, empirical data on VoIP issues, and that data allow you to decide when to escalate trouble issues and to whom when you experience SIP related call failures.

Wireshark is compatible with most of the available packet capture software on the market. If you have an office or device that uses Snoop, WinDump, or dsniff to capture the packets, Wireshark has no problem reading the file. Depending on the server that you use for your VoIP, you may find it easier to capture the data with one program and then transfer it to your PC, where you can read it with Wireshark.

You may want to use Wireshark because

- It's free.
- It allows you to see the inner-workings of your LAN.
- It easily identifies all packets associated with specific VoIP calls.
- It creates SIP trees outlining the messages used on a VoIP call.
- It allows you to easily find RFC2833 DTMF events.
- It provides a file that you can forward to your VoIP provider to aid in troubleshooting.

Installing Wireshark

You can find Wireshark at www.wireshark.org. Acquiring it for a PC that runs Window is as simple as clicking Get Wireshark Now for Windows on the Web site.

Downloading for Windows

The screen refreshes while the software downloads. A window appears, asking you to either Save or Run the program wireshark-setup-1.0.0.exe (or the latest update number). Select the Run option, and the software beings downloading to your PC.

After the software downloads, click the Next button to begin a standard installation process. It starts off with the standard terms and conditions of the software agreement that you must acknowledge by clicking on the "I Accept" button. Then, the next screen, where you must select the type of installation you want, appears. I recommend installing everything. It's much easier to go to your Control Panel and Add/Remove the specific program, rather than chase it down and add it later.

The available elements to install include

- **Wireshark:** The main protocol analyzer that you definitely need.
- **Tshark:** The command-line version of Wireshark that functions more like tcpdump in that you don't need an operating system that looks like MS Windows to run a capture.
- **Rawshark:** An advanced version of Tshark that you probably won't use for VoIP.
- **Plug-ins/extensions:** These are software elements that allow Wireshark to dissect the many varieties of software protocols in a capture.

  ✔ **Tools:** The tools allow Wireshark to easily analyze packet captures executed by other programs such as T-Shark or tcpdump.

  ✔ **User's Guide:** This is a very brief user's guide for the features and options of Wireshark.

Click Next after you select the options that you want to install. The screen that appears prompts you to install shortcuts.

The Wireshark installation gives you several shortcut options, so install them all — after all, it takes just a second to delete a shortcut if you decide that you don't want it. Select the shortcut options you want, and click Next to proceed.

The next screen identifies the destination folder where the file will be located, generally at `C:\Program Files\Wireshark`. You can browse and place the file anywhere you want, but it's always best to keep it in the program files to keep them away from the folders you use often where you could easily delete or move a section of the software on accident. Click the Next button to proceed.

The software finishes up by prompting you to install WinPcap before getting to the dirty work of extracting all the files and installing the software. WinPcap is a packet capture software that you can use with Windows. If you plan to capture packets on your PC, download it. Generally, you don't need it to analyze the captures for your VoIP calls.

Downloading for Linux

Linux is the main operating system used to run Asterisk. If you're familiar with Linux, you know that Linux doesn't have just one operating system. It's more like a family of operating systems that all share a common infrastructure. You can find many permutations of the standard Linux operating system. Each version of Linux is called a *distribution* (or *distro*) and can contain any number of features and supporting software called dependencies.

The many distros of Linux and their unique features and dependencies create a challenge when you want to either retrieve or install Wireshark. You may not know how many of the development tools your specific variety of Linux has until you start trying to download and install the software.

Hire the best person for the job to install Wireshark on your Linux server. If you don't have management rites to the system, and sufficient access to the main directory (the root directory) of the Linux server or aren't comfortable working in Linux, hire whoever installed your server, does have root access, and is comfortable with Linux.

The following sections give you enough information for a simple installation, but if it goes south, call in a professional for help.

Installing the easy way — YUM!

The easiest way to install Wireshark is by letting Linux do it all for you. The hundreds of Linux distros available complicate the simple task of ensuring that you have the right development tools and dependencies for a fast and easy installation.

You can use a process to identify the dependencies that you need for your specific distro of Linux, but you can most easily ensure that you have everything by installing (or confirming you already have) the Yellow dog Updater, Modified (YUM) package management utility.

YUM is the development tool package for Linux Fedora. If you aren't running a Fedora distro, this utility may not work. If YUM doesn't work on your distro, you need to do a normal, non-YUM installation, which I explain in the following section.

Do a Google search for "Linux YUM" to find a Web site from which you can download the software, if you don't already have it.

You must be logged in to the root directory to load Wireshark or YUM. If you don't have root level access to your Linux server, either use the `su root` command to gain temporary root access or have your Linux administrator handle the installation.

When you have root access, type the following:

```
yum install wireshark-gnome
```

The process to retrieve and install Wireshark is just that simple. YUM finds the latest version of Wireshark, and downloads and installs both Wireshark and its dependencies.

After you install Wireshark, skip to the section "Installing tcpdump," later in this chapter.

Taking the second option on a Linux installation

If you don't have YUM on your distro of Linux, don't fret. As long as you have a full compliment of development tools, the procedure is still straightforward. Execute the following commands from the Linux command-line interface (CLI) to install Wireshark on your Linux server:

```
mkdir /usr/src/tarballs
cd /usr/src/tarballs
wget http:///www.wireshark.org/download/src/wireshark-
          1.0.0.tar.gz
```

Wireshark is continually evolving, so check to determine the current revision available. Visit the `www.wireshark.org` Web site to find out which version of Wireshark is currently available. Then, replace the final portion of the `wget` command in the preceding code with it — `wireshark-X.X.X.tar.gz`.

The `wget` command accesses the Internet and downloads the `tar.gz` file that you specify. After the file is downloaded in the `/usr/src/tarballs` file that you created with the preceding code, you need to execute this command:

```
tar -zxvf wireshark-1.0.0.tar.gz
```

This command unzips the file, and all the contents of the `tar.gz` file race up your screen while also being placed in a directory named Wireshark-1.0.0. After all the individual files are open and available, enter the new directory and complete the installation process by executing this code:

```
cd wireshark-1.0.0
make
make install
```

If you have any problems executing the `make` or `make install` commands, you're missing some of the Linux development tools. Without all these tools, installing Wireshark becomes a long and drawn-out process. While still in the wireshark-1.0.0 directory, issue the following command:

```
./configure
```

More text flies up your screen while Linux runs through all the software elements required to install the program in the directory. It stops on the first element missing from the development tools that you need to install the package.

So, you know at least one tool that you need but don't have. But identifying all the missing pieces of software, downloading them from the Internet, and installing them all can take a lot of time and effort. And you may very well be unable to load one of the missing software pieces that you need because it requires you to install more dependencies first.

After you install each dependency, you must return to the Wireshark-1.0.0 directory, execute the same `./configure` command, and wait for the scroll of information to stop at the next dependency required. The process of installation and `./configure` provides the name of the next software element required that you must find, download, and install before continuing the process all over again until nothing stops the install.

Installing tcpdump

You must have a full set of development tools for your Linux distro if you want the acquisition and installation of tcpdump to come together quickly without spending time chasing down dependencies, and dependencies of dependencies.

Visit www.tcpdump.org before you begin downloading the tcpdump files. The software developers working on tcpdump are constantly revising and updating the software, so the versions of libpcap and tcpdump that you need may have changed since the writing of this book. Write down the name of the latest versions and modify the commands used to retrieve and install the software found below in this section to match the correct libpcap-*X.X.X*.tar.gz and tcpdump-*X.X.X*.tar.gz files to be downloaded.

tcpdump installation requires root level access in Linux. When you have logged in and gained root level access, execute these commands. The first line simply creates a directory to store the files you will retrieve, and the second moves you into that directory so you can retrieve the files into it. The wget commands are executed one at a time and if executed correctly, a lot of text files up the screen of your computer after you click the enter key at the end of them. The command sequence is:

```
mkdir /usr/src/tarballs
(if directory does not exist)

cd /usr/src/tarballs
wget http:// www.tcpdump.org/release/libcap-0.9.8.tar.gz
wget http:// www.tcpdump.org/release/tcpdump-3.9.8.tar.gz
```

The wget commands access the specific files at www.tcpdump.org and download them.

After both files are downloaded, issue the next set of commands:

```
tar -zxvf libpcap-0.9.8.tar.gz
cd libpcap-0.9.8
make
make install

cd ../

tar -zxvf tcpdump-3.9.8.tar.gz
cd tcpdump-3.9.8
make
make install
```

The first line of code unzips the tar.gz file and creates a directory called libcap-0.9.8. The second line of cd libcap-0.9.8 moves you into the libpcap-0.9.8 directory so you can execute the make and make install commands that, again, send text up the screen of the computer and install the software located in that directory. The cd ../ command sends you back to the previous tarballs directory so you can perform the whole procedure again on the tcpdump file.

Starting and Stopping a Packet Capture

You always want to capture packets as efficiently and concisely as possible. Starting a capture and leaving it unattended gives you a huge data file that you have to sift through for information. Start packet captures just before a test call, and then close the capture immediately after completing the test call.

The exact location of the packet capture command varies, depending on how you loaded the tcpdump software. A package management application may establish the packet capture command in one location, but you may have manually installed it somewhere else. Fortunately, you can easily track down the capture file by viewing the Linux command used to initiate it. The command commonly identifies the destination file location, allowing you to let the capture reside in the default directory (where you or your technician installed tcpdump or Wireshark) or in another directory that you specified.

Capturing packets with tcpdump

The tcpdump command-line syntax can be complex and includes many elements that you may never need to use. You execute the packet capture for tcpdump from a Linux session with this command:

```
tcpdump -w newfilename.log expression
```

The preceding command is made up of the following elements:

- **tcpdump:** Tells Linux the software you're using.
- **-w newfilename.log:** Identifies the name that Linux attributes to the capture file. Change the name for each packet capture by adding a number to them, such as capture1, capture2, and capture3. You can make multiple captures while identifying the chronology of those captures.
- **expression:** Identifies the specific elements to which you want to restrict your search. Do a little research of possible expressions in the manual page of tcpdump to figure out how to restrict your search to only the data you require. For example, the following expression captures data on only port 5060, to or from the specified host:

```
host 192.100.100.100 and port 5060
```

The capture continues until you stop it by pressing Ctrl+C.

Figure 11-1 identifies the participants of a VoIP call and the conversations that your VoIP proxy enabled with tcpdump can capture. The port or IP address that you specify as the basis for your capture restricts the data that the tcpdump receives.

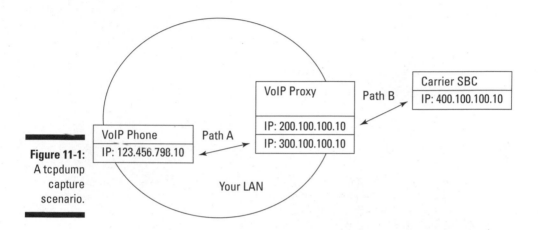

Figure 11-1: A tcpdump capture scenario.

VoIP Proxy

IP: 200.100.100.10

IP: 300.100.100.10

Path B

Carrier SBC

IP: 400.100.100.10

VoIP Phone

IP: 123.456.798.10

Path A

Your LAN

The most important information that you need when capturing data is the IP address or port from which (or to which) you want to focus the capture. To initiate a capture from the main IP address of 200.100.100.10 listed in Figure 11-1, execute the following command from the Linux CLI:

```
tcpdump -w Newtestfile.log host 200.100.100.10
```

Packet-capturing software can monitor a network interface, such as an IP port, in two ways:

- **Promiscuous mode monitoring:** Captures all packets traveling across the interface, regardless of whether they're originating from or terminating at the tcpdump's VoIP proxy. Tcpdump installed on your SIP proxy captures packets that pass through the proxy, but originate from other devices on the LAN, if the software is in promiscuous mode.

  tcpdump runs in promiscuous mode by default.

- **Nonpromiscuous mode monitoring:** Restricts the packets captured to only the data received by or sent from the specific interface identified in the capture.

The information gathered in the capture is saved as a file called Newtestfile. log that was specified in the line of code used to initiate the capture. As mentioned before, you can name the capture files whatever you want, and place their names in a sequence as well if you are executing several captures in rapid succession. The capture file tcpdump saves in the same directory as the rest of your tcpdump software (unless you specify a full path name along with your filename in the line of code you use to initiate the capture). The promiscuous mode capture file includes information about all data transferred through that IP address, not just the SIP, SDP, and RTP information for the test call.

Promiscuous mode monitoring captures every packet of data passing through the server running the capture. This can generate huge files of data due to other LAN traffic that isn't applicable to the research you may be doing. This could result in a slower response time when trying to open or analyze a packet capture. To avoid distilling the information after the fact, simply execute the command in nonpromiscuous mode, as follows:

```
tcpdump -w Newfilename.log -p host 200.100.100.10 or host
        400.100.100.10
```

Capturing packets with Wireshark

You may find capturing packets with Wireshark much simpler than with tcpdump, as long as your version of Linux has a GUI interface. If your distro doesn't have a GUI desktop that resembles the desktop of a Mac or Windows PC, then you need to use the command-line version of Wireshark called TShark. If your only Wireshark option is to use TShark, just use tcpdump to capture the data because the commands required are easier and presented for you in the previous section of this chapter.

To start and stop a capture by using the Wireshark GUI, follow these steps:

1. **Choose Capture⇨Options from the main menu bar.**

   A window pops up, identifying all the available capture options.

2. **Select the options you want and confirm the choices.**

   These options include the interface, capture filter, and any other specifics you require.

   The software provides drop-down lists whenever possible for you to use when selecting interfaces and IP addresses on the server. The interface option on the menu bar lists the network devices from which you can initiate the capture such as Internet Port 1 or Ethernet adaptor. Wireshark allows you to further refine the capture using preset *filters* available by pressing the Capture Filter: button revealing specific ports and protocols the capture will isolate, ignoring all other packets that don't meet the filter criteria.

3. **Click the Start button to start the capture.**

   The options window disappears when the capture begins.

4. **Choose Capture⇨Stop on the main Menu bar to close the capture.**

Or click Ctrl+E.

5. **Select File⇨Save As on the main Menu bar and save the file in a location from which you can move or e-mail it to your PC.**

You can also execute the packet captures by choosing Capture⇨Interfaces on the main Menu bar. A pop-up window appears, identifying all the available interfaces from which you can capture packets. This window has a Start button conveniently located jn the pop-up window identifying the interfaces on which you can execute your capture, which makes beginning the capture easier than using the previously mentioned multi-step process. You can stop the capture either by choosing Capture⇨Stop in the main Menu bar or pressing Ctrl+E.

Familiarizing Yourself with the Wireshark GUI

The Wireshark GUI is the gateway to unraveling the mystery of your VoIP calls. It allows you to start packet captures, end packet captures, and sort the data that you get from those captures. The main window for the Wireshark GUI consists of

- **Menu bar:** Contains drop-down lists of options for the standard applications. The only two items on this bar you use when capturing and analyzing VoIP calls are the Capture section (if you're starting captures from the GUI) and the Statistics section (to isolate VoIP calls).

- **Tool bar:** Provides buttons to quickly start and stop captures, as well as navigate quickly through a capture. These are great shortcut buttons that you should investigate after you're comfortable with the basics of Wireshark packet capture and analysis.

- **Filter bar:** You use this bar frequently. The `Filter:` button automatically generates the filters that Wireshark uses in many instances. You need to generate a filter manually only if you're isolating RFC2833 DTMF packets to investigate why your DTMF touch tones aren't being sent or received properly.

- **Data windows:** Wireshark displays the data from the packet capture in these three windows allowing you to analyze the SIP banter on the call between the SIP nodes:

  - **Summary:** Provides a summary of the packet captured. The SIP methods and responses are displayed in this section, allowing you to see a high-level overview of the packets that make up the VoIP call.

  - **Protocol Tree:** This window displays the nuts and bolts of the SIP information. Selecting a row in the Summary window populates the specifics for that packet in the Protocol Tree window. The Protocol

Tree window allows you to expand the SIP messaging, the SDP, and the RTP to view the specifics of each and validate the information provided and negotiated.

- **Data View:** The Data View window shows the raw data collected in the capture and highlights the information that corresponds to the element of the protocol tree you've selected. You don't use this section of the screen for VoIP call analysis because you can find all the data you require in plain English in the Summary and Protocol Tree windows.

Figure 11-2 shows a VoIP call capture displayed with Wireshark. Opening a capture with Wireshark is very easy. As long as the capture being opened has the `.pcap` suffix, Wireshark may be automatically selected to open it. If it doesn't default to Wireshark, you can either

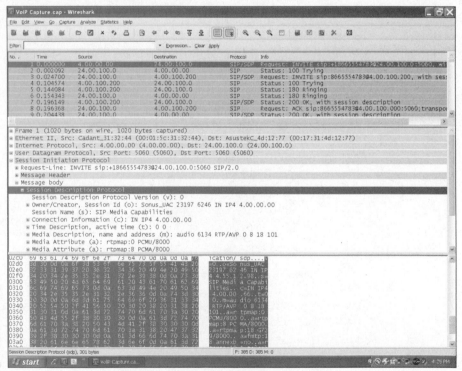

Figure 11-2:
The
Wireshark
GUI.

✔ Right-click the file and select Open With. As long as you have Wireshark loaded on the computer, it will be listed on the pop-up menu of programs, and you can click on it to select it.

✔ Open Wireshark and then choose File➪Open from the main Menu bar. A pop-up window allows you to navigate around your computer to find the Wireshark capture file you want to view. Highlight the desired file and click the open button to view the file with Wireshark.

After the file opens, the entire content of the capture is displayed, as shown in Figure 11-2.

Using the Summary window

The Summary window of Wireshark provides you with an overview of the packets in the capture.

The capture covers everything flowing through the device during the time the capture was open. If the capture was executed on your Internet facing router, it'll probably have TCP/IP traffic from Web surfing and e-mails, as well as the packets of your VoIP calls.

The data in the Summary section is grouped into six columns:

✔ **Number:** This column identifies the frame number of the capture. This very helpful section of the Summary window allows you to reference a specific line in the capture when speaking to someone. The capture in Figure 11-2 has an INVITE message sent in frame 1 and in frame 3. If you're sending the capture to your vendor for analysis, it's easier to speak about "the INVITE in frame 3" rather than "the second INVITE."

✔ **Time:** This column identifies the duration of time elapsed in the capture until the packet arrived. For example Figure 11-2 shows that, packet number 5 arrived 0.144084 seconds after the capture was started. This section provides the timeline from which you can track how much time passed between packets or events.

✔ **Source:** This is the IP address of the device that originated the VoIP packet listed.

✔ **Destination:** This is the IP address of the device to which the VoIP packet was sent. The INVITE packet in frame 1of Figure 11-2 was sent from the Source of 4.00.00.00 to the destination IP of 24.00.100.0.

✔ **Protocol:** This column identifies whether the packet listed was SIP, SIP/SDP, RTP, T.38, or UDPTL. Not every SIP packet contains SDP, so you can skip to the important packets as you need.

✔ **Info:** The Info column provides a summary of what's being said in the packet. In this column, you see whether the packet was an INVITE, 100 Trying, 180 Ringing, or 200 OK or ACK, to name a few.

The Summary window provides the general information allowing you to identify specific packets that need further investigation.

Branching into the protocol tree

Selecting a row of data in the Summary section of Wireshark populates the Protocol Tree window with all the information contained in that packet. The information is displayed from general to specific, and you can expand each section to reveal more detailed information by clicking the plus sign (+) to the left of the section.

The example provided in Figure 11-2 has the first INVITE message in packet 1 selected, displaying the specifics for it in the Protocol Tree window, including

- **Frame:** Lists the size of the frame captured.

- **Ethernet:** Covers data from layer 2 of the OSI model on the frame. (More information on the OSI model is available in Chapter 5.)

- **Internet Protocol:** The origination and destination IP addresses.

- **User Datagram Protocol (UDP):** This would be TCP in a standard Internet packet. The example in Figure 11-2 shows that the standard SIP signaling port of 5060 is being used for the source and the destination.

- **Session Initiation Protocol:** Used to research SIP and higher level VoIP issues. Expanding the lower-level section of the SIP protocol reveals the specifics of the IP addresses, ports, and codecs offered or established in the call. The SIP message in Figure 11-2 is expanded to show:

    - Request Line

    - Message Header

    - Message Body

    - SDP

Chapter 2 and Chapter 3 show normal SIP header and SDP information in detail. The Protocol Tree window of Wireshark allows you to see the specifics for the selected packet, ensuring that protocol mismatches or blatant SIP handshaking issues aren't affecting the packet.

Finding VoIP Calls

Digging in to a VoIP call is fun, but first you have to find the call. Not every capture you execute will be so clean as to start with the first INVITE message and finish with a BYE. The majority of captures you'll be looking at probably include ancillary TCP/IP information and other packets flowing through the LAN that may or may not have an impact on the VoIP call you're investigating.

Wireshark provides an easy way to isolate the individual VoIP calls in a capture, filtering out the unrelated packets. Click Statistics in the top menu bar and select VoIP Calls. Wireshark scans the entire packet capture, identifying all VoIP calls and populating them in a Wireshark: VoIP Calls pop-up window, shown in Figure 11-3.

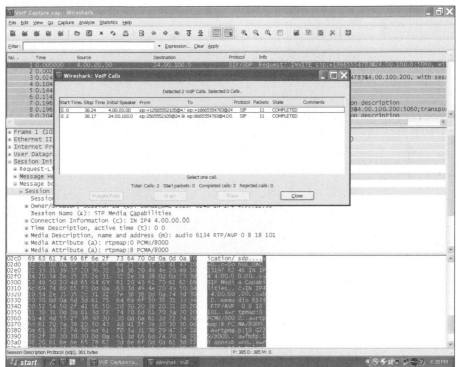

Figure 11-3:
Viewing
VoIP calls.

The window summarizes the calls by their general profile, allowing you to quickly see

- **Start Time:** This isn't the time of day the call began, such as 8:49 p.m. or 20:49 in military time, but the amount of time between the moment the capture being analyzed began until the call was initiated.

- **Stop Time:** The amount of time between the initiation of the packet capture and the final BYE message ended the call. This is not the duration of the call from INVITE to BYE, but the time in the capture when the BYE for the call was received.

- **Initial Speaker:** The IP address that originates the call. The first call in Figure 11-3 originated from the IP of 4.00.00.00.

✔ **From:** The origination SIP URI on the call.

✔ **To:** The destination SIP URI on the call.

✔ **Protocol:** Because you're looking at a VoIP call, it's listed as SIP. Despite the fact that only SIP is listed in the protocol, the call listed includes SIP/SDP and RTP packets.

✔ **Packets:** Provides the total quantity of SIP packets listed for the specific VoIP call. Other RTP packets may be associated with the call, but only the quantity of SIP packets are listed.

✔ **State:** Identifies the disposition of the call. The options include

   • **Completed:** Indicates a VoIP call that was established and was disconnected with a normal BYE.

   • **Rejected:** This call was refused by the receiving SIP node, most likely with a 404 Not Found or 503 Service Unavailable.

   • **Cancelled:** Identifies a call forcibly disconnected with the SIP method CANCEL.

   • **Call Setup:** The call listed in the capture was never established and includes only the initial INVITE message and provisional responses, such as 180 Ringing.

Graphing a call

The bottom of Wireshark's VoIP Calls window has four buttons that remain grayed out until you select a VoIP call to analyze.

The first button to select when analyzing a VoIP call is the Graph button. This option allows you to see a call tree for the specific VoIP call selected.

Figure 11-4 shows the call tree for a completed call, originating at IP 4.00.00.00 and terminating to IP 24.00.100.0 listed on the top of the graph. The dotted lines extending below these IP addresses function as a reference point for the IP as either the originator or recipient of each packet. The example is a very simple voice call running through the normal INVITE/200OK/ACK call setup.

The graph provides you more information about the call setup. Figure 11-4 shows that three codecs were offered in the initial INVITE — both versions of G.711 as well as G.729. The (5060) to the outside of each dotted line represents the SIP port used for signaling on the call. The 200 OK also provides more information, listing that the call was established as G.711u before the ACK was returned and the audio portion of the call proceeded. About 12 seconds later, the call concluded when the destination IP sent the BYE, responded to by the 200 OK.

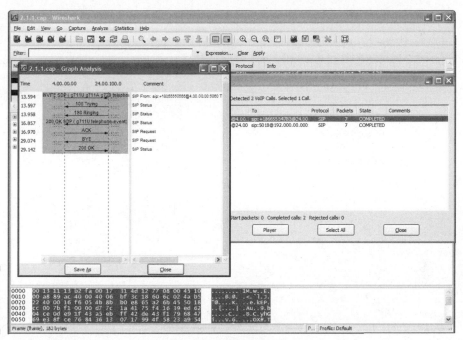

Figure 11-4:
A graph
analysis.

The example in Figure 11-4 is a simplified version of a normal VoIP call. The very nature of VoIP encourages the design of more complex networks. This frequently translates into the deployment of SIP proxies and intermediary SIP devices to facilitate connectivity. A single incoming VoIP call may then include two legs:

- Inbound from your VoIP carrier to your SIP proxy
- Outbound from your SIP proxy to the destination VoIP phone

In this example, both legs of the call are populated in the VoIP Calls pop-up window, but since they represent SIP messages cascading in from one leg of the call and out the other, it isn't helpful to look at each graph separately. You need to view both pieces as an integrated whole so you can instantly see how each call responded to SIP methods and responses that originated from the other leg of the call. Wireshark allows you to do this just as easily as viewing a single call graph.

Select both calls in the VoIP Calls window by clicking them individually or Alt-clicking the other call. After you highlight both calls, click the Graph button. The calls are now displayed together as one large graph with a different background color identifying each call.

Figure 11-5 identifies a call originating from IP 4.00.00.00 and passing through the SIP Proxy of 24.00.100.0 with a final destination at the VoIP carrier's IP of 74.100.00.00. This option clearly shows how the SIP messages bounce between the nodes.

This option allows you to view the SIP banter while it cascades across the SIP nodes from end to end on the call. This view makes it possible to find inconsistencies or portions of a VoIP call where a SIP method failed to receive a response. It's also a good place to identify when a SIP node continues to send SIP methods or responses, even after that node has received a legitimate reply from the far end.

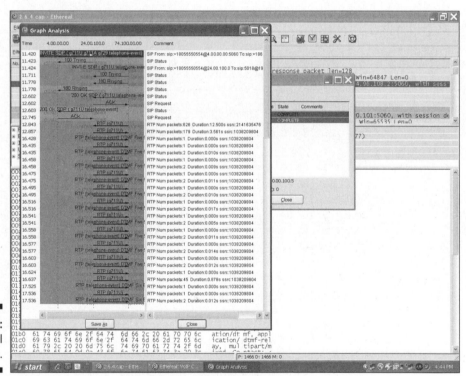

Figure 11-5:
Multi-call
graph.

Filtering down to one call

The call tree allows you to take a quick snapshot of the SIP messaging on the call before deciding to investigate it further. If you need to dig deeper into the individual packets of the SIP or SDP messaging, simply close the graph analysis with the `close` button at the bottom of the window and, with the individual call still highlighted in the VoIP Calls pop-up window, click the Prepare Filter button. A filter designed specifically for the selected call appears in the Filter toolbar of Wireshark.

Close the VoIP Calls window and then click the Apply button to the far-right of the Filter toolbar. The Summary window of Wireshark now includes only packets associated with that call. You can use this method to quickly and efficiently eliminate packets associated with other VoIP calls or auxiliary LAN traffic.

Now that Wireshark has filtered out all packets not belonging to the one call you're investigating, expand the sections of the packet in Wireshark's Protocol Tree window to display the Call Header, Message Body, or SDP sections, as you require. If you're attempting to follow the RTP port used for either the outbound or inbound stream, drill down into the SDP sections of the packet so that you can see the port number in the first line of the Media Description. After you expand the view in the Protocol Tree window, it displays all packets that you select in the Summary window expanded down to identify the first line of the Media Description if the highlighted packet has and SDP element to it. So, you can quickly scroll down packets in the Summary window, confirming that the details of the SIP methods and responses translated accurately from end to end.

Listening to a capture

A Wireshark capture doesn't only grab the SIP overhead messaging, it also captures the audio of the call in the RTP packets. You can listen to the audio of the call by using the Player button on the VoIP Calls window, located by the Graph and Prepare Filter buttons.

When you click the Player button, the VoIP RTP Player pop-up window appears, providing you the option to change the jitter buffer on the player before you click the Decode button. A new window now appears with both media streams displayed.

Figure 11-6 shows the RTP Player window in Wireshark with each stream identified below it. The RTP stream on the top of the window originates at IP 72.000.100.00 and is 20.66 seconds long. The small check box to the left of the identifying information provides you with the option to select one or both RTP streams to play at the same time. This option allows you to hear the exact conversation as it was experienced by the device from which the packet capture was executed. If the line experienced static, echo, or clipping because of packet loss, you can hear the degradation in sound quality for yourself.

Wireshark can play the audio on packet captures for only audio calls. If you're listening for handshaking or connection tones on a fax or a failed call, you don't get an RTP stream to listen to.

If you select a completed voice call to play and only one RTP stream is listed, that means you had one-way audio. Identify which RTP stream you have, either the outbound or the inbound. If only the outbound RTP stream was captured, you may have an issue with your firewall or Network Address Translation (NAT) blocking the incoming RTP. (NAT is covered in detail in Chapter 17.) If you have only the incoming RTP, check the Dial Plan for your VoIP phone system. Having only the incoming RTP indicates that something isn't mapping correctly between the phone on your LAN that originates the call and the part of your software that packetizes the audio for transmission in your SIP server.

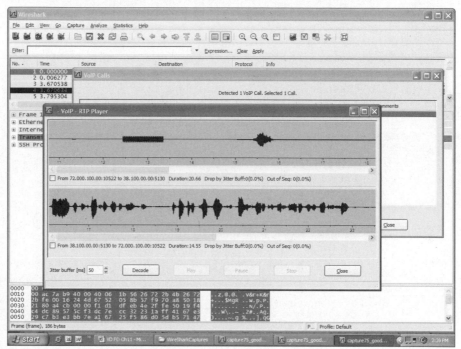

Figure 11-6:
The RTP
player.

Locating Touch Tones in a Capture

One of the challenges of VoIP is handling DTMF tones. They're used all the time, but they aren't really the ideal candidate for VoIP transmission. So, they come with their own set of complications.

Of the two types of DTMF transmissions currently promoted by the VoIP community, only the out-of-band RFC2833 DTMF tones are easy to find with Wireshark. You have the option to listen to in-band DTMF in the audio portion of a call with the player to confirm the receipt and transmission, but this option is available only if you use uncompressed codecs.

The RFC2833 tones are more mechanical. They aren't a tone at all, simply an event notification that your VoIP phone system reads to play the tone. Figure 11-5, which shows a multi-leg VoIP call, also shows another feature of

the graph — its ability to identify RFC2833 DTMF events. The graph identifies a long list of RTP Num packets associated with the number 5 being sent.
Viewing every RTP event packet sent with RFC2833 is a simple way to validate the transmission or receipt of DTMF packets, but you may need to drill
down on the individual packets to really see what's happening to the tones.

The easiest way to sort out the RFC2833 DTMF packets is with a filter. A filter
removes all the SIP and SDP packets, so you can't see when the DTMF packets begin in the flow of things, but the filter does allow you to focus on the
DTMF events themselves.

Type the following code into the window in the Filter toolbar:

```
rtpevent.event_id != 0
```

You know you've typed in the filter correctly when the background of the
window on the Filter bar turns light green. The background of the filter area
toggles from red to green, depending on whether the digits in the window
match a valid filter. Don't forget the space before the exclamation point and
the other before the final zero, or the filter will fail, and you won't get a list of
your DTMF packets!

Figure 11-7 shows DTMF digits displayed by using the preceding filter. You
need to pay close attention to three things on RFC 2833 DTMF events:

✓ **Sequence Number:** Located in the RTP section of the capture. It should
cascade up while other DTMF events are generated.

✓ **Event Duration:** Located in the RFC 2833 section of the capture. This
represents the duration of time the specific DTMF digit has been transmitted. Just like the sequence number in the RTP section, the value in
the Event Duration field should increase with each additional RTP event
for the same DTMF digit.

✓ **End Notifications:** Listed in the summary as DTMF Five 5 (end) in Figure
11-7. RFC 2833 specifies that there should be three end notifications for
every RFC2833-transmitted DTMF digit. Figure 11-7 matches the specification, so it includes everything you'd expect. The only difference on
the end notification of the DTMF event verses a normal DTMF event sent
is that the RFC 2833 section of the packet lists True instead of False in
this section of the code:

```
= End of Event:  True
```

Packets arriving out of sequence can be confusing for SIP. If one of the last packets of
a DTMF digit arrives late because of route flap, jitter, or any other reason, it can cause
some problems within your VoIP phone system. Ensure that your hardware is discarding out-of-sequence packets; your SIP server could perceive a DTMF end notification
followed by a late arrival as a second unique digit. Instead of discarding the packet
and understanding the transmission as 5, the wayward DTMF packet could make your

phone system read the transmission as 55. Reviewing the capture with Wireshark can very easily decipher this situation because the sequence number and event duration validate that the DTMF 5 packet that arrived late was a continuation of the original 5 DTMF digit and not a new transmission of the same digit.

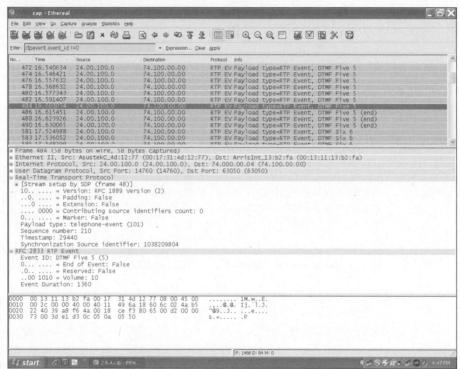

Figure 11-7:
A DTMF
capture.

TIP

If you need to view the DTMF event in context of the entire call, select a row in the Summary section and click the Clear button on the Filter toolbar. The selected packet in the Summary section remains in the same position in the Summary window, but all the other packets are now available to you, as well. So, you can place the DTMF packet in the context of the call or the flow of traffic on the LAN.

Checking a T.38 Fax Call

Faxing is the other telecom necessity that VoIP wasn't designed to handle. The transmission of faxing over IP is so specialized that it has its own acronym: FoIP (Fax over Internet Protocol).

Just like DTMF, faxes are transmitted over VoIP networks in two main ways. A VoIP network can either transmit the squeaks, squawks, and squelch of the fax in the audio stream of an uncompressed G.711 call, or it can convert the call into tiny .TIF files and send it with T.38. (You can find more information on general issues, challenges, and options concerning FoIP in Chapter 6.)

The basics of a T.38 fax call are very straightforward. The call is established as a voice call, either as G.711 or by using your choice of compressed protocol, and the RTP streams are established. After the call establishes RTP steams, one end sends a re-INVITE message that requests T.38, and the whole call is reconfigured in the same process of SIP methods and responses used to establish the call initially as a voice transmission, but this time negotiating T.38 as the transmission method and establishing UDPTL streams to carry the image data for the fax.

Despite the similarities in transmission options, sending a compressed fax is more complex than just sending DTMF digits. The T.38 protocol builds on and utilizes existing fax and modem standards to complete a transmission. This intensive protocol is built like Russian nesting dolls — the T.38 packets contain UDP Transport Layer (UDPTL) packets that in turn contain primary and secondary Internet Facsimile Protocol (IFP) packets.

The T.38 specification identifies the protocol as a two-phase protocol that includes the following steps:

- ✔ A primary IFP packet must be encoded (you also have the option to encode a second IFP packet).
- ✔ The encoded IFP packet is then installed into a UDPTL packet structure, which is also encoded, creating the finished T.38 message.

The stacking doesn't end there — a T.38 transmission may have two IFP packets, identified as a primary and secondary packet, each carrying a payload that uses yet another protocol called T.30 (a legacy fax protocol used for analog transmissions, as well as transmissions over IP with T.38). T.30 isn't the final supporting software of the transmission because it is in turn supported by a legacy modem format called V.21.

Figure 11-8 shows an expanded view of a T.38 UDPTL packet and the positioning of the IFP packets, T.30, and V.21 information. Each software element has its own job within the T.38 protocol.

The T.30 sets up the structure of the fax transmission, but it doesn't interact with the outside world — that's actually the job of T.38. T.30 instead establishes the rules of engagement, requiring an answering fax machine to send a CallEd station iDentification (CED) tone for about three seconds before the first handshaking message is transmitted. The CED tone is generally sent prior to the re-INVITE of the call to T.38; for outbound VoIP faxes, your carrier may use the CED tone to initiate the re-INVITE to T.38.

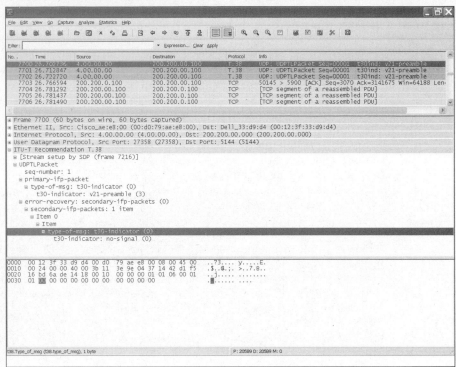

Figure 11-8:
A T.38
capture.

If you're sending a fax by using T.38, your VoIP carrier may initiate the re-INVITE to T.38 after it receives the CED. If not, your Dial Plan must include provisions to re-INVITE the call after it's established as a voice call.

Every SIP node interacting with the T.38 from your LAN to the network of your VoIP carrier must be employed to handle the protocol, otherwise the call will fail. You can easily see this variety of failure when you use Wireshark because you receive either

- 488 Invite Rejected
- 415 Unsupported Media Type

You must filter the packets by choosing Statistics➪VoIP Calls on the menu bar and either viewing the graph or employing the filter on the call to see whether the T.38 failed. The VoIP Calls pop-up window may display a failed T.38 call as COMPLETED because setup and tear down of the call were normal. The FoIP call was most likely established as a G.711 VoIP call and then re-INVITEd to T.38. If the T.38 fails, the call re-INVITEs to VoIP and issues a normal BYE. For this reason, you can see only the 4XX response code by viewing the filtered packets or the call graph.

Filtering a T.38 call by using the Prepare Filter button in the VoIP Calls pop-up window may result in only the SIP and SIP/SDP messages being displayed after the filter is applied, not the RTP and UDPTL packets. If you must drill down to that level, you can either

- ✔ Select a SIP packet in the summary section and click the Clear button in the filter toolbar.

- ✔ Select a specific SIP method or response in the Graph Analysis window (by selecting Graph in the VoIP Calls pop-up window) to locate a specific packet in the capture. You can scroll up or down in the capture to view the flow of information.

Using Wireshark to Troubleshoot

Wireshark allows you to see the messaging and signaling banter between your VoIP LAN and your carrier's SBC. This visibility was restricted in the days before VoIP to only large customers who used SS7 signaling to connect to their carriers and large dedicated circuits equivalent to 672 phone lines. Even if you had SS7, you still had to have capture software and a technician who could make sense of it all.

VoIP and Wireshark place the power in your hands. The more comfortable you are with pulling information in Wireshark and dissecting your calls, the more quickly you can resolve issues — and the less frustrated you feel.

You can best use Wireshark to troubleshoot call completion issues. You can't as easily identify call quality issues (for example, clipping, echo, and static) by using Wireshark, so either your carrier or your VLM software needs to pursue those issues.

Your VoIP carrier requests specific information from you when you report the issue. You may not have direct access to this information without a capture. You might not know exactly which outbound port it took. If you have a complex, least-cost routing configuration established, which routes calls by the area code and the first three digits in the phone number and includes roll-over to other providers if your primary VoIP carrier is maxed out, the Wireshark capture may be the only way to definitively identify which carrier processed the affected call.

When troubleshooting a failed VoIP call with Wireshark, follow these steps:

1. **Open a packet capture and redial the failing number.**

   If the call completes, then you have an intermittent issue. Continue to make test calls until you capture another failed call.

2. **Open the failed call in Wireshark.**

Open the file that contains the packet capture and identify all VoIP calls within the capture by choosing Statistics➪VoIP Calls from the main menu bar. Select the specific failed call in the pop-up window that appears.

3. **Graph the failed call, review the SIP methods and responses passed between your SIP proxy and the SBC of your carrier, and identify the source of the failure.**

   It may be as simple as your VoIP carrier responding to your invite with a 4XX response code or one end of the call issuing a CANCEL order. If the call failed because of a 4XX response from your carrier, open a trouble ticket with it engaging it for resolution. If the issue originated with your hardware, investigate the Dial Plan in your VoIP phone system.

4. **If the information in the graph is inconclusive, prepare a filter for the specific call and apply it.**

   Return to the main screen and review all sections of the packet to isolate any mismatch in the handshaking or negotiation by expanding all sections to include

   - **Session Initiation Protocol — Message Header:** Check the SIP URIs, IP addresses, and port numbers in the FROM, TO, and CONTACT sections.

   - **Message Body — Session Description Protocol:** Focus on the IP addresses and port numbers listed for the RTP, as well as the specifics of the media description, including the codecs offered and negotiated, as well as specifics for the RTP required in the media attributes section.

If you must open a trouble ticket with your VoIP carrier, it may ask you for specific information on the failed call. Figure 11-9 shows the information your carrier may ask you to provide.

Here's the information circled in the SIP message header, by location:

- ✔ **FROM field:** Origination IP address and phone number for the call

- ✔ **TO field:** Destination phone number and IP address for the carrier's SBC to which the call was sent

- ✔ **TO field (below the destination phone number and IP address):** The Call ID of the failed call

Your carrier also needs the basic information required in a call ID, which I talk about in Chapter 13, as well as one final piece of VoIP specific information — the 4XX or 5XX SIP response that results in the call failure. Not every VoIP call failure is rejected with a clean SIP response, but if one is presented, your carrier may ask for it.

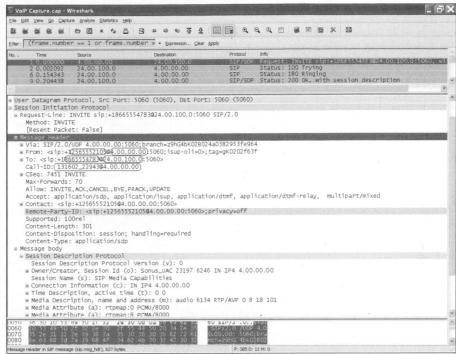

Part III

Maintaining Your Network and Service

The 5th Wave   By Rich Tennant

Don't worry, this is only temporary. Next week we plan to get you a chair.

BYG CALL CENTER

BYG CORP

In this part . . .

Troubleshooting is what you do after everything is deployed. It's an essential skill set for any technician, but very few technicians are trained in the theory and diplomacy of troubleshooting. This section breaks down VoIP calls into segments of responsibility. A phone call may span 1,000 miles from end to end, and you're only responsible for your section, so a step-by-step process is given to isolate and prove out each leg of the phone call.

The trouble reporting process is also covered in detail, identifying the information you must provide in order to open a trouble ticket, as well as some general guidelines for following up on issues once a trouble ticket is opened. The diplomacy of troubleshooting is woven throughout the section, because losing your cool during the process can make a bad situation worse.

A few problems specific to VoIP are identified, from fax failure and DTMF issues, to one-way audio caused by Network Address Translation (NAT) in your firewall. All the tools necessary to solve your problems are offered here in this section, so go forth and good luck.

Chapter 12

Troubleshooting Basics

• •

In This Chapter

▶ Getting the troubleshooting basics

▶ Figuring out a call problem's category and frequency

▶ Finding patterns in the frequency, geography, and time of day of a problem

▶ Defining your troubleshooting responsibility

▶ Reporting on VoIP crossed audio

▶ Troubleshooting logically

• •

You'll spend far more time troubleshooting and maintaining your VoIP network than you did preparing to deploy it. This period of time represents the final stage in VoIP Lifecycle Management and is punctuated by bursts of extreme stress and frustration in a landscape of otherwise mundane maintenance and review. I guarantee that, one day, all the planets will come into alignment, and it'll seem like every telecom catastrophe that could possibly happen is happening.

Troubleshooting doesn't need to be painful or frustrating, as long as you have a plan. This chapter gives you that plan and the standard rules of engagement necessary to reduce the impact of any problem on your network and your company. Keep your cool, use your tools, and you'll be back up and running in no time flat.

Understanding Troubleshooting Basics

Troubleshooting is a process in which you dissect a problem to identify the source of the perceived anomaly, which allows you to take actions to resolve the issues. It seems simple enough on the surface — a call is failing, so you need to find out why and correct it. The challenge comes when you have to decide the course of action to find the problem.

If you've been troubleshooting telephony problems for five or ten years, you may be able to tell the source of a problem before someone even finishes telling you the symptoms. If you haven't been doing it long enough to develop a sixth sense for it, you need a logical progression of tests to run through. Every test you conduct should build on your current information to further narrow down the source of the issue.

You're the beneficiary of a great gift — easy access to the overhead banter between your SIP server and your VoIP carrier. Traditional telephony lines or circuits don't allow you to gather information and pull it apart so easily. They don't have a Wireshark capture that you can download to gather up information in the overhead of your analog phone line or dedicated digital circuit.

Using diplomacy

The first rule of troubleshooting is that you must maintain complete objectivity. There's no better way to delay the resolution of a problem than to start the troubleshooting process with something fixed in your brain that "must be" the source of the problem. The worst part is that the data may outright refute what you believe the problem is. It's very common to jump to this type of conclusion, but you need to avoid obsessing that the problem must be a calls per second issue, or a carrier routing issue, or anything but your phone system.

In the end, you need to simply read and interpret the data. The data is the one thing in the whole troubleshooting equation that's unbiased and unemotional. Look at the information and pull it apart. It may lead you to one conclusion on Monday and in the opposite direction on Tuesday. Don't take it personally, the test results aren't lying to you, the conclusions drawn previously simply lacked the clarity brought to the issue today.

The main element of the troubleshooting process is people. The people working in the VoIP department for your carrier are nice people, just like you. I can assure you that they don't intend you to have problems, and they genuinely enjoy some aspect of the troubleshooting/repair process.

Your carrier's employees are human. They probably react coldly if you come in on a troubleshooting call with guns blazing and an attitude that "you guys are all screwed up." Someone can always find a way to spin a problem and make it "not their responsibility." If you strike up a good relationship with the technicians helping you, they respond to your calls more quickly and go the extra mile to solve your problem. If your conversations with your carrier are generally prefaced by you stating how worthless their network is and rhetorical questions about "why should I stay with you for service?", they avoid you and do their best to throw the blame on your hardware.

VoIP is still a relatively new technology, and nobody knows everything about it. Even if someone knows everything about VoIP today, a whole new realm of VoIP will emerge a few days from now about which he or she hasn't a clue. This fact makes everyone you chat with a potential resource of new information. The more the technicians and support staff like and respect you, the more apt they'll be to show you all the shortcuts and tricks they've figured out over years of working in their specific area of VoIP.

Troubleshooting can be a very emotional event. If you see the emotions getting too heated on a conference call, conclude the call and separate the two people fueling the argument. The main reason troubleshooting calls degenerate is because someone has decided that, whatever the problem is, it absolutely, positively can't be his or her hardware or issue. The finger-pointing mindset doesn't promote an environment in which people can effectively work together. You need to diffuse the situation and still get the requested tests done by following these tips:

- ✔ **Separate the antagonists.** End the conference call and act as the neutral third party. It may take a bit more time for you to relay information from your VoIP hardware vendor and your VoIP carrier, but in the end, it resolves your problem faster.

- ✔ **Tell your VoIP carrier that you know it definitely isn't its issue.** Even if every shred of data points to the fact that your VoIP carrier isn't processing the CANCEL request properly or that your software guy has an issue within your Call Plan, you can't tell him that. It might take a day for him to cool down, and you don't have that much time. It's always the most efficient to talk to each person individually and tell him, "I know this isn't your issue, but if you can just do this one test, we can prove that there's nothing in your system causing this problem." The opportunity to prove someone else wrong — and vindicate yourself in the process — is always a much better motivator than being browbeaten or threatened into doing a test.

Identifying the variables

Troubleshooting a phone call isn't as daunting as it may appear at first glance. The vast majority of the call path happens outside the realm of your LAN, over hardware that you don't own and through switches that you aren't responsible for maintaining. So, the quickest path to resolution is for you to do as many tests as possible to isolate the issue down to the responsible party, get the issue into it hands, and then empower it to resolve it.

Reviewing an outbound long-distance call

Before you can begin troubleshooting any call, you need to isolate the variables. The components of a call vary, depending on whether it's inbound, outbound, local, or long distance. The most common call you probably make is a standard outbound long-distance call.

If you want to know all the specifics of what qualifies a call as local, long-distance, outlying area, or international, *Telecom For Dummies,* by yours truly (Wiley), covers all this and much more.

Figure 12-1 shows the five main variables affecting an outbound call that's transmitted via VoIP and terminates to a non-VoIP phone number. Each segment in the call encounters a path for which a different entity is responsible. Starting from the origination of the call, the responsible organizations are

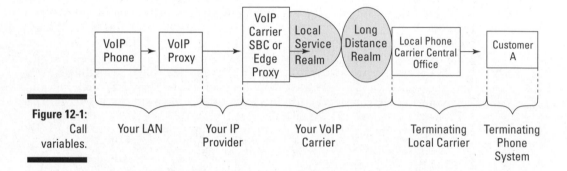

Figure 12-1:
Call
variables.

✔ **Your company:** The call originates from a VoIP phone, traverses your LAN, runs through your VoIP phone system, and finally leaves your responsibility when it's sent from your VoIP server to the SBC of your VoIP carrier. The majority of fluctuations in latency, jitter, and packet loss occur within your VoIP LAN. You need a fully-evolved VoIP Lifecycle Management (VLM) software package to effectively troubleshoot and manage this link in the call chain. I recommend the VLM solutions by Packet Island that are covered in detail in Chapter 9.

✔ **Your IP Provider:** It has the simple responsibility of transmitting your packets to arrive at the IP address of your VoIP carrier. It can potentially add latency and jitter to the transmission (sometimes caused by flap), as well as packet loss. It also has responsibility for delivering the packets sent to you in response by your VoIP carrier. Much of those transmissions traverse your VoIP carrier's IP provider, but your IP provider handles the final leg of that journey.

✔ **Your VoIP carrier:** Your VoIP carrier has the responsibility of receiving the VoIP call, transmitting it through its network, and potentially converting it from VoIP to integrate the call into the PSTN before delivering it to the local phone carrier that provides service to the phone number you dial.

✔ **The terminating local phone carrier:** The call is processed by the local phone carrier, which identifies the pair of wires belonging to the business or residence to which the phone number is assigned. After it identifies the phone number, the call is routed to ring at the recipient's site.

> ✔ **The destination phone system:** The telephone or telephone system of Customer A must ring, answer, route the call to the extension (if necessary) and send the proper signals back through the local carrier to indicate when the call is answered and hung up.

A call can fail because of problems at any point in this chain of events. Packet loss on your LAN or with your IP provider, SIP signaling issues, routing within any carrier along the way, or a bad phone at the far end can all kill a call.

Only the on-ramp to your carrier may be VoIP. Your carrier may convert your VoIP-originated call to traditional telephony directly after receiving the call. Your call may also be converted to and from VoIP several times during the transmission from end to end. The final leg of the call will probably be analog because most phones in America aren't using VoIP service yet (although the number of residences and small businesses making the switch is climbing).

Figure 12-1 isn't the only possible scenario for an outbound call. VoIP has been deployed within the network of long-distance carriers for years. Even before they released VoIP products to their customers, they were using VoIP internally. During those early years, many customers connecting into long-distance networks were surprised when troubleshooting issues with their carrier that their traditional telephony circuits were being instantly converted into VoIP after initial connection. The protocol flip-flop may have happened several times, when a carrier's internal network hardware converted the call back to traditional telephony, and then an underlying carrier converted it back to VoIP a second time. In international calls, VoIP is a common technology used to maximize the number of concurrent calls possible over a fixed bandwidth, because the cost of renting the circuit to the country it services is a huge expenditure and the more calls you can push over the same connection, the more money you make.

The good news is that you don't have to concern yourself with the sections of the call that are converted to or from VoIP. Your only focus is isolating an issue to a single company. It's the company's responsibility from that point to work through the complexities of its network and the networks of its underlying carriers.

VoIP technology changes some aspects of the troubleshooting process. Your VoIP provider replaces both the local phone carrier and long-distance carrier that you'd encounter in a normal telephony call. The local and long-distance functions are still separated, even within your VoIP carrier, because different hardware is required to provide local or long-distance service. If you're replacing your local analog lines, the VoIP carrier you select probably has a contract with one or several long-distance carriers to handle all your outbound calls. Even if you're paying a flat monthly rate for your service with no per-minute charges, they're still sending your call out to someone who's charging them a normal cost per minute.

Deconstructing a local call

Call quality issues, such as static, echo, and clipping, can occur at any stage in the call path. One of the easiest ways to eliminate some of the potential variables in the call equation is to see whether the same call quality issue is also present on other types of calls with different variables.

Figure 12-2 identifies the variables of a call to your VoIP phone from a normal analog phone in a neighboring town. The call flows from the analog phone, through its long-distance carrier, into the local service side of your VoIP carrier, and finally to your VoIP LAN.

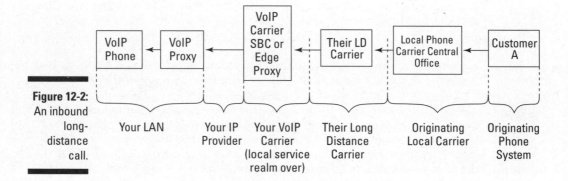

Figure 12-2:
An inbound long-distance call.

Your LAN — Your IP Provider — Your VoIP Carrier (local service realm over) — Their Long Distance Carrier — Originating Local Carrier — Originating Phone System

You can use the two call types represented in Figure 12-1 and Figure 12-2 to qualify or rule out similar and dissimilar variables. If you have static every time you call Customer A, but Customer A never has static when she calls you, you can rule out every similar variable as a possible source of the static. Simply comparing the two different types of calls allows you to remove the following elements as potential sources of the static:

- ✔ Your VoIP phone
- ✔ Your VoIP proxy
- ✔ Your IP provider
- ✔ The local service realm of your VoIP carrier
- ✔ The local carrier for Customer A
- ✔ The phone system for Customer A

This side-by-side analysis is sometimes referred to in telecom as *stare and compare.*

The simple act of placing the two calls next to each other provides you with the data that you need to *prove out,* or eliminate, some variables. If every call outbound to a certain phone line has static, but no inbound calls from that same phone line have static, then any piece of hardware that's used in both calls is vindicated as a potential source of the static. This logic isolates the issue down to the one dissimilar variable present on the affected calls, the long-distance side of your VoIP carrier.

Many call issues reside within the realm of the long-distance portion of the call, for no other reason than that leg of the journey usually covers the greatest geographic distance. The call may progress a few miles from your office through your Internet provider to the SBC of your VoIP provider. It starts the second leg of its journey when your VoIP provider sends the call to the long-distance carrier, which is responsible for transporting it across the United States (or across the world) before terminating it to another local carrier. The miles over which the long-distance carrier transmits the call means that the call potentially encounters more hardware and cabling while it spans from end to end. Every new piece of hardware or cabling is another aspect of the call that can fail and cause problems.

Now, not only does the long-distance portion of the call cover a lot of distance, so can the VoIP portion of your call.

Figure 12-3 shows what may be hidden behind the curtain of your VoIP provider. It may not be the only VoIP entity in the equation. The current market of VoIP providers allows for several layers of telecom carriers in the mix. The call represented in Figure 12-3 is a local call and never reaches a long-distance carrier's network. It might be an extremely local call, traveling only down the block to your office. The close proximity between the origination point of the call at Company A and the termination of the call at your office doesn't guarantee a geographically stunted transmission. This simple call in Figure 12-3 hits the following entities:

- **Company A:** Its analog phone dials your VoIP-provided phone number.

- **The local carrier for Company A:** The call hits Company A's local carrier, which identifies the call as being local and then queries the national database to determine who owns the phone number. In the example in Figure 12-3, the local carrier that actually "owns" the phone number is Level 3 Communications.

- **The VoIP carrier:** The actual VoIP carrier recognized as the legitimate owner of your phone number. It's easier to sign a contract for service with a VoIP carrier than it is to go through all the certification required to be a recognized local carrier, so most VoIP companies that sell you service don't go through the hassle. Because the VoIP carrier in this example is an established local carrier, it has presence in New York, and the call traverses only a few miles before it hits its network.

- **The VoIP reseller:** This VoIP middleman is named Juggernaut Telecom in Figure 12-3. Juggernaut Telecom is located in Dallas, so the call is sent to the switch that it uses to aggregate its traffic before sending the call on to your VoIP provider. This company doesn't own the phone numbers in the eyes of the national database, but it isn't the company you bought your VoIP service from, either. It's a VoIP reseller, among other telecom services, and it has enough traffic with the VoIP carrier to accomplish two important business functions:

- It can easily cover the minimum monthly payment that the VoIP carrier requires. The commitment always boils down to an expected level of revenue from the reseller. For instance, it must either have $25,000 in usage per month or pay the difference.

- The amount of traffic it has with the VoIP carrier is substantial enough that it can negotiate an aggressive rate structure, making it cheaper for your VoIP provider to buy service through Juggernaut Telecom than go directly to Level 3.

✔ **Your VoIP provider:** The wonderful guys and gals at VoIP R Us provide all the great features available with VoIP in this example. They don't own your phone number, and they don't have direct contact with the Level 3 — but they have a contract to provide service for you. The only problem is that they're located in San Jose, where their soft switch aggregates their calls and gives you all the fun VoIP features. So, the local call from Company A across the street from you in New York is now sent to California.

✔ **Your company VoIP server:** In Figure 12-3, the VoIP R Us server in San Jose sends the call all the way back to your office in New York, where it rings your phone, and you pick up to speak to the guy across the street. Maybe you can see him through the window, and you wave, completely unaware of the fact that your call has run all the way to California and back.

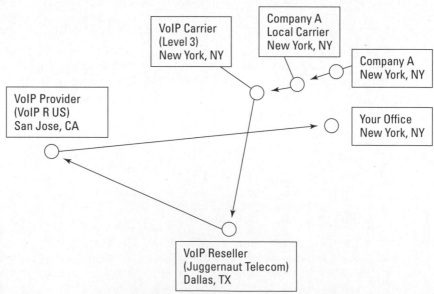

Figure 12-3:
A local
VoIP call.

The distance that your VoIP call may travel doesn't have to be a frightening thought. As long as every leg along the way allows the RTP portion of the VoIP call to be re-INVITEd, only the SIP messaging has to take the circuitous route through the layers of your VoIP supply chain. In the end, the audio portion of the call may be traversing only from the Level 3 site in New York to your office. This short distance is preferable because every hop induces more latency and adds another potential variable to the equation that can cause latency, jitter, packet loss, and call failure.

Identifying the Categories of Call Problems

Trouble issues fall into two categories — call completion and call quality. These types of issues are different in both how they manifest themselves within the reporting of the network and the troubleshooting techniques required to isolate and repair them. You can generally find and resolve call completion issues easily, but call quality issues are more subtle and require more intensive research.

Digging in to call completion issues

Call completion issues refer to any call terminating in a manner other than a standard answer at the far end by either a person or a phone system. A call failure can be the result of SIP messaging issues, packet loss (within the VoIP portion of the network) or non-VoIP issues within the long-distance side that affect all calls to the destination phone number. You can quickly and easily isolate all the potential variables that can cause a call failure issue, from routing through the PSTN, to the terminating local carrier, to the recipient's phone or phone system.

It isn't your responsibility to fix issues within the networks of your VoIP carrier, the local carrier, or the destination number. But your carrier always greatly appreciates information that you can provide to unequivocally narrow down the source of the issue to one of these variables, and this information expedites resolution.

The specific nature of call failures are further identified by their *call treatment,* the symptoms of the failed or substandard calls. Call treatments don't have to relate to only call completion issues — the term is also used to describe call quality issues. The main call treatments you encounter are listed in the following sections.

Understanding why "your call cannot be completed as dialed"

If you hear a recording that your call can't be completed as dialed, you may have mis-dialed the number, the area code of the number you're dialing may have changed, or a translation problem may have occurred in a carrier network along the line. This issue is generally confined to a single phone number that you're calling and isn't a systemic problem.

If you had no problems dialing phone numbers yesterday or this morning, and now every call attempt made to any phone number fails to this recording, you need to dig deeper and begin the troubleshooting process.

Understanding why "the number you have called has been disconnected or is no longer in service"

A recording that says a number has been disconnected or is no longer in service might be legitimate. The local phone carriers post this recording for cancelled phone numbers after the three- or six-month courtesy period is over, during which you would have heard the recording "this phone number has been disconnected, the new number is . . . "

If you know that the phone number isn't disconnected, either you misdialed the number, or there's a translation issue at some point after the call enters the long-distance network.

Handling an "all circuits are busy" message

On rare occasions, you may hear a recording that tells you that all circuits are busy. This recording rarely means that all the circuits available in your carrier's network are occupied, unless you're trying to call your Mom at 9 a.m. on Mother's Day, along with everyone else in the world.

This recording is generally played when your carrier has an outage of some sort and a portion of their network is down. If a backhoe accidentally cuts through a section of your long-distance carrier's fiber optic cable, that cable disconnect can potentially take down service for an entire city. In a situation like this, you probably hear this recording when you try to dial out (the carrier doesn't have a "sorry, our main fiber optic backbone has been cut by a backhoe" recording).

Listening for tones and tags

Tones and tags are supplemental sounds or recordings that can be attached to a standard recording. Tri-tones are three tones in ascending pitch that generally sound like they're being played by a cheap synthesizer. They precede a recording played by a local phone carrier, as opposed to something added by a long-distance carrier. The tri-tones let you know that you've reached the wrong local phone carrier, or the wrong Central Office (CO) at the correct local carrier.

The tags are more important than the tones because tags frequently provide valuable information to your carrier. Tags are attached to the end of a recorded message and usually consist of a group of numbers. A tag may be added onto the end of a recording, such as, "Your call cannot be completed as dialed. . . . 17-2."

The tag of 17-2 usually identifies the specific switch in the long-distance carrier's network that's playing the message. This information helps your carrier troubleshoot because it can go directly to the switch that's playing the recording to find out why the call failed, instead of chasing down the call example to finally determine the final switch.

Despite the wealth of information in SIP, it doesn't directly translate tones or tags into a SIP response. Your carrier may not provide you with the audio recording, it may respond with only an appropriate SIP code, preventing you from receiving this additional tone and tag information. Your carrier can still find the call and resolve the issue; the process simply takes a bit more time if you can't relay the tag information.

Understanding the fast busy signal

A *fast busy signal* is a busy signal that sounds twice as fast as the normal busy signal. You probably hear a fast busy signal when part of your carrier's network is down (that pesky backhoe again — see the section "Handling an 'all circuits are busy' message," earlier in this chapter), so your call can't be completed. Because this call treatment is interchangeable with the "all circuits are busy" recording, your carrier invariably gives you the same SIP response messaging identifying it.

Dealing with dead air

Dead air is when you hear nothing on your call after you dial a phone number. You don't hear the dial tone anymore, but you also don't hear any ringing; you just hear nothing. When you have a call with dead air, stay on the line for 30 to 60 seconds; the call treatment usually reverts to a fast busy signal if you wait long enough. It is possible for the call to eventually complete, despite not hearing any ringing on the line, or could fail to a recording. It's worth the minute or two of waiting to see what happens. The additional information could be the key to a quicker resolution.

Dead air is generally caused by a translation or routing problem that caused your call to be transferred to a piece of hardware or a circuit that no longer exists. Because the hardware no longer exists, nothing is there to send you a polite recording, busy signal, or anything. All you get is dead air.

Dead air isn't the same thing as Post-Dial-Delay (PDD). PDD is the silence you hear that usually lasts a few seconds between when you finish dialing the phone number and when you hear ringing from the far end. Every call has some PDD, thought it might last only a second. International calls are notorious for long PDD; anywhere from 15 to 30 seconds may pass before you hear the phone ring on the far end.

Encountering the aberrant recording

Each long-distance and local phone carrier has a handful of standard record-ings. Any other recordings that you hear probably come from your phone system. Almost every VoIP phone system has a library of recordings for almost every occasion. They may even have specialized recordings that exist only in your brand of VoIP software. Some of the aberrant recordings you might encounter are ones that say, "We regret that you were unable to access an outside line" or "Your long-distance carrier is currently rejecting your call."

If you receive any recording referring to your carrier, it probably wasn't made by the carrier's network. Always start your investigation by checking with your VoIP provider to ensure that it doesn't have the recoding in its library. If it confirms that it doesn't have it on file, then capture a bad call with Wireshark, or watch a bad call in the command line or console view of your VoIP phone system. See whether your phone system shows the name of a file in your recordings library that's being played.

Picking up dropped calls

Phone calls that are disconnected before either person hangs up are deemed *dropped calls*. If your phone system loses power while you're talking, it drops your call. The same thing happens if you're calling over a dedicated circuit that suddenly fails, whether it's the Internet circuit over which your VoIP is running or a circuit within your long-distance carrier's network.

The good news is that every call is monitored to see who disconnects the call. Your long-distance carrier's network records whether your SIP server sends the BYE or the analog phone on the other side hangs up and sends a disconnect signal. The switches handling the call actually have three possible options that it can use to identify the disconnect call:

- ✔ Origination end disconnect
- ✔ Termination end disconnect
- ✔ Other

The first two options are pretty self-explanatory. The switches saw either the originating or terminating party hang up. One of these results generally moves the troubleshooting along quickly. If you were dialing out from your VoIP server and the person you called had a power outage, the call could drop, and the network would see a disconnect signal from the far end.

The third option of Other indicates something curious — this option tells you only that the disconnect wasn't the result of one of the ends hanging up or sending a BYE or CANCEL. An Other indicates that the call ended because of a problem in the middle of the call path.

The good news is that a network event large enough to disconnect a call also generates errors within the switch that your carrier's network technicians can easily identify. The issue probably happened to many other people's calls, as well, increasing the reports of the problem and allowing your carrier to quickly triangulate the issue and resolve it. The bad news is that dropped calls are generally the result of a failing piece of hardware, and you can expect the failures to become more frequent until the carrier's network technicians find and correct the source of the problem.

Understanding call routing

Every long-distance carrier that receives a call must determine the local phone carrier that it needs to send the call to, and then it must deliver the call to the correct circuit to reach that local phone carrier. These activities represent two of the most common areas that cause call failures. Your VoIP provider generally handles the routing of your outbound calls by sending them over the carrier or underlying carrier that offers the least expensive rate for the phone number dialed. The level of complexity of the Least Cost Routing (LCR) configuration of your VoIP carrier depends on how advanced your carrier is and how many carriers it has available. If your VoIP provider is a standard carrier, such as SPRINT or QWEST, it has a very complex LCR and overflow routing system. If your carrier is a smaller reseller of one of these carriers, it probably has a few carriers at its disposal for a more modest LCR scheme.

The level of LCR complexity impacts you when you dial a phone number that has just been released, or is in a new area code that's been opened but hasn't yet been loaded into the routing tables of your VoIP provider. In these cases, the call may fail before it even leaves your VoIP provider's switch, responding to your INVITE with a 404 Not Found.

Translation is the process that a carrier undertakes to identify the destination or the network that must receive your phone call. Long-distance networks don't send calls directly to the end telephone that's receiving the call — the final leg of the call is actually the job for the local carrier. The long-distance carrier processing your VoIP call sends it to the local carrier's specified *central office* (CO). If the local carrier decides to change the CO that provides service to your phone, your long-distance carrier may send the call to the wrong CO, and the call fails. The translations department at your long-distance carrier corrects the problem because the translation of the number you dialed to the correct CO must be resolved.

Analyzing call quality

Both VoIP and non-VoIP issues can potentially cause call quality issues. Each technology has its own propensity for call quality issues. A short on the line can much more easily generate static on an analog call than the SIP side of the call can produce anything remotely akin to it.

Hearing the echo

Echo (also called *audio gain*) occurs when the audio portion of the call has excessive amplification that causes an audio reverberation the listener perceives as echo. Echo can be a VoIP-related issue, but it's more commonly associated with the long-haul section of the call while it routes through the PSTN. The main challenge with echo is that, like latency concerns in VoIP, it's a cumulative issue that collects from one end of the call to the other. Every piece of telecom hardware that processes your call adds a bit more volume to it, compensating for the audio loss while the signal is pushed from the originating local carrier through the PSTN to the terminating local carrier. This issue is more common with calls that cover long distances (such as coast-to-coast calls).

Usually, only one person on a call hears the echo. Carriers have specific pieces of hardware installed throughout their network called *echo cancellers* (or *echo cans*) that eliminate echoes on calls. These devices can fail over time, be mis-optioned, or be mistakenly installed backwards. If one person hears an echo on a call, a bad echo on the other end of the call is probably causing that echo. Sometimes, both people can hear the echo, but it isn't as common.

Echo doesn't manifest itself in a way that's immediately visible to the technicians at your carrier. If your call fails to a fast busy signal, your carrier can pull the call record and find the piece of hardware in its network where the call failed. Some issues, such as dropped calls or static, are visible in a circuit's performance report, which indicates an electrical or protocol-related anomaly. Echo on a call doesn't leave a trail of breadcrumbs, so it's a difficult issue to isolate and repair.

Clipping bits of your call

Clipping is the telecom term used to identify when random portions of your call are dropped. If you've ever spoken to someone on a cell phone in an area with bad coverage, you've experienced clipping when you lose bits and pieces of the other person's words and sentences.

In the non-VoIP world, clipping is seen as the mechanical opposite of echo. An amplification of the signal causes the reverb-generating echo; insufficient or negative amplification results in clipping. Communication between traditional analog land-line phones don't often have to deal with clipping and echo because the amplification levels of the carrier's switches and the local carrier COs have been refined over years to ensure sufficient signal strength without echo or clipping.

Packet loss within your VoIP LAN is the most probable cause of clipping in a VoIP-originated call. For this reason, any investigation into clipping should begin with your VoIP LAN, move out through your IP provider, and finally include your VoIP carrier. You must rely on your VLM software to isolate the issue. Excessive latency, jitter, discarded packets, a mis-optioned VoIP phone, or a failing piece of hardware that's throwing away packets without any good network reason can all cause packet loss. Finding packet loss on your VoIP LAN without proper diagnostic tools will be exceedingly difficult. Chapter 9 covers the best VLM software and the benchmark for what you use to manage your network.

Finding static

Static is the loud white noise you hear on the line, at times overpowering the conversation and forcing you to hang up and try your call again. This isn't a VoIP issue. It's generally caused by an electrical short in a specific section of cabling or hardware in the call path. The most challenging aspect of static is that you hear it only when your call passes over that one failing piece of hardware or cabling. So, the problem is generally intermittent because not every call to a specific destination takes the same path. Even if you call the same phone number ten times in a row, you may hit the identical path only twice. If you have static on 5 percent of your calls, the mathematical possibility of capturing one of the bad calls and getting it resolved in 24 or even 48 hours is slim.

The silver lining to this cloud is the fact that the electrical short generating the static is also sending errors into the network. Almost all circuits in the United States can be monitored for quality. This doesn't mean that someone from your phone company is listening in on your calls to ensure that they sound clean, but computer files can capture any unexpected electronic or protocol activity on a circuit. The networks use diagnostic files called *performance monitors* (PMs) that record electric and protocol anomalies. The PMs categorize potential trouble issues and any *erred* or *severely erred seconds* generated by a failing switch generally identify that switch as a potential source of the static you're experiencing.

Identifying the Frequency of a Call Problem

After determining what the problem is, your next job is to estimate the consistency of the problem. Can you get the same call treatment or call quality issue 100 percent of the time, or is this more of a 20-, 10-, or 5-percent issue? The frequency of the issue has a large impact on how you go about troubleshooting. The larger the problem, the easier it is to find and fix. Smaller issues that affect less than 10 percent of your calls can linger for months without being resolved unless you stay diligent and keep very good notes.

The key to resolving these kinds of issues is to be in full communication with your carrier and provide as much information as possible about both affected and unaffected calls.

Figure 12-4 shows the paths taken by three calls, all originating in Portland, Oregon, and terminating in Miami. The first call (represented by the single solid line) experienced static, but the second and third calls didn't experience any static. Your carrier can analyze these three calls to locate the path they took and then isolate or eliminate legs of the call, depending on whether the calls had static.

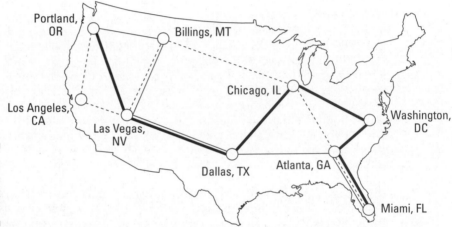

Figure 12-4: An intermittent call issue.

Laying the individual call paths over each other, you can see that the affected call took only two legs of the path that the two unaffected calls didn't take. Your carrier can assume that every leg of the unaffected calls is clean, so only paths that aren't shared with a clean call are identified as *suspect.* Your network technician can therefore isolate the sections of the network (in this case, the leg from Portland, Oregon, to Billings, Montana, and the leg from Dallas to Atlanta). You can see how more information helps to isolate an issue because every affected or unaffected call further clarifies and reduces the possible variables.

Figure 12-4 is a simplification of the possible route choices available on each call and indicates the calls being routed within the carrier's network, which allows your long-distance technicians to see the exact path. In reality, a call can take a multitude of possible routes, depending on the route cost, quality, and congestion.

Beware the underlying carrier. No long-distance carrier has direct connectivity to all destinations. So, it uses other carriers to transmit calls in areas in which it doesn't want to install fiber, switches, and service. Every carrier operates this way for the simple reason that it's a very good way to do business. The downside of these arrangements is that your network technicians can't see a call after an underlying carrier takes it. If a problem is specific to one underlying carrier, your long-distance provider can easily take it out of route or open a trouble ticket with it, alerting it to the problem and requesting resolution.

Isolating a Pattern

The process of qualifying a problem should progress from general to specific. After identifying the problem and its frequency, look for a pattern in which calls are affected. Depending on the depth and breadth of a problem, you may need to look beyond what you've identified in the general troubleshooting to find the source of the issue.

Any consistent problem is easy to find and track down. If every one of your outbound calls are failing 100 percent of the time, you can bet that something at your SIP server, IP provider, or the SBC of your VoIP carrier is causing the problem. Not being able to place calls is a huge problem that can have a sizeable impact on your business, but you can generally find such a problem easily. The smaller the problem, the more difficult it is to correct. If you experience a troubling but intermittent issue, you can help the repair process along by providing as much detailed information as possible.

Narrowing down the geography

A phone number that you've been dialing for the past three years probably won't suddenly start failing. Unless that phone number was being migrated to a new carrier and got hung up somewhere in the process, you should be able to consistently reach it. You likely can't reach your favorite client because of a larger issue covering his or her geographic area, rather than a problem with that individual number. These issues can include

- **An area-code split:** The widespread use of faxes, modems, cell phones, and pagers has dramatically increased the quantity of phone numbers used in any given market. You can create only so many combinations of phone numbers on the back end of an area code before you use them all. After that happens, North American Numbering Plan Administration (NANPA) has to release a new area code for the area. The geographic region covered by the old area code can either be split (with half of the territory receiving the new area code), or as an *overlay area code* that deploys the new area code in the same geographic territory. In either case, your call will fail unless you use the correct (new) area code.

- **Fiber cut/network outage:** This geographically sensitive issue occurs when the fiber backbone is severed, eliminating service to a specific area. The affected carrier usually take a few hours to find fiber cuts, a few more hours to dispatch technicians, and (in a perfect scenario) another few hours to repair the cut. If the fiber was crushed by a large tractor that needs to be extracted first, or if the fiber was washed out by a flood, the down time can easily span in excess of 24 hours.

✔ **Reallocation to a new central office (CO):** Local phone carriers are constantly responding to market demands. If you used to live on the outskirts of town five years ago, and now all the rural land around you is developed, your local carrier is providing service to many more homes and businesses than when you first arrived. It may have even deployed another CO to cover the increased demand and reallocated your phone number to that site. The information that specifies the exact CO that provides service to your phone is updated in the national database, but until all the other carriers download the information, it may send your calls to the old CO. The other carriers can easily fix the issue after they know that they have a problem, but if you know about any of these kinds of changes, you can greatly shorten the amount of time required to resolve the issue.

Area-code splits, overlays, and other changes that affect the CO that provides service to a phone number generally include a duration of time when the call will still complete, even if you dial the old phone number. This *permissive dialing period* lasts three to six months, during which you can reach a phone number by dialing either the old or the new area code. After the permissive dialing period ends, your call is rejected by a "your call cannot be completed as dialed" recording.

Matching up the time of day

One of the last troubleshooting patterns you'll use to troubleshoot a failed or affected call is the time of day at which it occurs. When the call occurs is just as important within your VoIP LAN as it is for your VoIP carrier. Say that you start your network backup at 4:30 p.m,. and your outbound VoIP calls begin to experience packet loss around the same time. If your call quality consistently, and only, drops during the back-up, you need to reschedule the back up or identify the bottleneck in your LAN caused by the increased packet flow. Be aware of the peak traffic times on your LAN because they can have an overall impact on your call quality and completion. It's better to know the times of day or days of week when the LAN is busy to avoid a long troubleshooting process. If you are unaware of the cyclical ebb and flow through your LAN, you could spend weeks chasing down a LAN congestion problem that only occurs once a month when you perform your monthly billing.

You need to view any problem that's time-of-day specific in the context of whose peak time is it. Carriers use underlying carriers based on call flow. They may have an underlying carrier that they use only when connectivity to all other carriers is full. This scenario of an underlying carrier that's only used for a few hours a day, and only for overflow can result in a failure or call quality issue that occurs only during peak calling times. These underlying carriers used only in overflow conditions aren't necessarily sub-standard. They may actually have a better call completion than the primary underlying carriers used, but are further down the routing preference because they are more expensive. The companies that can impact your calls based on the time of day include

- **Your company:** If your VoIP is integrated with your data LAN, you need to see whether the times when the issue occurs match peak times for data transmission. You may not see your LAN straining to generate the month-end invoices, but you sure can hear when it starts knocking out VoIP packets. If your peak calling or LAN usage time is 7:30 a.m. or 6 p.m., and you have staff reporting call completion or quality issues during that time, you most likely have an issue within your LAN because neither of those times match the standard peak calling time for long-distance networks.

- **Your IP provider:** It's the conduit between your VoIP server and the SBC of your VoIP provider. If it has a client that blasts it with spam every day at 11 a.m., the huge flow of packets running over its IP network may impact you, as well.

- **The long-distance network side of your VoIP provider:** Calling issues that crop up daily between 10 a.m. and 11 a.m., then again between 3 p.m. and 4 p.m. correlate to the peak calling times within long-distance networks. If your call quality or completion issue occurs only during these peak times, open a trouble ticket with your VoIP carrier.

Time-of-day-related call quality or completion issues have a distinct profile. You may be able to dial a specific phone number at 8 a.m., but if you dial it again at 10 a.m., you probably get through only half of the time. If you wait until noon, the call completes without incident. The same problem can affect call quality — you may have calls with clipping, echo, or static only during a few hours of the day, and aside from that, the call quality is acceptable.

Performing Your Due Diligence

Your network is your responsibility. Every link in the chain of your VoIP communication has a point of demarcation beyond which one company's responsibility ends and another company's begins. Your VoIP carrier isn't responsible for correcting problems in your Dial Plan or how your VoIP phone system responds to specific SIP methods or responses. As long as it follows the RFC as it relates to the situation, it doesn't want to make changes for your specific needs. Before performing all of the required testing to ensure a call quality of completion problem is not within your area of responsibility, you need to know where the responsibilities reside:

- **Your company:** You're responsible for sending accurate SIP and RTP packets with the correct headers, structure, and information. You also need to make sure that your Dial Plan or SIP server responds to all incoming RTP, as well as SIP methods and responses, according to the latest RFC.

> ✔ **Your Internet carrier:** It must transmit the packets sent from you to your VoIP provider and similarly route the incoming packets from your VoIP provider back to you.
>
> ✔ **Your VoIP provider:** It shoulder the greatest range or responsibility because it must respond to your SIP and RTP packets; convert them, as necessary; and complete your calls to the destination by accurately sending them through the PSTN.

Before you open a trouble ticket with your carrier for any issue, perform at least the most basic troubleshooting on your VoIP network to ensure that whatever's affecting you isn't an internal issue. The five or ten minutes you spend doing a cursory examination not only provides direction to the trouble-shooting, it also shows your VoIP provider that you know what you're doing.

Worrying about what your carrier thinks of you may seem odd, but the big faceless company that provides your VoIP service is run by people, just like you. If you call them up screaming because all your outbound calls are failing, they may drop what they're doing and call in all their best technicians to look at it. They'll work over the issue, and if they discover that they aren't receiving any packets and your IP provider is down, they're going to be less inclined to jump through hoops for you the next time you call.

To do your call-completion due diligence follow these steps:

1. **Pull a Wireshark capture of the failed call.**

   If you don't have Wireshark on your SIP server or your PC, go to Chapter 11 right now. No VoIP LAN should be without a packet capture software.

2. **Read the Wireshark capture.**

   Review the banter between yourself and your VoIP provider. Identify where the call fails, and the specific SIP response you're receiving on the failure. If you're getting a SIP response of 503 or 404, note it. Look at the last packet before the SIP failure response to determine whether it may be a response to something you sent. Do you think it came from the far end of the call on the other side of the PSTN?

Try to have a capture of a completed call to review next to any failed call you're investigating. You can much more easily stare and compare the two calls when they're sitting side by side, instead of trying to remember whether you were supposed to send +1 before the phone number in the TO field=. The side-by-side comparison allows you to check every aspect of how the call, the SIP, and the RTP is handled.

To perform your due diligence for call quality issues, especially clipping, follow these steps:

1. **Pull a Wireshark capture.**

You need a file to work with, and it always helps your carrier if you can provide a capture for any SIP issue.

2. Listen to the Wireshark capture.

Listen to the RTP and confirm that you hear the call quality issue. Wireshark should be loaded on your SIP proxy server, or the last piece of hardware on your LAN before the packets are sent off to your VoIP carrier. Executing a packet capture from your SIP proxy allows you to hear the quality of the call after it has passed from the originating VoIP phone through your LAN, and before it is sent to your VoIP carrier. If the call quality is poor before it even leaves your LAN, you can rule out any issues with your IP provider or VoIP carrier as neither of them have done anything to impact the call quality yet.

3. Leverage your VLM software.

Check the logs, reports, and available information from your VLM software. You especially need to use this software with instances of clipping on a call that's probably the result of packet loss. Check your latency, jitter, packet loss, and bandwidth use during the affected time.

Call quality issues are, by their very nature, more difficult to find than call completion issues. You may be able to identify the source of static through errors on a piece of hardware or a circuit, but echo and clipping can be virtually invisible to your carrier's network. Perform analysis on your network before you hand the issue off to your carrier so that it can focus fully on its portion of the call without lingering doubts that the whole problem resides within your LAN.

Reviewing a VoIP Curiosity

VoIP has many structural similarities with the SS7, the predominant signaling method within the PSTN. Both technologies utilize a call structure in which the *overhead* of the call (the SIP information in VoIP calls) is transmitted through a different path or circuit than the media/audio of the call. The fact that the overhead of the call and the audio of the call are split makes for a potential issue that can't happen in simpler telephony protocols — the audio of one call can potentially be swapped with the overhead of another call.

Figure 12-5 demonstrates the progress of two VoIP calls. Call A originates from 714-555-1212 and is calling out to 305-555-1212. The SIP header information and RTP have been given a background to differentiate them from Call B, which comes from 805-555-1212 and terminating to 212-555-1212.

The calls leave their SIP proxies and land at the SBC of their VoIP carrier, which transmits the individual streams to their gateway. The SIP and RTP streams are independent, so I grouped the SIP messaging and the RTP streams together in Figure 12-5 because the SIP messaging for both calls probably terminates to the same port on the SIP gateway.

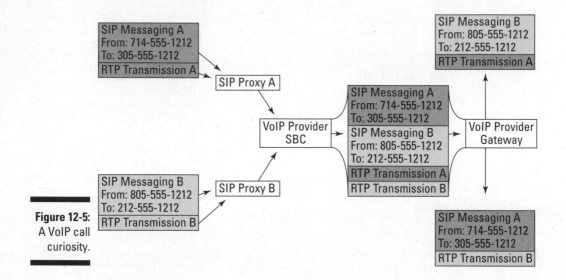

Figure 12-5:
A VoIP call
curiosity.

After the calls are received by the VoIP provider, everything gets a bit interesting. For some reason, the VoIP provider gateway in the example in Figure 12-5 mismatches the SIP headers and the RTP streams. You end up with a very challenging problem for two reasons:

- **The callers connect to the far end, but not to the numbers that they dialed.** The back end of the calls at SIP Proxy A and SIP Proxy B see the call intact, and the people originating the calls have those calls answered, but they have no idea why they reached the numbers that they did.

- **The calls appear to be fine, from a carrier-network perspective.** Because the SIP overhead of the call remains intact, the FROM, TO, and all associated SIP information looks fine. The call can be accurately traced back to its point of origin, and there's no evidence of crossed audio.

I've seen this issue twice; both times, it was deferred to an underlying carrier of the long-distance company with which I was working. The issue is difficult to isolate because the calls look fine on the surface. Crosstalk doesn't happen often in non-VoIP telephony, and it's generally caused by exposed or poorly insulated wires touching together, allowing the signal from one pair of cables to invade the other pair of cables. The issue is generally linked to electrical shorts on the line, and one person can almost always hear both parties on the other conversation.

The VoIP variety of an crossed-audio situation is completely different. It's a wholesale swap of the audio, in which both origination points make clean connections to the other's dialed number, just as if they initiated the call themselves.

The only way to positively identify what's happening is to have the offending VoIP carrier capture the VoIP calls with Wireshark. It can then read the capture to track the destination ports that the RTP of each call used so that it can follow how those RTP streams are handled. If an underlying carrier is causing the issue, your carrier generally can't easily accomplish this task. Your carrier has to open a trouble ticket with the underlying carrier, and then you execute test calls until the issue crops up. Your carrier can more easily route off the underlying carrier to resolve the problem.

If you experience this issue, copy Figure 12-5 and fax or e-mail it to your carrier. Not many people have heard about this problem, and carriers certainly don't want to admit to it. SIP does a really good job of linking together the SIP and RTP for a call, but with a rash of incoming calls into the SBC of an underlying carrier, things can get skewed.

Although I use SIP in the examples in this chapter, the issue can just as easily occur if you're using H.323 or any other VoIP protocol. I use SIP simply for the sake of continuity in this book.

Using Logic when Troubleshooting

Nothing happens in a vacuum. The process of troubleshooting involves finding a pattern for the issue that fits a profile. Chapter 13 covers troubleshooting and the trouble-reporting process for your carrier, but you need the correct mindset before you even open the trouble ticket with your VoIP provider.

Troubleshooting should progress from general to specific, with each test building on the knowledge of the previous test, further eliminating variables. To hit all the targets of troubleshooting, follow these steps:

1. **Identify the variables.**

   Draw how all the business entities engaged in the call interact with the call.

2. **Isolate the variables.**

   Confirm that every section in the call path is either suspect or proven good based on a comparison of call types (for example inbound calls have slightly different variables than outbound calls) or testing.

3. **Find the level of the issue.**

   Is this a global issue affecting all calls, or is it isolated to one phone number or region? You can link the profile of call failure or poor call quality to the level of the OSI model in which the problem exists. Chapter 5 covers the OSI model in depth, but if you have static that's most likely caused by an electrical short (a Layer 1 issue in the OSI model), don't waste time analyzing your IP addresses or SIP messaging (at higher levels in the OSI model) because they aren't the source of the static.

4. Identify a pattern.

If the problem always crops up at 5 p.m. on Friday or only when you call to New Jersey, you can refine your data to eliminate more variables, making it easier for your carrier to identify the issue.

5. Trace back to when the issue first began.

If your call quality issues began immediately after you installed a new piece of hardware on the LAN or upgraded your software, investigate those points first. You need to factor in any change made to your VoIP LAN, from the addition of a VoIP hardphone to the installation of routers or switches, when you're troubleshooting. The person who's responsible for reporting phone-system issues may not be the person responsible for maintaining the LAN. A little communication between these two people goes a long way in reducing the overall stress of VoIP deployment and maintenance.

VoIP can seem to disconnect at times. While you're dialing out, a port may suddenly seem to lock up. As far as you know, your server is sending the SIP messages, but your VoIP provider isn't responding anymore on a specific RTP port. Whenever you have an issue where the communication seems to have just stopped on a specific call for a duration of time, you have to dig in a bit deeper to the issue. Don't waste too much time looking into the connection between your SIP server and your VoIP carrier for that specific call — instead, check the last call sent on that specific RTP port. The SIP level interaction between your proxy server and your VoIP carrier's SIP server is very methodical. If you send a SIP method, you receive a SIP response. If you don't receive a response, something has gone awry. The issue is probably related to how the last call ended, rather than a failure in sending packets through your IP provider or a glitch in the SIP stack at your VoIP provider.

You can find a trouble issue only when it's present. Call captures of completed calls don't help unless you also have a failed call to look at, which is why large issues that affect 100 percent of outbound calls are so much easier to troubleshoot than a 5-percent issue.

Avoid any method of troubleshooting that resembles grasping at straws. A random series of "well, let's try this" attempts doesn't isolate or eliminate variables — and it's a sure-fire way to prolong the issue and increase your frustration. Before you dive in to a problem, make a plan that allows each additional test to build on the knowledge of the previous test. Each new action that you take must further isolate the issue or prove out variables — anything else is just an exercise in futility.

Chapter 13

Troubleshooting and Reporting Process

....

In This Chapter

▶ Reviewing your carrier's trouble reporting structure

▶ Giving your carrier a call example or two

▶ Managing your trouble tickets

▶ Troubleshooting outbound calls

▶ Troubleshooting inbound calls

....

*T*his chapter begins with an introduction to the trouble reporting structure of your VoIP carrier. I cover the information it requires when you open up a trouble ticket. That information is essential for it to solve the problem. I explain where to find the data, why it's necessary for resolution of your problem, and how to manage the trouble issues and your trouble ticket history.

The second half of the chapter covers the methodical testing process that I advocate in Chapter 12, fleshing it out for standard inbound and outbound calls. You isolate and resolve issues with the individual legs of calls, down to the companies responsible. The testing in this chapter isn't focused only on your VoIP LAN, but also the entire call path. The investigation of areas of the call outside your network consumes only a few more minutes but can greatly reduce the amount of time required for your carrier to correct the problem.

Depending on the size of your company and VoIP deployment, you may be troubleshooting a new issue every day, or you may have to troubleshoot only once a year. Regardless of how often you need this information, you'll be glad it's here waiting for you.

Investigating Carrier Trouble Reporting Structure

Most carriers have a two-tiered structure for handling problems. The first tier is the entry-level customer service folks. These people generally work from a script and ask you specific questions to qualify your issue. The customer service agent works through all the required questions and then gives you a *trouble ticket* number for tracking purposes.

Depending on your VoIP provider, this first line of defense may be able to pull packet captures on VoIP calls and do rudimentary troubleshooting, or it may simply be an interface to begin the entire process. Speak to your carrier to find out the testing and visibility capable that their first tier of support has. If it can pull packet captures and see detailed information, it may be able to resolve most of your problems without having to complete a trouble ticket and relay it to a technician — which can save you time and frustration.

If the first tier of customer service can't resolve the problem, the trouble ticket is sent to the VoIP network technicians, who make up the next level of support. These people can manipulate the network, update switches, and perform more intrusive tests, and they're empowered to fix the complex things that go wrong. You want to speak with this group of people when you have a complex issue.

If you have a difficult and intricate issue, give the first-level customer service people just enough information to open the ticket and then ask whether you can chat with a technician as soon as possible. If you begin trying to tell the customer service representative all the minutiae of the problem, it might get lost in translation from you, to them, to the notes, to the tech. Simply get the ticket open, press for a tech, and then explain it all after you're speaking to someone with knowledge of the technology and a few years in the industry under his or her belt.

Keep three facts in mind when chatting with the first-tier customer service representative:

- ✔ **The rep you talk to is probably working off an interactive script that has required information.** The system is constructed in such a way that you can't be issued a trouble ticket number unless all the required fields are populated. If you don't have all the information you need, things won't go far. Make sure you gather as many details as you can before you pick up the phone. For example, if you have a problem dialing a phone number in Cincinnati, but you don't know the number you dialed because you lost your notes, the carrier can't open the trouble ticket.

✔ **All the information you give guides how your problem is handled.** If you call in and report that your call to a specific phone number is failing to a fast busy signal, it's going to send the call to its routing department to research that one specific call. It looks at all the routing information from the IP of its SBC where your call was received, going from your SIP message to the final local carrier that should be completing the call. If you realize that all your calls are failing, you have to call back in and update the ticket, and the issue is sent to another department to check the SBC and the interaction of the SIP stack. All the updating and redirecting takes time — a luxury that you don't have when your service is down.

✔ **The person who opens your ticket is one of your greatest allies.** He or she can escalate the ticket on your behalf, monitor its progress, and call in favors to resolve your issue. Because the customer service rep is capable of doing so much for you (and has the power to do nothing at all), always be nice. If the customer service person you're chatting with doesn't understand what you're requesting or the specific complexities of it, graciously ask for a supervisor.

Providing a Call Example

A call example contains detailed information that allows your carrier to follow the call's path from the moment the INVITE message was received by its SBC to the point where it either completed or failed. As technical as the idea sounds, a *call example* is just basic information that you've written down about a failed call. After you dial out and get a "cannot be completed as dialed" recording, dial the number again and write down the necessary information (see the following sections for more information about what to include in your notes). When the carrier finds the call's endpoint, the technician can begin correcting the issue.

Call examples tell the technicians where to look for the problem and also allow the customer service rep to categorize the issue. Based on the information you provide, the customer service rep sends your issue to a specific department for repair.

Call examples might not be easy to come by in all instances. If you're calling a number that you dial often and the call fails, you have all the necessary information at hand to open a trouble ticket. The challenge comes when customers who are dialing in to your VoIP phone numbers have issues. Most people won't dial back into your company to report a problem that they had in reaching you. Unless they have your cell phone number, they may not have another way to reach you to report the issue. Even if they get through to you, you probably don't want to begin your conversation with a quiz about the specifics of a failed call attempt. As a result, you might have to ask one of your customers to make test calls for you.

Call examples have a shelf life of about 24 hours. The specific information about how the call is routed is kept in your carrier's switches for a finite amount of time before it's overwritten with new, more recent calls. If an issue crops up on Friday at 5 p.m., you need to relay it to your carrier immediately. If you provide the call example from Friday when you come into the office on Monday, your carrier will probably reject it and ask for a fresh example from within the past day.

Providing call example basics

Every call example, whether VoIP or non-VoIP, must begin with basic information:

- **Date and time of call:** The technicians at your carrier must look for your specific call on a switch that processes millions of calls per day. Each switch stores call information in individual folders broken down by time. Telling your carrier that the call was placed at 10:05 a.m. CST today gives them the information necessary to go directly to the correct file within the switch.

- **Origination phone number:** Your carrier needs to know the phone number from which you were dialing when the failed or affected call was made. In pre-VoIP days, a carrier used this information to identify the carrier's switch that was geographically the closest to where the call originated. The new VoIP world still needs this information to isolate your call from all other calls on their network that called the destination phone number that same day.

- **The number dialed:** The dialed number indicates to your carrier's technician the most likely final switch in their network that would have processed the call.

- **The call treatment:** Your carrier needs to know what it's looking for — is it a failed call to a fast busy signal or a completed call with static? The call treatment tells the carrier the real reason why this specific call example is of interest.

The physical origin and termination of the call gives your carrier a place to begin searching for your call example. It knows its network switches, and it can methodically run through them at either the origination or termination of the call. After it locates a likely switch, it uses the origination or termination phone number to query the file in the switch for the specific time the call was made so that it can find the call. In instances in which you're calling a popular number, your carrier needs the phone number from which you originated the call to differentiate it from the hundreds of other calls terminating to the same phone number. You may need to pull a Wireshark capture for a failed call to identify the specific originating phone number used on the outbound call because VoIP is dynamic and you can populate any phone number you want in this field.

The fresher the call, the easier to find. The easier to find, the faster your carrier can resolve your issue. If every call you make to a specific phone number fails, make another test call right before you call into your carrier to make it easier for it to find the call.

Introducing VoIP-specific call example requirements

Because your calls are being delivered as VoIP, your carrier most likely also wants this information:

- ✔ **The IP address from which you originated the call:** If you're a large company or VoIP reseller, you may have an array of five or ten different servers from which you originate VoIP calls to your carrier. Your origination IP address is used just like the origination phone number in a non-VoIP call. It provides an origination point to query in the carrier's SBC to find the specific call. Even if you aren't a huge VoIP carrier or reseller, you may still have more than one SIP proxy on your VoIP LAN, simply for the sake of redundancy.

- ✔ **The IP address of your carrier's SBC to which the call was sent:** Your carrier may have several different and geographically unique SBCs assigned to you. It may have deemed it necessary to accommodate your volume of calls or simply to provide redundancy in case one of its SBCs fails. Each SBC may be located anywhere in the country, so it has to know which one you sent your affected call to in order to have any chance of finding the call.

- ✔ **The SIP reject sent for the failed call:** If your call was rejected to an "all circuits busy" recording, the specific SIP response provides information to your carrier about which it can query the SBC.

Capture a failed call with Wireshark or your favorite packet capture software before you call your carrier with the issue to ensure that the origination and termination phone numbers, IP addresses, date/time of the call, and SIP response that you're providing to your carrier are accurate. Guessing that the origination phone number was probably the main one for the office only makes more work for your carrier, prolonging the time it takes to resolve your issue. The Wireshark capture can also help you if your carrier requests the call ID for the failed call or the capture itself to compare against its switch records that show how the call was handled.

Providing Multiple Call Examples

A single call example sometimes isn't enough to resolve complex issues — especially with intermittent issues. You may have ten different SIP proxies from which you can originate a call, and your carrier may have ten different SBCs to which the calls can be sent. Those two variables already provide 100 different combinations that can affect your outbound calls, before even calculating the multitude of possible routing options after your VoIP carrier receives the calls.

Any intermittent issue may be caused by any one leg of the journey, any one piece of hardware, or a cumulative response to multiple issues along the way. These intermittent issues require you to provide multiple call examples to your carrier. It may ask for only two or three examples of affected calls, as well as two or three examples of unaffected calls. Even if the initial customer service representative opening the trouble ticket doesn't want the other call examples or doesn't have room in the ticket to input the information, keep those call examples handy. The technician who picks up the trouble ticket and eventually calls you back will appreciate your diligence and gladly take down the information.

Intermittent issues are the most troublesome because they can easily persist for weeks or months. By keeping an accurate log of both affected and unaffected calls, and maintaining a consistent dialogue with your carrier, you can generally resolve the problem in a matter of days.

The reason intermittent issues persist is because people lose focus. After the initial report of the problem, your carrier responds by attempting to bypass a specific portion of its network or re-option a suspect piece of hardware. Its fix may not be complete and may remove only one more variable from the equation, so it asks you to retest after it completes the changes. It's difficult to maintain focus on a problem that takes days or weeks to work through, and the transition point between the carrier and yourself can cause the problem to drag on.

Your job probably isn't devoted to chasing down 15- or 5-percent trouble issues on your phone system. You're taking the emergencies of the day and doing your own version of triage. If a customer has an emergency because something was shipped late or to the wrong address, or it arrived broken, or the wrong thing was sent, you can't make those test calls on the 5-percent static issues and get back to your carrier in a timely manner. You might take three or four days to work your way down to the issues that affect 5 percent of your life. By then, your carrier has closed the original trouble ticket, and you have to start all over again. Stay focused, make the five or six test calls, and reply to your carrier in less than 24 hours to put the phone-issue ball back in its court. Its technicians do nothing but work on trouble issues, so you can go on with your normal job and expect a call back in about another eight business hours for the next round of testing.

Managing Trouble Tickets

You may open several trouble tickets per month or only one a year. The more calls you send, the more likely to have one fail or experience poor call quality. You need to track your trouble ticket and keep a good log of how it progressed.

If you work for a VoIP carrier or reseller, create a database to log in all the trouble tickets, identifying

- **The customer reporting the issue:** This information can include the specific origination or termination phone number or IP address. You need this field populated so that you can pull reports to see whether any customer is experiencing chronic issues. Either he doesn't know his hardware, or a network issue may be frustrating him. If anyone has a high incidence of reported troubles, he or she may be growing unhappy and will probably stop being your customer.

- **The carrier to which the issue was reported:** If you have multiple VoIP carriers, this field allows you to view the volume of problems on each carrier. If you have too many issues with any one carrier, you probably should move your traffic off that carrier and find another.

- **Call treatment:** This field allows you to find trends. One carrier may be great on completion, but the last 15 trouble tickets opened with it were for clipping, probably caused by packet loss. Reports pulled from this field help identify troublesome areas of your carrier or end user's networks.

- **Notes/resolution:** List how the trouble issue progressed, who you spoke to at your carrier, what he or she said, and at what time you had the conversation. Every time you call in for status, write another note, listing the date and time. After the troubleshooting process is complete, write down how it was resolved. This information is invaluable for chronic issues or if anyone gets into a finger-pointing match a year later.

- **Other fields:** You can add additional fields to identify the time to repair and the frequency of trouble issues, but most companies don't need anything that detailed.

 If you don't expect to have more than a few trouble tickets per year, you don't need to make a database to track them, but keep your notes. You can simply jot everything down on a piece of paper and stick it in a Trouble Tickets folder in your desk. Even if you put in only one new piece of paper per year, I guarantee that you'll need to know the specifics of the trouble issue at some time in the future. If you need some guidance on how to structure the information on your trouble tickets, check out the Cheat Sheet in the front of this book.

Understanding the timelines

The service side of telecom ebbs and flows based on the triage of incoming trouble issues. If someone has a huge circuit failing that normally sends out a million calls a day, he or she is going to be pushed to the top of the list, and a 5-percent Post-Dial-Delay issue goes to the bottom of the pile. The telecom triage is a way of life in the industry — and a large outage or issue can, and should, get people out of any staff meeting or conference call to jump in on the problem and work it to resolution.

Every carrier has a different timeline for response, but somewhere in every company, that timeline exists. Ask the customer service rep when you open your ticket when you can expect a call back from a technician. You may have to wait as little as two hours for a large network issue or as long as a day or more for international completion or call quality issues.

Just because the carrier makes you wait to speak to a technician, you don't have to sit around twiddling your thumbs for that duration of time. You can call back to get an update — just be aware that he or she may tell you, "You just opened the ticket an hour ago, and a technician hasn't picked up the ticket yet."

The time that the customer service rep gives you when you open the trouble ticket is generally a response interval. That doesn't mean that they can resolve the issue in two or four hours. It simply means that a technician should call you back in two to four hours for testing, for clarification, or to provide an update. The technician may be able to fix the problem at that time, but don't base the life or livelihood of your company on it.

If you need to know an average time to resolution, ask your carrier for that information in a generic context, not specific to your trouble issue. You probably won't be able to get an Estimated Time to Repair (ETR) for your specific trouble issue. If you're trying to decide whether to send your staff home or make a business decision about when a telecom issue will be resolved, ask your customer service rep (in your most relaxed and non-accusing tone of voice), "How long do these problems usually take to get fixed?" If the rep doesn't think that you're going to use the information against him or her in a court of law, you can probably get a ballpark time frame that you can use to make a decision.

Working your escalation list

Every company that provides telecom service should have a solid structure for reporting problems and escalating issues. The telecom carrier or provider should have provided you with an escalation list when you first activated service with your carrier. If you ever lose your copy, it should be able to send you a fresh copy via e-mail within minutes.

Some companies have strict rules of engagement for escalations, especially when it comes to the traditional local phone carriers, such as Bell South and Verizon (formerly GTE). It may specify that a customer can escalate a call quality trouble ticket only once every four business hours. Other companies allow you to escalate as you see necessary. Remember these bits of advice when you're escalating a trouble ticket:

- **When you go higher up the escalation list, you don't necessarily reach more sophisticated technicians.** The tier 1 and tier 2 technicians can solve the majority of issues handed to them. Escalating up to their manager may put you in contact with the most senior technician in the department, or you may just reach someone who has good management skills and only basic troubleshooting prowess. Escalation to director, senior director, and vice president levels doesn't put you in contact with a more skilled technician, it simply raises the visibility of the issue.

- **A tier 1 or tier 2 technician eventually does the work and resolves your issue.** Maybe his or her manager steps in to offer some guidance, but the nuts and bolts of fixing something falls back on that technician's shoulders. Don't be surprised if you're speaking to a vice president one minute, and then you get a call back from someone two rungs down the escalation ladder. You may have been de-escalated, but you're probably in better hands.

- **If you leave a message for someone on the escalation list, wait for him or her to call you back.** If you don't have the luxury of giving him or her 60 minutes to call you back, don't leave a message. If you end up leaving a message, or you realize that she isn't going to get back to you (because she's at off-site meetings or training, for example), tell her in the message that you plan to call the next person up the chain of command. If you leave a message with a manager, and then immediately call that manager's director and leave another message, and then immediately call the vice president and leave yet another message, you put three people to work on the same issue. This process is commonly referred to as *working the system*. Eventually, all three of these people show up at the desk of the technician working the trouble ticket, and they wonder why they're all doing the same thing. When you call (one person!), tell him or her that it's an urgent issue and say, "I don't know whether you can get back to me in an hour, but I need to get this rolling, so if you're tied up, I'm going to call Ms. Director at whenever o'clock and see whether she can help us out."

✔ **Escalating a trouble issue can raise or lower your carrier's perception of you.** Never forget that people work in the Network Operations Center (NOC) for your VoIP carrier, not robots. If you work up the escalation list in a respectful way, nobody will think evil of you.

You can go about escalation in two ways: properly or improperly. The proper way to go about escalation is in an inclusive way, in which you always refer to your carrier's staff as part of your team. Keep your carrier on your side during an escalation by talking about how "we" need to get some more visibility on this issue and "our" customer is having a rough time of it. Tier 1 (and even tier 2) technicians know that they don't know everything. You might even ask them, "Should I escalate this and get you some more help?" You want to foster as much good will during escalations as possible. The staff at your carrier will do everything in their power to help you, as long as you keep them as part of your team and respect them in the process.

The wrong way to escalate is by making your carrier the enemy. It's possibly the only entity that can fix your problem, and at the least, you need its cooperation in testing to resolve an issue, even if that issue isn't directly within its specific area of responsibility. Pointing the finger at the carrier, screaming, and threatening is no way to enlist it to go the extra mile.

The end result of an escalation is that you resolve your situation, and you build a stronger working relationship with your carrier. VoIP issues can quickly escalate to the realm of the technically esoteric. You need every resource available to unravel some of these mysteries, and alienating your carrier (one of your largest technical resources) is never helpful. You can make your life much easier by establishing a healthy working relationship with all your technical support staff.

Troubleshooting an Outbound Call

Although you can have many types of calls — inbound local, outbound long-distance, toll-free, international, and so on — the only classifications that you need to worry about for VoIP are inbound and outbound calls. All the other permutations of calls, including international and toll-free, are simply add-on steps to deliver an outbound call or receive an inbound call. The VoIP interaction between your carrier and your SBC is of greatest importance to you in the troubleshooting process. If you're looking for a step-by-step breakdown of all varieties of calls, as well as a detailed troubleshooting process, pick up a copy of *Telecom For Dummies,* which I also wrote (Wiley).

The majority of the calls running through the average business phone system are outbound calls. These calls begin at your VoIP phone, traverse your LAN, are aggregated by your SIP proxy, and are sent via your Internet provider to your VoIP carrier.

Figure 13-1 shows the variables in a standard outbound VoIP call. The level of troubleshooting available to you depends on the complexity of your network design. The more redundant carriers and ISPs you have, the more opportunity you have to surgically isolate and prove out each section of your call.

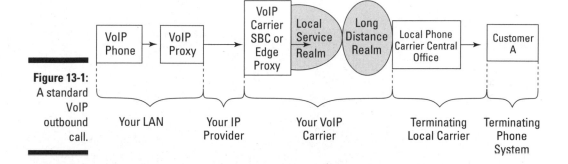

Figure 13-1:
A standard VoIP outbound call.

Troubleshooting must follow a logical progression in which each test proves out another section of the call, removing it as a potential cause of the issue. Troubleshooting individual call issues should begin by proving out your own hardware and then moving out through all other variables until you reach the phone system at your destination.

Troubleshooting Step 1

You must make an outbound call to the same dialed number that experienced the failure or call quality issue, but execute it in a way that changes one of your outbound variables, keeping all other variables the same. This first test may not be easy if you have only one VoIP carrier, one Internet provider, and no analog lines connected to your VoIP phone system.

If you have any redundant services connected to your VoIP phone system, have the programmer who set up your phone system create extensions that are dedicated to specific IP providers, VoIP carriers, or ports on your system (including analog). That setup allows you to hit the extension, dial the phone number experiencing the issue, and ensure the call is sent over a specific carrier. The more extensions that you can set up to direct your call over a specific route, the more quickly you can isolate an issue.

Bypassing your Internet provider

Your Internet provider is a small but vital variable in the outbound dialing equation. It has the simple task of routing packets between your VoIP proxy and the SBC of your VoIP carrier. It probably doesn't indiscriminately lose hundreds of packets, unless it's experiencing a huge outage or congestion.

Figure 13-2 identifies the area being tested when you send your calls over an alternate IP provider. The call still originates from the same VoIP phone, goes through the same VoIP proxy, and arrives at the same VoIP carrier. If your call treatment is correct, then the only possible source for the issue is your Internet provider. Call it to open a trouble ticket and push through for resolution.

Figure 13-2:
An alter-
native IP
provider.

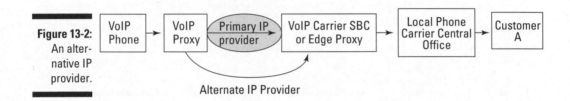

If your test call yields the same result, then you know that your Internet provider definitely isn't causing the issue. Proceed to your next test call described in the following section to further isolate the issue.

If you have an issue with call completion, rather than call quality, you can record and convey the performance of your Internet provider by creating reports in your VLM software. Latency injected by your Internet provider may be preventing SIP messages from being properly transmitted or received.

If your VLM software doesn't have any features to identify latency caused by your IP provider, execute a Wireshark capture on a failed call. The capture should show normal SIP banter from your VoIP proxy to the SBC of your carrier. If every SIP packet sent has an appropriate response, you can reasonably deduce that the call failure is related to something other than latency induced by your Internet provider.

Don't assume that every packet you believe you're sending is being properly sent. If your VoIP provider doesn't respond to the INVITE packets that you send, you might incorrectly assume that either your Internet provider isn't delivering the packets, or your VoIP carrier isn't responding to them. If you're seeing packet loss across the board on random outbound packets, and not just INVITE packets, then your Internet provider could be causing the issue.

Your VoIP carrier's SBC is designed to respond to every INVITE with a 100 Trying before it even . . . well, tries to do anything. If you claim that you're sending calls and your VoIP carrier claims it isn't receiving the INVITE, you have one of two possible problems:

✔ **You're overloading your VoIP carrier's SBC.** The accidental equivalent of a Denial of Service (DOS) attack where you are sending so many packets to your carrier that it can't respond to anyone else. Your VoIP carrier may have provisioned you for both a specific limit of concurrent calls and a number of maximum allowable calls per second that you can transit. If you exceed the calls per second, you may overload its switch. You could send so many calls in such a short duration of time that you eventually send INVITE messages to which your carrier doesn't respond, but that's unlikely. Before it gets to that point, you can expect this kind of evolution of the problem:

1. The increase in incoming INVITE messages prevents other customers assigned to the SBC from having their calls processed. Their calls are rejected with a 487 Request Terminated SIP response.

2. Your excessive call attempts are rejected with a 487 Request Terminated SIP response.

3. You push through and continue to ramp up the volume of calls being sent, overloading every resource on your carrier's SBC. Finally, after thousands of INVITE messages have been sent by you, receiving the 487 Request Terminated, a few begin to see no response at all. The SBC has run out of processor strength, and you've outstripped its ability to generate enough 487 responses.

4. The NOC at your VoIP carrier realizes that you're overrunning its SBC with INVITE requests. It sends an urgent e-mail or call you, demanding that you throttle back your traffic or face it turning your service off.

✔ **Your SIP server is having an issue and isn't clearing the last completed call.** If you don't see the progression of 487 messages being returned to your INVITEs, followed by a stern call from the VoIP NOC, then you haven't overloaded your carrier's SBC. You aren't seeing responses to your INVITE messages for another reason. Your VoIP carrier can run a capture for the same duration of time that your INVITE messages were sent to confirm that it saw the INVITE messages arrive. The INVITE message may not be arriving at your VoIP carrier's SBC because your SIP server may block it. In this case, check the last call transmitted before the problem occurred on the specific port that's failing the call. That call probably ended in an abnormal manner. Your VoIP server may have cleaned up the call by sending a CANCEL or timing out, but that doesn't mean that your SIP server is ready to go. Your IP provider probably can't successfully deliver all the SIP banter between you and your VoIP provider on every completed call — but likely just drops some random INVITE messages. Also, your VoIP provider probably can't respond to every SIP message on active calls, so it likely just ignores random INVITE messages.

If your issue is intermittent, whether call completion or call quality, you have to make several test calls to validate whether the issue is gone. If you have a 5-percent issue, make 20 to 40 test calls to validate that it's been resolved.

Bypassing your VoIP carrier

Unless you're a large company, you may not have an alternate Internet provider. But you can easily set up additional VoIP carriers to provide redundancy, which allows you to pick and choose the best rates from more than one carrier for outbound calling.

Figure 13-3 shows the area of the call that you isolate when you send your call over an alternate VoIP carrier. If the problem you're experiencing is related to how your primary VoIP carrier handles your SIP methods and responses, you should see an improved response when transmitting to another VoIP carrier.

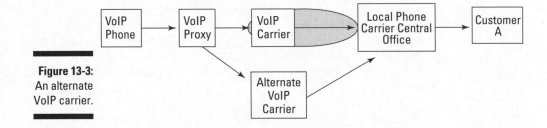

Figure 13-3: An alternate VoIP carrier.

Unless you're using VoIP service rolled out by a traditional long-distance carrier, you're probably in the dark about who your VoIP provider uses to handle the long-distance portion of the call. It may use one long-distance carrier or several. This long-distance question affects the troubleshooting process because if both your primary and secondary VoIP carriers use the same long-distance carrier, your test call over the alternate provider isolates only the front-end SIP interface section of its service. Only when you know for certain that they use different long-distance carriers does this test actually isolate the area form your VoIP carrier's SBC to the point at which the call is dropped off at the local phone carrier for the phone number dialed (represented in Figure 13-3).

Take a Wireshark capture of the failed or affected call over your primary VoIP carrier, as well as over the alternate VoIP carrier. You can much more easily identify a problem with the specific details of the call when you can look at these calls side-by-side, going through every layer of every SIP message sent and received.

If your call treatment improves when you dial over another VoIP provider, then you need to call your primary VoIP carrier to open a trouble ticket. Give it all the information that it needs, and it should be able to resolve the issue quickly.

If the issue you identify is a SIP interaction problem, your VoIP carrier may or may not make changes. If your alternate VoIP carrier is a smaller boutique carrier that set up its server to your requirements, it may have modified its SIP protocol stack specifically to handle your configuration requirements. If your configuration needs a SIP response or method to be treated in a way that doesn't follow the RFC, a small boutique carrier probably sets it up for you. After you identify the same issue with a large VoIP carrier, it probably tells you to modify your SIP stack to accommodate the RFC because it won't install a change specific to your hardware.

If you experience the exact same call treatment or call failure when you send the call over an alternative VoIP carrier, all isn't lost. You may not have positively identified the specific source of the issue, but you've eliminated a large section of it as the possible source. You've just validated the entire center section of the call, from the millisecond that the packets reach your VoIP carrier to the millisecond that they're delivered to the local carrier at the terminating end, so it's no longer in question.

Trying it on an analog line

If you work in a small company that has only five or six phone lines, you probably don't have either an alternative Internet provider or another VoIP carrier. But you may still have an analog phone line connected to your VoIP server, which handles faxes, modems, or security systems, or is just a general backup in case your IP provider or VoIP carrier have a catastrophic failure. The monthly charge to have an analog phone connected to your VoIP phone system is an inexpensive insurance policy that allows you to route local calls less expensively over the traditional telephony network.

Figure 13-4 identifies that all external SIP messaging, as well as your Internet provider, VoIP provider, and the long-distance network they're using are all bypassed when you execute an analog test call. Going analog cuts out a huge section of your outbound call and quickly narrows down the potential sources of the problem. The analog bypass allows you to definitively prove out your Internet provider, as well as the variables isolated on the test call to the alternate VoIP carrier.

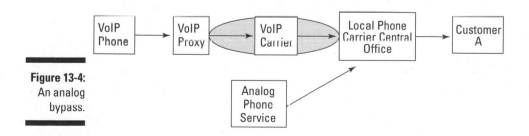

Figure 13-4:
An analog bypass.

Calling out over another long-distance carrier

The non-VoIP world has an easy way to bypass the long-distance portion assigned to your phone line. Almost all local phone carriers allow you to place your call on another long-distance network by dialing their access code prior to the phone number you want to reach. These 1010+ codes were promoted on television a lot in the 1990s. You may be able to use this option to force your call onto AT&T (by dialing 1010288), SPRINT (by dialing 1010333), or QWEST (1010432) when making a test call out over your analog line.

A full phone number dialed with the AT&T access code is 1010288-1-414-555-1212.

Your VoIP provider probably doesn't allow the use of 1010 access codes because it most likely has an advanced LCR table set up to find the cheapest route for any phone number you dial.

Remember, unless you have a contract for service with the long-distance networks that you can reach by entering their access codes, they charge you the highest rate possible for any completed call made over their network — frequently $3 to $5 per minute for domestic calls. And the international rates, if they don't simply block you, can be excessive.

In the end, if the call issue persists on either test, you're left with only three possible sources for the issue:

✔ Your LAN
✔ The terminating local carrier
✔ The phone system of the person you're calling

If the problem you're chasing down is a call quality issue involving clipping, investigate your LAN first. Fully integrated voice and data networks aren't easy to build or maintain. Engage your VLM software, tracking down the specifics of your LAN at the time the calls were made. Check for latency, jitter, and packet loss because of hardware and bandwidth constraints and potential hardware mis-optioning or failure. If the issue is static or echo, which isn't normally associated with VoIP, move on to Step 2 in troubleshooting, discussed in the following section.

Troubleshooting Step 2

Of the three remaining variables in the outbound call problem, you have an alternative to only one of them. No matter how you dial a phone number (whether with a VoIP phone, an analog phone, or a cell phone) and which long-distance carrier transports the call, eventually, all the calls terminate to the exact same Central Office (CO) of the exact same local phone carrier. The CO then identifies who owns the phone number and sends the call down the exact same set of fiber or cables to the company's building and rings their phone system. Most companies and residences don't have redundant phone systems or local phone carriers. If they have a separate VoIP phone system running through an IP provider, you probably avoid using a VoIP carrier whose purpose is to connect your calls to traditional analog phones, and instead send your calls directly to the IP address of their SIP server over the Internet. However, every office and home in America doesn't have an alternative VoIP system, so for now, it isn't a common option.

With that in mind, the one piece of technology that nearly everyone has access to is the cell phone. Calling from a cell phone doesn't change the local carrier's CO or the phone system of the person you're calling, but it does prove out every other variable in the call stream.

The gray oval in Figure 13-5 shows the area of the call tested when you dial the destination number with a cell phone. If your call fails with the same echo or static, or terminates to the same error recording, then you know the problem, unfortunately, has nothing to do with any company or hardware with which you have the authority to open a trouble ticket.

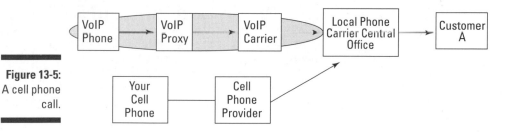

Figure 13-5:
A cell phone call.

The recording you're given may vary, depending on the long-distance carrier that you use to place the test call. For example, if your VoIP carrier uses QWEST, you receive a fast busy signal, but the analog line at your office uses SPRINT and plays a recording of "all circuits are busy." If you call to the exact same number with your cell phone that uses AT&T for the long-distance portion, you may get the message that "the number has been disconnected or is no longer in service." If you make three test calls over three different long-distance carriers and they all fail, you can only believe that it's a valid failure. If not a single long-distance network can complete the call to anything but a recording, then the local phone carrier for that phone number is having an issue.

Even if you call the local phone carrier for the company you're trying to reach, it still won't help you. You may be able to ask it general questions, such as, "Are you experiencing an outage in the Cudahy, Wisconsin area?" But that's about it. You can't open up a trouble ticket on the specific phone number that's failing unless you're the end user of record for that phone number. The *end user of record* is the entity paying the invoice for the phone service and is the only person/group that can open a trouble ticket on the phone lines.

In this way, the world of telecom delineates responsibility for phone service and with whom the carriers are legally authorized to speak. Depending on whether the owner of the number pays extra for line insurance or has some sort of maintenance contract, the local carrier may charge if a technician needs to be dispatched to a site. If local carriers didn't uphold the relationship with their end user of record, then anyone could call in at any time to request technicians be dispatched, new hardware installed, and intrusive testing conducted — all tasks that have a financial and/or service impact on the phone lines.

The person you're calling at Company A may already know that his or her phone system is down, and it's actually the hardware on site (not the local carrier) that's ultimately at fault. If you have the person's cell phone number, call that before you worry that Company A has gone out of business. If you don't have a Company A cell phone number, send an e-mail with a subject of Your Phone System Is Dead. That e-mail generally gets people's attention and quickly results in someone from Company A calling you back.

Troubleshooting international issues

From your perspective, troubleshooting an international call is just like troubleshooting any domestic call. You can run through the outbound troubleshooting steps in the preceding sections to isolate the issue, just as if you were calling New Hope, Minnesota. The only twist to troubleshooting international calls is that you might find some interesting similarities when your call hits different long-distance carriers.

Call treatment similarities over different long-distance carriers occur because your long-distance carrier doesn't use its own network to complete calls to every country in the world. I guarantee you that MCI, Sprint, and AT&T don't own all the phone cables and hardware in the world, and they probably don't have a staff of technicians in every country to connect your calls into Senegal, Papua New Guinea, and India. The long-distance carriers that your VoIP provider uses in turn use an underlying carrier that's a company specifically designed for delivering international calls from the United States to a specific country or region in the world. Only so many underlying carriers provide service into each country, and every large domestic long-distance carrier probably has a contract for service with every large underlying carrier. In other words, more that one long-distance carrier uses the same path to complete calls to Tokyo or Prague.

Carriers monitor their completion rates daily to every country in the world. If you try hard enough, your VoIP carrier may even send you a list from the long-distance carrier that it uses, identifying what that long-distance carrier considers to be acceptable completion rates. Don't be shocked if you see that a completion rate of 60 percent for Western Europe is acceptable; the rate drops to around 7 percent or less for some African countries.

The long-distance carrier that your VoIP provider uses can route your international call over several underlying carriers. The choice of underlying carrier depends on the underlying carrier's completion ratios, compared with all the other carrier choices at that time, as well as the price you're paying for your international calls. Some carriers have a premium group of underlying carriers available for international calls, but they can't place you on that group of carriers because they'd lose money. If your business is focused on international calling, you might want to pay a few pennies more per minute for your calls, if you can get a better call quality or completion rate. If you're opening more than one trouble ticket every few months on international issues, speak to your carrier about a better route.

Troubleshooting an Inbound Call

Many VoIP providers use different carriers or providers for their local services, as opposed to the long-distance services. Each group (local and long-distance) requires different classes of hardware and different types of federal certification. So, a recognized local carrier that uses a class 5 switch must handle the ownership of a phone number and accept the responsibility for terminating calls to the phone number. Keep this fact in mind because your VoIP provider probably uses a minimum of two different companies to supply both the inbound and outbound VoIP service. A long-distance carrier handles all your outbound calls, and a local phone carrier receives and routes your incoming calls.

Inbound calls can come from local points of origin, long-distance points of origin, or through toll-free numbers. Regardless of how the call arrives at your office, you have to worry about only a few variables when troubleshooting:

- ✔ Your VoIP provider
- ✔ Your Internet provider
- ✔ Your VoIP LAN
- ✔ The individual VoIP hardphone receiving the call

Figure 13-6 shows the standard variables of an inbound call. The call originates to the right of the diagram when Customer A calls you, and it goes through his local phone carrier and his long-distance carrier before it even hits the first company with which you have any direct business contact. You can't have an impact on any problems that the call experiences before it hits your VoIP carrier (because you aren't the end user of record for service with any of those companies).

The figure would look only slightly different if the call originated locally. In that case, the call doesn't use a long-distance carrier, and the company's local phone carrier connects the call directly to the circuit that it has pointing to your VoIP carrier or the local carrier that your VoIP carrier uses to receive calls. Please check out Chapter 12 for a detailed look at the complexity of handling a local VoIP call.

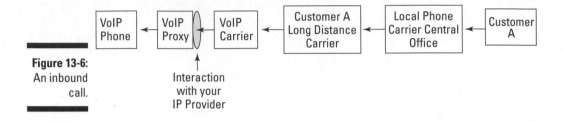

Figure 13-6:
An inbound
call.

Interaction
with your
IP Provider

Briefly touching on toll-free

Toll-free calls are just inbound calls for which the receiving company pays the per-minute charges. Many companies have and use toll-free numbers every day, but the calls don't function any differently if they terminate to an analog phone line or a digital circuit, or if they're converted to VoIP and sent over your Internet provider.

This book focuses on VoIP, so I gloss over the other aspects of the traditional telecom market and focus only on the point at which they interact with VoIP elements that you have visibility over. Toll-free calls add one more variable to the normal processing of an standard inbound call. Your toll-free call must first be sent to your long-distance carrier who is listed as the "owner" of the toll-free number. Your long-distance carrier receives the call from the originating local phone carrier and delivers it into the VoIP portion of its network, sending it to you via its SBC. The call could potentially fail or be affected during the long-distance portion, before it hits the SBC for your VoIP carrier, but that's uncommon.

Toll-free numbers don't physically exist. They aren't assigned to a pair of wires on a phone jack in your office, just like a normal phone number. But they're actually virtual numbers that direct inbound calls to a *ring-to-number,* a phone number that's wired to a phone jack in your office which acts as the recipient for the calls. The ring-to-number is generally your main office line used by local callers when they dial your company. The shorthand version of troubleshooting a toll-free number is to call the ring-to-number of the toll-free number and see whether you have the same call failure or call quality issue. If you have the same problem, then the issue has nothing to do with the toll-free number and everything to do with some variable within your area of control on the inbound call. Follow the troubleshooting procedure outlined in the section "Troubleshooting an Inbound Call," in this chapter.

The subject of toll-free numbers, their ordering, routing, and troubleshooting, as well as the layers of responsibility for each variable in a toll-free call, involve too many non-VoIP elements to include in this book. If you have specific questions regarding how to order new toll-free numbers, migrate existing toll-free numbers to a new long-distance carrier, or troubleshoot a toll-free number, I recommend the only book that covers this industry information, *Telecom For Dummies,* by . . . well, me (Wiley).

Identifying global issues with your cell phone

Troubleshooting inbound calls is frequently more difficult than outbound calls. If someone can't complete a call to you, she generally won't track down a cell phone or get access to e-mail so that she can reach you. When she finally reaches you, unless she's a long-time customer, she probably won't have all the information necessary for a complete call example — especially if a first-time customer is calling into your office. She might easily perceive your questions about when she called, what phone number she called from, and the call treatment she received to be invasive — some salesman's ploy to get her phone number.

You need the same information to open a trouble ticket on an inbound call to your VoIP-enabled phone number as you do for an outbound call (which is covered earlier in this chapter). Your VoIP carrier may be more lenient on the questions that specify the IP address of the SBC that sends the call and the IP address of the server that receives the call, but the rest of the information is essential. If you know only that calls into your phone number are failing, but you don't have a single phone number that's tried to call you and couldn't complete, I regret to inform you that you're S.O.L (Simply Out of Luck).

Figure 13-7 shows the easiest way to test a problem with an inbound call. Just pick up your cell phone and dial the number yourself. This test quickly tells you whether the problem that people are having when they try to reach you is specific to their local phone carrier or their long-distance carrier, of whether it's a global issue.

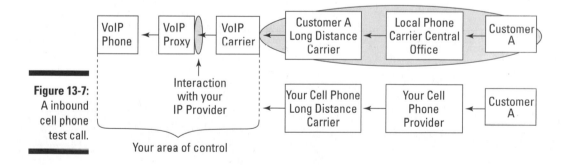

Figure 13-7: A inbound cell phone test call.

If the test call from your cell phone fails, you're probably looking at an issue where nobody can connect to your phone number from anywhere. But at least you can easily make test calls and be confident that you're giving your VoIP carrier the correct origination phone number, time of call, and call treatment when you open a trouble ticket with it. You can also quickly validate any repair after your VoIP carrier makes changes.

Before you make the call to the trouble repair department of your VoIP carrier, pull a Wireshark capture of the call attempt. If your hardware sees the INVITE message from your VoIP carrier, determine why the call is being rejected. The simplest answer might be that the phone number simply isn't listed in your phone system, and so the system doesn't know where to route the call. Regardless of what internal workings are going astray, if you see the call attempt reach your phone system, read the call capture to determine what failed the call and why.

You don't have to execute a full-blown Wireshark capture on a failing inbound call. Many VoIP phone systems allow you to view all the activities happening within them in real time by logging in to the console for the phone system. This view shows the hardware responding to inbound and outbound call requests, sometimes showing the exact port from which an inbound call was received. Because you need to see only whether the call attempt ever hit your server, you can frequently most easily view the phone system in the console mode and then make a test call to the failing phone number. If you see the call attempt, make another test call and capture it with Wireshark. If the call attempt never hits the phone system, you know that your VoIP carrier isn't getting the call to you.

Determining whether it's trouble or provisioning

You absolutely must determine whether the phone number you're dialing has ever worked since you converted it to VoIP before you call into your VoIP carrier to open the trouble ticket. If the number never worked, your trouble issue probably isn't technically a trouble issue — it's a provisioning issue. This gray area between determining if a problem belongs in the trouble repair department, or if it legitimately exists within the scope of the order entry/provisioning side of the company is where things can get messy. A simple problem that may take 15 minutes to resolve if it was a legitimate trouble issue, may take days to fix if the root cause is actually associated with order entry/provisioning.

Telecom carriers identify trouble issues as a failure to complete successful calls over phone service that is active, installed, and established. Carriers have shifts of people who do nothing except unravel and resolve problems work these issues 24 hours a day, seven days a week. These people are fully empowered to fix any and all problems in the shortest time possible, and when it comes to VoIP, they can usually resolve most normal issues in a matter of hours.

Provisioning issues involve any problem on service that hasn't yet been established, including pitfalls that can happen during the transfer of your phone line from your old carrier and the establishment of service at the new

VoIP carrier. Don't handle these situations as emergencies, instead treating them like business as usual. Getting provisioning issues fixed is more like scheduling a doctor's appointment to have your cholesterol checked, as opposed to an emergency room visit for a broken arm. The provisioning department usually consists of one shift of employees who work a standard eight-hour day. If your phone number was rejected, lost, or snapped back to your old local carrier, you may need to begin the entire provisioning process all over again. You may need to fill out a new Letter of Authorization for your new VoIP carrier, and wait through the standard time intervals for the response from your old local carrier to the newly submitted order, as you're starting over from the beginning. Chapter 1 covers the process for migrating phone numbers from one carrier to another if you would like additional information on how it works. If the phone number has successfully migrated to your VoIP carrier, it may be able to refresh the routing for the phone number within its network and resolve the problem instantly.

All the features attached to your normal, analog phone line are removed when it's migrated to another carrier. If your traditional local phone carrier had voicemail, international blocking, and a distinctive ring on your phone number when someone called for your officemate, you lose all those features when your old carrier no longer services the number. Your new VoIP carrier may replicate all those services and give you a handful of additional features, but remember that you're getting *new* services from your VoIP carrier that are replacing the old features you lost. The migration process for phone numbers essentially converts the phone number from a bi-directional number, capable of originating and terminating phone calls, to a Direct Inward Dial (DID) line that points to the IP address of your VoIP proxy.

Looking at the source

If the test call from your cell phone completes without a problem, then the issue is most likely restricted to the specific local carrier that provides service to the customer who can't get through to you. This situation isn't common because most local carriers keep close tabs on where phone numbers are and to which local carrier they belong. That's the realm in which local carriers function, so they don't often send a call destined for you to the wrong local carrier.

But problems do crop up. The reality of the situation is always more complex than the boxes in call diagrams. These diagrams represent the simplified flow of the call and don't include the multitude of underlying carriers. Local phone carriers don't have dedicated circuits from every CO they operate out to every other local and long-distance carrier in the United States. They actually use a more business-savvy approach of routing outbound calls through underlying carriers. Even if you're receiving a local call from across the street, your neighbor's local carrier may not have a direct connection to your new-fangled VoIP carrier.

Figure 13-8 shows a slightly more detailed view of a local inbound call. This call originates in San Luis Obispo, California, and travels two blocks to your office. The curious thing about the call is that your phone number was with Pacific Bell until a few weeks ago, when it migrated to Level 3 Communications (your VoIP carrier). This fact is interesting because you know that Pacific Bell is fully aware that the phone number is no longer with it. It couldn't give your phone number to Level 3 and not realize it.

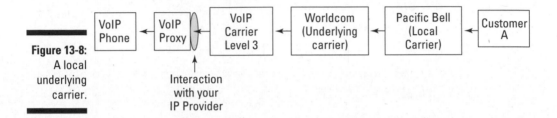

Figure 13-8:
A local
underlying
carrier.

You've made good test calls to your phone number from your cell phone, and you've received calls from friends and family across the country. The only person who can't call you is the guy across the street, whom you could hit with a Frisbee if you really wanted to. Pacific Bell doesn't have a direct connection to Level 3 in your town; in fact, it uses an underlying carrier (Worldcom) to reach you. That's where everything gets awkward. Pacific Bell says that it knows your phone number belongs to Level 3, and it confirms that it sent the call to Worldcom to deliver it to you. But Worldcom hasn't updated its database yet with the new routing for your phone number, which is now in the ownership of Level 3 Communications, so your local customer's call is failing.

So, Worldcom looks at your phone number and routes the call back to Pacific Bell. Pacific Bell, of course, knows that it doesn't have your phone number anymore, identifying that it went to Level 3, and it again routes it to Worldcom to complete the call to Level 3. The call is resolved by Worldcom again, and the cycle continues until the call times out, never to be completed.

Call your VoIP carrier to confirm that it isn't receiving the call, and then decide how you want to deal with the problem. Resolving this type of issue requires patience, diplomacy, and the ability to convey information in a clear manner. You face these hurdles:

✔ **You can't troubleshoot the issue directly because your carrier (Level 3 Communications) never receives the call.** It's your carrier's job to deliver to you all inbound calls that it receives for your phone number. Because this call never reaches the carrier, it can't do much to force the issue.

✔ **You can't call Pacific Bell on behalf of your customer because you aren't the end user of record.** Because you aren't listed on Company A's account to authorize repair with Pacific Bell, it won't talk to you. Your customer at Customer A is busy, knows nothing about telecom, and decides that it's your issue because he or she can call everyone except you.

✔ **Pacific Bell can only see as far as they route the call.** If you could reach Pacific Bell, it would probably see in its records that the phone number belongs to Level 3 and routes to Worldcom. Because Pacific Bell is both resolving and routing the call fine, the problem isn't with its network, so it isn't its issue. Its responsibility is to route the incoming call from Company A in the most direct route to Level 3 as possible, which it's doing.

✔ **You aren't the end user of record for Worldcom either.** Worldcom definitely won't talk to you because its end user of record on this issue is Pacific Bell. Because you don't work for Pacific Bell and aren't even its customer, it can't help, even if it wants to.

You have two possible solutions to this situation. The first involves you waiting until Worldcom updates its routing (in a week or month) with a fresh download from the national database, which tells it the local carrier that owns every phone number in America. If you don't have the time to wait, you need to get creative.

Call into Pacific Bell and ask about Company A's phone number. Muddle through its voicemail routing system until you reach a live human and then explain the situation to him or her in the nicest attitude that you have. Go with something like, "Gosh, you won't believe this — it's so strange, it's almost funny." You have to win over this technician enough to enlist his or her help. Phrase all your questions as procedural, not as specific to Company A's phone number. "Because my number is ported and I suspect you're routing the call to me, it seems like it's getting lost in the mix. Is there an underlying carrier you use to reach Level 3 that might be misrouting the call? How would we go about getting this fixed?"

The technician might indicate that you need to set up a conference call with your technician at Level 3. He or she may also just open a ticket with Worldcom and get it fixed. The technician you speak to knows that you aren't Pacific Bell's customer, but he or she may still go the extra mile for you to make it work (trust me, these people exist — one helped me on this issue). As soon as the ticket is opened with Worldcom and it updates its routing, the call completes — and you're back in business.

Chapter 14

Handling VoIP-Specific Problems

*T*his chapter fits perfectly at the end of the troubleshooting part of this book. Just like your investigation of any issue should begin by looking at general concerns and working your way to a specific issue, this part progresses in the same manner. Chapter 12 covers the theory of troubleshooting, Chapter 13 talks about the troubleshooting tools, and this chapter covers the specific issues that can plague your VoIP traffic.

Problems such as one-way audio (or no-way audio) can crop up during a VoIP deployment, and additional maintenance issues can appear when you add on more phone lines and services. Every new VoIP phone that you install should progress through the exact same testing and burn-in procedure, executing a five-minute call from the new phone to confirm configuration and call quality. Performing your due diligence at the time that you make changes and additions prevents those new components from causing trouble down the road.

Handling One-Way Audio

VoIP is a unique creature because it consists of four completely separate flows of information. The overhead of the each call and the outbound audio from each end are all potentially sent on a unique path from end to end. Even the SIP and media sent from the same end over the same Internet provider may traverse different routes before landing at the SBC of your VoIP carrier.

This route variation generally has minimal impact on how the streams of information work together, but the way in which the streams interact with the intermediary VoIP nodes can have a large impact on your call quality and completion. One of the issues associated with the unique nature of the individual data paths that you may encounter during implementation is one-way audio.

One-way audio isn't an uncommon problem when deploying VoIP because one RTP stream carrying the audio portion of the call can be misrouted or blocked. So, the correct IP address and port can't receive the audio, leaving only one active outbound audio stream.

Figure 14-1 identifies the most common reason for one-way audio on VoIP — Network Address Translation, otherwise known as NAT. You can hide the IP address that you use within your LAN from the outside world by using NAT. NAT literally translates public IP addresses and ports visible to the public Internet into internal IP addresses and ports used within your LAN. It establishes a translation table between these IP addresses and ports, keeping the data present and available for use as long as the active transmission of data needs the connection. NAT refreshes that data every time it receives another packet from the origination site.

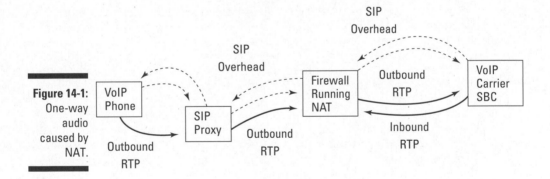

Figure 14-1: One-way audio caused by NAT.

The initial INVITE message sent by the VoIP phone in Figure 14-1 identifies the RTP IP address and port of the phone to which the far end should direct its RTP. The aggregating SIP proxy takes that information and replaces it with its own RTP IP address and port to receive the media while it initiates the INVITE message sent to the VoIP carrier through the firewall. If the IP address assigned to the SIP proxy is an internal IP address and not a public IP address, the firewall blocks the incoming RTP stream from the VoIP carrier's SBC, and the audio stream is rejected because

✔ The incoming RTP stream is of a different protocol than the SIP messaging that initiated the response.

✔ The IP address and port that receive the RTP stream didn't initiate the transmission.

The call setup in Figure 14-1 progresses normally with the originating VoIP node sending the INVITE, and receiving responses of 100 Trying and 180 Ringing. But when VoIP carrier's SBC sends the 200 OK, the firewall intercepts the audio, and the caller who originated the call doesn't hear any audio back from the far end.

A firewall is designed to prevent uninvited media streams from entering the LAN based on standard firewall processes of validating the origination and destination addresses, as well as the traffic type, whether TCP, UDP SIP, SDP, or RTP, and deactivating sessions that appear to be discontinued. The SIP messaging that initiates the call can traverse the NAT firewall more easily when the destination SIP node directs response transmissions to the same originating IP and port, as well as transmitting in the same protocol.

Your SIP proxy should be running on a public IP address where it can manage the keep-alive messages that maintain the NAT translation table. A phone conversation has two participants. If one person is long-winded and the other is simply listening, the quiet person's SIP may not be sending any packets because his or her end of the conversation has no audio and RTP isn't sent. The router that receives the incoming call may consider the data transmission complete and tear down the IP address and port information in the translation table, preventing the RTP from re-establishing, leaving the callers with one-way audio or tearing down the call entirely.

NAT isn't an indiscriminate feature thrown onto your LAN for the sole purpose of creating one-way audio on your VoIP calls. It's actually a useful tool used by network administrators to either hide the internal structure of their network from the outside world or so that they can use more IP addresses than the block of public IPv4 addresses they've been given by their IP provider or purchased directly. The additional benefit of NAT is that, after you have it working correctly with your VoIP, it makes changing IP providers or VoIP carriers much easier because you only have to re-establish the connection between the server and your carrier, as opposed to the challenge of migrating IP addresses and reconfiguring all your hardware to connect to the new IP provider.

The benefits of NAT mean that you need to find a way to keep it intact, but still be able to complete VoIP calls. The industry has responded with several options for NAT firewall traversal:

- ✔ **Application Level Gateway (ALG):** The ALG firewall replaces the standard NAT firewall and recognizes protocols flowing through it, managing the traffic based on protocol and application. It's a nice superficial bandage, but it doesn't provide a high level of security on these transmissions, aside from qualifying that they're sending SIP, UDP, or RTP.

- ✔ **Session Boarder Controller (SBC):** You can deploy your own SBC. Many carriers use them to regulate huge volumes of calls interfacing with their networks.

✔ **Manual configuration:** The easiest way to avoid the problems with NAT is to assign a public IP address to your VoIP proxy server. You can just open up a specific range of port numbers on your firewall, but leaving any ports unprotected by the firewall opens a security risk. Also, this manual process may be a bit more advanced than you're inclined to try. NAT is more of a concern with VoIP connections that mimic traditional telephony, where you're expecting calls from a wide range of IP addresses, just as you expect to receive calls from a wide range of phone numbers across America and the world. The evolution of the VoIP market has created a scenario in which the VoIP connection you have more resembles the configuration for a dedicated long-distance circuit because your VoIP comes in from a single point at a carrier who aggregates your incoming and outgoing calls. The single IP point from your VoIP carrier for receipt of outgoing calls and the source of all incoming calls allows you to open up your firewall for the one or series of addresses representing their SBCs, from which you can potentially receive RTP, and still maintain an acceptable level of security within your LAN.

✔ **Simple Traversal of UDP through NAT (STUN):** Designed by the IETF, STUN allows the SIP messaging to identify a public IP address and port that can be used to effectively communicate with the far end of the VoIP conversation.

✔ **Traversal Using Relay NAT (TURN):** This NAT traversal method was also developed by the IETF and provides multiple IP addresses as potential candidates to ensure connectivity. The IP addresses offered may include public IP addresses geographically spread out between the origination and termination VoIP endpoints. Because the incoming VoIP call may traverse several VoIP nodes before reaching your VoIP server, this method can greatly reduce delay because the TURN selects the IP address with the least amount of delay and latency to establish the RTP.

✔ **Interactive Communications Establishment (ICE):** A NAT traversal solution proposed by the IETF that allows the process of negotiating NAT traversal between VoIP nodes to use either STUN or TURN. A VoIP endpoint lists a group of possible IP addresses and ports where the SDP of the INVITE message could reach it. The connection points can be addresses available with STUN or TURN. You may not know whether the SBC of your carrier is using STUN or TURN, so ICE provides addresses for each category. The far-end VoIP endpoint then sends test messages to the proposed IP addresses to validate which one it can reach. The first successful reply is used to establish a media path for the call. The IP addresses provided with ICE can be

• **Local candidate:** The local IP address of the VoIP endpoint. This address would be useful only if the call was internal to the LAN.

• **Reflexive or STUN candidate:** A public IP address of the NAT server.

 • **Relay or TURN candidate:** An address on a SIP node between the final SIP endpoints that acts as a relay server.

The relay candidates are the easiest to use because the Reflexive and Local candidates may be unreachable from outside servers.

As VoIP evolves and becomes more widespread, VoIP connections look more like they did at the beginning of VoIP. The entire VoIP call consists of only two VoIP endpoints and the public IP between them, instead of incorporating the legacy PSTN and traditional local and long-distance carriers. That reality opens up a whole new challenge with NAT because NAT has so many different configurations that negotiating between firewalls becomes more complicated while your potential endpoints increase.

Realizing Why You Have No-Way Audio

No-way audio is more likely to occur with VoIP calls than with traditional telephony calls. The independent nature of the media streams give them much more potential to go wayward than traditional telephony, in which the audio is attached to the overhead of the call, at least for the start and finish of the transmission.

No-way audio, or the blocking/misdirection of both audio streams, can occur because of NAT traversal issues (which I explain in the preceding section) or because your VoIP proxy server runs out of G.729 licenses. Many VoIP phone systems, such as Asterisk, require you to purchase licenses to use compressed codecs, such as G.729.

Unless you're re-INVITE-ing the media on every call to the final VoIP node, your proxy server uses two G.729 licenses for each compressed call that it handles — one for the incoming leg of the call into the SIP proxy and one from the SIP proxy out to the final SIP node.

After all the G.729 licenses are employed, the next incoming call that arrives as G.729 in the SIP INVITE negotiates fine, but when the RTP stream hits your VoIP proxy, it realizes that it doesn't have any more licenses, and the audio portion of the call fails in both directions.

So, always re-INVITE the media of the call, if possible. If you also use your SIP proxy as an additional line of defense to manage incoming data streams, double up on the number of G.729 licenses you have. They're inexpensive, and because they don't come with an alarm when you're about to use up your final licenses, you don't have an easy way to alert yourself when you're running out.

Working Outbound Call Failures

I talk about outbound calling issues, in general, in Chapter 13, but what happens when the calls fail before they ever leave your SIP proxy? Software such as Wireshark allows you to capture the data and realize that the call never left your LAN. The challenge is answering this question — why?

Your outbound call failures may be the result of an overcomplicated and insufficiently designed Least Cost Routing (LCR) system. It may have been designed so tightly that calls are routed based on the first 6, 7, or 8 digits of the phone number. Building an LCR system to this level of detail isn't inherently bad, it simply creates more work for your programmer in charge of maintaining your Dial Plan when a new area code is released and he or she must update the entire matrix.

When you build an LCR, make it as granular as you can, assigning a default path for all calls that don't fit the profile in the pattern matching. If you're a smaller long-distance customer, select a carrier that can provide a flat rate or a simple rate deck that you can easily replicate in your phone system. If you're a large VoIP carrier, pay the money to access the national Local Exchange Routing Guide (LERG) database and update the LCR once a month or, at least, once a quarter.

An LCR matrix that has holes in it isn't the only reason that outbound calls can fail before they leave your LAN. Other Dial Plan issues can cause the same failure. You need to investigate further on these issues internally to determine the true source of the issue. If a central routing matrix isn't blocking your outbound calls, the problem may be specific to a single phone. You can easily validate whether a particular phone is causing the problem by attempting to dial the same phone number from another phone in your VoIP LAN. If the calls complete when you dial out by using an alternative phone, you've narrowed down the issue to the initial phone from which the calls failed. The problem may be that the failing phone

- ✔ **Hasn't yet been built in to your phone system:** Until your phone system is aware of a new VoIP or analog phone in the system, it doesn't accept any calls from that phone.

- ✔ **Doesn't have the permission to place the call:** The phone may be set up in your VoIP phone system, but it isn't assigned any outbound calling permissions. If the phone is in a publicly accessible place, your VoIP install tech may have programmed it to allow only incoming calls to be received and local calls to be made outbound. If the specific extension is recycled for a new employee later, he or she won't be able to dial long distance until your VoIP install tech, or the programmer who manages your dial plan, adds that capability.

Getting the full scoop on LCR design

Least Cost Routing tables are generally built on the basis of the first six digits of a phone number, called either the area code and prefix, or the NPA-NXX. These tables were effective in 2000, and even in 2003. The challenge with creating an LCR based on the NPA-NXX is that it's a blunt instrument for grouping calls. In the days before phone numbers were in short supply, phone numbers were assigned in 10,000 blocks in which every phone number in a specific area code and prefix belonged to a single local phone carrier. That's no longer the case.

The demand for phone numbers has caused many carriers to give back portions of the numbers assigned to them for a prefix so that the local phone carriers that own numbers may be differentiated in smaller groups, to the NPA-NXX-X or NPA-NXX-XX level. Most rate plans that long-distance carriers provide for their larger customers are broken down by either individual rates for each individual local carrier or by a tier system that consists of several local carriers grouped together. The bottom line is that the local carrier for the phone number inevitably dictates the per-minute price charged to the call. If you're attempting to predict the local carrier for a call based on only the first six digits of the phone number, you may well be incorrect.

Your long-distance carrier probably identifies the local carrier that owns the phone number you've dialed based on the full ten-digit phone number dialed. They do this to

- Ensure the correct carrier is identified if the specific area code and prefix are broken down beyond the NPA-NXX level.

- Identify ported phone numbers.

The widespread adoption of VoIP has created a secondary challenge because many more phone numbers are being migrated to alternative carriers. The current trend is for the migration of phone numbers from traditional local carriers (which normally charge the lowest rates to terminate calls to their numbers) to alternative VoIP carriers (which normally charge some of the highest rates to terminate a call). Depending on your normal call profile, who you call, and the volume of calls you make, this issue can either have a negligible effect on your phone bill or a significant one. I've seen this issue have an impact upwards of 17 percent on a $35,000 phone bill. The lowest impact I've seen is 50 cents.

Diving In to Inbound Calling Issues

The largest VoIP problem with incoming calls is simply ensuring that your programmer whose managing your Dial Plan has completed programming the new phone number within your phone system. Your phone system must have all your phone numbers built in and related to extensions, either for a VoIP phone or application (such as voicemail or a conference room) before those numbers can accept an incoming call. The establishment of these routes must be completed by your VoIP technician, regardless of how you're receiving your phone numbers, whether you're migrating phone numbers or your carrier is assigning new numbers to you.

The key to avoiding inbound calls that fail is to build all the required inbound routing for the phone numbers before they're even active at your VoIP carrier. If you're receiving new phone numbers and they won't be active for two or three days, build your phone system immediately and have it waiting for the numbers to activate. Then, schedule a test call and view the incoming call on the day it's supposed to cut over. You need to either watch your incoming call attempt through the command-line interface of your phone system or execute a Wireshark capture during the test call to ensure you're receiving the incoming INVITE and that your phone system is responding to it properly.

If you're running an array of Asterisk servers, update each and every server with the new routing information. Asterisk is an amazing software package, but it doesn't have the innate ability to network itself together through a cluster of servers. Each server running Asterisk is an island unto itself, and data cascades through the servers only if you design your own after-market software to make it happen or manually input the new routing information into each server. If you install the new phone number on only one server, your calls fail whenever a non-updated Asterisk server receives the incoming call. Again, pull a Wireshark capture to see which server received and failed the call. It should be pretty obvious because your server is probably responding with a 403 Not Found SIP response.

Looking Over Non-Voice Issues

VoIP is designed to transmit voice calls, but fax and DTMF tones have to fit within the VoIP structure the best they can, making them prime candidates for problems. The main thing to remember about faxing over IP is that you can use the features available with your hardware only if you integrate them into the outside world with your Dial Plan. Just because your hardware says it can transcode from T.38 to analog doesn't mean that it automatically knows which phone numbers you've set up for your fax machine and automatically re-INVITEs to T.38. That's still a function of your Dial Plan, so you must design and build that out to tie the fax machine extension together to the re-INVITE to T.38.

Wireshark captures are essential in troubleshooting T.38 issues because the banter between your SIP proxy and the SBC of your VoIP carrier is more involved during this type of call than any voice call you may have.

DTMF issues are another challenge. The specific connections between the long-distance provider that your VoIP carrier uses and the local carriers that your calls use can make receiving DTMF continuity a challenge. It seems like a simple enough task, but some of these connections aren't perfectly established, so you may experience challenges in receiving consistent DTMF from and to all locations. If your phone systems depend on DTMF digits (for example, if you're running a calling card platform or other service), speak to your carrier about the DTMF transmission to ensure that it can provide consistent coverage.

Wireshark can easily capture DTMF tones. If you want the specific code required to filter for the out-of-band RFC2833 tones, flip back to Chapter 11. You can verify the in-band tones by listing to the RTP in the outbound transmission (also covered in Chapter 11).

The most challenging aspect of DTMF is transmissions that include packets being sent over more than one route from your VoIP proxy to the SBC of your carrier (also called route flaps), resulting in DTMF packets arriving out of sequence. This isn't an issue as long as the receiving DTMF collector discards any packets that arrive out of sequence. If the wayward packets aren't discarded, the DTMF digit may appear to be two digits because DTMF packets interspersed with END notifications (or vice versa) make one DTMF digit appear like two.

Dealing with Progressively Diminishing Returns

Economists talk about the law of diminishing returns. It's based on the fact that when you get to the end of your inventory, you'll have spent more on warehousing, maintenance, insurance, and the general overhead associated with doing business on the oldest items that you have in inventory, translating into less profit when those items sell. VoIP can experience a similar dynamic when you load up more and more consecutive calls across your network. Eventually, you hit the saturation point for your hardware, bandwidth, carrier SBC, or connectivity into the terminating local carrier, so your calls begin to experience increasingly poor call quality or simply fail altogether.

Any issue that appears when your call volume or LAN activity increases identifies a systemic bottleneck in your VoIP environment. Figure 14-2 identifies the variables to take into account when you try to resolve problems that exhibit this pattern. Your own LAN isn't the only variable that can affect your calls when your total concurrent call count increases, but it does contain the largest group of elements that must struggle with the increased data flow. As Figure 14-2 indicates, begin troubleshooting within your LAN and work your way out to the last point at which the issue is present.

The increased stress on your VoIP LAN can manifest itself as either a drop in call quality when individual packets are lost or a drop in call completion. Depending on the call volume that you generate and where you're calling, you need to consider three possible sources of failure, with two of them being VoIP-specific:

✔ **Your LAN:** You may be maxing out the processing strength of your server — or you may have outstripped the available bandwidth on your LAN. Begin your investigation of any problems that occur only at peak time within your LAN. Use your VLM software to identify existing or growing issues. Every piece of hardware that interacts with the call, including routers, switches, cabling, and the VoIP phone itself (as well as the configuration and design of all these elements) affect the efficiency of the calls. Your VLM software should be able to indicate the source of the latency or the spot at which you're outstripping the capacity of your LAN, causing calls or packets to be discarded.

✔ **The SBC of your carrier:** Many carriers allow only a low rate of calls per second to hit each SBC on their network, generally maxing out at eight to ten calls per second. Check with your carrier to confirm the maximum calls per second and concurrent calls available for each SBC. If your average call duration is longer than three minutes, you shouldn't have to worry about the calls per second concern. If you're exceeding the calls per second, you should be receiving 487 responses back from the SBC. You may get the same response if you're trying to send more concurrent calls than you're allowed. In either of these cases, you carrier doesn't open a trouble ticket on the issue and tells you to temper the speed and volume of the calls you're sending. Check the math — pencil out your average call duration and the total quantity of consecutive calls that you're planning to hit. You may not need to have 50 or 60 calls per second available to you. Just because your array of seven Asterisk servers can pump out that many calls doesn't mean that you need them.

✔ **The tandem or IMT (Inter Machine Trunk) from your carrier to the terminating LEC:** Most carriers have only a limited amount of available bandwidth, maybe enough to handle 24 or 48 consecutive calls at best, to small local carrier central offices over the normal usage level they expect. If you inundate the central office for Red Oak, Iowa, or Snook, Texas, with 100 calls, you could blow out the local carrier's switch and prevent all calls to that area from completing.

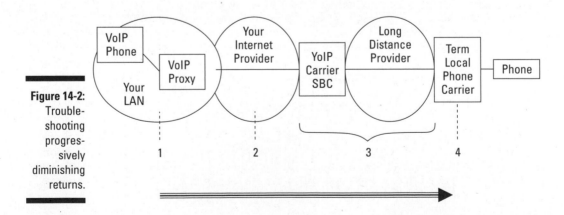

Figure 14-2: Trouble-shooting progressively diminishing returns.

Troubleshooting should always progress from the most likely to the least likely cause of the problem. Your carrier is designed to handle calls from you and thousands of other customers at the same time. Its hardware and connectivity are rated to process more calls than you could ever send to it, so its incoming VoIP interface probably isn't restricted.

The most robust section of your VoIP carrier's network is the long-distance portion. It's built with multiple routes and overflow carriers to terminate calls to any location in the world. The only way that you may experience an issue of call completion or call quality degradation when you place a high volume of calls is if a large outage takes down a section of your carrier's network.

Throttle back your calls for a few minutes to see whether the problem goes away. You need to accurately diagnose the problem — your call volume issue may actually be a time-of-day issue, not your LAN or one of the networks you encounter hitting a capacity limit.

Just because your VoIP carrier's network may be able to handle 10,000 calls per second and a million concurrent calls, you may not have access at that level. Your carrier most likely restricts you to both a maximum rate of calls per second and a maximum total of concurrent calls. If your company has grown and you've built your network and bandwidth to allow for twice the volume of calls, be sure to double your Internet bandwidth with your IP provider and order more sessions with your VoIP carrier. Just because your IP bandwidth may be "burstable," where you pay a monthly fee for a set amount of bandwidth, but you can exceed that limit at which time you pay an additional fee per megabit of use, doesn't mean the same goes for your VoIP sessions or calls per second.

Handling Curious Caller ID Names

The VoIP marketplace is dynamic. Its complexity sometimes has unexpected side effects. One of the places in which this shows itself is in the alpha character name presented on your outbound Caller ID. When you call to someone within the United States from the new VOIP line you've had installed at your business, Maureen's Flowers, the person receiving your call may see in his or her Caller ID window

- ✔ MAUREENS FLOWERS 805-555-1212
- ✔ JOHNS TOWING 805-555-1212
- ✔ 805-555-1212

The first Caller ID display in the preceding list is accurate and probably what you want the person picking up your call to see. The second Caller ID display lists the previous owner of your phone number, and the final Caller ID doesn't list any name, just your phone number. Despite the variety of information that Caller ID can display, two important universal truths pertain to Caller ID:

- ✔ **You can't input an alpha character name into the Caller ID stream.** Even if you could send the company name that you want to identify in the call stream, maybe putting it somewhere in the FROM section of the SIP INVITE, your VoIP carrier's SBC ejects it.

- ✔ **The local phone carrier populates the Caller ID window.** The company or residence name that appears next to your phone number in the Caller ID window of the person who receives your phone call is populated by its local phone carrier. If you were to call from Miami to New York City, Nynex in New York (or whoever the local carrier for the phone number you're dialing may be) actually pulls the name attributed to your Miami phone number from the national database.

The two Caller ID maxims in the preceding list can cause variations in the name presented in the Caller ID window. If the national database isn't updated from when the previous company had your phone number, whenever you call out, it's going to display the previous owner. That may be JOHNS TOWING or SUN VALLEY DRY CLEANING, but it isn't your company name. If the phone number assigned to you hasn't been used in six months or more, or is brand new, no company or residence name may be attributed to it, so the Caller ID simply displays the phone number and nothing more.

These Caller ID display discrepancies occur because of your relationship with the local phone provider that's identified as owning your phone number. The VoIP market frequently has several layers of companies between the actual end user who dials out and the carriers that provide the local and long-distance features for the line. Chapter 12 delves into this layering of VoIP carriers and VoIP service providers that may be involved in providing inbound service, illustrating how the layers of VoIP service providers interact, as well as their visibility and impact on your calls.

When all is said and done, one local phone carrier owns the responsibility of your phone number. It's the one company identified in the national database of phone numbers as the provider, and all incoming calls are directed to its network. This company must provide a white pages listing for your phone number if you want to update the company name that appears on your outbound Caller ID. It's the one company that interacts with the national databases to identify how to reach your phone number (more specifically, how to reach its central office that provides service to your phone number). Because only it has the authority to change the national records on your phone number, it needs to update the database to reflect your new company name.

The logistics of inputting your phone number into the national directory alongside your company name is the first challenge. The process of updating the white pages listing for a phone number is time consuming and requires manual labor — someone has to key in exactly what you want. She can't make any typos or mistakes; otherwise, she has to do the whole thing over again. The constant pressure to provide phone service at a lower price has made this little luxury a non-standard add-on for many local phone carriers that provide phone numbers to VoIP carriers. They may not provide a white page listing for your phone number at all, or it may be available for a fee.

The second challenge is that the local phone company responsible for your phone number probably doesn't have a direct relationship with you. You usually receive VoIP service through one or more intermediary aggregators or service providers who may not know the white page listing policy of the true local carrier. Even if the carrier that its use to provide the local phone service does offer white page listings, it (or another intermediary company) may elect to not offer the service because of the increased manpower and overhead required to support it.

If your VoIP carrier doesn't provide white page listings, expect the Caller ID name on your outbound calls to reflect the last company that did have a white pages listing. If you have a new phone number that's never been issued, or your phone number has been deactivated for so long that the previous white page listing has been expunged, then only your number is listed, without your company name.

If your business requires your company name to appear next to your phone number in the Caller ID of all outbound calls, ask your VoIP carrier about this feature before you migrate your phone numbers to them. If you're an established company and plan to migrate all your phone numbers, you may not have to worry about this potential issue. Your phone numbers have been active for years, and you've had white page listings for them over that duration of time, so you don't need to change the current name displayed. If you're starting a new company or your existing company was purchased, you may have to interview a few VoIP companies before you find one that can provide the directory listing service for your numbers.

Troubleshooting Wisdom

Every telecom company has its strengths and its weaknesses. Some companies have an efficient troubleshooting structure, some don't. Unless you plan on buying your telecom provider and re-vamping its trouble reporting system, you have to make do with the level of service it provides — and also keep it as your friend and troubleshooting partner. If your level of service drops completely, you need to look for another carrier.

Because you're using VoIP, you have so many more options available to you than the average person who uses traditional telephony. This chapter, as well as Chapter 12 and Chapter 13, allow you to narrow down almost any issue to the specific carrier responsible. If you take the time to pull the Wireshark capture, analyze it, and work through your VLM software, you can remove almost all the guesswork in troubleshooting.

In every troubleshooting conversation between technicians, someone always knows a little more than the other person. If you're the one with the more extensive knowledge, be gracious. Remember the point in time when you weren't the smartest one on the call. If you aren't the guru on the call, that means you're speaking to someone who can show you a thing or two, so ask every question about VoIP that crosses your mind. Even if it doesn't relate to the issue at hand, he or she may be able to answer it for you.

If all the troubleshooting you've done has been inconclusive, go back and start all over with a clean slate. Identify the variables, isolate them, and prove them out one by one. After you validate a carrier or a leg of the call, don't look at it anymore. Then, narrow down the issue based on where it fits in the OSI model (see Chapter 5 if you'd like to know more about the OSI model). List all the potential variables that interact at that level and narrow down the trouble-shooting some more. You can find the problem and fix it. Really. Stay persistent, take good notes, and there's no issue you won't be able to unravel.

Part IV
The Part of Tens

In this part . . .

Every pearl of wisdom regarding VoIP has been carefully identified and presented to you in this section. The early days of VoIP saw it growing, evolving, and working through its gawky stage where everything didn't work as well as it does now. That time made a lasting impression on some, and the ten common misperceptions of VoIP are tackled in the very first chapter of this section.

I run through the ten things that make VoIP great next, that can be used as a checklist of VoIP features you really should be exploiting. The next chapter covers the ten things about VoIP you should NOT be exploiting. These are the pitfalls, and loopholes people sometimes use with VoIP that they shouldn't. Some of the points listed will simply cost you money, or irritate your carrier if you do them, while others may land you in jail. It's a good thing to peruse before you abuse the technology.

The final chapter of this section, and the book, identify ten places to go for help. This is an evolving technology and everyone is at a different level of education in every aspect of it. There are times when you need to unravel a mystery and you're at your wits end. There are other times when you might need to learn another layer of information in order to use VoIP more fully. Regardless of why you need the information, the final section provides resources to find it.

Chapter 15

Ten Common Misperceptions

*V*oIP is a victim of stereotyping. All the challenges, problems, and growing pains it went through in its evolution have stigmatized it in the eyes of many people. They don't see it as an evolved technology working hand in hand with traditional telephony, but simply the clumsy, awkward protocol used by techno-hobbyists to make static-filled calls to friends overseas by using their dial-up Internet connections.

VoIP has come into its own. It's a tested and true technology that can do everything traditional telephony can do, and more. This chapter covers the lingering misperceptions about VoIP, explaining their truth, their half-truth, and their complete lies. Believing that any of these ten VoIP fables are true only leads to frustration. The widespread acceptance and adoption of this technology, and the maturity of the market, has established it as a legitimate protocol that's the basis for future telephone communications.

Banking on Saving Money

The first and largest misperception about VoIP is that it's free, or at least cheaper than traditional telephony. VoIP used this battle cry when it was first released. The entire industry was abuzz with stories of how VoIP was going to wipe out the long-distance industry. The theory was put out to the masses that all calls would eventually span from VoIP device to VoIP device, and the traditional PSTN carrying all the phone calls would become instantly obsolete. Phone calls were going to be just another Internet service like e-mail, where you can send as much as you want without a per-minute, per-meg, or per-transaction cost.

Well, it was a beautiful dream. Reality began to set in when the companies marketing this fantasy started paying for the per-minute fees to complete the calls into the PSTN, the hardware to facilitate the calls, and the technicians to service the hardware needed to facilitate the calls. All the real-world costs reigned in the idea of free phone service.

The costs in the VoIP market have always been more reactive than proactive. VoIP providers and carriers provided services for free until the overhead became too expensive to ignore. Migrating phone numbers from one carrier to another used to be free. The Local Number Portability (LNP) departments of large phone carriers consisted of one person who wasn't busy enough to worry about the cost. That didn't last long, and soon hundreds and thousands of phone numbers per day were being transferred between carriers. That one person who started the department now manages a staff of ten that is probably struggling to keep up with the demand. The increased labor required to manage the ancillary elements of VoIP translated to increased cost for the VoIP providers, and the number portability charge was established to ensure profitability.

This reactive process of realizing the costs and responding to them after they could no longer be ignored was a reoccurring theme in the VoIP industry while it evolved. The technology allowed for companies to enter a niche market that was previously unreachable — the local carrier arena. Many companies tried to compete with the Baby Bells, GTE (now Verizon), and Ameritechs in the past, but the cost to replicate their infrastructure, bringing wiring into every home and business in America, was just too difficult and expensive. When the Internet gained force and everyone in America suddenly had the ability to buy cheap, dedicated Internet bandwidth, that hurdle was removed. Small VoIP companies could use the DSL or broadband connections purchased by the residences and small businesses to provide their service.

But the companies that heeded the VoIP call were, unfortunately, not telecom companies. A great many of the companies jumping into VoIP were made up of the leftover dreamers from dot-com companies that went bust only a few years earlier. They had no experience in telecom, but they were well-versed in marketing new and cutting-edge technology companies to investors. They saw VoIP as the next big wave of easy money and simple profits. The path seemed clear and just like the dot-com run before it. Many founders of the new VoIP companies were determined to ride this technology to the top and sell the company for top dollar.

The VoIP companies started up the marketing machine, and VoIP was touted as the free alternative to traditional phone calls. Articles were published on the death of long distance and prophesized how the service would soon be marginalized to a line item on a bundled monthly bill covering your Internet and TV, as well.

VoIP companies tried to continue to push the idea of free long distance until they realized that it wasn't gong to be free any time in the immediate future. They feared losing the customers they were gaining, so they reworked the old free-long-distance gimmick by saying that the usage and monthly charges are less with VoIP than traditional telephony. This seemed like standard math because you can get twice as many calls out of the same bandwidth by using VoIP with compression, so at least the monthly fees must be cheaper. The cost savings on the monthly fees may be true some of the time, but not all the time.

If you're buying digital cable Internet from your cable TV provider, you pay only one fee every month, which covers the cost to deliver the copper cable to your home and the Internet service. On the other hand, purchasing a dedicated Internet connection from a large carrier such as MCI, Sprint, or QWEST actually involves two charges:

- ✔ **A monthly fee for the *local loop* (wiring from its POP to your office):** This charge varies, depending on how far your office is from the POP. The further away you are, the more you pay.

- ✔ **A monthly fee for the Internet port after you reach its POP:** This charge also varies, depending on how much bandwidth you need.

Depending on the cost of the local loop and the Internet port, VoIP may offer you a better deal than traditional phone service, or it may not. The cost for both the loop and port varies, depending on your requirements and distance from the POP, so you have to crunch the numbers to identify whether the switch would actually save you any money.

Don't forget about the hardware. If you have an existing phone system, you have to replace it with VoIP hardware and software, and hire someone to deploy and validate it. If you don't have a phone system and are starting from scratch, the hardware costs might be the same as a traditional phone system, or a bit less due to the availability of open source software such as Asterisk. Weigh all the costs before assume that VoIP is a better deal than traditional phone service.

Expecting Bandwidth Savings

VoIP is an amazing technology that can cut down on your bandwidth requirements, or it can consume more bandwidth than traditional telephony. The myth comes from the marketing. VoIP is sold as an extremely efficient, cutting-edge technology, which it can be in the hands of a skilled technician.

A standard call that uses traditional telephony consumes about 64 Kbps for the audio portion of the call and precious little bandwidth for the overhead. An uncompressed VoIP call uses the same 64 Kbps for the audio portion of the call, but it also has to grapple with the additional overhead required to form RTP, UDP, and IP packets. All this overhead translates into a single, uncompressed VoIP call that can use up to 83 Kbps, which effectively knocks out any idea of a 1:1 ratio for bandwidth use when comparing VoIP and traditional telephony.

The rumor of bandwidth-efficient VoIP does have some truth to it. Unlike traditional telephony, you have several options for compressing the audio portion of the call for transmission. Table 15-1 compares the bandwidth requirements of traditional telephony and the VoIP codec options available.

Table 15-1	VoIP and Traditional Bandwidth Use		
Transmission Method	*Audio*	*Overhead*	*Total*
G.711 Codec	64 Kbps	19 Kbps	83 Kbps
Traditional Telephony	64 Kbps	0 Kbps	64 Kbps
G.726 Codec	32 Kbps	19 Kbps	51 Kbps
G.728 Codec	16 Kbps	19 Kbps	35 Kbps
GSM (Global System for Mobile communications)	13 Kbps	19 Kbps	32 Kbps
G.729 Codec	8 Kbps	19 Kbps	27 Kbps
G.723 Codec	6.4 Kbps	19 Kbps	25.4 Kbps
iLBC (Internet Low Bit Rate Codec)	6.6 Kbps	19 Kbps	25.6 Kbps

All VoIP codec information listed in this table is based on a 20-ms packetization interval

Despite the variety of codecs available, don't choose one solely on the compression available. The logic used for each codec dictates the amount of time required to code and decode the voice (which creates latency), as well as the expected audio quality. All these factors reduce the field of codecs that most companies use to either G.711 or G.729.

Every VoIP carrier supports these two codecs. But if you're offering G.729 and G.711 in your INVITE message, your calls may negotiate to either one, depending on the far-end requirements. The industry standard is for the first codec choice offered in the INVITE message to be accepted, as long as the far end supports it, so keeping G.729 as the first option forces more calls to the compressed codec, and you'll see the bandwidth savings.

G.729 codecs usually require you to purchase a license for each concurrent call active on your VoIP phone system that uses them. You don't get a warning when you run out, so ensure you have more than you need.

Believing in the Homogeneous Route Path

Customers who used traditional telephony circuits in the early days of VoIP believed that their non-VoIP connection to the long-distance carrier ensured their calls would remain a traditional telephony call from end to end. This perception was shattered when their dedicated circuits were wired to their long-distance carrier through a VoIP-enabled NGS (Next Generation Switch). Many of the customers believed that their traditional telephony calls were being corrupted by this potential conversion to VoIP, and they were determined that because they ordered a digital circuit, they wanted the calls to be digital from end to end.

The truth of the matter is that regardless of how a call reaches a long-distance carrier, either from an analog or a VoIP phone, it's routed and processed in exactly the same way. The call is converted to or from VoIP when it flows through their network and delivered to an underlying carrier. After the call is with the underlying carrier or carriers, it may be converted to or from VoIP again and again until it reaches the local phone carrier, which rings the phone belonging to the number dialed.

If any end of the call is embedded in the PSTN with a traditional phone number, the call will be traditional telephony at some point in time and may be VoIP for at least one leg along the journey. Carriers don't separate their networks, with VoIP traffic running through one side of it and all the traditional telephony calls sequestered someplace else. It costs too much to build a redundant network just to accommodate a different protocol, especially with VoIP because the telecom switches that make up the long distance carrier's network can relatively easily convert the VoIP traffic into or out of the protocol.

The only time you can guarantee a homogeneous route path is when you're sending a call from a VoIP point of origin to a VoIP endpoint, without referencing anything that looks like a traditional phone number in the INVITE message. The PSTN is built and designed to locate and route calls to phone numbers. VoIP interfaces with the PSTN to exploit the existing infrastructure for calls, so the only way to avoid the PSTN is to avoid anything in your call that looks like it belongs in the PSTN.

No current mechanisms allow you to start a call from an analog telephone in the PSTN and ring into a VoIP phone that doesn't have a phone number assigned to it. You can't just grab the rotary dial phone at grandmother's house and dial a SIP URI of `stephen@wiley.voip`. You may be able to place calls from the PSTN to a SIP URI in the future, but right now, no one has established a national routing guide for SIP URIs. PSTN-originated calls are connected to VoIP phones by referencing the phone number assigned to them, and they're routed just like a traditional phone call. The local carrier that owns your phone number finally converts the call to VoIP only in the last leg of the call, then sends it to your URI.

Suffering through Poor Call Quality

This specter of poor call quality was the biggest threat used against VoIP when it was first released. This myth, like the others, began a long time ago with a grain of truth. In the early days of dial-up Internet connections, people used to design their own VoIP software and call other techno-hobbyists around the world. In these early times, programmers and technicians were working through the algorithms for compression and only just discovering the impact that latency, jitter, flap, and packet loss had on call quality. In this wild and wooly time before the concept of VoIP Lifecycle Management, half the fun was just making an international call for free, even if you could make out only every third word spoken.

The technology and the industry have grown since those simpler days. Your VoIP-originated call probably is converted to traditional telephony and delivered through the PSTN to an analog phone. So, all the threat of latency and jitter is stopped when the call is converted to traditional telephony. After the call hits your long-distance network, regardless of whether it arrives VoIP, analog, or digital, that call experiences a standard call quality while it travels through to the PSTN and the terminating local carrier.

Therefore, the only specter of VoIP-induced call quality issues exist within your LAN or en route to the SBC of your VoIP carrier. You have complete control over how efficiently or inefficiently your LAN functions. If you're overloading the network and losing packets during peak data transfer times, resulting in poor audio quality, you have the power to resolve the issue.

VoIP does have more potential variables that can impact call quality than traditional telephony. These elements of VoIP calling brought about the concept of VoIP Lifecycle Management and advanced software packages that allow you to track down these issues. Call quality should no longer be a concern for any VoIP deployment, as long as you have

> ✔ A well-engineered and -managed network
>
> ✔ A connection to a quality IP provider that has sufficient bandwidth
>
> ✔ A VLM software package that allows you to manage your LAN after VoIP deployment
>
> ✔ A minimal number of hops required to reach the SBC of your VoIP carrier

All these factors allow you to reduce the potential that your LAN or IP provider is the source of a call quality issue. After you clear that hurdle and the call reaches the SBC of your VoIP carrier without excessive latency, jitter, or packet loss, everything else in the call path is the same as if you were calling from an analog phone.

Dreading the InterOperability

Every new, cutting-edge technology goes through the awkward adolescent stage in which it can't seem to communicate well with its peers. Sometimes, all the hardware, software, and interfaces are different. One format may be Mac, the other a Windows PC. Maybe one was VHS, and the other Beta Hi-Fi. Regardless, the hardware market is always full of competitors running on different platforms or interfaces when any technology emerges. So, some hardware simply can't work with other hardware. As much as you try, that old 8-track cassette doesn't fit in your CD player.

Fortunately for VoIP, VoIP devices don't have a hardware compatibility issue. As long as each device has connectivity to the Internet, it doesn't matter whether it's a fiber-optic, co-axial, or copper connection. The IP platform that VoIP uses paved the way and eliminated these physical barriers to connectivity.

But VoIP still had challenges in the beginning. The challenges weren't that dissimilar to when ISDN was released back in the early 1990s. The industry had some uniformity for the cabling required and standards for how information would be sent. The problem cropped up because, like every written standard, two different manufacturers wouldn't necessarily interpret the specific requirements for how the overhead was going to control the individual channels in the same way. Despite the fact that you have everything set up exactly as it should be for your ISDN line, your Motorola Bitsurfer may still not work with the Livingston router that your Internet provider uses.

Many worried that the new and emerging VoIP technology would spawn hardware equally as incompatible. Yes, VoIP was amazing, and everyone who could write code was capable of drawing up their own SIP software from scratch. But on the downside, everyone who could write code *was* drawing up their own SIP software from scratch. The VoIP world ended up with a multitude of custom-built software phone systems, all using someone's personal interpretation of the RFC standard.

During that time, if you fired up your Linux server that ran the personal SIP code drawn up by your techie friend next door, it could very well *not* work with your boutique VoIP carrier. Even after modifying settings and working through all options for codecs, sampling rates, and dial plan settings, you might not have sufficient common ground to consistently pass good completed calls.

Many VoIP carriers were acutely aware of this reality and created InterOperability (InterOp) testing, which they used before releasing a prospective customer into full production because it didn't make sense to build out VoIP ports and allocate resources if the end user couldn't even complete test calls consistently.

Those days are now behind us. Open-source SIP software is readily available, and the fun of hacking your own VoIP code has been exchanged for time spent evolving an amazing dial plan based on the Asterisk software you downloaded. Asterisk, and other open source software packages, allow programmers to build on them, adding the features and enhancements that they want while leaving the nuts and bolts of the VoIP software alone.

After a relatively short period of time, carriers have now done away with the pre-installation InterOp testing regime. VoIP hardware is now as likely to function with the software on the SBC of any VoIP carrier as if it was a traditional telephony connection. The standardization is complete within the VoIP protocols, and any two VoIP platforms should be able to work together seamlessly, after all the standard parameters and options are configured correctly.

Cringing at Complexity

The people who work with VoIP can be more intimidating than the technology itself. They speak a strange English that's peppered with acronyms, programming terms, and LAN-speak. So, getting an intellectual understanding of VoIP can be challenging because every question that you ask to clarify an acronym seems to lead to a definition in tech-ese that requires yet more explanation. The same can be said for VoIP information that you can find on the Internet or in many books (aside from this one, of course).

Most of the available information sources assume that you've spent several years writing software, programming, and designing LANs. All these areas of study support VoIP, and that's just the technology part. After you understand all the technical elements enough to do something with them, you still need to figure out the industry information. If you're going to use VoIP, you need to know how carriers work together to deliver a VoIP call from end to end and how the calls are rated and billed. That mountain of information still leaves room for the finer points of Local Number Portability, Caller ID transmission, and setting up a white page listing for your phone number.

Well, you don't need to know everything about all the elements used to build VoIP. After VoIP is deployed, you can use it just as easily as your standard analog telephone. Think of VoIP like an automobile — you may not know anything about electrical systems, hydraulic systems, computer programming, or internal-combustion engines, but you have no problem putting gas in the car and driving it.

The one aspect of VoIP that frightens people the most is the dial plan. You may find the design and construction of the internal routing of calls and the allocation of telecom services daunting if you're starting from scratch. Phone vendors and hardware technicians had to do the same programming for traditional telephony phone systems, but those systems' configuration was simplified to limit your options and designed to make you pay more money if you need more capacity or features.

VoIP phone systems are accomplishing the same tasks as the traditional phone systems, simply allowing you to deploy it yourself. If you need a specific setup for your phone system, hire a programmer to design it for you. If you need only a basic configuration with nothing special, you can find plenty of move-in-ready, open source phone systems available, such as AsteriskNOW and trixbox. These software packages auto-locate any installed hardware, configure it, and provide you with a simple Web GUI that you can use to fine-tune all the extensions, voicemail boxes, call queues, and conference rooms that you may need.

I have found one downside to AsteriskNOW — the version of Linux that it installs lacks most of the development tools that you need to retrieve and successfully install Wireshark. For any VoIP deployment, you must have some packet-capture software running on your VoIP server. Otherwise, you're at the mercy of the availability and motivation of your carrier's technicians whenever you have an issue.

The one shred of truth to the fear that VoIP is more complex than standard telephony is that, as a customer, you shoulder more responsibility for the call. Anything that impacts the call within your own network is your responsibility to identify and repair. But if you can defrag your computer's hard drive and use standard virus protection software, you can successfully use the VLM software available to clean up your LAN.

If you're looking for some VLM software, I recommend only the best — a solution offered by a great company in Cupertino, California, called Packet Island (www.packetisland.com). Check out Chapter 9 if you want to see it in action.

Fearing Troubleshooting

Troubleshooting, in and of itself, is a challenge, and troubleshooting a new technology is frequently a daunting task. The problem isn't that VoIP technology is inherently more difficult to pull apart and analyze, but simply that it's new. You invariably find yourself trying to build test scenarios about something, only to realize that you don't even know what you don't know about it. Huge variables could be impacting your calls that you haven't even identified as being involved in the calls.

When VoIP was initially released, the VoIP carriers and resellers probably didn't have a battalion of technicians with complete knowledge of SIP, SDP, RTP, H.323, T.37, T.38, and every codec in the industry. VoIP is a specific technology that's a hybrid of so many other disciplines that long-distance carriers rolling out VoIP service often can't find staff who have enough varied experience to quickly grasp the totality of it.

In regards to experience, everyone in the VoIP world benefits from the intense growth that the market has experienced over the past few years. The technicians have had time to figure out all the aspects of VoIP, and they've trained a new batch of technicians who may have never known anything before dealing with VoIP.

The majority of any telecommunications services troubleshooting isn't your responsibility. Do your best to help your carrier narrow down the location of the problem, but most of the standard telephony issues you encounter are probably the same ones you encountered before you switched to VoIP.

The data-centric and packet-based nature of VoIP makes it much easier to troubleshoot than traditional telephony calls. You don't have an equivalent to Wireshark or tcpdump for calls in the non-VoIP world. Your carrier must do any kind of call traps or analysis in the traditional telephony, after you open a trouble ticket, and after a technician calls back, and after that technician sets up the capture. If you have an intermittent issue, the tech might not be able to capture the data before the data they receive overloads the capture buffer of the specific program used.

VoIP allows you to execute captures on the entire call or just the overhead, and the capture remains open until you use up all the remaining available memory on the server (unless you set a limit within the capture software). If you're running SIP, you can then easily open up the capture by using Wireshark and read all the banter that's running through your VoIP server. And you can do all this yourself, in probably the same amount of time it would take to call your carrier, reach a customer service rep, and simply open a trouble ticket. If you need to open a trouble ticket with your carrier after you execute a packet capture, you can provide that capture to it, which can help focus its efforts and shorten the time to resolution.

Expecting a Simpler Phone Bill

This theory is still up for debate. Here's a more accurate question: What's a simpler phone bill? Many companies bundle services into one big lump and offer a single invoice for your cable TV, Internet connection, and phone service. If you want to pay $125 per month for all that and enjoy the luxury of having your invoice arrive on a single piece of paper, then this myth may be true for you.

If you dig down into that combination invoice, you may find that it isn't as great a deal as you thought. The company from which you're getting all these services isn't a charity, so it's obviously making a profit on this bundled package. Package deals are considered good for the service provider because

- **The more services a customer has, the less likely he or she is to move to another company.** Trying to replace any one service provider is a hassle. The resistance to jump ship increases exponentially when the number of services increases. If you have to replace your phone company, Internet company, and cable television provider, you may prefer to just pay a little more per month and have slightly less service, rather than go through the hassle of moving everything.

- **The service providers expect you to use much less phone service than you're paying for.** The majority of your total phone bill, local and long-distance, is probably the local portion. You pay a monthly fee for your phone number to your local phone carrier. Your local phone carrier has no real reason to charge $25 or $35 per month for local phone service, aside from the fact that it used to be a monopoly and was federally authorized to get away with it. Your VoIP provider knows that the local-service side of providing phone service costs much less than what the traditional local carrier charge, and it expects you to spend about $10 per month on long distance, so a package deal in which it charges you $35 for everything is a good deal — for it, and maybe for you.

Even though your new VoIP provider probably says that it offers unlimited calling, check the fine print. Every call that you make to a traditional phone number must be sent over the PSTN, and at some point in time, it's charged a per-minute fee that your carrier recovers in your flat-rate fee. If you suddenly make hour-long calls to a cell phone in South Africa or a ship in the Pacific, I guarantee that your new VoIP provider will find a way to roll those additional charges to you. Be sure to read everything thoroughly before you decide that any deal is a good deal for you.

Disregarding Traditional Long-Distance Carriers

Traditional long-distance and local phone carriers are conservative entities. They run new technology through a series of tests before they release it internally for their own use. After they work out all the bugs, they release that technology to a few select and friendly customers for testing and feedback. While they do this test-and-release process, they watch the market and crunch the numbers. They have more overhead than a small boutique carrier that's running one VoIP soft switch and has a handful of technicians.

Because of this need to run through a slow and methodical deployment of VoIP, the big long-distance companies, such as QWEST, Sprint, and Verizon, didn't offer VoIP when VoIP was still evolving. They knew that they hadn't figured out all the costs yet, and they wanted to see how big VoIP was going to be before they jumped into the market.

Well, they've jumped into the market now, every company in different ways. Some chose the high road, offering VoIP to only other carriers that use their service, and others took the low road, rolling out residential packages for homes across America. The VoIP market has by no means matured. Multitudes of VoIP offerings still have yet to be released that will come to the market in the next three to five years. The natural shift in the industry is toward VoIP, and if your long-distance carrier doesn't offer VoIP access today, just wait a few years.

One of the main reasons that some carriers are slower to enter the VoIP market is because of the hardware cost required to open up the technology. The existing networks for every carrier in America have evolved over decades, all designed around the idea of supporting traditional telephony calls. VoIP does have benefits that traditional telephony doesn't, so companies feel a definite pull to provide service. The downside to rolling out VoIP is that it entails the addition of VoIP gateways in front of the long-distance carrier's existing network backbone. So, the long-distance carriers must pay capital expense to purchase these expensive gateways and hire additional technicians to deploy them. At the same time, their long-distance customers expect them to provide the VoIP service at the same cost per minute as traditional telephony. Finally, many companies are moving to VoIP or opening up new offices with VoIP, so the market to make money exists. The migration moves on slowly.

Expecting Non-VoIP Phone Features

All phone numbers aren't the same. Some do more than others. When a phone number is migrated from a traditional local phone carrier, such as Bell Atlantic or Nynex, it loses more than all those fun features you had on it (such as distinctive ringing, voicemail, and Caller ID), it's also stripped down to the lowest common denominator of what a phone number can do.

The one function that the phone number still retains is the ability to act as a routing reference point for incoming calls. Any feature that you have with your new VoIP carrier, aside from the ability to receive incoming calls, is a replacement feature that it's providing from its VoIP soft switch. Its hardware provides your new voicemail, sends you Caller ID, and gives you any other spiffy features you have. The stripped-down version of your phone number that does exist is actually viewed as a Direct Inward Dial (DID) number that's only purpose is to receive incoming calls.

The new local carrier that received ownership of your phone number publishes it in the national Local Exchange Routing Guide (LERG) database so that everyone in the world knows how to find you. A call coming into your phone number flows through the following steps. From the time that your phone number is dialed by the originating phone, the call follows this path:

1. The originating phone's local carrier receives the call.

2. That local carrier routes the call to its assigned long-distance carrier.

3. The long-distance carrier checks the LERG to identify your new local carrier.

4. The long-distance carrier delivers the call to your new local carrier.

5. Your local carrier delivers the call to you, ringing your phone.

That's all your phone number is empowered to do in the eyes of the PSTN. Your outbound calling may list your phone number as the originating phone number, and that number is probably displayed in the Caller ID of anyone you call.

Despite that fact, your phone number has nothing to do with your ability to dial outbound over your VoIP line. The Caller ID that the recipient of your calls sees is derived from the phone number identified in the FROM field of the INVITE message initiating the call. The phone number listed in the FROM field *isn't* branded to your telephone or the phone line. It's probably either input into the INVITE message by the ATA delivered to your home by your VoIP provider or after your outbound call hits your VoIP provider, when it cross-references your IP address to your phone number.

The phone number listed in the FROM field is completely open to manipulation. Anyone with access to the calling profile or dial plan can place any phone number that he or she wants in the FROM field. It could be

- ✔ Your legitimate phone number

- ✔ A valid call-back number for your office that *isn't* your phone number

- ✔ A toll-free number

- ✔ A phone number that has nothing to do with your company (generally a bad idea and sometimes illegal if you're telemarketing)

- ✔ A bogus phone number that doesn't exist (123-456-7890, for example)

After your telephone phone number migrates to a VoIP carrier, it affects only your incoming calls. All outbound services are provided by your VoIP carrier, and it can deliver those services to you, regardless of whether your actual phone number has ported to it.

The migration of your phone number to a VoIP carrier removes it from the standard support infrastructure that you've enjoyed for so many years. You may no longer have access to some features through standard channels that you took for granted with your traditional telephony. The federal government has dictated that all VoIP providers that have the ability to provide outbound VoIP service must provide emergency 911 service to their customers. This huge step had to be accomplished in order to pave the way for the current expansion into VoIP.

Despite the mandated features, you may still have a difficult time establishing or modifying a white page or directory assistance listing. Your VoIP provider is not required to offer white page listings, and if it's essential to you or your business, be sure to ask about it before you sign a contract for the next 12 months.

Chapter 16

Ten Great Advantages

*V*oIP is the telecom wave of the future. No technology on the horizon is set to eclipse the development of VoIP in the next decade. Carriers are deploying more VoIP-enabled equipment right now than traditional telephony hardware, and that trend shows no sign of changing. The industry is moving toward VoIP every day, and the movement is gaining momentum.

This chapter covers ten reasons why VoIP is growing so quickly. The nature of its structure allows it more flexibility, features, and visibility at all levels. The widespread deployment of broadband Internet has fueled the VoIP fire and opened up a whole new realm of viable competition to local phone carriers that previously maintained a stranglehold on that market.

Freeing Yourself from Your Local Carrier

Local carriers, such as Pacific Bell, Bell Atlantic, Nynex, and the old-time GTE, all had geographic areas over which they were required to deliver service. If you lived in the middle of a city (or in the middle of nowhere) and wanted a phone, they had to pull cable to your house. Pulling cable for miles to wire up a single farm on the outskirts of town cost a lot of money, but they offset that cost with subsidies or with all the money made on residential customers packed into subdivisions. They didn't have to worry about any real threat to their profit because they were a government-sponsored monopoly, so they had a guaranteed specific rate of return on their investment.

Time went on, and other phone companies wanted a piece of the pie. They leveraged the federal government to allow competition into these local markets, and before long, Competing Local Exchange Carriers (CLECs) began cropping up to go head-to-head with the traditional local carriers.

The biggest hurdle to competing with the existing local carriers was the simple fact of logistics. The incumbent carriers had many years to deploy their networks and install cable, all under the protection of the federal government, ensuring their profit margin. So, they had time to pay off most of the initial deployment costs and build all the required infrastructure to provide connectivity to every telephone in their geographic region. The CLECs entering the market years later had neither a widespread network nor a protected profit margin during their deployment, forcing them to incur enormous start-up costs.

The only other option for competing with the local carriers was to contract with them to use their network. The incumbent carriers were eventually forced by the federal government to provide this option, so they eventually complied. This approach wasn't viable, either, because the reseller arrangements involved processes so constricted and convoluted that the new competing local phone carriers posed no real threat to the market share of the incumbent carriers.

Then came the Internet. Everyone ordered a second phone line and got a dial-up connection. Then, the local cable TV companies realized that, over the years, they had developed a network with access to every home in America. They also realized that the cable they used to deliver the video for television had enough spare bandwidth on it to also provide Internet access. In a few years, both the traditional television companies and the local telephone carriers were offering dedicated Internet access through the same wiring used to deliver their primary service. The bundled service package was born, marketed, and sold to millions of homes across America.

The ubiquitous availability of broadband Internet was the back door that VoIP needed to open up the market for local phone service. Dedicated Internet connections were seen as an add-on service by cable TV and local phone providers, both of which were almost unaware of the growing strength of VoIP. By the time the cable TV and local phone providers realized what had been brewing, it was too late. An entire network of redundant cabling from cable TV providers had been installed across America, giving VoIP the vehicle that it needed so that it could deploy and opening the doors to competition with the local carriers.

Today, you can leave your old local carrier behind. You no longer have to deal with its inefficient business model with a federally mandated rate of return. Many VoIP carriers are providing aggressive rates for standard phone service, so look them up, read the fine print, and go forth to a smaller phone bill with more services.

Enjoying VoIP Compression

Traditional telephony has only two bandwidth options. You can use 56 Kbps for the voice portion of the call and about 8 Kbps for overhead, or you can use 64 Kbps for the voice portion and dedicate another phone line for the overhead. Regardless of which option you use, you still can't squeeze any more than 24 concurrent phone calls out of a standard T-1 digital circuit.

Allocating 64 Kbps to a phone conversation for every millisecond the call is active does seem a bit of a waste. During a call, one person has to stop speaking so the other person can talk, or maybe both people don't say anything from time to time. Although absolutely no sound needs to be transferred, an entire 64 Kbps are locked up sending white noise. The packetized nature of VoIP can reduce your overall bandwidth consumption by simply not sending packets when nobody speaks on one or both sides of a call. If nothing else changed on the call for bandwidth use, you'd still save bandwidth.

The great news is that VoIP doesn't restrict you to only two options that, in the end, both use up the same amount of bandwidth. An uncompressed VoIP call that uses G.711 does use a bit more bandwidth than a traditional telephony call, but other codeccs allow you an amazing level of compression. G.729 is the industry leading compression codec. It uses only 8 Kbps to transmit the voice portion of a VoIP call.

Conserving bandwidth translates into a lower phone bill, as well. One of the biggest monthly expenses for companies with a lot of phone lines is the rental of their local loop (the cabling used to connect them to their local or long-distance carrier). Depending on how many miles your office is from the nearest POP, the monthly fee could be $200 or $5,000. VoIP compression allows you to more than double the volume of calls possible with traditional telephony through the same volume of bandwidth. So, by converting to VoIP, you may be able to eliminate some unnecessary circuits and thus pay for fewer local loops.

Growing with VoIP

Business changes fast. At the beginning of the year, you may be in a small office with a handful of people, and by the end of the second quarter, you may have hired ten more employees. In the old days before VoIP, you had no choice but to call into your local phone carrier, order up ten new phone lines, and wait a week or so for a technician to come out and drop new phone jacks on the wall. After the lines were delivered to your office, your hardware vendor would have to show up, wire into the new phones, and program all the additional extensions in the phone system.

If your proprietary phone system runs out of lines, ports, or capacity, you have to buy more cards, or scrap the old system to replace it with something more robust. If the phone line you have is a dedicated digital connection, such as a T1, you have to order an additional T1, which you can't activate into the new phone equipment (you need to buy that equipment, as well) for 30 to 45 days.

VoIP is much more accommodating when you're growing. The total number of concurrent calls you can send with VoIP, after your LAN is designed to avoid being a limitation, is only restricted by

- ✔ The codec used to transmit your calls
- ✔ The size of the connection you have to the Internet

If you have a T1 of bandwidth to the Internet, 1.544 Mbps, and minimal other usage on it, you can easily add ten more concurrent calls. These calls may just barely fit in if you're using the uncompressed G.711 codec because the overhead needed to packetize G.711 data fills a T1 at about 18 calls. You can easily overcome this limitation by upgrading to G.729. With G.729, you can add the 10 new employees, and another 15 employees before you even have to think about expanding your Internet connection.

T1 lines are the smallest dedicated circuit you can receive, delivering 1.544 Mbps of bandwidth on two pairs of twisted copper wires. The next larger size of circuit is delivered on coaxial cable and can support up to 35 Mbps of connectivity (typically called a DS-3). So, if you order 5 Mbps of bandwidth to the Internet, your carrier can't deliver it on T1 cables because you need more bandwidth than a single T1 can provide. Your carrier delivers the service to your office on DS-3 coaxial cable where you are only using a portion of the total bandwidth that the physical cable can handle. When you place the order to open the bandwidth from 5 Mbps to 10 Mbps, you don't need to arrange to have your existing cable replaced or modified. The Internet provider simply makes the change to open up additional capacity at the far-end connection within its POP. If you're only opening the IP connection, your Internet provider may be able to make this change in a few hours or a couple days.

Opening up IP bandwidth and adding additional VoIP sessions are two different things. If you have an IP provider that simply provides the path through which you reach your VoIP carrier, you must also order more VoIP sessions for each additional concurrent call that you're planning to send. If you want to add 50 or 100 more sessions, adding these sessions may take some time because your carrier must design the sessions, build the routing, and establish a billing reference point for these new calls. This process can take time, possibly as much time as ordering another new dedicated circuit, because the design and deployment portion of the service may go through the exact same process.

The hardware for your VoIP server is easy to find, see, and understand. Most of the open source, VoIP phone systems, such as Asterisk, use cards that you can purchase on the Internet and install as simply as a video card. As long as you have slots available in your server, you can add more cards.

When you're purchasing analog cards for your VoIP phone system, don't forget to choose cards with the correct port configurations. Cards have either Foreign Exchange Office (FXO) or Foreign Exchange Station (FXS) ports on them. FXO ports connect to the cable on the wall that your local phone carrier provides, and these ports speak to its Central Office for all transmissions. FXS ports connect into cables that terminate at the analog phones within your office that need access to the system. If you're using one large Internet pipe and need a card to support four new analog phones, make sure it has four FXS ports on it.

Finding Yourself with VoIP

VoIP allows calls to have more than a 1:1 ratio when it comes to origination and termination points. SIP can route a single incoming call to multiple endpoints, either all at the same time or in a set sequence. The SIP server that manages the call flow can either let the person calling you hear the phone(s) ring or just give him or her some lovely music and a message, such as, "Please wait while we find your party."

This is the basis of the *find-me-follow-me* service that has been a major draw for many emerging VoIP carriers. This service can include as many different phone numbers and levels of complexity as you desire. For example, if you're a consultant who works from home some days, you could have the routing configured to

- ✔ **First:** Ring your office extension.
- ✔ **Second:** Ring your cell phone.
- ✔ **Third:** Ring your home phone.
- ✔ **Fourth:** Send the call to your voicemail.
- ✔ **Fifth:** Save the recorded voicemail message as a .WAV file and e-mail it to your office and home e-mail addresses.

If you don't want the people who call you to wait, you can have your office extension, cell phone, and home phone all receive the incoming call at the same time. The caller would hear normal ring-back, but three phones would actually be ringing at the same time. The call connects to the first device that you answer.

You can also modify this type of service to change the destinations for the call, depending on the time of day (with a different setup for after-hours calls) and the day of the week, as well as special holidays.

Taking Control of Your Phone System

Traditional phone systems consisted of sealed hardware boxes with a fixed number of ports or expansion slots, and proprietary software rigidly establishing all the parameters of call handling and routing. Voicemail boxes, duration of outgoing messages, duration of incoming messages, and the number of rings allowed before a call is sent to voicemail were all hard coded into the system.

Traditional phone systems weren't only rigid in their configuration and limited in how they could be expanded, they also rarely offered more features than basic call routing and voicemail. VoIP opens up a wealth of applications to any business that has the ambition to download some open source software such as Asterisk onto a server, and then buy the analog or digital cards required to connect to existing phones.

Unlike the limited features available with traditional phone systems, most open source VoIP packages include

- Voicemail
- Standard incoming call routing
- Standard outbound call routing
- Conference call capability
- Call queues with advanced features
- Advanced routing with pattern matching
- Interactive Voice Response (IVR) capabilities
- Blacklisting of incoming calls
- Restrictions on outbound access by extension

You can find details about all these call features, their benefits, and some potential pitfalls in Chapter 4.

Phone systems are no longer prohibitively expensive and complex proprietary systems. You can now build them yourself by using a standard server and interface cards.

If you don't want to key in all the code required to fully flesh out your phone system, you can go the short route by using an all-in-one solution such as AsteriskNOW. You can download a burn file (designed to be placed on a CD-ROM) at www.asterisknow.com that gives you almost all the power of Asterisk without the need to be an advanced computer programmer to make it work. After you burn the file onto a CD-ROM, simply place it in the server that you want to use as your phone system and re-boot that server. It takes about an hour for the software to find any cards that you've installed, program those cards, and give you the Web link to the GUI, where you can finish the configuration. It's just that easy to get your own VoIP phone system up and running.

Analyzing Your Calls

In case you skipped the entire book up to this point, VoIP works in conjunction with packet capture software, such as Wireshark and tcpdump, which allows you to see every overhead message sent between your SIP server and the SBC of your carrier. You get hard data that proves which server sent which message/method/response that resulted in a failed or impaired call. Check out Chapter 11 for a crash course in how packet capture software empowers you when you're troubleshooting.

The open source phone system that you're running probably makes its own Call Detail Records (CDR) for every call you place. CDR is a single line of text (which may or may not be delimited by commas, tabs, or anything else) that contains all the pertinent information on a phone call, generally including the

- ✔ Origination Phone number
- ✔ Termination Phone number
- ✔ Date of call
- ✔ Time of call
- ✔ Call duration
- ✔ Call completion code
- ✔ Port/channel/extension from which (for an incoming call) or to which (for an outgoing call) the call was placed

You may find this information extremely useful when you're troubleshooting a call issue to a specific terminating phone number. You need to investigate whether the call was sent over the expected carrier. The routing logic within your phone system may not be readily apparent to you, and maybe the call was directed out over an analog line or sent to a secondary carrier in your Least Cost Routing (LCR) table because all the sessions on your primary carrier were active. (The specifics on LCR tables are covered in detail in Chapter 4.) You can find the CDR and validate the egress point listed in the line of date displaying all of the information regarding the call.

You can also use CDR to validate your phone bill. I wish I could say that every phone bill is 100-percent accurate, but that simply isn't true. Telecom billing has so many nuances that providing a bill without any flaws at all is exceedingly difficult. Depending on how much money you're spending on your phone bill every month, reconciling the total number and duration of calls made during a month's time may be an essential exercise.

You can perform the simplest check by tallying up the total number and duration of all calls made for the month (or for the days covered in your billing cycle) that you have in the CDR from your phone system and compare those numbers with the numbers that appear on your bill.

The total number of calls charged to you by your carrier probably doesn't exactly match the total number of calls you see recorded on the CDR in your VoIP phone system. Some calls that you place to outlying areas, such as the Bahamas, the Caribbean, Alaska, and Hawaii, may stay stuck in the POP for over a month before they download and appear on your invoice. Every phone call is valid and can be billed up to 90 days after it's made, so some calls may appear on your invoice the following month.

How your phone system logs in calls can affect the number of calls that appear in your CDR. If your phone system generates a CDR for every call attempt, regardless of whether the call completes, you have many more calls on your CDR than appear on the bill from your carrier.

The total number of minutes that your carrier charges just can't exactly match the total call duration that your phone system logs in. No two systems ever register the start and stop times of calls in an identical manner. One system may start the clock for duration as soon as you finish dialing (such as when a cell phone company bills you for air time, rather than the duration of the call when you're actually connected to the other person). Another system may begin the duration counter only after it receives a connect signal from the far end of the call once the recipient picks up their phone, or ACK, representing the same start point triggered by a completed call. Also, one system may bill in one-second increments, and the other bills at six-second increments. Before you start obsessing about the minutiae of call clocking, identify how both your phone system and your carrier log call durations.

To reconcile an invoice, you need to recognize that these variations occur. If the invoice from your carrier doesn't match your CDR by 3 to 7 percent, you're probably okay. If the carrier invoice doesn't match by more than 7 percent, analyze the invoice down to the individual call level to find out why you have such a large discrepancy.

Converging Technology on Your LAN

Your network designer may not have had VoIP in mind when he or she established the core structures in your LAN, but it's definitely welcome to the packetized neighborhood. The real-time application aspect of VoIP is the one element that prevents it from looking like any other data flowing on your LAN. You have to make some adjustments to your LAN to accommodate VoIP, but with proper analysis and structuring before you start deploying VoIP, you can make your newly designed, or fortified LAN a cost-effective combination of data and VoIP.

Only a handful of years ago, a company would have to pay for both an Internet connection and a dedicated circuit for its phone system. Both services may even have come from the same long-distance carrier, resulting in two monthly charges for each local loop — one for Internet and one for the voice service. VoIP changes that setup. Now, you can eliminate half of those local-loop costs and run everything over your Internet connection.

You probably weren't pushing the limits of your Internet usage, anyway. You may have your Web surfing and e-mails delayed by another second or two because VoIP gets priority on the LAN, but you probably won't even notice. Integration of VoIP onto an existing data LAN allows you to use your Internet connection more efficiently than the bursty traffic that was hitting it previously.

VoIP conserves your bandwidth by sending nothing during times of silence on a phone call, which leaves more bandwidth available for Web surfing, e-mails, or someone else on a completely different call who's talking at that moment. VoIP's use of 20-millisecond packets use bandwidth much more fully than a simply configured LAN that runs only data traffic.

Moving Your Phone Number

The widespread availability of broadband Internet and the evolution of VoIP have brought viable competition to the local phone carriers. Local Number Portability (LNP) increases competition and lowers price for local service. The old system for porting phone numbers was, at times, more of a shell game than an actual migration. If you were moving your phone line to a company that was reselling your existing local carrier, your number would never change location or ownership in the eyes of the world. . . . But you would lose your voicemail, distinctive ringing, conference calling, call forwarding, and that really cool feature you used once but forgot how to use but can't live without because you don't remember want it does but you know it sure is cool. You lose all these features, in spite of the fact that your phone number didn't even leave the company with which you originally had it. Because the reseller didn't negotiate these features in its contract with the local carrier, the reseller couldn't provide them to you.

VoIP prevents this stranglehold on your phone number. You can now move your number to a completely different local carrier. You still lose your voice-mail, distinctive ringing, conference calling, call forwarding, and the really cool feature you forgot how to use, but your VoIP provider can replace them all and even give you two or three cool features that can make you not care about the one you already forgot.

VoIP also allows you to move your phone number further than you ever could before. If your office converts to VoIP and you plan to spend three months at an affiliate location overseas, your SIP proxy back at the main office can simply route the calls to you, wherever you are. Granted, this routing would be more seamless if your home office was in New York and the remote office was in London (where the time zones are relatively close together), rather than your home office in Los Angeles calling you at the remote office in India. The technology that allows you to log in to a VoIP phone overseas, build that phone into the dial plan at your home office, and send and receive calls from it exists.

Not only does a VoIP call forwarded to a remote office logistically work the same as if you were at your cubicle down the hall because your SIP phone logs in with the SIP registrar at your corporate office, it also bills the same. Because the leg of the call from the SIP server at corporate to your office in London is IP to IP, the call isn't processed by a long-distance carrier, and so there isn't any company to assess a per-minute fee. The call is seen by your IP provider as packets traversing the Internet, so neither your IP carrier or any other carrier for that matter, doesn't levy any additional fees on these extended long-distance calls, and you still have connectivity.

Just because you can swing calls to addresses other than where the national Local Exchange Routing Guide (LERG) believes the phone line exists, don't do it as a way to skirt billing issues. Sending a call to Germany while you're there for ten days is legitimate, and as far as the LERG or the world of telephony cares, the call ended in your office in New York. If you're trying to avoid paying intrastate rates by dialing out to a phone number in Pennsylvania that's forwarded to an IP address of a VoIP phone in New York, you're skirting the rating issue, and the FCC frowns on that kind of behavior. As long as you remember that willfully manipulating call information to secure an interstate rate and avoid the (sometimes much higher) intrastate is illegal, you should be able to keep yourself away from FCC entanglements.

Recession-Proofing Your Career

The company that you're working for today probably won't be the company you work for five or ten years from now. The information you're gathering about VoIP makes you a much more desirable employee to anyone who works with or provides this new technology. Telecom companies sought out the programmers who made their own SIP code in the early days. Those programmers who figured out the landscape of telephony rose in the ranks, teaching the new employees.

Going from keying code to understanding how phone numbers are ported, phone calls are routed, and all the different companies and telecom entities work together may not seem like an obvious transition. The big Internet boom is over, and everyone who did programming or LAN design work needs to find a position in which they're guaranteed work in the future. VoIP is one of the fastest growing sectors in the technology market, and despite the fact that nothing can guarantee you a paycheck, having knowledge of VoIP is a big plus in the job market.

I haven't hired an employee in the past three years without asking whether he or she knew VoIP. I think that, going forward, a candidate with VoIP experience will always receive preferential consideration over an applicant who has worked with only traditional telephony. Soak up all the VoIP knowledge that you can like a sponge because you're in the right place at the right time.

Enjoying VoIP's Future

VoIP is a revolution of technology, fed by engineers and enabled by ubiquitous broadband Internet availability. It's an amazing tool that seems to grow faster than you can figure it out. When you think you've mastered the aspects of voice transmissions, you have to contend with DTMF. After you get DTMF down, you need to look into faxing, T.37, and T.38. After you're comfortable with fax, you must deal with local number portability.

Every element of VoIP, from the signaling, to the DTMF and fax are rooted in a wider based of intellectual disciplines when compared to traditional telephony. By figuring out one aspect of VoIP, you're opening the door to the other supporting technologies and areas of information. Despite the fact that everyone refers to it collectively as VoIP, in order to be well versed in using VoIP in the real world, you must learn the supporting industry and technical underpinnings of it, including:

- **Traditional telephony:** Where VoIP ends and the PSTN begins. VoIP is based on the SS7 signaling of traditional telephony, so you need to be familiar with it's interaction with the PSTN.

- **Computer programming:** Programming terminology and skills shed light on the configuration of SIP, SDP, and RTP, as well as how they work with each other to accomplish a unified goal.

- **LAN design:** An essential aspect of a successful VoIP deployment because you must think through and validate every section of cabling, router configuration, and bandwidth allocation. If you're integrating VoIP into your existing LAN and don't really know LAN design all that well, you will be well acquainted by the time you finish. As long as you have a fully featured VLM software package to help you, you'll be just fine.

✔ **VoIP nuances:** All the programming, LAN design, and basic telephony help build the foundation for VoIP, but you can still find a wealth of information about VoIP itself. If you're deploying VoIP, you need someone on staff who knows about SIP, SDP, RTP, DTMF, and fax, as well as any obscure features that you want to pull from the traditional PSTN or get as a part of your phone system.

✔ **Industry diplomacy:** Companies have to work with other companies in every industry. In the telecom industry, even if you're in direct competition with another company, you must still interact with them in an honest and professional manner. While Level 3 is migrating a handful of phone numbers from Verizon, Verizon is also migrating some numbers back from Level 3. This situation requires diplomacy on every interaction because, in two more months, you may need to ask the person whom you want to read the riot act to today for a favor.

Whatever your background is when you begin using VoIP, the ease with which you use VoIP can only increase by finding out more about the other elements that support it. If you've been thrown into VoIP after a lifetime working in traditional telephony, take a basic class in programming and LAN design. The ability to install and effectively use packet capture software allows you to conduct intensive troubleshooting before you even engage your carrier. Similarly, if you've come into VoIP from years as a programmer and Web designer, spend some time figuring out how the telecom industry is structured and how the companies work together. You need to know who has the responsibility for doing what when you provision a new service or troubleshoot an existing service.

Whatever you knew before, expect to acquire the same quantity of information all over again in three more realms before you can translate your old level of efficiency to VoIP as a whole. Don't settle for just being a programming whiz because the telecom industry aspect of it will drive you to distraction.

The technology is a hybrid. It's evolving, and it requires a great deal of brainpower to keep up with it. As long as you work with VoIP, you'll never be bored. And you might not feel that you've figured out every aspect of VoIP for 20 years. By then, hopefully, you can retire.

Chapter 17

Ten Common Pitfalls

The Internet used to be the Wild West. It was open terrain without laws. There were no taxes on it, no laws governing it, and in many respects, it was an environment where "anything went." By and large, in the early days, it was a sane and friendly place. Online stores were popping up, search engines such as Yahoo and Google were just forming, and VoIP was being hammered out and constructed by an international community of programmers, technicians, and engineers.

This environment, and the flexible nature of the open source software that evolved along with it, made VoIP very dynamic. Aspects of the technology allow you to do things that are impossible with traditional telephony. Also, elements of the VoIP industry are evolving and haven't settled into the comfortable procedural rut of analog service. All the flexibility of VoIP allows VoIP practitioners to engage in undesirable behavior that was previously impossible. This chapter covers these bits and pieces of VoIP that you should avoid. They may be specific to the technology, the industry, or the psychology encompassing it all.

Launching Denial of Service (DOS) Attacks

A Denial Of Service, or DOS, attack refers to a situation in which a barrage of packets come from some unknown source, flying at a server so fast and with such volume that nobody else can interact with the server. The legitimate devices attempting to reach the server are, literally, denied service because that server's too busy trying to fend off the unwanted packet stream(s). VoIP servers at customer sites don't commonly receive this type of attack, but you may unwittingly be replicating a DOS attack toward your carrier.

Normal offices that have 10 to 20 employees probably can't ever replicate anything that remotely resembles a DOS attack to your carrier. Even if everyone tried to place a call at the same time, you still might be sending only two calls per second. This inadvertent DOS attack is more of an issue for companies that are either VoIP resellers that run their own VoIP soft switch or telemarketing companies. Both of these kinds of company have the potential to flood a VoIP carrier's SBC with upwards of 100 calls per second.

Some telemarketing companies seem determined to deliver as many calls as their hardware can possibly send. If their combined server array can send 80 calls per second, they'll push for 81. The truth of the matter is that, depending on the maximum sessions you've been allocated, 80 calls per second may be overkill.

A standard, voice marketing call, which aims to leave a recorded message on your answering machine, typically has a 30-second duration. After you add the amount of time it takes the call to connect after three to six rings, the total *off-hook* time is close to a minute. Table 17-1 shows the maximum number of sessions you can potentially reach at different call-per-second rates.

Table 17-1	Call-per-Second Rates' Maximum Sessions
Calls per Second	**Maximum Sessions**
5	300
10	600
15	900
20	1,200
25	1,500
30	1,800
35	2,100
40	2,400

The chart is based on a total off-hook time of one minute. A true telemarketing company may have an average off-hook time of only 45 seconds. In that instance, you can reduce all the numbers listed in the maximum sessions column by 25 percent to adjust for the shorter duration. A telemarketing company also expects to have up to 25 percent of its calls fail instantly because of bad numbers in its dialing list, so the total sessions possible can potentially be cut in half with both of those factors.

You still have a maximum consecutive call level in the hundreds for almost anything over eight calls per second. Here's the moral to the story: If you don't need to besiege your carrier's SBC to fill all the sessions allocated to you, don't do it. If you decide to make a habit of flooding your carrier's SBC with calls at rates faster than it's expecting, you can expect any or all of the following outcomes:

✔ The Network Security department of your carrier calls you, expressing its displeasure with the volume of calls you're sending.

✔ Your carrier may throttle down your service, lock it to a lower CPS than you previously enjoyed, or take more forceful action and temporarily shut down your service.

✔ If you make a habit of ignoring its requests to maintain an acceptable CPS rate, it may deactivate your service permanently.

✔ You run the risk of legal action from your old VoIP carrier (whose SBC you locked up) and all its customers who were playing by the rules and suffered an avoidable outage because of the DOS attack.

There's a huge difference between an unintentional DOS attack (such as a rogue RTP stream flailing through the Internet to some unsuspecting IP address) and a premeditated one in which you're just trying to cram as many calls as you possibly can through your carrier. Unintentional problems are irritating, but they rarely result in successful litigation.

Manipulating Your Caller ID for Cheap Long Distance

You can almost always call from one state to another more cheaply than you can call within the same state because of the rates that the local carriers charge to terminate calls. They've always charged more for intrastate calls than they have for interstate calls, which has been the logic in telecom for many years.

The flexible nature of VoIP creates a loophole that many unsavory companies use to beat the system. The origination phone number listed in a VoIP call is usually derived from the phone number listed in the FROM field of the SIP header in the INVITE message. The loophole comes into play because the phone number listed in the FROM field has no other purpose in the outbound VoIP call. Outbound VoIP calls are most likely attributed to you by your IP address and the dialed number, and not by the phone number populated in the FROM field. The phone number you list in the FROM field could be anything — a toll-free number, a bogus number, or a partial number — and your outbound VoIP call may complete just fine, especially if you have a large VoIP connection to your carrier that has one or several SBCs allocated to you, with several hundred sessions running per SBC.

Morally bankrupt companies try to exploit this flexibility by sending toll-free numbers, bogus phone numbers, or even legitimate phone numbers from another state in the FROM field to trick the system into charging an interstate rate. This number shifting may work for a while, but if you're sending a toll-free or bogus phone number, your carrier deems the calls as *indeterminate jurisdiction* and applies the intrastate rate as a default. Check your contract because how your carrier deals with indeterminate-jurisdiction calls is most likely covered in the fine print.

Don't manipulate your origination phone number for the sake of cheaper rates. Such actions can lead to a host of negative side effects, such as

- **Losing service:** Your carrier may identify the anomaly and instantly discontinue your service. The carrier is culpable for fraud after it realizes that you're manipulating your Caller ID, so it has no other option. It can't change the Caller ID back to something legitimate, so as soon as it's aware of the situation, it becomes an accomplice in fraud if it doesn't do something about it.

- **Paying strange taxes:** Placing an out-of-state phone number into the FROM field of your INVITE message doesn't only identify a new point of origin when your carrier determines jurisdiction, it also establishes a new location for taxation. If your office is in Los Angeles, but you decided to use a New Jersey point of origin, your calls are now marked for all eligible New Jersey taxes made by these calls. Tax rates vary by state, county, and city, so by indiscriminately choosing a different phone number for your FROM field, you may be incurring more cost in taxes. If you dispute those taxes because you physically don't exist in New Jersey, then you've just alerted your carrier that you're cooking your Caller ID, and it may take action against you.

- **Getting into trouble with the FCC:** Your carrier may identify the anomaly and alert the FCC. Any help that your carrier provides to the FCC can potentially prevent it from being dragged into an FCC investigation for fraud (which is what this type of call stream manipulation is) or lessen the impact on it. Your carrier is just helping itself in this matter by turning off any offending circuit known to be manipulating the FROM field. It can even take the moral high ground by then reporting you to the FCC. This type of action shows the FCC that a carrier is doing everything it can to comply with the rules, and assist in upholding them.

When the FCC starts investigating a company, the end is near. If you've manipulated the Caller ID with one carrier, you've probably done it with others, as well. You face a painful existence from that point forward if you've willfully engaged in deceptive manipulation of the call stream information.

In a certain scenario, a telemarketing company can manipulate the Caller ID stream legally. A telemarketing company can display the phone number of its client's local store, providing a valid phone number for everyone receiving the call, which the recipients can dial to ask for more information or request that their phone numbers be placed on the Do Not Call (DNC) list.

The federal government requires that all telemarketing campaigns provide a valid call-back number in the Caller ID field.

If the telemarketing company is located in Dallas and the Caller ID that Juggernaut Electronics wants to send is for its store in Boston, it has a problem. The calls are legitimately interstate and should be charged the lower rate because they originate from Dallas, not Boston. Some carriers don't care because they may rate the call based strictly on the phone number in the FROM field and the dialed number listed in the TO field of the SIP header of the INVITE message. This is the only scenario in which you can supplement the call stream information to establish a correct billing reference point.

SIP provides additional fields that can be used as a billing reference point. The phone number in the FROM field of the SIP header is still used as the Caller ID of the call, but these other fields can be used to identify jurisdiction (interstate or intrastate):

- ✔ P-Asserted ID
- ✔ Remote Party ID
- ✔ P-Charge Info (proprietary to some networks)

Check with your VoIP carrier to see whether it uses any of these fields to usurp the jurisdiction of the phone number in the FROM field. It may use one or all in cascading preference. Get the whole story before you use the fields and expect to be invoiced based on them.

Creating One-Way Audio

The essential pieces that make up a phone call are the ability to send overhead information from one end of the call to the other, and, just as important, to send audio between these same two points. Traditional telephony makes this task easy by packaging all this in one contiguous section of bandwidth, for most of the life of the call. VoIP, on the other hand, isn't as rigid and allows each stream of information to find its own way from end to end.

This doesn't pose a problem in most instances, except when you're using Network Address Translation (NAT) in the firewall of your VoIP-enabled LAN. The NAT functions to translate the public IP address and port of your firewall into public IP addresses and ports of your SIP proxy, feature servers, or individual VoIP phones. The firewall itself is a formidable challenge to VoIP, anyway, because the firewall is designed to reject any unsolicited data streams from entering the LAN. Figure 17-1 shows a standard problem with a firewall that uses NAT.

The call begins at a VoIP phone, which uses the internal IP addresses. Those addresses are converted to a public IP address at the firewall. The SIP messaging is sent out from the external IP address and port of the firewall, the same firewall that also receives the response messaging from the SBC of the VoIP carrier. The SIP messaging is accepted and sent on by the firewall for two reasons:

 ✔ The return messaging is sent as a response to the same IP address and port that originated the INVITE (generally).

 ✔ The return messaging is of the same protocol as the outbound packets.

The two reasons that allow the SIP messaging to pass through the firewall and be successfully NATed to the VoIP phone in the LAN are the same two reasons that the incoming RTP never reaches the VoIP phone. The IP address presented in the INVITE message to your VoIP carriers SBC may not have been modified by your firewall from the internal IP of the VoIP phone to the external IP address of your firewall. The SBC at the VoIP carrier can't locate the public IP address to which it should send the RTP, so the return stream of audio is lost.

If the RTP IP address was modified in the INVITE message by a SIP proxy with a public IP address located behind the firewall, the inbound RTP may still fail. The incoming RTP stream will be directed to a unique port on the public IP address that hasn't transmitted any RTP outbound. This classifies the incoming RTP stream as an unsolicited transmission of a dissimilar protocol, and again, the firewall blocks it.

NAT isn't the death of VoIP. It's actually a common issue with several solutions, all covered in detail in Chapter 14.

Figure 17-1:
A NAT firewall causing one-way audio.

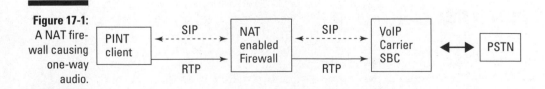

Ignoring Hidden Costs

VoIP is an evolving technology in an evolving market. The industry attempted to handle it, just like any other telecom product, but quickly realized that providing VoIP service has additional costs that don't exist in almost any other section of the industry.

This wisdom wasn't immediately understood by most VoIP carriers, so they've been reacting to these increases in overhead only after the overhead grew so large that the carriers couldn't ignore it any longer. The first big wave of new fees for VoIP customers was associated with Local Number Portability. VoIP carriers can move your home phone number or office lines away from your current carrier so that the VoIP carrier can provide you service, but at the same time, that process comes with considerable costs.

Most companies now charge a one-time fee for the migration of each phone number, as well as a monthly fee for maintaining the records in the national database for each number every month. In addition to the standard one-time and monthly fees, you could also see charges for

- ✔ White page listings
- ✔ Expedited orders
- ✔ Cancellation orders
- ✔ Expedited cancellation orders (called Snapback)
- ✔ Port out fees
- ✔ Delivery of new phone numbers from a new market or rate center

If you're a VoIP carrier, provider, or reseller, you need to factor in additional business costs to your business plan. You probably need more employees to handle the migration and resolution of rejects in the LNP process than you anticipated. In addition to the LNP staff, you need provisioners to build the service, install the orders, and troubleshoot any issues. You need a solid database to manage the flow of phone numbers, identify to whom they belong, and specify any special features they may be allocated. Finally, you have to purchase the VoIP hardware. Even if you have an entire multibillion-dollar long-distance network deployed, you still need to spend a few million dollars installing VoIP gateways to enable the network to interface with your new techno-savvy customers.

The billing on VoIP is still in flux, and new fees will invariably crop up. Review your invoice every month and read any billing notices or contract amendments sent to you from your carrier. Business is busy enough without having to spend time focusing on your telecom costs, but you need to do it every now and then.

Many VoIP providers use the same VoIP carriers to provide their service. Speak to your new VoIP provider and inquire whether your phone numbers are currently with the carrier they use, simply under the account of your current provider. If they are, you may be able to reduce the charge for an internal migration between account numbers.

Sacrificing Your Carrier

This situation starts out simple enough. Your VoIP service is working fine except for one small thing — maybe you can't receive DTMF, maybe you receive DTMF but it looks like you're getting two tones for every one that's legitimately sent, or maybe you're just frustrated and can't figure out why your calls aren't completing. With all the troubleshooting and business options available to you, don't decide to just not troubleshoot it and vehemently pronounce that your LAN, servers, and configuration are flawless, and it *must* be a problem with your VoIP carrier.

This shift of blame is referred to in the industry as *throwing your carrier under the bus*. This act of desperation is usually preceded by a half-hearted attempt at troubleshooting by individuals without enough technical expertise to conduct a full examination of the problem. A cursory examination identifies that, yes, the VoIP phone is plugged in, and yes, the power is on to both the phone and the router, so obviously, you can't have a problem within the LAN. The president of the company then demands resolution on the issue, and shortly thereafter, an e-mail nasty-gram is fired off to the VoIP carrier claiming it's ignorant, has poor service, and uses a sub-standard network. The chain of events progresses rapidly from that point in time and generally follows a typical path:

- The carrier opens a trouble ticket.
- The carrier investigates any call examples provided.
- The carrier engages the customer in head-to-head testing in which a network technician at your carrier (and preferably your hardware vendor at your office) capture and analyze individual calls that exhibit the issue.
- The captures identify that the customer isn't sending accurate information in the SIP INVITE, the customer isn't responding properly to a SIP response, or packets believed to be sent by the customer's proxy never seem to have arrived at the carrier's SBC.

✔ The testing concludes that, just like for the 10,000 other customers that use VoIP with the carrier though an identical configuration, the VoIP carrier is processing everything according to the RFC, and the anomaly lies within the customer's realm of responsibility.

✔ The customer then breaks off communication with the carrier after at least one more e-mail or correspondence in which the customer vents more anxiety and frustration on the carrier. This communication generally contains an assertion that even if the problem is within the customer's LAN, it's still the carrier's fault or responsibility to fix it (which isn't true).

✔ The customer hires a VoIP guru to analyze the situation, and after two days of analysis, a small configuration issue is uncovered and resolved, correcting the problem.

✔ The carrier is never given a call, e-mail, or notice that the issue has been repaired. It's also never informed that the problem was found to be entirely within the realm of responsibility of the customer.

✔ Finally, the carrier sees traffic resume on the VoIP ports and knows that the issue was both (A) resolved and (B) not its problem. But the customer never sends the carrier an apology for throwing it under the bus when the issue was first reported.

This cycle of events leaves a damaged relationship with your VoIP carrier. You definitely don't want any damage to that relationship because it's your best, and least expensive, ally in VoIP troubleshooting. It isn't charging you an hourly rate to fix the issue, and everyone in the troubleshooting department does nothing aside from troubleshooting VoIP all day, every day. If you have a problem, they've probably seen it before at least ten times and worked it through to resolution. They're constantly receiving new trouble tickets for every possible problem that can go wrong with VoIP, so they're continually refining their skills at resolving these issues.

Don't write angry. The more emotion in an e-mail, or phone call, the less productive it is. The president of the company may be screaming to get something fixed, but you must act as a buffer between the emotion from your boss and the people working for the VoIP carrier, who are only there to help you.

Maintaining a good relationship with your carrier's troubleshooting people can only make your life easier. A good working relationship allows you to bounce trouble issues off them, even when you suspect it may be caused by something within your LAN. The issue very well may reside within your VoIP carrier's area of responsibility, but even if it does, you can always resolve the problem more efficiently by providing data, not emotion.

Forgetting that VoIP Is Still Telecom

The tasks required to deploy VoIP onto an existing LAN are data-centric in nature. Setting up the VLANs, reducing router hops, and traversing the NAT in your firewall can focus your mind on VoIP as a solely packetized transmission from end to end, just like surfing the Web or sending e-mail. You can easily forget that VoIP is still a part of telecom.

VoIP is rarely an end-to-end medium for voice transmissions, especially when you call out to a traditional phone line. After your call is converted to traditional telephony, it has to play by the same rules as every other phone call in the PSTN. It's charged based on the same rating structure, uses the same termination agreements with the local phone carriers, and is governed by the same FCC regulations.

View VoIP as an on-ramp to the PSTN to help keep it in perspective, so that when you want to order a new toll-free number or migrate an existing one, you don't find yourself wondering, "How do you do this with VoIP?" The process is exactly the same, regardless of the method of connection you use, whether VoIP, analog, or digital.

Expecting Uniformity of Process

Every carrier handles billing, provisioning, and troubleshooting aspects of VoIP differently. They all strive to provide the same service, but the manner in which they do so can vary widely from carrier to carrier. They all have their own business plans, target customers, network designs, and history that have shaped the infrastructure that they use to deliver service today.

Each carrier uses its own VoIP questionnaire because each carrier weights the value of information differently. One carrier may require you to supply a 30-day Minutes of Usage (MOU) summary if you order more than 500 sessions, another carrier may request the MOU for as little as 300 sessions. In addition to the logistics of paperwork, codec selection, and standard configuration issues, some carriers may not offer the same features as others.

Write a list of all the features that you need from a new carrier before you move all your service onto its network. Ensure that you clarify

- ✔ LNP process and fees
- ✔ LNP services such as white page listings

- ✔ Utilization of P-Asserted ID fields and/or Remote Party ID fields for billing
- ✔ Any PSTN features you may require thought SIP-T
- ✔ DTMF types available (in-band and RFC 2833)
- ✔ Codecs available
- ✔ T.38 and fax transmission options

If you're considering a move from a boutique VoIP provider to a VoIP service through a traditional long-distance carrier, you may not be able to get some of your current fun features. The smaller VoIP providers frequently make changes to work with a customer, even if the change means deviating from the RFC for the feature. Large carriers don't offer this kind of tailor-for-each-customer service.

Planning for an InterOp Testing Environment

InterOperability (InterOp) testing was a necessary part of VoIP in the early days. The number of people writing their own SIP code based on their interpretation of the RFCs created an environment in which you could have two VoIP systems that were incapable of working with each other.

Also, you couldn't find many VoIP testing software packages available, and the concept of VoIP Lifecycle Management was still in its infancy. These factors contributed to the need for, and frequent abuse of, InterOp testing.

The stated purpose for InterOp testing was to confirm that the VoIP hardware at the customer location and the VoIP hardware at the carrier could successfully complete VoIP calls. The testing follows a simple process that requires a handful of calls of modest duration. In the perfect scenario, a company could complete InterOp in eight hours. You can construct only a finite number of combinations t to test the connection and disconnection of calls.

The InterOp testing environment was usually loosely structured and allowed a company to progress at their own pace. Some customers remained in InterOp for months because they used the testing environment and free calls to prove out internal features of their dial plans. The longer that customers stayed in InterOp, the more the InterOp testing system bogged down. The carriers realized that customers weren't using the testing platform for its intended purpose, but simply as a lab to work through development issues.

InterOp testing was phased out shortly thereafter. The widespread use of open source software such as Asterisk as the basis for SIP servers has provided consistency in VoIP activations. Your chances of hardware incompatibility are now the same whether you're using VoIP or traditional telephony, so the vast majority of VoIP carriers have eliminated the InterOp testing and established a standard service installation.

Anticipating Use that You'll Never Have

VoIP is a product provided by businesses. Carriers, resellers, value-added resellers, aggregators, and service providers supply it. Every layer of the VoIP supply line has its own niche market, defined by specific parameters of overhead and projected profit. End users pay the most per phone number (or consecutive SIP session) to ensure the profitability of the VoIP service provider that must cover the cost they have to pay to LNP and provision the phone number, process the monthly billing, pay for the support staff, and field customer service calls from potentially each and every customer. The further up you go the supply chain, the dynamics change from the high price, high service, low monthly commitment arrangement with the end user to a lower cost per line with support service only offered on trouble issues.

The first VoIP provider that faces the actual end customers who use the service fields all the customer service calls and relays to their internal staff only the trouble issues requiring that the VoIP carrier take action. The dynamic of cost and responsibility moves toward less service, lower price, and a higher revenue commitment as the mid-level VoIP providers get closer to the actual VoIP carrier.

This dynamic of lower price and technical support that only covers trouble reporting is the basic logic behind all telephony contracts, in general. Where VoIP customers can get into trouble is the revenue commitment. An individual customer with Vonage may be on the hook for only $25 per month, but the contract with the actual VoIP carrier may require a monthly commitment of $30 to $50,000.

Companies frequently agree to a commitment level way beyond their existing billing. They generally present a business plan that projects immense growth over the next six months, doubling or tripling their revenue, and so the carrier and customer strike a deal, and the customer is allowed 90 days to ramp up to the $30,000 in usage.

Many of the small VoIP carriers that entered the market when VoIP was still brand new got into trouble with their usage commitment levels with their VoIP carriers. The projections that these new start-up VoIP carriers assumed weren't based in reality, and after six months, they were still using only 10 percent of their total monthly commitment. Those companies are now in a bad situation. Their carriers may be gracious enough to work with them and offer these options:

> ✔ Keep the same rate structure and pay a shortfall fee every month for the difference between what was billed and the commitment level.

> ✔ Accept new, more expensive rates based on the commitment level they were meeting.

> ✔ Move all traffic to another carrier within a specified amount of time or face either of the first two options until the migration is complete.

Contracts are based on business plans. If you sign up for a $5,000 monthly commitment with a VoIP reseller, the rate package provided factors in the cost of the expensive technicians it has on staff to support you, the sophisticated billing system, and all the infrastructure it put in place to ensure quality service and an accurate invoice. If you bill out only $200 per month, it's losing money because one or two hours of that account manager's time may eat up all the profits for the month, and they may have had to spend ten hours to simply finish your VoIP activation. You're a profit-negative customer, and the VoIP reseller has no hope to recover the costs. Always quote realistic projection numbers and commit based on what you know you can deliver. Signing a contract for monthly amounts ten times your current level of usage simply places everyone in an uncomfortable situation.

Drowning in the Sea of VoIP

You may feel overwhelmed by the enormity of VoIP. It's supported by and based on so many different disciplines that nobody knows all aspects of it. Even if you could know everything about LAN design, programming, SIP, SDP, RTP, UDP, T.38, T.30, and DTMF, the industry would evolve tomorrow and present a whole new world of information on some evolving aspect of VoIP.

Three centuries ago, you could devote yourself to study and eventually know everything. You could read every last page of every worthwhile book printed. But knowing everything is just an impossible feat today. You'd need 100 lifetimes of devoted study simply to understand the discoveries of the past 100 years.

VoIP is a similar, ever-expanding pool of knowledge and information. You may be able to reach a level where you know enough to use and manage VoIP, even if you can never know everything. If you get information from everyone who knows more than yourself and maintain good relationships with these people to help you out when you get stuck, every challenge you encounter will be swiftly resolved.

Chapter 18

Ten Ways to Get Help

Sooner or later, everyone comes up against a problem that gets the best of them. As much as you slice it, dice it, and break it down to the molecular level, the solution eludes you. Even in traditional telephony, the tenants of which have remained mostly unchanged for decades, problems exist that take the best technician and test his or her limits.

VoIP has its own unique set of variables and encompasses so many other disciplines, aside from telephony. Every person has his or her specialty, and unless you saw this technology developing and spent several years programming, working in telephony, and finally doing a stint in LAN design, some aspect of VoIP just isn't your forte. Do as must testing as you can within your LAN and pull Wireshark captures before you start calling in favors. When you hit that wall and don't know where to go, dive in to this chapter. It provides ten places to turn to for help, guidance, or at least a bit of augury.

When you contact anyone for help, make him see himself as secondary support rather than your first line of defense. You need to perform your own essential tests on all issues before you turn to anyone else for free help. Performing your own tests demonstrates to him that you know what you're doing and that you've worked through every test case you can think of. The process of explaining all the testing you did also brings him up to speed on the variables that you've isolated and eliminated, preventing him from wasting time suggesting options you've already tried. If you're bringing on a consultant, it's doubly important to exhaust all options before contracting with him so that you can avoid paying for information that you may have been able to get for free from another source.

Dialing Your Vendors

The companies from which you purchased your hardware and software are your first line of inquiry if something goes wrong within your LAN, especially if you purchased any type of service contract from them.

If you hired a consultant to design or redesign your LAN who also provided the hardware, developed the software for your dial plan, and loaded up your VLM software, she is your best choice for an inquiry into any LAN-related issues. Fly any issue by her that you suspect may be related to your LAN. Some problems may manifest themselves on your LAN but be the result of some outside force. You'll probably hire your consultant to fix the issue if the problem is in your LAN, so a five-minute call with her should yield some general feedback about whether the problem is a LAN issue.

If you assembled the bits and pieces of your VoIP network yourself and don't have a guru-consultant who orchestrated the whole thing for you, you can still find help. The manufacturers of the hardware you purchased may be able to provide some level of support regarding configuration and troubleshooting. They may not be able to directly help you because the hardware is too old, you purchased it as refurbished, or they don't have you on record with a current service contract. Even if they can't help you directly, they can still be a valuable resource. You just have to ask different questions. Ask the manufacturer who its authorized resellers are in your area that sell or have sold the model you're using. The manufacturer probably also has a list of local companies that service its product to which it can refer you.

 Start by describing the issue and the troubleshooting that you've already done to isolate it. The details you give them can help them determine whether the problem is within their realm or whether they should refer you to someone else. Because they work in the industry, they probably have other companies, consultants, and individuals they've worked with whom they can refer you.

Rallying Your Industry Buddies

Telecom is a small world. If you've been working in it for more than two years, you've run into interesting and intelligent people employed by your VoIP carrier, hardware manufacturer, and software company, who would all be more than happy to give you ten minutes of help.

The entire communications and VoIP industry is in an amazing state of flux, expansion, consolidation, and reorganization. The people you met last year at the trade show are probably wearing the shirt of another company today, or at least a new title. All the good technicians find their way up the chain of command, which is good news for you. Those techs have moved on, figured out even more about SIP messaging, FoIP, and the industry in general, and can provide you with an even better resource today than they did two years ago. Good technicians don't jump to another company or position in which they have less responsibility and no growth potential. They move from one position as an entry-level technician to another job in which they can discover even more in a new field.

Keep track of all the technicians you stumble across who are good at what they do. They tend to rise to the top, get promoted, and continue to figure out what's required to be a success in their field. Keep their business cards, e-mails, and phone numbers someplace safe. As long as you have a good relationship with them, based on mutual respect and professionalism, they'll be more than happy to give you 10 or 20 minutes of their time to solve a problem or at least give you some direction. Your problem may be as simple as the specific router that you have doesn't support the function or so complex that they refer you to a technician they've worked with in the past who knows that aspect of VoIP inside and out. Regardless of the solution, you can always find it more easily when you have access to people with experience in the area.

Digging In to the RFCs

A Request For Comments (RFC) is an Internet Engineering Task Force (IETF) memorandum that describes procedures, research, and advancements for Internet and Internet-based systems. The RFCs are identified by a memo number and generally pertain to a small aspect of Internet-based transmissions. My favorite RFC is RFC2833, which covers the transmission of DTMF digits in SIP transmissions. The RFCs are the de facto industry standards for VoIP interaction, and despite having no enforcement bureau, the VoIP carriers have all adopted the RFCs as their guidelines.

The RFCs aren't only the standards for the VoIP protocols, they're also useful tools. You may find them especially useful if your VoIP provider is a large carrier and not a small boutique provider. The larger carriers don't have the flexibility to adjust every SIP method and response to accommodate the vagaries of your interpretation of SIP. They take a hard line on upholding the RFCs for the code, and your only hope to budge them into making accommodations for you is by proving to them that your interpretation is more in keeping with the spirit of the RFC than theirs.

You can find the RFCs at www.ietf.org/rfc.html. This page gives you a few options on how to gain access to the specific RFCs. The lower half of the page is devoted to tools that allow you to retrieve specific RFCs of interest. If you already know the RFC number that you need to investigate, you can simply input it into the RFC Number text box and click the Go button to retrieve the document. If you aren't sure which RFC you need to research, click the RFC Index hyperlink. It sends you to a page that lists every RFC currently on file with the IETF, from RFC 0001 (which covers host software) to RFC5280 (regarding Internet X.509 Public Key Infrastructure Certificates and a Certificate Revocation List Profile).

If you don't have the time to scroll through the 5,000-plus RFCs, conduct a quick search on the Web page by simply pressing Ctrl+F and entering a key word or phrase in the text box that appears. Enter **DTMF** in the text box and click the Find Next button to quickly go to RFC 2833, as well as RFC 4733. A similar search for **t38** yields RFC 3362 and RFC 4612. Use this search box to quickly focus on the specific documents from which your carrier is inevitably establishing their method of engagement. You may have to read through a few RFCs to find the specific one that references the exact aspect of the DTMF or T38 you're interested in knowing. Your VoIP carrier may even be able to direct you to the specific RFC as well if it is holding a hard-line and making you modify your SIP or RTP software.

Hunting on the Internet

Aside from the IETF Web site, which offers access to the RFCs, you can use the Internet, in general, as a great resource for investigation. Wikipedia (www. wikipedia.org) is a wealth of information on VoIP generally written in straightforward English. The people who add information to the site may use some buzzwords here and there, but contributors tend to write for a general audience and don't make things so complex that you need an advanced degree in computer programming to make sense of it.

Check out the more technical VOIP Wiki at www.voip-info.org/wiki.

Use this wiki to research more complex issues. The site has a search engine at the top of the page that pulls published data from theVoip-Info.org Web site (www.voip-info.org) and offers links to other Web sites on the related topic. A search for **T.38**, for example, yields both links to documentation on the protocol and lines to VoIP service providers that offer T.38 service.

You can find the British version of the wiki at www.wiki.voip.co.uk.

The widespread adoption of Asterisk as the basis for VoIP phone systems (either by itself, or in the trixbox and AsteriskNOW versions) has given Asterisk a large presence on the Voip-Info.org Web site. It even has its own wiki at www.voip-info.org/wiki-asterisk.

Working a wiki

A *wiki* is a collection of Web pages constructed in such a way that anyone with access to the pages can submit changes and update the content. It's an open and dynamic structure that allows for mass collaboration on an area of research. This type of national and global cooperation is an interesting characteristic of the Internet and one of the things that makes it the great place that it is. Linguistically speaking, the term Wikipedia is rooted in *wiki,* the Hawaiian word for *fast.* Despite the claim that wiki is an acronym for What I Know Is, that definition was constructed to fit the root work after the first wikis were already established.

As much fun as wikis are, you can also find information and FAQs on manufacturer Web sites. The companies that build and distribute VoIP phones; VoIP feature servers; interface cards for VoIP phone systems; and VoIP-enabled routers, firewalls, hubs, and switches all have service and support information on their Web sites that cover general information and questions that you may have. Some of the larger manufacturers, such as Cisco, also have online libraries of documents that you can access, as well as training opportunities posted.

The manufacturers' Web sites may be written for the highly technical market of developers, programmers, and engineers whom they expect to be using their products. If you encounter a section of their Web sites or a linked document that's over your head, try to absorb what you can, and write down the key words or phrases that are foreign to you. Then, research those individual concepts until you get a solid working knowledge of the situation. It may take several hours to interpret the initial Web site or document, but eventually it all makes sense.

Joining a Local Users Group

Many people who work with computers just want to talk to a live human about their technical issues. You may have had to suffer through a carrier's automated troubleshooting in which the speech recognition program doesn't seem to realize that what you're reporting isn't in its menu of standard questions. There's no substitution for a good-old one-to-one conversation with someone. So, you need to find someone whom you can sit across a table from, or in a comfy chair next to, and pick his or her brain for about an hour. Look no further than a local VoIP user group.

The good folks at Voip-Info.org (www.voip-info.org) list local user groups in many metropolitan areas. Many of them are Asterisk Users Groups, but don't let that scare you off, even if you aren't using Asterisk anywhere in your VoIP LAN. These groups are generally comprised of highly skilled programmers and engineers whose latest passion is VoIP, Asterisk, trixbox, or maybe even YATE (Yet Another Telephone Engine). Just because the name on the user's group is Asterisk doesn't mean that some of the members haven't mastered SIP, RTP, SDP, UDPTL, Wireshark, and T.38.

The users groups represent a small community of individuals who are interested in VoIP and Asterisk, and also have a strong base of knowledge in these subjects and most likely have a few years under their belt developing the technology.

If you don't have a users group in your area, establish one. I'm sure that you can find people who use VoIP in your town — people who either know the technology or want to know the technology. Talk to the professors who teach computer programming at your local university or city college to drum up some people who may be interested in sharing what they know. Then, post your group on Voip-Info.org and wait for people to begin signing up. This technology is too new and interesting for everyone to already be complacent, and (just like they said in the movie) if you build it, they will come.

Troubleshooting by Other Means

Sometimes, you may feel like you've exhausted all your troubleshooting options. You've done everything you can to isolate and prove out every variable that you can think of, but one small section of your network or element of the transmission is invisible to you. Maybe you installed Wireshark too far in your LAN and therefore can't see the packets that are actually leaving your SIP proxy, or maybe you have a bug in your dial plan. The problem now shifts from the actual call failure or quality issue to the lack of definitive testing on that area. Because you're making a stab in the dark at the problem anyway, you might as well use some tested methods of augury.

Going for the Magic 8 Ball

You may know the Magic 8 Ball as a small toy made by Tyco Toys (a subsidiary of Mattel, Inc.), but to the universe of telecom, the Magic 8 Ball is the oracle of the greatest possible likelihood. The little 20-sided die inside the blue inky fluid may have a 50-percent representation of positive outcomes, but it's still an enjoyable and quick answer to any question you have.

Question: Is the packet loss on my LAN caused by a failing router?

Answer: Don't count on it.

The Magic 8 Ball doesn't work only for troubleshooting — you can also consult it for provisioning issues, billing concerns, and assistance in determining the best lunch option. If you don't have a Magic 8 Ball handy, you can always find one online at `www.magic8ballonline.com/8ball` or simply enter the phrase **magic 8 ball online** in the Google search engine to find any of the other sites that provide the same service.

Runing your chances

If you aren't a Magic 8 Ball kind of person, maybe you can try runes. Most of us don't have a bag of Anglo-Saxon, Teutonic, or Scandinavian letters carved in bone, stone, or wood lying about. If you have a nice bag of runes, then you probably already know the meanings of each Anglo-Saxon, Teutonic, or Scandinavian letter and have a general idea of the methods of interpretation.

If you don't have a ready bag of runes and the time to figure out how to interpret them, you can still do the modern day expedient for it. It's a little diversion I've heard referred to as consulting the Webster runes.

The idea is simple. Find the largest dictionary you can and set it before you on a table, holding it closed with the spine resting on the table and the pages pointing skyward. Then, ask it a simple question — maybe, "Why is my call quality dropping?"

Close your eyes, let go of the dictionary covers so that the book falls open on the table, and randomly push through the pages until you think it's time to stop. Scroll your finger down the pages until you feel you have the answer and then press your fingertip against the page. Open your eyes and read the one or two words directly above your finger. If you're pointing at the words Keystone Kops, then the reason your call quality is dropping is probably because someone in your office is downloading stupid videos off the Internet. If JibJab has released a new comedy song and dance, you may have found your culprit.

I don't recommend using augury to run your business or as a replacement for actual testing, but I do recommend engaging in some activity to bring a degree of levity to your office. The process requires concentration, effort, and energy for the sole purpose of simply returning the system to normal. A group of people who are upset, depressed, and anxious surround any problem. You want to do what you can to keep everyone stabilized until the problem's fixed.

You're not doing something where everyone starts out in a good mood, then you all burst into cheers and high-fives after you solve the issue. The people you're working with see the problem as an inconvenience, and they just want to get back to normal. At the end of the day, they go on like nothing happened, and you feel like you've been run through the ringer. The only thing that can fill you up after you've poured all your energy into a problem is a good laugh. Take it where you can, go looking for something funny, and soak it up because tomorrow, it might start all over again.

Soliciting Help from Your VoIP Carrier

You can find a distinct point at which the responsibility of one entity ends and the responsibility of another begins. It's your responsibility to send accurate SIP messages and responses from your VoIP proxy. It's your IP provider's job to deliver those messages to your VoIP carrier. It's your VoIP carrier's job to accurately interpret the information in the packets and respond in an accepted manner according to the RFCs.

Your VoIP carrier is keenly aware of these points and may either use them to shield itself from you or may only mention them to you after identifying possible solutions. A strong relationship with your carrier makes your life much easier. If you've been regularly throwing the carrier under the bus, flying off the handle, and screaming at it, I guarantee you that if you ask for assistance on anything that can be construed to be "not its problem," it will most likely tell you bluntly that, whatever it is, it's "not its problem." At the same time, if you're a customer who always does your own essential testing on trouble issues and starts off any troubleshooting conversation with the carrier by running down all the testing you've done to isolate the issue, it'll have a much higher level of respect for you. As long as it doesn't feel like it's your first line of defense for every new issue, or your most productive unpaid employee, it'll probably make time for you. Even if the issue obviously isn't its responsibility, it may give you some of its time and assistance.

The greatest thing about network troubleshooters is that troubleshooting is all they do for eight hours a day, every day. Enlisting their help on a problem is like the difference between taking your car to a certified mechanic with ten years' experience and letting your buddy next door take a shot at it because he's good with tools. The network technicians see VoIP issues every day and have developed the skills to quickly resolve them. Even if your issue is within your LAN or dial plan, they may have some experience in how their last customer running Asterisk or Cisco fixed the problem. If you're on good terms with them, they may even refer you to their other customer who had the problem for some guidance on how that customer fixed it.

Your carrier is an outstanding resource for all things VoIP. I recommend developing the skills to ask it any VoIP-related questions you may have during troubleshooting, installations, or provisioning. Technical conference calls always seem to have some dead time, in which someone has to wait for a server to be rebooted or a download to complete. Use that time to ask questions and find out all you can. As long as you do it in a respectful manner, she'll be happy to share what she knows.

Pushing Through with Your Escalation List

An escalation list is a section of a company organization chart. The main difference being that the company level organization chart identifies every employee in every department, and the branching hierarchy of its managers, directors, and vice presidents, all the way up to the CEO or president. An escalation list is only a slice of that organization chart, focusing on a specific section of the company. The list represents a single chain of responsibility for a function, whether troubleshooting or provisioning, and the list ignores all the other employees in unrelated jobs within the company.

As a customer who uses VoIP service, your carrier should provide you with an escalation list that covers

✔ **Provisioning issues:** You use this part of the escalation list for any pending order (adds, moves, or changes) that haven't been officially completed or accepted. The staff on this part of the escalation list work normal business hours because you can't really have a legitimate after-hours provisioning issue situation. If, through some freak occurrence, your service does become discontinued at 2 a.m. on a Sunday, you're S.O.L (Simply Out of Luck) until Monday morning.

✔ **Trouble reporting issues:** This section of the escalation list never sleeps. The list may have phone numbers on it for both normal business hours and after-hours staff, or you may simply be given cell phone and pager numbers for after-hours situations.

The standard escalation list begins at the lowest level of escalation, that generally identifies the standard phone number for the customer service or provisioning queue, and progresses to the highest level that's usually the vice president over the department. You can see a simple escalation in Table 18-1.

Table 18-1	A Sample Escalation List	
Escalation Level	*Contact*	*Phone Number*
First	Customer Service Representative	888-555-1212
Second	Customer Service Manager	888-555-1212
Third	Service Delivery Manager	916-555-1212
Fourth	Director of Voice Service	916-555-1234
Fifth	VP of Operations	916-555-9876

You can use an escalation list to raise the visibility of an issue in an attempt to accelerate resolution. You aren't encountering more intelligent, seasoned, and ingenious technicians while you move up the chain of command. The individuals at the director and vice-president levels probably didn't get those jobs because of their superior VoIP troubleshooting skills, but because of their superior management skills. They may know how to spell VoIP, but they probably don't know how to read a Wireshark capture. The reality of escalating any issue is that the first- or second-level technician on your escalation list does the real work of resolving a problem. The managers and vice presidents of the company can more easily help by bringing in additional technicians or authorizing overtime. In the end, the problem will be resolved by a technician who sits at level 1 or 2 of your escalation list working through the issue.

Escalation lists are like antibiotics. If you use them all the time, your issues become immune to the treatment. A more real-world explanation is that the staff on the escalation list begin to see you as an alarmist, so they treat all your escalations like fire drills and, even though you're trying to escalate something, they don't handle it with any more urgency than if you didn't call everyone and their VP.

To prevent rampant abuse of escalation lists, ask yourself the following questions to qualify the situation:

✔ **Do I really have to escalate this issue?** The individuals you're employing to move the problem along faster are going to be asking the same question. If you sent in a request to migrate a phone number from your old carrier this morning and you're pushing to have it installed by close of business tonight, rethink using the escalation list. You should let any task that routinely has a timeline of more than 24 hours run its course before escalating.

✔ **Have I waited long enough before escalating to the next level?** Some carriers, especially local phone carriers, have specific time limits that you must meet before they allow an additional escalation. The specific timelines they hold before an issue can be escalated to the next level allows the existing escalation level to make progress and respond to you before you ratchet the situation up another notch. Calling a second-level escalation person, leaving a message, and then immediately calling the third-level escalation person simply causes a duplication of efforts. Unless you tell the second-level escalation person that you're going to call the next person up the list in five minutes, both individuals start working on the issue. Eventually, they're both standing next to the technician who's actually working on the issue and realize that one of them is wasting their time.

✔ **Are you escalating out of anger or frustration?** You may happen to get a technician on an off day, and he or she seems wholly apathetic. In this case, ignore the technician's behavior and just ask to speak to his or her manager. He or she is probably glad to get you off the line. The goal of escalating is to move the issue to people who can assist you and resolve the problem sooner than if you let it follow the normal drift. Escalating past the technicians who are working on the problem only raises the visibility of the issue within your carrier. The vice president may now be aware of it, but he or she isn't going to run to the tech department, edge out the technician, and start pulling packet captures. Escalate issues beyond the technicians only when you believe it can help prevent similar situations in the future. A vice president isn't going to personally fix your problem, but by bringing it to his or her attention, you may encourage him or her to build infrastructure in the company to keep it from happening again.

Your escalation list is an effective means of resolving problems if you use it correctly, but it's a sure way to destroy your relationship with your carrier if you use it improperly. Escalations don't have to be contentious. The more you enroll your carrier to help you, in a firm but engaging manner, the faster things progress toward resolution.

Going Back to Square One

Some issues seem to drag on for forever, especially with intermittent issues. The 5-percent static issue can linger for months while you provide call examples, your carrier works through them, and it asks you to retest.

After you finish every testing scenario you can and still have no definitive answer, start all over again from the most basic level. Any problem that can possibly befall your VoIP has a logical explanation. Looking too intently at the details may have caused you to miss the bigger picture, so review the results of all your testing based on the following perspectives:

- ✔ **Find a pattern to the problem.** Look at time of day, day of week, geographic area, association of the problem with peak calling times, peak data transmission times, anything that links the occurrence of the issue to a larger environmental situation.

- ✔ **Review all configurations.** The packet sampling size, codecs offered within the SIP server, hardware settings on VoIP phones, VLAN configurations on your LAN — everything.

- ✔ **Look at your network layout.** If you haven't drawn a diagram of your network, do so. It doesn't have to be pretty. Simple boxes and lines work. You want to look at every piece of hardware and cable that connects it. Reviewing the network design may identify a bottleneck in the system that you were unaware of.

- ✔ **Identify all variables.** Remember, not everything can cause a problem. If you have static, you're looking for an electrical short functioning at the first layer of the OSI model. If it's packet loss, you're looking at the IP layer. After you identify the strata in which the problem is occurring, write down every potential piece of hardware, software, and cabling from your VoIP phone to the SBC of your carrier that are potential sources for the issue.

- ✔ **Isolate the variables.** Construct tests to bypass the individual variables or use your VLM software to gather data on them so that you can either prove them to be clean or indicate whether they're potentially the source of the issue.

Do the testing twice as methodically and twice as slowly the second time around. Something obviously slipped through the cracks, so write down all the testing that conduct, including the time, date, and result. Follow your testing where it leads. The truth is out there.

Glossary

- -

A

ACK: A SIP Method sent to acknowledge the final response to an INVITE message. Listed in RFC 2543.

ANI (Automated Number Identifier): A fancy way of referring to your telephone number. (Pronounced *Ann'EE* or *Ay-En-I.*)

ANI II (also called ANI InfoDigits): Two-digit numbers that identify the type of phone originating a call, for example an ANI II of 29 identifies a call originated from a prison, and an ANI II of 70 specifies a call made from a payphone.

Annex: A revision or update to a protocol designed to provide an additional feature not available in the initial release. The Annex B release of the G.729 codec, for example, has additional code to enable silence suppression on calls utilizing this codec.

Area code: The first three numbers of a domestic phone call identifying the general geographic area in which the phone number resides.

Area code split: The division of a geographic area previously serviced by a single area code due to an increased demand in the region for new phone numbers. The region covered by the old area code can be split, with half of the territory given to the new area code, or the new area code can be deployed in the same territory as an *overlay area code.*

Asterisk: A very popular open source software allowing a standard Linux server to be converted into a feature rich telephone system, supporting both analog and VoIP calling.

ATA (Analog Telephone Adaptor): A small device to convert the signal required by your traditional analog phone into a VoIP protocol allowing VoIP provided service to be used.

AVP: Audio-Video Protocol is a transmission protocol for multimedia communications to be transmitted over the Internet.

B

BTN (Billing Telephone Number): The phone number linked to phone service and acting as either a billing reference point or main account number. Individual phone lines may all be referenced by a local phone carrier to a single BTN as well as being used to establish a geographic point of reference for outbound calls over dedicated digital circuits.

BYE: The standard SIP method sent to terminate a call *after* the bi-directional media stream is established on a call. It is similar to the disconnect notification in an analog call and is defined in RFC 2543.

C

Calling footprint: Identifies the local phone carriers in the cities, states, and countries where your calls terminate on average over the course of a month.

CDR (Call Detail Record): Listing of an individual phone call with your invoice containing the origination phone number, termination phone number, date, time, and cost for the call.

Call example: The detailed information of a call that is required to open a trouble ticket on a call completion or call quality issue. The call example must be less than 24 hours old and contain at least the origination phone number, termination phone number, date and time of call, and a legitimate call treatment to warrant opening of a trouble ticket.

Call Plan: The software within your phone system designed to route calls and provide features such as call queuing, voicemail, and conference service.

Call queue: A Call Plan feature allowing multiple calls to be placed on hold before being connected to an extension or set of extensions. The call queue can be designed to hold calls until an operator at one of the assigned extensions becomes available or provide the caller with the option to go directly to voicemail. Multiple distribution methods are available to deliver calls to the prescribed extensions from round-robin to most idle, least idle, and circular.

Call treatment: The way in which a call is completed. This is most commonly used when reporting trouble on a call, whereby the call treatment may include static, echo, clipping, or call failure to a recording or fast busy signal.

CANCEL: SIP method used as a direct command to the cancellation of a session. It is the only option for tearing down a SIP call prior to receiving a 200 OK response to the initial INVITE message from the far end. This method is defined in RFC 2543.

CED (CallEd station iDentification tone): The initial audible squeal sent by an answering fax machine for about three seconds before the first handshaking message is transmitted.

CIC (Carrier Identification Code): Three numbers that identify the network of a carrier. This is the main method that local phone carriers identify the long-distance carrier to which all of your calls are delivered.

Class 5 switch: The switching hardware used by local phone carriers, such as the traditional "baby Bells" (Pacific Bell, Bell Atlantic, and Southwestern Bell), that provides local phone services such as dial tone, emergency 911 service, 411 information service, and access to toll-free numbers and long-distance carriers.

Class 4 switch: The switching platform used by long-distance carriers geared toward finding the local carrier owing a dialed number, and routing calls to that carrier. They structurally differ from class 5 switches and cannot provide local carrier features.

Clipping: A call treatment characterized by the loss of portions of the audio transmission of a call. The condition is caused by an under-amplification of the call signal in a traditional telephony phone call and is more common in VoIP as the result of packet loss.

CO: Central Office is a building that contains a class 5 switch and provides local services to businesses and residences in the surrounding area.

CODEC: Coder-Decoder algorithms for packaging and un-packaging the voice portion of a VoIP call so it can be transmitted over an IP network. Codecs are available using different algorithms, each allowing the call a different level of compression.

Comfort Noise: The soft static or white noise you hear during a call when nobody is speaking.

COS (Class of Service): An Ethernet frame field that can be populated with a value of 0 to 7, representing the priority level of the data. 7 is the highest priority; 0 is data that can be sent with "best efforts."

CPN (Called Party Number): The number processed in the call stream of a phone call used to display in the Caller ID window of the phone dialed. This number can be either derived from the FROM number in the INVITE message of a SIP call or translated from ancillary fields populated in the INVITE message for the specific purpose providing a unique CPN.

CPS (Calls Per Second): Identifies the rate at which calls are sent. This is most frequently used to regulate the flow of VoIP calls from a customer's VoIP server to the SCB of their carrier.

D

Datagram: Self-contained packets of data containing a header and payload information located in the third layer of the OSI model. Datagrams are the basic element sent with UDP (the User Datagram Protocol that functions within the fourth layer of the OSI model).

Dead Air: A call treatment whereby no ringing or other sounds are heard after completing to dial a phone number. The dead air usually persists for only about 30 to 45 seconds before reverting to a fast busy signal or the call disconnects.

Dial Around Code: The seven-digit number consisting of "1010" and the three-digit Carrier Identification Code identifying a long-distance carrier. It is used to bypass the default routing within your local carrier to force your call over another long-distance carrier.

Dial Plan: The software in your phone system designed in a logical and orderly piece manner to provide such features as call queuing, voicemail, and conference calls.

DID (Direct Inward Dial): A phone number that can only receive inbound calls and is incapable of dialing outbound. Migrating standard phone numbers from a traditional, local phone carrier essentially converts them to DIDs, as all other service is stripped when the numbers are ported.

DNC List (Do Not Call): A database of phone numbers compiled by residential customers who wish to be removed from the call list of telemarketers. A DNC list may be an industry DNC list, a state-level DNC list, or a DNC list collected and maintained within the telemarketing company itself. Placing your phone number on a DNC list does not prevent you from receiving calls from non-profit or political organizations.

DNS (Domain Name System): A reference model used to link Web site URLs to their public IP addresses.

DOS Attack (Denial of Service): A malicious hack whereby a stream of packets is directed at an IP address with the intent to overload the server and crash it. VoIP creates the potential for this to occur without malicious intent in the event that a company inadvertently overruns its CPS and maximum concurrent calls, bombarding its carrier's SBC.

Dropped Call: Phone calls that are disconnected before either person on the call intends to or physically hangs up.

DSCP (Differentiated Services Code Point): A set of QOS values that can be used to prioritize traffic using four classes of service with three priority levels.

DS-0: The standard 64Kbps of bandwidth used to facilitate a single phone call over an analog or digital circuit.

DS-1: The basic unit for a dedicated Digital circuit. It is called a T-1 in American systems, consisting of 24 individual DS-0s; an E-1 in Europe consists of 32 DS-0s.

DS-3: An aggregated circuit containing 28 DS-1s, and a total of 672 DS-0s.

DTMF (Dual Tone Multi Frequency): The sounds you hear when pressing the digits on the keypad of your phone. They are called Dual-Tone because they actually consist of two separate tones to distinguish them from a normal human voice.

E

Echo: Reverberation caused by over amplification of signal strength during the transmission of a call. This is more common on calls traveling a longer distance as the signal requires more modifications to keep it within acceptable parameters.

Echo Chancellor: A device to eliminate echo on a dedicated circuit or individual call. If installed improperly or backwards, it can generate echo or cause call quality issues.

E&M (Ear and Mouth): Old bi-directional protocol used in traditional telephony whereby each end of the call interacts to set up and tear down every call.

EPS (Edge Proxy Server): A VoIP server sitting on the edge of network used as an aggregation point for incoming and outgoing VoIP calls.

ETR (Estimated Time to Repair): The projected timeline to resolution of a trouble issue. This is a mythical creature and is rarely, if ever, provided by a telecom carrier out of fear or legal reprisals if the ETR is not met.

F

Fast Busy Signal: A busy signal twice as fast as a normal busy signal that normally identifies a network outage and is sometimes replaced with a recording that *all circuits are busy.*

Feature Server: An independent server that isn't used to process every VoIP call, but instead is installed to handle specific calls and provide specialized services such as voicemail, conference calling, or call queues.

FEC (Forward Error Correction): A method of preventing and qualifying data transmissions by sending additional redundant data to provide guidelines to replace any data lost during the transmission.

Fiber cut: The unintentional severing of a section of fiber optic cable that usually results in call failures both into and out of the area serviced by the connection. Fiber cuts usually require 3 to 8 hours to repair unless they are the result of catastrophic damage.

fmtp: Format parameters that are located in the SDP packet of a VoIP transmission and usually identify the codec offered or negotiated within a VoIP call.

FOC (Firm Order Commitment): A generic term for any document that stipulates the date by which a provisioning order is committed to be complete. The FOC may be for the installation of a traditional telephony dedicated circuit, like a DS-1, or the porting of a local phone number to a VoIP carrier.

FoIP: Fax over Internet protocol either utilizing an uncompressed VoIP codec of G.711 or a specialized FoIP protocol such as T.37 and T.38.

Fraud: The unauthorized access of a phone system. The fraud could be the result of someone taking a lineman's butt-set and connecting to your phone line at the junction box (called *clip-on fraud*) or the result of the malicious hacking of a phone system for more aggressive *PBX fraud.*

FXO port (Foreign Exchange Office): Ports are installed in your phone system and face your local phone carrier. They receive both power and incoming calls through the cabling that terminates at the jack on your wall.

FXS port (Foreign Exchange Station): Ports are installed in your phone system and face the analog phones, fax machines, and other devices within your office or LAN.

G

Gateway: A device that converts the languaging or protocol of the data received on one side to a different protocol or even variant of the same protocol on the other side.

Groundstart: A traditional telephony protocol used to establish calls whereby the customer's hardware dictates that it is sending a call, as opposed to asking the carrier if it is ready to receive one.

G.711: The industry standard Codec used to transmit uncompressed calls. It changes only slightly across the world, with the United States and Japan using a variant called G.711μLaw (generally referred to as G.711u) and the rest of the world using G.711a (generally referred to as G.711A-Law). The variation in the codecs is based upon the logic used by each to sample the audio that it packetizes.

G.729: The most aggressive codec in regards to the realized compression on the audio portion of the call while retaining a consistent and acceptable call quality. It boasts an 8:1 compression and can be utilized without incurring excessive delays in the process.

H

H.323: One of the oldest sets of VoIP guidelines designed by the International Telecommunications Union working group that supports the transmission of voice and video.

Hardphone: Any phone that has matter, takes up space, is used to send and receive phone calls, and isn't simply software on a computer.

I

ICE (Interactive Connectivity Establishment): A framework utilizing both the STUN and TURN protocols to solve the NAT traversal problem. ICE chooses the best possible interconnection method between two users.

IETF (Internet Engineering Task Force): An international coalition of technicians, network designers, researchers, vendors who collaborate to evolve and refine transmissions of data through the Internet. It accomplishes this through the promotion of industry standards called RFCs.

IFP: A method of fax transmission utilizing IP packets and separating the transmission overhead from the fax image. The first IFP packet holds the payload, transmitted with the legacy fax protocol of T.30.

IJ (Indeterminate Jurisdiction): A call classification characterized by the geographic location of at least one end of the call being masked or hidden. The transmission of calls over dedicated digital circuits and the flexibility of identifying the origination phone number of choice in VoIP calls allow either toll-free or bogus phone numbers to be populated in this field. Toll-free numbers are not geographically tied to any area, unlike a phone number that can be attributed to a physical phone line at a home or business. This causes calls employing a toll-free or bogus number as the origination Caller ID to be tagged as Indeterminate Jurisdiction and are generally billed at the highest rate allowable.

International dialing prefix: The 011 that must be dialed from the United States before calling any international destination. The international dialing prefix is different when placing international calls from other countries.

Internet: A global array of interconnected computer networks utilizing IP protocol to send and receive packets of data.

InterOperability or InterOP test: A series of compatibility tests executed between a company's VoIP hardware and the VoIP network of its carrier ensuring that the two systems were capable of functioning together to pass toll-quality voice calls. InterOP testing is no longer supported by most VoIP providers as the widespread adoption of open source software systems such as Asterisk has greatly reduced the likelihood of hardware incompatibility.

INVITE: The SIP method used to establish a VoIP phone call as defined by RFC 2543. The INVITE provides all of the introductory information for the call and initiates the negotiation of all aspects of the transmission from the accepted SIP methods and codecs used to the transmission ports for the SIP and RTP.

IP (Internet Protocol): The basic protocol used to transmit data across a packet switched network. It functions at the third layer (Network) of the OSI model and facilitates the transmission of VoIP, FoIP, and TCP.

ISDN (Integrated Services Digital Network): An out-of-band signaling protocol used in traditional telephony whereby the overhead of the phone calls is located on a separate channel from the audio portion of the call.

ITU (International Telecommunications Union): A United Nations agency established to assist in the development and standardization of communication technologies.

IVR system (Interactive Voice Response): Complex telephone systems allowing incoming callers to reach their desired extension by responding to questions by either pressing digits on the keypad of their phone or speaking keywords.

J

JBIG (transcoding): A compression technique for the data used in a fax transmission. The technology was developed by the Joint Bi-level Image experts Group (JBIG) and bears their name.

JIP (Jurisdictional Indicator Parameter): A phone number assigned to cell phone calls by a cell tower or switch servicing the cell phone identifying the physical location of where the call originated. The JIP can then be used to determine the true jurisdiction of a call to or from the cell phone. The JIP was developed and deployed to correct billing issues caused by international travelers utilizing their cell phones in the United States and being charged international, as opposed to domestic, rates.

Jitter: The variations in transmission latency that can cause packet loss and degraded call quality in VoIP calls, also sometimes called *delay variation.*

Jitter buffer: A device installed on a LAN that collects the individual VoIP packets, arrange them in sequence, and then send them out in a uniform cadence. This can be a solution to jitter, but if improperly deployed, it can result in increased latency and eventual packet loss. Jitter buffers are also sometimes referred to as *Packet Loss Concealment (PLC)* devices.

K

Key system: A basic phone system that may provide voicemail and rudimentary features while allowing you to dial out through it without the need of pressing "9" for an outside line.

L

LAN (Local Area Network): A computer network that typically exists within a small geographic area such as an office or campus environment.

LATA (Local Access Transport Area): A geographically defined region that may include hundreds of miles of territory in which a local phone carrier can independently complete a phone call. If the call must terminate outside of the originating LATA, a long-distance carrier must be utilized to cross the LATA boarder.

LCR (Least Cost Routing): The rates for a multitude of carriers to which a company has access are programmed into a database enabling the phone system to route any call dialed over the carrier with the least expensive rate to that terminating location.

LERG (Local Exchange Routing Guide): A national database identifying every phone number in America, along with specific information such as its associated local phone carrier, vertical and horizontal positioning for the local carrier's CO, and routing information.

Linux: A free operating system similar to Unix and created by Linus Torvalds. It has evolved to offer many variations called Distributions (Distros) and is the operating system of choice for many open source VoIP phone systems, such as Asterisk.

LNP (Local Number Portability): The process by which a phone number is moved from one local phone carrier to another.

LOA (Letter of Authorization): A document you must sign in order to authorize a phone company to either change the long-distance carrier on your phone line or to move your phone number to another local carrier. Some states, such as California and Georgia, also require validation of the transfer through the use of a third-party verification system.

Local Loop: The cabling required to connect a dedicated circuit for voice or Internet from your business or residence to your carrier. It spans from the Network Interface Unit at your premise to the interface card within your carrier's switch.

Loopstart: A protocol used in standard telephony whereby the carrier is always offering to initiate a call to the customer's hardware.

M

Managed Devices: Unique devices that are unlike ordinary hubs, routers, printers, bridges and switches in that they have a software element installed in them called an *agent* allowing them to gather management data and relay it up to the NIMS in an SNMP managed network.

Maximum concurrent calls: The maximum quantity of calls you expect to have active with your carrier at the same time. This is sometimes translated into the maximum concurrent sessions with a VoIP provider establishing the ceiling for concurrent calls they will accept.

Media: The payload portion of a call that can contain the audio portion of a voice call or the image portion of a fax transmission.

MMR (Transcoding): The Modified Media Read (MMR) compression format used for faxes to reduce the required bandwidth of the transmission.

MOS (Mean Opinion Score): A rating structure used in telecom identifying the overall quality of a phone call. The rating is between 1 and 5; 1 is the lowest rating, and 5 is the best rating.

N

NAT (Network Address Translation): A common way of hiding the IP addressed used within your LAN from the outside world. NAT translates public IP addresses visible in the public Internet to internal IP addresses used within your LAN. A NAT firewall protecting your LAN intercepts unsolicited data types entering it from reaching your internal servers.

NIMS (Network Management System): A device that's responsible for controlling and monitoring SNMP-enabled Managed Devices in a SNMP-managed network.

NIU (Network Interface Unit): The final piece of hardware installed on a local loop for which the local carrier is responsible. All cabling beyond the NIU is the responsibility of the building owner and is referred to as *inside wiring*.

NOC (Network Operations Center): The main building or center where the troubleshooting hardware and technicians are located for a long-distance, local, or VoIP carrier.

Nonpromiscuous mode monitoring: A packet capture setting that restricts the packets captured to only the data intended to be received by or sent from the specific interface identified in the capture.

NOTIFY: A SIP Method used to keep the PINT client updated on the disposition of the PSTN feature for which the PINT client is SUBSCRIBEd. A NOTIFY update is sent to the PINT client whenever the disposition of the monitored service session changes and is defined in RFC 2848.

NPA: Numbering Plan Area code is a three-digit number where the first digit is 2-9, the second digit is 0-8, and the third is 0-9, used to identify geographic regions in America. This is more commonly referred to as the area code.

NTP (Network Time Protocol): An extremely accurate method for determining the time. Times identified by NTP are accurate to within 10 milliseconds over the public Internet. This is extremely important in VoIP transmissions, whereby a standard packet of voice only represents 20 milliseconds of sound.

NXX: The Central Office or Exchange code identifying the local phone carrier central office that provides the dial tone to all phone numbers within the NXX. This is the second set of three digits on a phone number after the area code with the first digit being populated with a 2-9 and the last two digits listed with 0-9.

O

OCN (Operating Company Number): An identifying identification number that links a phone number to the local carrier which provides service to it.

Open source software: Software available to download for free which can be modified and built upon such as Asterisk.

OPTIONS: A SIP method used to query the options and capabilities of a far end VoIP device. This method is defined in RFC 2543.

OSI Model: The Open Systems Interconnection model, also called the Open System Interconnection Basic Reference Model. A standardized system whereby the individual elements required to support network transmissions are defined and categorized into seven layers.

Outlying areas: The calling area outside the continental United States, but that doesn't require an international 011 prefix such as Alaska, Hawaii, U.S. Virgin Islands, Guam, and the Caribbean.

Overhead: This is the section of bandwidth used for call set-up and tear-down, as well as general housecleaning of the call. It is where everything that isn't the voice portion of the call is transmitted.

p

Packet Island software: The industry leading VoIP Lifecycle Management software allowing for the highest level of visibility into the LAN sources of latency, jitter, and packet loss.

Packetization time (ptime): A parameter within a VoIP call that defines the duration of audio used to make each audio packet sent in the RTP stream. The number listed next to the ptime parameter in a SIP message identifies the number of milliseconds used for the audio sampling. The most common duration for ptime is 20 ms.

P-Asserted ID headers: A supplemental field used to identify the geographic point of origin of a phone call. The data may be used as a billing reference point in the event that the phone number listed in the FROM field is invalid or ignored by the privacy indicator.

Pattern matching: A type of logic used to identify similar strings of data. This can be used to match up the phone numbers dialed on outbound calls to an LCR table or can also be used to route incoming calls.

PBX (Post Branch Exchange): A more complex variety of phone system that generally provides a large quantity of features to include not only standard voicemail but also conference calling, call queues, and account codes.

PDD (Post-Dial-Delay): The 5- to 35-second period of silence you hear after you finish dialing a phone number and before you hear ringing from the far end. It is a common condition when dialing someone internationally and is frequently more than 15 seconds in duration for calls to some countries.

Permissive dialing period: The duration of time spanning from three to six months whereby you can call a phone number that has been changed to a new area code before receiving a recording of "your call cannot be completed as dialed."

PFM (Pure Friggin' Magic): The mystical event whereby a problem that had persisted previously simply vanishes and resolves itself without anyone acknowledging that he or she has made any changes whatsoever.

POP (Point of Presence): A long-distance, Class 4 switch location where services can be received from the carrier and into which circuits to them can connect.

PIC (Primary Interexchange Carrier): The long-distance carrier assigned to a phone number within the CO of the local carrier providing service to the number.

PIC freeze: A logistical security device that many people have on their phone lines to prevent their long-distance carrier from being changed without their consent. This provision also applies to the migration of local phone numbers as well.

PINT (PSTN/Internet iNTerworking Service): A protocol that translates information from within the PSTN into a format that can be used and processed through SIP.

PINT client: A SIP end point that originates a request for PINT service that is sent to the PINT server to set up a session and deliver the requested service.

PINT gateway: SIP node that translates the PINT requests from the SIP messaging from which it is received by the PINT server and translates it to a traditional telephony protocol to interact with the PSTN.

PINT server: A server used to receive a service request from a from a PINT client, functioning as a proxy to deliver information to the PINT gateway.

PMs: Performance monitors are passive diagnostic reports available on most dedicated circuits throughout a carrier network used to record electric and protocol anomalies such as erred seconds, unavailable seconds, and frame slips.

Port Out Notification: A notice that should be sent out and received whenever a phone number is migrated away from one local carrier to another.

PPS (Packets per Second): Rating standard for traditional servers routers and hubs, identifying their maximum throughput before they fail.

Progressively diminishing returns: Also know as the Law of Diminishing Returns. An economic law that asserts that if only one input in production increases while everything else remains the same, a point will be reached whereby additional output yields smaller yields in production and profit. VoIP networks experience the same effect as VoIP call volume increases and all other constraints and limitations on the LAN remain constant.

Promiscuous mode monitoring: A packet capture setting whereby all packets of data traveling across the server are captured for analysis, regardless of whether they were specifically originating from or terminating to the capture server as any packet that is passing through to another destination will also be captured.

Propagation/Packetization delay: The amount of time required to covert a voice signal either to, or from a codec for transmission with VoIP.

Proxy server: A server acting as an aggregating point and link between the SIP devices on a LAN and SBC or EPS of a VoIP carrier.

PSP (Payphone Service Provider): A company that owns a payphone and to which the federally mandated payphone surcharge must be paid for all revenue-producing calls originated from its payphones to toll-free numbers.

PSTN (Public Switched Telephone Network): The interwoven network of long-distance and local phone service providers utilizing traditional telephony and a cascading array of carriers and underlying carriers that allows any phone in the United States to reach any phone in the world.

Q

QOS (Quality of Service): An aspiration of LAN design whereby applications, users, and data flows are prioritized through resource reservation control mechanisms to maintain bit rate and reduce delay, jitter, and packet loss.

R

RBOC (Regional Bell Operating Companies): The local phone providers initially assigned to provide service to specified geographic areas by the federal government, such as Pacific Bell, Bell Atlantic, and Southwestern Bell.

REFER: SIP method used to redirect both the SIP and RTP stream of a VoIP call to a new destination and covered in RFC 3515.

REGISTER: SIP method used to register the URI of a VoIP phone on a LAN with the SIP Registrar server. Defined in RFC 2543.

Re-INVITE: Issuance of an INVITE message on a VoIP call after the initial INVITE message was sent. Re-INVITEs are used to redirect all or a portion of a call, request additional features, codecs, or protocols, or solicit information.

Remote Party ID: A supplemental SIP header that can be used to transmit a different telephone number to provide an additional geographical reference point for a phone call. The Remote Party ID field can be used as a reference point to determine the jurisdiction of a call (interstate or intrastate) in the event that the phone number listed in the FROM field is to be ignored by the privacy indicator and if the Remote Party ID filed is acknowledged by the VoIP carrier.

RFC (Request For Comments): An IETF memorandum describing procedures, research, and advancements for Internet and Internet-based systems. The RFCs are identified by a memo number, such as RFC2833 that covers the transmission of DTMF digits in SIP transmissions. The RFCs are the de facto industry standards for VoIP interaction, and despite having no enforcement bureau, the VoIP carriers have all adopted the RFCs as their standards.

RFO (Reason For Outage): A justification or explanation of the events leading up to, during, and after a service impacting outage. Any customer can request an RFO after a problem has been resolved, but carriers are generally resistant to providing any more information than was already known and released during the repair process.

Ring to number: The phone number that wired to a phone jack in a building acting as the recipient of calls to a toll-free number.

RJ-45 jack: The standard jack used to deliver dedicated digital DS-1 service to a business or residence.

Rogue RTP: An RTP stream sent to an undesired IP address resulting in a flow of audio data being delivered to the remote server, potentially overloading it in a manner similar to a DOS attack.

RTP (Realtime Transport Protocol): A standardized packet format used to deliver audio and video over the Internet and is described in detail in RFC 3550.

rtpmap: RTP mapping assigns RTP information to a specific CODEC and ensure that both ends of the call are sampling at the same rate. It is listed in the media-description section of the SDP on a VoIP call.

RTP PT (Realtime Transport Protocol Payload Types): Shorthand in the form of numbers corresponding to specific CODECs offered for use during a VoIP call.

S

SBC (Session Border Controller): A device used by some VoIP providers as an interface for their individual VoIP customers. The SBC sits on the edge of the VoIP carrier's network, in a similar position to an EPS, but has additional call management features allowing it to control the sessions at a higher level.

SDP (Session Description Protocol): Coordinates the connection of the media and negotiation of the media format for a VoIP call. It only manages the media of the call, but does not packetize it, a task it delegates to RTP.

SIP (Secession Initiation Protocol): Guidelines established by the Internet Engineering Task Force, covering the transmission of voice, video, and Instant Messaging over an IP network. It is more efficient and easier to work with than older protocols such as H.323.

SIP method: Specific messages sent with SIP protocol that initiates a request for information or action in a VoIP call such as INVITE, ACK, REFER, and BYE.

SIP node: Any hardware device that interacts with a SIP call during its transmission from the VoIP phone making the call, the SIP proxy sending the call from the LAN to the SBC or EPS receiving the call within the VoIP carrier's network.

SIP registrar: A database server used to log in the SIP URI information of a VoIP hardphone using SIP.

SIP response: A SIP packet sent in response to a received SIP method indicating varying levels of success, disposition, or failure.

SIP-T: An interface protocol used to gateway a call between VoIP and the non-VoIP Public Switched Telephone Network in order to pull information from the call stream that is not normally available with VoIP. The most common reason SIP-T is employed is to receive the ANI II from the standard telephony call stream.

SIP URI: A SIP Uniform Resource Identifier is an address used to identify a VoIP end point that can look like an e-mail address, such as stephen@wiley.com. When dialing a phone number in the PSTN to be completed by your VoIP carrier, the URI may be identified as +14145551212@VoipCarrier.com.

SIP user agent: A generic term used for any hardware device that interacts with a SIP call and contains both a UAC and a UAS.

Snapback: A return process used in the process of local number portability to allow for an instant return of a phone number to a previous local carrier. The process is frequently quite costly and can only be executed within the first 24 to 48 hours from the time the phone number is successfully ported to your new local phone carrier.

SNMP (Simple Network Management Protocol): A team of software elements residing in nodes on your LAN that collect management data on the health of the LAN, recording network events that indicate the presence of congestion and packet loss.

Softphone: Software-based applications that display a small dialpad on your computer screen similar to the calculator you find in the Microsoft Windows Accessories folder. The mouthpiece and earpiece of a traditional phone are replaced with the microphone and speakers on your computer.

SOL: Simply Out of Luck is a condition present in telecom when the expectation level of an individual is outstripped by the real-world limitations of a situation.

SS7: The predominant signaling protocol used in the PSTN that is very similar to VoIP in structure and cadence. The overhead of calls is transmitted on a separate path, independent of the media of the call and the banter of INVITE and response is also similar.

Static: An undesirable call treatment where white noise is present at a volume where it makes hearing the person at the far end of the call difficult or impossible. Static is most frequently the result of an electrical short somewhere in the hardware or phone line between the two ends of the call.

STUN (Session Traversal Using NAT): A NAT traversal solution whereby a public IP address and port mappings are identified for the end of the call residing behind a NAT. This traversal method allows the public IP address and port to be used for the VoIP transmission, facilitating a successful transfer of data from one VoIP end point to the other.

SUBSCRIBE: A SIP method used to interact with a PINT server, requesting an update on the status of a service request, and defined in RFC 2848.

T

T-1 circuit: A dedicated circuit containing 1.544 Mbps of bandwidth and 24 individual DS0s over which calls can be made. It is the standard for digital dedicated circuits in the United States.

T.30: A legacy fax protocol used for analog transmissions as well as being integrated in the use with FoIP transmissions such as T.38. The T.30 protocol establishes the rules of engagement, for the fax call, requiring an answering fax machine to send a CED tone for about 3 seconds before the first handshaking message is transmitted.

T.37: A FoIP fax protocol whereby an entire page of a fax is collected, converted to a .TIFF and transmitted across an IP backbone. It is a very functional program but requires the T.37 server to have both, sufficient memory to hold the TIFF before transmission and enough processor strength to devote to the conversion of the incoming data to a TIFF file.

T.38: A newer FoIP protocol that resolves the buffer and processor issue by treating a fax transmission more like a voice call. The T.38 protocol doesn't store the pages while it spools the entire fax document into a TIFF. It simply converts the document as the data is received, sending small TIFF packets representing a sequenced portion of a fax page instead of waiting for all of the data to be translated.

Tags and tones: Leading or following information presented.

TCF (local): An indicator that the Training Check (TCF) message identified by the receiving machine or gateway will be used to identify the Bit Error Rate (BER) of a FoIP transmission.

TCF (transferred): An indicator that the Training Check (TCF) message sent by the originating device must be used at the receiving machine or gateway is to be used to identify the Bit Error Rate (BER) of the FoIP transmission.

TCP (Transmission Control Protocol): The primary protocol used to transmit data across the Internet.

TCPdump: A free packet capture software that can be used to gather data on VoIP calls through a command line interface.

TOS (Type Of Service): An older networking tool used to prioritize data flow to prevent the loss of packets in real-time applications while allowing lower priority transmissions such as e-mail and Web surfing to be delayed or retransmitted.

Troubleshooting: The process of resolving call quality and completion issues by identifying the variables, isolating them, and proving them as clean or suspect. It is best if executed in a methodical manner whereby each subsequent test builds on information learned in previous tests.

Trouble ticket: A tracking tool used within carriers to record trouble issues and their resolution. They are generally referenced by a trouble ticket number.

TURN (Traversal Using Relay NAT): This is a NAT traversal method whereby the NATed end allocates a public IP/port on a globally reachable server to be used to relay media between communicating parties.

U

UAC (User Agent Client): The portion of a SIP user agent that initiates communication to the next node in the call path and requests information or acknowledgements from it.

UAS (User Agent Server): The portion of the SIP user agent that receives the communication from the UAC of the device upstream on the call, processes the request, and responds back to it.

UDP (User Datagram Protocol): A leaner version of TCP used to transmit SIP packets with less overhead and doesn't allow for retransmission of packets, making it ideal for real-time transmissions like VoIP.

UDPTL (UDP Transport Layer): The transmission method used with T.38 FoIP in lieu of standard UDP that would be employed in a normal VoIP call.

UNSUBSCRIBE: A SIP method sent to a PINT server requesting the termination of a monitoring session and defined in RFC 2848.

URL: Universal Resource Locator such as `www.msn.com` is a string of characters used to identify a stationary resource on the Internet.

V

VLAN: A virtual LAN that acts like a physically separate network, despite the fact that it is riding on the exact same switches as your primary.

VLM (VoIP Lifecycle Management): A network management philosophy designed to manage and anticipate the impact of the VoIP deployment on an existing LAN prior to deployment and conduct systematic and periodic testing on the LAN once deployed.

VLM software: A software package designed to pre-qualify a LAN prior to VoIP deployment, validate configuration and quality during deployment, and monitor network conditions once VoIP has been successfully deployed. The premier software available at this time is created by a company called Packet Island.

VoIP (Voice over Internet Protocol): A collection of supporting protocols and software elements allowing voice phone calls to be executed over an IP-based platform.

V.21: A legacy modem protocol used within the T.30 portion of a T.38 FoIP transmission.

W, X, Y & Z

White noise: The type of soft droning static categorized as desirable that is input in a call during the moments when nobody is speaking, also called comfort noise.

WireShark: The industry leading network protocol analyzer. It is free software that should be deployed on every VoIP server in the world, or at least on the PCs of any technician responsible for a VoIP network to analyze packets.

Index

• Q •

Notes

Notes

USINESS, CAREERS & PERSONAL FINANCE

ccounting For Dummies, 4th Edition*
8-0-470-24600-9

ookkeeping Workbook For Dummies†
8-0-470-16983-4

ommodities For Dummies
8-0-470-04928-0

oing Business in China For Dummies
8-0-470-04929-7

E-Mail Marketing For Dummies
978-0-470-19087-6

Job Interviews For Dummies, 3rd Edition*†
978-0-470-17748-8

Personal Finance Workbook For Dummies*†
978-0-470-09933-9

Real Estate License Exams For Dummies
978-0-7645-7623-2

Six Sigma For Dummies
978-0-7645-6798-8

Small Business Kit For Dummies,
2nd Edition*†
978-0-7645-5984-6

Telephone Sales For Dummies
978-0-470-16836-3

USINESS PRODUCTIVITY & MICROSOFT OFFICE

ccess 2007 For Dummies
8-0-470-03649-5

xcel 2007 For Dummies
8-0-470-03737-9

ffice 2007 For Dummies
8-0-470-00923-9

utlook 2007 For Dummies
8-0-470-03830-7

PowerPoint 2007 For Dummies
978-0-470-04059-1

Project 2007 For Dummies
978-0-470-03651-8

QuickBooks 2008 For Dummies
978-0-470-18470-7

Quicken 2008 For Dummies
978-0-470-17473-9

Salesforce.com For Dummies,
2nd Edition
978-0-470-04893-1

Word 2007 For Dummies
978-0-470-03658-7

DUCATION, HISTORY, REFERENCE & TEST PREPARATION

frican American History For Dummies
8-0-7645-5469-8

lgebra For Dummies
8-0-7645-5325-7

lgebra Workbook For Dummies
8-0-7645-8467-1

rt History For Dummies
8-0-470-09910-0

ASVAB For Dummies, 2nd Edition
978-0-470-10671-6

British Military History For Dummies
978-0-470-03213-8

Calculus For Dummies
978-0-7645-2498-1

Canadian History For Dummies, 2nd Edition
978-0-470-83656-9

Geometry Workbook For Dummies
978-0-471-79940-5

The SAT I For Dummies, 6th Edition
978-0-7645-7193-0

Series 7 Exam For Dummies
978-0-470-09932-2

World History For Dummies
978-0-7645-5242-7

OOD, GARDEN, HOBBIES & HOME

ridge For Dummies, 2nd Edition
8-0-471-92426-5

oin Collecting For Dummies, 2nd Edition
8-0-470-22275-1

ooking Basics For Dummies, 3rd Edition
8-0-7645-7206-7

Drawing For Dummies
978-0-7645-5476-6

Etiquette For Dummies, 2nd Edition
978-0-470-10672-3

Gardening Basics For Dummies*†
978-0-470-03749-2

Knitting Patterns For Dummies
978-0-470-04556-5

Living Gluten-Free For Dummies†
978-0-471-77383-2

Painting Do-It-Yourself For Dummies
978-0-470-17533-0

EALTH, SELF HELP, PARENTING & PETS

nger Management For Dummies
8-0-470-03715-7

nxiety & Depression Workbook
or Dummies
8-0-7645-9793-0

ieting For Dummies, 2nd Edition
8-0-7645-4149-0

og Training For Dummies, 2nd Edition
8-0-7645-8418-3

Horseback Riding For Dummies
978-0-470-09719-9

Infertility For Dummies†
978-0-470-11518-3

Meditation For Dummies with CD-ROM,
2nd Edition
978-0-471-77774-8

Post-Traumatic Stress Disorder For Dummies
978-0-470-04922-8

Puppies For Dummies, 2nd Edition
978-0-470-03717-1

Thyroid For Dummies, 2nd Edition†
978-0-471-78755-6

Type 1 Diabetes For Dummies*†
978-0-470-17811-9

Separate Canadian edition also available
Separate U.K. edition also available

vailable wherever books are sold. For more information or to order direct: U.S. customers visit www.dummies.com or call 1-877-762-2974.
K. customers visit www.wileyeurope.com or call (0)1243 843291. Canadian customers visit www.wiley.ca or call 1-800-567-4797.

 WILEY

INTERNET & DIGITAL MEDIA

AdWords For Dummies
978-0-470-15252-2

Blogging For Dummies, 2nd Edition
978-0-470-23017-6

Digital Photography All-in-One Desk Reference For Dummies, 3rd Edition
978-0-470-03743-0

Digital Photography For Dummies, 5th Edition
978-0-7645-9802-9

Digital SLR Cameras & Photography For Dummies, 2nd Edition
978-0-470-14927-0

eBay Business All-in-One Desk Reference For Dummies
978-0-7645-8438-1

eBay For Dummies, 5th Edition*
978-0-470-04529-9

eBay Listings That Sell For Dummies
978-0-471-78912-3

Facebook For Dummies
978-0-470-26273-3

The Internet For Dummies, 11th Edition
978-0-470-12174-0

Investing Online For Dummies, 5th Edition
978-0-7645-8456-5

iPod & iTunes For Dummies, 5th Edition
978-0-470-17474-6

MySpace For Dummies
978-0-470-09529-4

Podcasting For Dummies
978-0-471-74898-4

Search Engine Optimization For Dummies, 2nd Edition
978-0-471-97998-2

Second Life For Dummies
978-0-470-18025-9

Starting an eBay Business For Dummies, 3rd Edition†
978-0-470-14924-9

GRAPHICS, DESIGN & WEB DEVELOPMENT

Adobe Creative Suite 3 Design Premium All-in-One Desk Reference For Dummies
978-0-470-11724-8

Adobe Web Suite CS3 All-in-One Desk Reference For Dummies
978-0-470-12099-6

AutoCAD 2008 For Dummies
978-0-470-11650-0

Building a Web Site For Dummies, 3rd Edition
978-0-470-14928-7

Creating Web Pages All-in-One Desk Reference For Dummies, 3rd Edition
978-0-470-09629-1

Creating Web Pages For Dummies, 8th Edition
978-0-470-08030-6

Dreamweaver CS3 For Dummies
978-0-470-11490-2

Flash CS3 For Dummies
978-0-470-12100-9

Google SketchUp For Dummies
978-0-470-13744-4

InDesign CS3 For Dummies
978-0-470-11865-8

Photoshop CS3 All-in-One Desk Reference For Dummies
978-0-470-11195-6

Photoshop CS3 For Dummies
978-0-470-11193-2

Photoshop Elements 5 For Dummies
978-0-470-09810-3

SolidWorks For Dummies
978-0-7645-9555-4

Visio 2007 For Dummies
978-0-470-08983-5

Web Design For Dummies, 2nd Edition
978-0-471-78117-2

Web Sites Do-It-Yourself For Dummies
978-0-470-16903-2

Web Stores Do-It-Yourself For Dummies
978-0-470-17443-2

LANGUAGES, RELIGION & SPIRITUALITY

Arabic For Dummies
978-0-471-77270-5

Chinese For Dummies, Audio Set
978-0-470-12766-7

French For Dummies
978-0-7645-5193-2

German For Dummies
978-0-7645-5195-6

Hebrew For Dummies
978-0-7645-5489-6

Ingles Para Dummies
978-0-7645-5427-8

Italian For Dummies, Audio Set
978-0-470-09586-7

Italian Verbs For Dummies
978-0-471-77389-4

Japanese For Dummies
978-0-7645-5429-2

Latin For Dummies
978-0-7645-5431-5

Portuguese For Dummies
978-0-471-78738-9

Russian For Dummies
978-0-471-78001-4

Spanish Phrases For Dummies
978-0-7645-7204-3

Spanish For Dummies
978-0-7645-5194-9

Spanish For Dummies, Audio Set
978-0-470-09585-0

The Bible For Dummies
978-0-7645-5296-0

Catholicism For Dummies
978-0-7645-5391-2

The Historical Jesus For Dummies
978-0-470-16785-4

Islam For Dummies
978-0-7645-5503-9

Spirituality For Dummies, 2nd Edition
978-0-470-19142-2

NETWORKING AND PROGRAMMING

ASP.NET 3.5 For Dummies
978-0-470-19592-5

C# 2008 For Dummies
978-0-470-19109-5

Hacking For Dummies, 2nd Edition
978-0-470-05235-8

Home Networking For Dummies, 4th Edition
978-0-470-11806-1

Java For Dummies, 4th Edition
978-0-470-08716-9

Microsoft® SQL Server™ 2008 All-in-One Desk Reference For Dummies
978-0-470-17954-3

Networking All-in-One Desk Reference For Dummies, 2nd Edition
978-0-7645-9939-2

Networking For Dummies, 8th Edition
978-0-470-05620-2

SharePoint 2007 For Dummies
978-0-470-09941-4

Wireless Home Networking For Dummies, 2nd Edition
978-0-471-74940-0

PERATING SYSTEMS & COMPUTER BASICS

ac For Dummies, 5th Edition
8-0-7645-8458-9

otops For Dummies, 2nd Edition
8-0-470-05432-1

ux For Dummies, 8th Edition
8-0-470-11649-4

cBook For Dummies
8-0-470-04859-7

ac OS X Leopard All-in-One
sk Reference For Dummies
8-0-470-05434-5

Mac OS X Leopard For Dummies
978-0-470-05433-8

Macs For Dummies, 9th Edition
978-0-470-04849-8

PCs For Dummies, 11th Edition
978-0-470-13728-4

Windows® Home Server For Dummies
978-0-470-18592-6

Windows Server 2008 For Dummies
978-0-470-18043-3

Windows Vista All-in-One
Desk Reference For Dummies
978-0-471-74941-7

Windows Vista For Dummies
978-0-471-75421-3

Windows Vista Security For Dummies
978-0-470-11805-4

ORTS, FITNESS & MUSIC

aching Hockey For Dummies
8-0-470-83685-9

aching Soccer For Dummies
8-0-471-77381-8

ness For Dummies, 3rd Edition
8-0-7645-7851-9

otball For Dummies, 3rd Edition
8-0-470-12536-6

GarageBand For Dummies
978-0-7645-7323-1

Golf For Dummies, 3rd Edition
978-0-471-76871-5

Guitar For Dummies, 2nd Edition
978-0-7645-9904-0

Home Recording For Musicians
For Dummies, 2nd Edition
978-0-7645-8884-6

iPod & iTunes For Dummies,
5th Edition
978-0-470-17474-6

Music Theory For Dummies
978-0-7645-7838-0

Stretching For Dummies
978-0-470-06741-3

Get smart @ dummies.com®

- **Find a full list of Dummies titles**
- **Look into loads of FREE on-site articles**
- **Sign up for FREE eTips e-mailed to you weekly**
- **See what other products carry the Dummies name**
- **Shop directly from the Dummies bookstore**
- **Enter to win new prizes every month!**

eparate Canadian edition also available
eparate U.K. edition also available

ilable wherever books are sold. For more information or to order direct: U.S. customers visit www.dummies.com or call 1-877-762-2974.
. customers visit www.wileyeurope.com or call (0) 1243 843291. Canadian customers visit www.wiley.ca or call 1-800-567-4797.